Grassroots Marketing

Grassroots Marketing

Getting Noticed in a Noisy World

Shel Horowitz

CHELSEA GREEN PUBLISHING COMPANY

White River Junction, Vermont

Totnes, England

Printed in the United States.
First printing, May 2000.

03 02 01 00   1 2 3 4 5

This book is printed on acid-free, recycled paper.

Many of the designations used by manufacturers and sellers to distinguish their products
are claimed as trademarks. Where those designations appear in this book and Chelsea
Green was aware of a trademark claim, the designations have been printed in initial capital
letters.

Library of Congress Cataloging-in-Publication Data
Horowitz, Shel.
   Grassroots marketing : getting noticed in a noisy world / Shel Horowitz.
     p. cm.
   Rev. ed of: Marketing without megabucks. c1993.
   Includes bibliographical references and index.
   ISBN 1-890132-68-3 (alk. paper)
    1. Marketing--Management--Cost effectiveness. 2. Nonprofit
organizations--Marketing. I. Horowitz, Shel. Marketing without megabucks. II. Title.

HF5415.13 .H675 2000
658.8 dc21

                                        00-022133

Chelsea Green Publishing Company
Post Office Box 428
White River Junction, VT 05001
(800) 639-4099
http://www.chelseagreen.com

To my amazing wife, D. Dina Friedman,
partner in love, in work, and in family,
light of my life, my reality check and best critic, and
a joy in every part of my world.

Contents

Acknowledgments

There are always many people to thank—starting with my "research team," Elise Bernier Feeley and Elise Dennis of the Forbes Library Reference Department, who tracked down answers to difficult questions on this and many other projects.

Thanks also to all the people who consented to be interviewed: Lois Barber, Honoré David, Frank Fox, Stanley D. Friedman, Jordi Herold, Anne Kousch, Dave Lannon, Dr. Jeffrey A. Lant, Georg Schlomka, Bob Wieler, and Amy Zuckerman.

Finally, thanks to all those who allowed me to use their material: Jaffer Ali, Cliff Allen, Eric Anderson, R. David Andrus, Thomas L. Ashley, Wanda Atkinson, John Audette, Larry Aynesmith (White Cliffs Media), Lorilyn Bailey, Ned Barnett, Evelyn Lee Barney, Lee Barstow, Angela Barth, Kathy Barthen, Jeffrey Baumgartner, Rick Beneteau, David Beroff, Rynn Berry, Adam Boettiger, Kathleen Buckley, Brad Byrd, Campus Design and Copy (and its designer, Lynne Chinigo), Linda Chestney, Brian Chmielewski, Luis F. Clement, Sonny Cohen, Diane W. Collins, Neil Connors (Bell Atlantic Information Resources), Brent Cook, Bob Cortez, Wayne Corwin, Jim Daniels, Walter Daniels, Jeanne Dietsch, David Doggett, Alvin Donovan, John Ebbets (*Daily Hampshire Gazette* advertising department), David Farkas, Terri Firebaugh, James Foudy (*Daily Hampshire Gazette*), Frank Fox (Professional Association of Résumé Writers), Rob Frankel, Alan Friedman, Dina Friedman, Sherree Geyer, Teri Gidwitz, Peter Gill, Jerome Gold, Tom Golden, Lawrence Goldman, Dan Goldstein (New York Press and Graphics), William Greene, Merril D. Grohman (Datawise Publishers), Monique Harris, Charles Hayes, Greg Hayward, Bill Hunt, Tordis Isselhardt, Stephen Jackson, Suzanne Jackson, Evan Jennings, Brian Jud, Lynda Karr, Lorna Kepes, Mark Ketzler, Shannon Kinnard, Terry Kluytmans, Gene Kroupa, Paul Krupin, Jane I. LaForce (and her design team of Petula Stanley and

Janet White Associates), Carole B. LaKind (Platinum Treats), Dr. Jeffrey A. Lant, Bob Leduc, Muhammad Lee, John Lustina, Dave Majercik, Bonnie Marlewski-Probert, Howard Meibach, Becca Merrill, Mary Morris, John D. Morrison, David Needle, Brook Noel, Dr. Kevin Nunley, Ray Owens, Nancy E. Paglia (and her designer, Joan Linden), Bob Pardue, Jerry Parkins, Lisa Pelto, Melvin Powers (Wilshire Book Company), Plake, Paul Purdue, Jim Reardon, Josh Reynolds, Gail Robinson, Linda Robinson-Hidas (and her designer, Leslie J. Hollis), Nancy Roebke, Eva Rosenberg, Georg Schlomka, Harvey Segal, Hon. James L. Seward, Paul Siegel, Nina Silver, Judith H. Solomon, Jared Spool, David Stansel, Joan Stewart, Michael Stewart, Jay Steinfeld, Alice Stelzer, Jim Sterne, B. Taylor, Donald Todrin, Corvan Heumen, Raymond L. Warren, Dan Wasserman, Sheila Webber, Mark Welch, Janet Westergaard, Mary Westheimer, Gloria Wolk, Robert J. Woodhead, Leah Woolford, Michihiro Yoshida, David Zinman, Natalie Zubar, and Simon Zylph.

Portions of the chapter on sales presentations were originally published in *Related Matters,* the newsletter of the University of Massachusetts Family Business Center. If you own a family business, you'll find about fifty of my articles on various family business topics and the FBC Web site, <http://www.umass.edu/fambiz/relatedlist.htm>.

Some of this material was originally published in my 1993 book, *Marketing Without Megabucks: How to Sell Anything on a Shoestring.*

If You've Already Read
Marketing Without Megabucks

Since I first wrote *Marketing Without Megabucks: How to Sell Anything on a Shoestring* in 1991, I've been keeping files of new developments in marketing. When I took the book back from Simon and Schuster, I put together the first 12,000 words of an update that eventually grew to 22,000 words by January 1998.

Still, I couldn't incorporate everything I'd learned, because the scope of that book was not as comprehensive. By my best count, there are over 70,000 words of new information in this book, as well as a completely new way of conceptualizing the material. The additional material alone is as lengthy as many entire books. In short, even though some chapters are taken from the old work, this really is a brand-new book.

A portion of the material in the book will be familiar to you, especially if you bought recently enough to get the 1997 or 1998 update. However, much is different, as well.

The entire section on the Internet (part 4) is new—and vastly expanded over the update to my previous book. Also, much of part 5, Phone and Face, is brand new. Much of the chapter on electronic media has been expanded, as this universe continues to grow and change. Even the chapter on writing press releases has been vastly enlarged.

And, of course, every single chapter has been gone over thoroughly, to incorporate new information, delete obsolete material, and change the tone to be consistent with this new and very differently organized book.

1

Skeptics—Please Start Here

A ten-dollar marketing budget—are you kidding? No, and I'm not crazy either.

In 1981, I started my business with an initial marketing investment of twelve dollars. It was enough to get started and keep me going over the first few months, until I could afford to put more into promotion. I didn't get my first computer until 1984.

Nearly twenty years later, I'm still running my business on an annual marketing investment of under two thousand dollars, or less than forty bucks a week. Yet my business is the busiest shop of its kind in a three-county territory, and I have clients on three continents. You too can learn to get this kind of return with easy and straightforward marketing.

Even in the year 2000, ten bucks is enough to get started. Obviously, your own marketing mix will vary depending on what you're selling, and to whom. But here are some ideas:

THE $10 MARKETING BUDGET

- Free e-mail and a free Web site
- A series of press releases, faxed locally, e-mailed, or hand-delivered
- Appearances as a talk show guest

- A well-designed and compellingly written flier, photocopied on eye-catching paper and distributed on bulletin boards or under doorways
- Articles in trade publications, on- or off-line
- Free classifieds

THE $100 MARKETING BUDGET

As above, but also including:

- Your own actively promoted Internet domain, with a small Web site and a newsletter
- Wider geographic reach for press releases and articles
- Conducting a small local seminar
- Walking the floor at one or more trade shows
- Ad swaps with other newsletters

THE $1,000 MARKETING BUDGET

As above, but also including:

- Sponsorship of targeted e-zines
- A carefully crafted in-column Yellow Pages ad
- An active program of appearances as a radio guest
- Bigger seminars

- A well-written and beautifully designed brochure

THE $2,000–$10,000 MARKETING BUDGET

As above, but also including:

- Small-space classified ads
- Experiments with short-run direct mail
- Radio advertising on shows that are a perfect fit for your message
- An active referral/affiliate program

By the time you're done reading this book, you'll know how to do all these, and a whole lot more.

— Why You Need — This Book

If you've ever tried to get people interested in what you do, you know it can be difficult to motivate them. Whether you're trying to market a product, service, idea, or personality, you need to find the right people, and convince them you have what they want.

Let's face it, you've got lots of competition for their attention. The average adult in the United States is exposed to some two thousand messages per day. One issue of the Sunday *New York Times* contains more raw information than George Washington and his era absorbed in a lifetime. You have to somehow stand out in this information deluge so that your customers can find you.

This book will help you stand out in the crowd, at the lowest cost. We won't make any assumptions about what you already know, so there are step-by-step instructions and examples, as well as plenty of commonsense advice.

If you consistently have as much business as you can possibly handle from word-of-mouth referrals and you never want to expand, pass this book on to a friend. But if you have any slack time, or you want to slash your current marketing costs and increase your return, everything you need is in these pages.

— Overview —

Marketing is the combined ability to:

- Identify the exact members of your audience,
- Get the right information out to them, and
- Motivate them to deal with you.

Whether you're a business owner, artist, human-services worker, educator, or organizer, if you are marketing any product, service, or idea, you can benefit from the same easy and inexpensive marketing techniques used by full-time marketing professionals. These tools are there for the taking, but far too few businesses and service providers use them. If you take advantage of them, you'll get the customer's or client's call.

Even if you already use some of the techniques covered in this book, you will learn how to increase your effectiveness while lowering your cost. You'll also learn how to expand your marketing in new directions.

Specifically, you will learn how to:

- Turn newspapers, magazines, radio stations, and online communities into your own *free* international publicity bureau
- Enlist your customers, vendors, and others in your network to bring you a steady stream of new business
- Slash the cost of print and radio advertising while zeroing in on the exact people you want to reach
- Harness the awesome marketing power of the Internet with a coherent, integrated, and *successful* strategy
- Create and distribute a wide range of effective do-it-yourself promotional materials: direct mail, fliers, brochures, and much more
- Get free exposure nationwide, in any medium
- Evaluate every marketing and advertising purchase for appropriateness and cost-effectiveness

- Become known as an expert in your field and be quoted frequently in the media—at no cost to you
- Enhance all your marketing by developing and maintaining a consistent and appropriate image
- Track the results of your marketing campaign so that you know which tools are working most successfully for you

Traditional business thinking focuses on increasing efficiency and reducing costs. Standard nonprofit thinking stems from community service. And artistic thinking is based on creativity. *Grassroots Marketing* combines the best of business, nonprofit, and artistic thinking.

— My Credentials —

This book is a comprehensive guide to low-cost, efficient marketing: thorough and clear but upbeat, easy to read, and full of examples. My goal is to help you without intimidating you, and to provide you with a one-volume reference source for a wide range of marketing approaches.

It is based largely on my own experience, running a diversified service and information business and growing it from extremely humble beginnings. In just one week recently, I had clients in London, Cyprus, Boston, Alaska, Arkansas, and my own home base in western Massachusetts.

This book is also based on my considerable knowledge of how to work the media. I have published some eight hundred articles; appeared as a guest on close to two hundred radio stations on three continents (and a few TV shows); developed and manage a 350-page Web site including three magazines and two monthly tipsheets (with zero setup cost except for my domain registration); been featured in national print media from the *Christian Science Monitor* to the *Cleveland Plain Dealer;* spoken before groups as diverse as the American Marketing Association, National Association of Home Remodelers, and Publishers Marketing Association; published books with a major New York house, small publishers such as Chelsea Green, and even my own publishing company; been asked to write jacket quotes for several books . . . I'll stop there; I don't want to bore you!

This book is not based only on my own experience, but also on extensive research. I've read a library's worth of books on marketing, kept up with the latest developments through daily monitoring of close to two dozen Internet newsletters and discussion groups, interviewed celebrity marketers as well as ordinary folks, searched far and wide for examples . . . in short, I've done a lot of work so that you don't have to do it again.

— How to Use This Book —

At first, you may want to explore only a few of the ideas here, and that's fine. If, for example, you base your current marketing on media publicity and fliers, but later want to learn about direct mail or paid advertising, the information will be there when you need it.

Ultimately, I really believe in "entrepreneurial thinking"—applying creativity to solving a problem, and then letting people know you've done so. This is not only the best approach for small business, but also for human-services agencies, grassroots community groups, and yes, even large corporate or government agencies. Unfortunately, too many organizations are set up to stifle creativity instead of enhance it. This book is designed to help you open up your thought processes—not just about marketing, but about creativity and productivity in many aspects of your organization.

Meanwhile, are you ready to get out there and build the most effective, least costly marketing program you can? Fasten your seat belts; we're on our way!

2

Image and Market

Image encompasses your firm or agency name, letterhead, logo, slogan(s), the appearance of your office, your Internet presence, any printed material or advertisements, and so on. A consistent image or set of images is crucial. If you design publicity materials with your overall image in mind, all the publicity works together as a "family" and the message is stronger. Every piece you create reinforces your overall image.

You cannot avoid a corporate image. Human-services agencies, political action groups, and sole proprietorships all have their own image. Either you deliberately anchor your operation together in the public eye, or else by default you present chaos.

— Matching Image and Market —

Stop a moment and consider what your image has to encompass. What specific products, services, and/or ideas are you offering (or might you offer in the future)? Perhaps the best way to answer that question is to ask yourself—in the clearest possible terms—*what problem(s) can you solve?* All your marketing must focus on the answer to that question; that's how you will attract clients, customers, or converts.

Next, what makes you unique? Do you offer a truly rare product? Quality service? Personal attention? Fast turnaround? Custom quantities? Enormous selection? Discount pricing? Professional credentials? In other words, why can *you* solve your clients' problems more effectively than someone else?

Answering this question determines your Unique Selling Proposition (USP)—why someone would want to do business with you instead of with someone else. Once you've identified your USPs, both for your company as a whole and for each individual product or service your offer, all your marketing should be built around them.

Although price is a strong influence in marketing, don't be afraid to market aggressively on quality instead. Dave Lannon, manager of Bread & Circus, a natural-foods supermarket in Hadley, Massachusetts, expresses it like this: "If you're buying a car, you don't say, 'I'm going to buy the cheapest car.' You buy the best car for the money. If you're going to buy the cheapest food, you're also going to get the worst food. Price isn't what we focus on; you know if you buy it from us, it's a good, healthy product."

Take every feature of your product or company and express it as a specific benefit. Potential customers are not going to care, for instance, if you sell a new fuel-saving carburetor; they will care that it gives 60 miles per gallon with no loss in performance.

But don't stop there. Marketing guru Dr. Jeffrey Lant notes the importance of "Ultimate Benefits"— the things we all really want out of life. Let's put this in concrete terms. Say your product assembles in three minutes, whereas competing products require an hour. The specific benefits are time saved and reduced frustration; the Ultimate Benefit is more time to enjoy life. If you sell aerobic exercise equipment, you're really selling the Ultimate Benefits of health and longevity. Life insurance? Your Ultimate Benefit is peace of mind.

Ultimate Benefits include health, leisure, sexual fulfillment, prestige, physical, emotional, and intellectual satisfaction . . . but not money; it's just a means to an end. The real Ultimate Benefits result from the ability to spend the money (travel, support your favorite charities, buy a fine home, etc.).

You should be able to tell a potential customer in one or two sentences how he or she can benefit from working with you instead of someone else. Once you've got those two sentences, you can build an entire marketing campaign around this summary. If you can't do this, subdivide the categories of benefits into separate but related marketing campaigns, each of which can be expressed in two sentences or less.

Obviously, this focus will shift with time; you will continually gain experience, determine your strongest likes and dislikes, refine your pricing and selection structure, and so forth. Therefore, do this exercise at least every year.

Now that you know what you're really offering, identify your audience. *Who has the problem(s) you can solve?* Who comprises your market? Potential customers can be grouped in three ways:

Geographical

For some businesses, territory might be just a few square miles. For instance, a village general store will generally draw most of its customers from residents of that village. The major draws are convenience and a sense of community, not price or se-

lection. A large regional supermarket in the next town might draw from a twenty-mile radius; the same people who would stop at the village store for milk and a newspaper will load up on staple items a couple of times a month at the larger store.

For other businesses, it might not be so cut-and-dried. My own shop varies according to the service. Our business marketing and consulting clients come from around the world, and we never meet most of them in person. For résumés and creative writing courses, most of our clients come from within forty miles. However, when we used to offer typing and word processing—services available in many communities—we drew about 95 percent of our base from within ten miles.

The more specialized your offering, the less geography is a factor. For the corner convenience store, geography may be the only selling point. But a specialty bakery offering premium, all-natural food products can probably serve wholesale accounts within a five-hour drive. And a producer of nonperishable goods can sell wherever you have distribution.

Horizontal

In traditional business lingo, horizontal integration refers to marketing several competing products. For instance, General Motors markets several different brands of similar cars; Procter and Gamble produces two of the three most popular brands of diapers.

I'm using the term "horizontal marketing" a little differently here—to mean the various types of people or groups who can use you. Some items can be marketed to everyone; other products will be marketed only to a particular audience.

Say you're marketing a cookbook of recipes featuring plantains. Fruit can be marketed all across the horizontal spectrum—almost everyone buys some kind of fruit. But plantains, for the most part, are sold to Latin American and Caribbean cooks. So your primary market would be the horizontal slice that already uses plantains.

To reach other horizontal slices, distribute your cookbook at ethnic restaurants, gourmet shops, and international community fairs. But to expand into the mainstream, you would have to convince non–plantain-eaters to try your recipes—through cooking demonstrations in supermarkets, for instance.

Mainstreaming a subculture item is a hard task, but not impossible. Who would have predicted in 1975 that tofu would become popular outside of Asian and health food circles? Now tofu—even tofu yogurt and ice cream—is widely available. And look at the influence of subculture groups on clothing: haute boutiques show clothing derived from cowboys and miners, flappers, beatniks, hippies, and punks.

Vertical

A vertical market refers to a particular industry. Companies that are vertically integrated control production from start to finish—for example, steelmaking from mining the ore to stamping out the finished product. Your piece of any vertical market will be a slice of this larger picture. But unlike the broad base of a horizontal market, vertical marketing only addresses consumers within one industry.

For instance, if your product is an integrated bookkeeping, billing, and file-management software package for commercial photographers, then your marketing will be to commercial photographers. Going beyond this market involves retooling the product to fit the needs of other vertical market segments—audiovisual film producers, for instance.

Applying vertical market thinking in human services, you identify people needing a specific type of service: housing assistance, job training, drug counseling, family systems assessment, and so on. Rather than trying to serve everyone, find one area with gaps in service and try to fill the gap.

(There is, of course, a place for the holistic, horizontal, human-services agency that serves its clients in several areas. If your aim is to treat addicted women on public assistance, you might provide drug rehabilitation, career and life skills training, personal counseling, family therapy, and day-care referral within the context of your mission. But you would not offer the same services to homeless men without substance abuse problems—you'd refer them to another program.)

Putting It All Together

Remember learning about sets? Your teacher drew overlapping circles to show the intersections. If you had a set representing the color red, and another representing food, the overlap included tomatoes, apples, and radishes.

Your current target market is the intersection of your slices of territory within geographical, vertical, and horizontal markets. When you are ready to expand, plan a strategy to widen your circles. A counseling agency might service high school students (horizontal) from troubled families (vertical) in Los Angeles County (geographical). If this program were to expand, it could train staff to handle issues of college student and adult family life (horizontal); work with new immigrants (vertical); and set up a satellite office in the neighboring county (geographical).

If you manufactured filters for gasoline pumps, you would aim at vertical markets such as gas stations, fuel-distribution depots, and highway department garages throughout the country.

*O*nce you've established your product/ service line and target market, you're ready to create a consistent, appropriate image.

If you're marketing a cassette tape by a local ethnic artist, you start with limited market penetration: horizontally, the performer's ethnic group; vertically, the genre of music; and geographically, your local area. The present audience for this tape is the overlap of these three areas, but you want to expand. Your goal is to encourage "crossover" among other listeners and make the tape a national hit. So you'd widen one circle at a time by focusing:

- In the performer's ethnic group but outside your local area

- On people within your area who like similar music but don't know your artist
- In mainstream channels new to that type of music

— Back to Your Image —

Once you've established your product/service line and target market, you're ready to create a consistent, appropriate image.

This is the single most important factor in the way you will be perceived. Do you want to emphasize warehouse bargain savings on off-brand discontinued merchandise? Print your fliers on cheap newsprint and list lots of specials under a big banner headline.

Are you aiming for a teenage crowd? Get a teenager to let you in on the latest lingo—and use it, even though it might seem completely indecipherable (just keep updating your teen-slanted materials as the slang changes).

Is a professional image important? Make your prospects aware of your credentials: degrees you hold, recognized experts you've trained under, professional organizations you're involved with. Frank Fox, who heads two national trade associations (Professional Association of Résumé Writers and National Association of Secretarial Services), notes that membership in a trade group can be an asset. "Members are able to put [the organization's] logo in ads and promotions. It sets them apart from competitors. If they are marketing to people in some other professional association, it can be a very important credential—they recognize that the service cares enough about their clients to continue professional development."

Do you want to puff up your one-person, home-based business to make yourself sound like a well-established larger outfit? Create a firm name and logo that reflects this, put everything in the plural, and find a graphic designer to make you look properly corporate.

Want a homelike, personal touch? Decorate the inside of your business like a cozy New England inn.

Aiming for the high-priced, quality-seeking crowd? The right motto or slogan on an understated publicity handout might do the trick.

— Choosing a Name —

The core of any identity is the name that holds it together. Names should receive careful thought, as they have ramifications in every other aspect of your marketing. Check any name for trademark infringement before committing to it; litigation and forced name changes are expensive headaches.

Evaluate these eight aspects:

Alphabetical Placement

If Yellow Pages or other directory advertising is *ever* going to be a part of your marketing plan, a name at the beginning of the alphabet has major benefits. Most people start with the first name on the list, or at least the first name that's geographically convenient. A much smaller percentage start at the bottom and work their way up. Either way, if there are more than five to ten listings in your category, most people will not call everyone. So if you're in the middle of twenty-five names, you'll get a lot fewer calls than if you were first.

My own experience bears this out. I was aware of this consideration when I started my business in 1981, but at that time I didn't expect to use the Yellow Pages. My company's original name was Writing & More, and we solicited business entirely through fliers and press releases. Three years later, we entered the Yellow Pages and quickly realized it was outpulling all our other marketing combined. After some agonizing, we changed our firm name to Accurate Writing & More—a name that built on the reputation we had established, but moved us from last to first in nearly all Yellow Pages categories. To protect our existing client base, we continued to list the old name for a couple of years.

The results were dramatic: We immediately saw an approximately 30 percent increase in bookings out of the Yellow Pages, and many clients continue to tell me, "Well, you were the first one listed in the book."

Tone

Your image may have absolutely nothing to do with your actual structure. Even if you are one person operating out of a toolshed, if you answer the phone with a business voice and a professional sounding name, you can compete in the big leagues. Of course, for some businesses—a barbershop, family restaurant, or corner grocery—an informal name may be a marketing benefit.

Personalization

Every business or agency chooses between two types of names: (1) one that includes the operator's name(s), and (2) one that doesn't.

Some people's names lend themselves well to integration into a business identity; others don't. It will also depend on the type of business.

A first name conveys a down-home, mom-and-pop image—appropriate if you stress personalized service and a convivial atmosphere. Garrison Keillor's mythical "Bob's Bank" always gets a laugh; bank names are formal, corporate.

Say you run a gourmet food store. If your name begins with A, even better. Call yourself something like "Ann's Fine Foods" and you'll contrast sharply with large chain supermarkets. A last name sounds more formal, but still lets the business feel personal and approachable.

Of course, if you're well known, a personalized name will build on your existing reputation. Actor Paul Newman succeeded with specialty foods because he had name recognition. Many celebrities go into some kind of business or lend their endorsement to someone else's. Even if your reputation only extends within your own community, it's something to consider.

A straightforward fictitious name could be The Gourmet Shop, International Cookery, or Food Specialties, Ltd. Of course, there are other approaches. Sound, imagery, rhythm, and cleverness can all come into play. You could be Aromatic Aristocratic Food Specialties; An Exotic Place to Eat; or Asparagus Gourmet Foods.

You can still have a personalized name while maintaining a professional image. Compare the tones of these variations: Abe's Camels; Abe, Ike and Jake; Abraham, Isaac & Jacob, Inc.; Three Guys from the Middle East; Abraham and Sons; Abraham and Associates; Camels and Desert Sands; A. Isaac, Jacob, and Partners—Camel Dealers; AIJ Associates; AIJ Desert Transportation Specialists, Inc. . . .

Incidentally, you don't have to use your own name. One firm began as Sandy's Secretarial Service. When the business was sold, the new owner cleverly dropped the leading S; Sandy's became Andy's. This tiny name change moved the business from the dregs of the Yellow Pages to second place, while maintaining a clear identity to previous customers.

Descriptiveness

In the above list of possible business titles, only a few give any indication of what Abraham, Isaac, and Jacob actually do. Although that ambiguity may be an advantage if you're not sure of your direction, ultimately you're a step ahead of the game if your business or agency title gives some clue. That way, every time your firm name is listed—in the Yellow Pages, a newspaper, a flier, a tourist brochure, a search result on the Web—people who see it will associate your business name with your product, service, or idea.

I opened my Yellow Pages at random to the category of Plumbing Fixtures, Parts and Supplies—Retail. These businesses are listed: Cowls Building Supply, Inc.; Greenfield Supply Co.; Grossman's Lumber; Haberman Hardware Co.; H. A. Knapp & Sons, Inc.; Necessities for the Bath; W. S. Pickering & Son, Inc.; Richard's Plumbing and Heating; Rocky's Home Center, Inc.; Serv-U Hardware Homecenter; Springfield Plumbing Supply Co.

If you were looking in the Yellow Pages, which one would you choose? If I wanted some fancy yuppie bathtub with all the trimmings, I would pick Necessities for the Bath. But I'd pick one of the home or hardware stores if I wanted some basic plumbing hardware. If I had heard of them, I might pick one of the firms that used only a person's name.

Now think about trying to get the same product out of the White Pages, where remembering a firm name is the only way to look someone up. The nondescriptive names lose out. There is no clue in the names Knapp or Pickering about what these people do. Greenfield Supply is almost as vague—they could be supplying all manner of things. But if I'd already heard of a place called Springfield Plumbing Supply—perhaps from passing it on the road and seeing a sign—I'd almost certainly start there.

Cleverness

Puns, wordplays, and the like may either help or hurt your cause. If you're aiming at the "average Joe," it's probably best to stay clear of cuteness. But if you cater to a tourist crowd in a resort town, a clever name can help set you apart and build name recognition. How far to go may largely depend on your market niche and the fashions of your geographic area.

In any case, the name should have something to do with what you're selling. An office temporary service specializing in publishing might call itself Temp-Prose. A transportation broker could be Ship to Shore Transportation, Inc. An herb store might use the name Allspice & Thyme. But avoid purely artistic names, with no functional link.

Sometimes, clever names can be very appropriate for expanding in new directions. For instance, several years ago, a local seafood restaurant began offering dancing. The Fishcotheque was immediately popular.

Before developing a clever name, do some market research. Conduct a survey of your existing or potential clientele, asking them to rank five or six names (including your current one) in order of preference.

Expandability

While descriptiveness is important, make sure not to get too specific. Think of the difference between Floral Wreaths by Marie and Floral Designs by Marie. If Marie decided to diversify, she'd be severely limited by "Wreaths." She'd have to name a new sideline and reestablish her identity, continue to use a name that didn't match her expanded product line, or go through the hassles of changing the name as she expanded. But the second name allows her to go into landscaping, macramé, painted flowers, or many other directions.

My own business name, Accurate Writing & More, allows virtually unlimited room to grow. In addition to the professionalism and alphabetical advantage conveyed by "Accurate," the word "More" allows us to keep changing the mix of services without affecting our image. Our slogan, "Ideas into words; words onto paper," reinforces our multifaceted image. Could we have attracted international business clients with a restrictive name, such as "The Résumé Shop?"

If you've been in business for a while, examine the name you operate under. How effective is it? If it needs improvement, how hard would it be to change it? How much more effective would you be under a new name? Can you notify your existing client/customer base? Does it make sense to keep both names running for a while?

If starting over is more than you're willing to bear, consider creating a subsidiary. If you've been doing auto repairs and you want to expand to fixing lawn mowers and outboard motors, turn it into "A-Plus Small Engine Repair Center, A Division of Joe's Garage."

Trademarkability

If you create an entire new category, consider registering a trademark. This is a complex process involving intellectual property lawyers (not cheap!) and the need to rigorously defend your trademark once you establish it. It's probably only worth the hassle if you think you're going to have a very big seller—but pick a name that can be trademarked. In general, this means a coined name with certain distinct characteristics, rather than a combination of existing words.

If this is a factor for you, do some research on what's involved and consult with a lawyer who specializes in trademarks—*before* you commit to a name.

*L*ook around, listen. When something strikes you as effective, examine it.

Internet Domain Availability

Since many people enter a company name or product type into a Web browser navigation bar (the part at the top of the screen that shows the address of the current site), the best name is one that is still available as a .com domain. If the name is still available, register it right away before someone beats you to it—even if you have no immediate plans to market on the Internet. You won't be sorry; we'll talk more about this later.

— Logos —

A logo is a symbol that represents your firm or organization (or your membership in a larger network).

A logo may be completely pictorial, a mixture of graphic and letters (or even letters formed into a graphic), or purely verbal—your organization's name or initials in a certain typeface. Study the ads in any magazine and you'll see examples of logos.

To create your own logo, sit down for a minute and think about what you offer. How might it best be graphically represented? Do some rough sketches and see which gets the best response. Find a competent commercial art student who can inexpensively but effectively translate your ideas into a good piece of art. If it's in color, make sure it also looks good in black-and-white.

Alternatively, computer special effects or drawing software can make fast, elegant logos. The examples that follow took less than fifteen minutes each to create, using PostScript special effects programs and a PostScript laser printer.

Some common logo tricks:

- Stylized initials in a geometrical shape
- Graphic representation of a product or service
- Graphic interpretation of firm name
- Graphic depiction of a goal
- Incorporation of a common image or icon (or a representation of it) into the logo (two obvious examples are the Christian cross and the Jewish star, both of which have been used in countless logos)

Mascots/Symbols—Logos in 3-D

A firm's symbol can have three dimensions, and can even walk and talk. A local used-car dealer has a car on the roof; no one knows their firm name, but everyone knows how to find them. On the same

street, a muffler shop built a humanoid figure out of old mufflers and parts and named him "Marty the Mailbox." Needless to say, Marty provides visibility—and when he got stolen and was later recovered, it was front-page news. Once a symbol is designed, it can also be used in a logo.

When a recognizable human, humanoid, or animal figure is identified with an organization, we call that figure a mascot. Ronald McDonald and the A&W Root Bear are examples from the corporate world. For special events, hire someone to wear the costume, and let the mascot shake hands, cuddle children, and serve refreshments.

— Slogans —

The right slogan or motto can be very effective in developing an image. Large corporations provide us with examples such as: "It takes a tough man to make a tender chicken"; "Bet you can't eat just one"; "The power to be your best."

A slogan can be used as a headline, a photo caption, a radio jingle, or—most commonly—as a summation, in fairly small type, at the end of an ad or poster. Mottoes are also great on business cards, brochures, and advertising specialties (handouts such as pens and calendars). Often, a motto and a logo are used together; the graphic could even be incorporated into the slogan.

For small businesses, a slogan probably best emphasizes the high quality of a product or service, its affordability, and/or the personal touch that sets you apart from larger, more sterile competitors. Don't be afraid to use corny devices such as repetition, alliteration, and rhyme; they work. Look around, listen. When something strikes you as effective, examine it. Find a copywriter who's clever with words and check out a few proposals.

— Letterhead —

Like everything else you send out, your letterhead should be a marketing tool. Emphasize services by listing them, give your organization more credence

For small businesses, a slogan probably best emphasizes the high quality of a product or service, its affordability, and/or the personal touch that sets you apart from larger, more sterile competitors.

by listing names of prominent people, or simply reinforce your image by restating your logo in your standard typography. Your letterhead, business cards, display ads, brochures, fliers, newsletters, and so on should all work together to reinforce your image.

There's no need to spend a lot of money to create a letterhead; any word-processing service with a laser printer and scalable type should be able to create a serviceable letterhead for you in five minutes or less. Rather than printing up a batch, keep the letterhead as a computer template file and write letters directly into the template.

— Multiple Campaigns —

Earlier, we discussed keeping a campaign's salient points to one or two sentences. If you have too many good points for that, break them up into different marketing campaigns, all tied together by common typeface, logo, and/or slogan. Apple Computer is an excellent real-world example. Over the years, Apple's ads have stressed power, ease of use, the ability to share software across virtually the entire product line, innovative applications for computers, and lots of other attributes. But each advertisement focuses on only one or two of these benefits.

Although Apple's direct-mail brochures list many points, they're cleanly divided into sections, with each benefit discussed in one or two pages.

Clearly, as you increase the variety of products and services you offer, and aim for ever wider diversity of clients you'd like to reach, you will need a greater number of approaches. Apple's example is a good way of handling it if you have too many benefits to cover in a single ad. Instead of trying to cram it all in together and overwhelm the reader, be selective in ads and fliers, but put together a more comprehensive piece for serious inquiries.

— Changing Your Image —

Although your marketing pieces should all echo your central image, you are never locked into one format. There's a lot of flexibility, and images can either be modified or completely replaced at any time. Huge corporations, who pay more and closer attention to image than the rest of us, do this all the time. Remember when every McDonald's had blazingly bright white exterior walls, topped by enormous golden arches? In the 1980s, the company's image was more subdued—red brick buildings retained the pair of arches, but shrank them down almost to a garnish. But those arches were constantly reinforced—as a logo on the wrapper of every hamburger, on the workers' uniforms, and in all the company's ads. (More recently, the company has returned to a bold, garish look.)

Like McDonald's, many companies gradually shift their image but maintain an underlying unity that stays over time. Other companies undergo more thorough and abrupt transformations. When Esso became Exxon in 1972, the firm abandoned its friendly, family image in favor of high-tech—almost clinical—expertise.

In fact, since the 1970s, there has been a general shift in corporate America's imagery, away from traditional, humanistic concerns and toward high-tech impersonality—right down to architecture.

Yet, other successful companies have created a very different kind of image: that of the old-fashioned, quality-conscious, personable family operation. Some very large and successful companies, from Volvo to Jack Daniels, use this technique. Pick up a copy of any back-to-the-land magazine and look at the woodstove ads; numerous companies fight to present themselves—in subtle, soft-sell ads—as the choice for workmanship, quality, and individualized attention from a small company, combined with the latest technological advances.

Big corporations are willing to spend countless millions of dollars for a complete image makeover. But if you're smart, you'll position yourself with an image you can grow with, and not have to undo all your hard work later.

⊀

Now that you know who you are, and what and to whom you're marketing, it's time to learn the territory.

3

Copywriting 101

To put together good marketing, you need to write strong, persuasive copy and create attractive, effective visuals. Most of this book is based on a clear understanding of this and the next chapter; please refer back whenever you need to.

For brevity, I'll refer to your audience as "the reader" and your marketing piece as "the ad." The same principles apply when addressing listeners, electronic visitors, and viewers, and in creating any marketing materials designed to sell directly rather than generate publicity.

A good marketing piece pays attention to both content and design. But always, always, always, write the copy *first*. The design must reemphasize the strongest points in the copy and never be created independently of it. Otherwise, your stuff might look great but have too little substance, or have a visual message at odds with the text, or force your most important points into some hard-to-read corner.

Copywriters often have a sense of good design, and may prepare a rough layout for the designer to work from (or, if the design is simple, actually create both elements together). But trying to fit words to suit illustration and design is a definite no-no.

The only exception is in a very small piece. In some instances, such as a business card with a strong graphic, you may have a very clear idea of the graphic look before you write the words. If the whole idea is to dominate the page with a graphic, such as your company logo, and fit in contact information around it, obviously the words come second. But always ask yourself whether this card is doing the strongest selling job it can. Maybe you need a sales sentence and should shrink the logo down a bit—unless your product, too, is graphically oriented. Make sure the graphic is appropriate to your message—and if it isn't, junk the concept.

— Effective Copywriting —

Many experts cite the AIDA formula: Attention, Interest, Desire, Action. I've expanded this to ten points. Great copywriting:

1. Catches the reader's attention with something relevant;
2. Addresses the reader's fears, anxieties, and/or aspirations;

3. Stresses specific benefits to the user, not the features that lead to those benefits;
4. Offers to solve the reader's problem, in the most specific terms possible;
5. Provides the reader with a chance to acquire something of clear value—but only for a limited time;
6. Pulls the reader toward immediate action;
7. Shows the consequences of a failure to act;
8. Includes solid, substantial validation of your claim by someone else (a customer, an expert);
9. Backs up claims with comparisons to competitors; and
10. This should be obvious—provides the necessary order form, address, and/or telephone number to allow the reader to move forward.

You probably won't get all ten in every marketing document, but strive to include as many as you can. These group together into several bunches:

Attention, Aspirations, Benefits

If you don't grab the reader, your money is wasted. Think of the most important thing you are offering the reader: What fear are you allaying or what Ultimate Benefit can you provide? Now, write a headline that stresses the core of your offer, in one to eight words.

Remember, the reader is not reading your ad in order to buy your product. He or she wants to overcome a fear, aspire to something greater, or solve a particular problem.

Let's examine some sample headlines. Rank them in the order of which ones work best for you:

**New Detergent Leaves Clothes
Whiter, Brighter**

Get Clothes 30% Whiter

Try Our New Detergent

**Clothes Come Out 30% Whiter, Fabrics
Last Longer**

I'd rank the bottom one first, then the second, then the first, and last, the third headline. The first focuses on the product—on the feature, not the benefit. The reader is not interested in the detergent, but in cleaner clothes.

The second one is clear and specific. The benefit is enumerated, and that's where the focus is. But the fourth example fits in two benefits that work together to reinforce each other.

The third headline only wastes space. There's no reason to try the detergent, and the focus is entirely on the product—not even on the features, much less the benefits.

Here's another round of examples:

Make Money in Your Spare Time

Make $200 Extra This Week

**Make $200 Extra Every Weekend
Recycling Packing Materials**

The third example provides a clear, specific benefit (extra income of $200 per week), the inducement of repetition (week after week), and some idea of what's involved (recycling packaging). Furthermore, by changing week to weekend, the copywriter shows this money-making opportunity can be done in just a few hours—a clever way to get extra mileage out of the same number of words.

Learn to transform features into benefits not only in headlines, but in body copy. For example, see the table on page 15.

Limited-Time Offer, Failure, Follow-through

Your marketing must culminate in action from the reader. You want either a sale or a solid inquiry that you can transform into a sale. So ask for it! Force the reader to take action quickly, either to gain an incentive ("If you mail in your order within the next ten days, we'll send you a free _____, which is usually sold separately for $34.95"), or to avoid losing out ("Prices are going up at the end of the month, so act now and don't miss these big savings"). Let

FEATURE	BENEFIT(S)	TEXT
Easy to assemble	Avoid frustration. Save time for more important things.	"Don't tear your hair out for six hours putting together Brand X. Our Brand Y snaps together and is ready to use in just 10 minutes."
More power for the money	Able to accomplish more	"Our 35 hp motor lets you cut twice as much grass in the same time."
Money-back guarantee	Protects customer's investment	"Try it in your home for a full year. If you don't like it, send it back! You risk nothing."
Expandable	Protects customer's investment	"You never have to worry about being stuck with a product that can't grow with you. Upgrading to the next model is as simple as popping out three screws and replacing the assembly."

the prospect feel the pain of failing to act: "You could enjoy a cozy, warm winter around our fuel-efficient stove. But act now, before the heating season starts. Otherwise, as you shiver on your way to pay your outrageous heat bill, you'll know you could have been saving money and keeping warm. Don't be left out in the cold!"

Substantiate Claims, Use Testimonials

An unsubstantiated claim is an empty assertion. And why should the reader believe you? After all, you have a clear vested interest. Back up your claims with pull quotes from media reviews, article reprints, feature-comparison charts covering you and your competitors, and, of course, specific testimonials from satisfied users. Get your referees to restate the claims you make—as benefits you helped them achieve! Identify the writer by name, city, and possibly job title.

Obviously, the better known your endorser, the more useful it will be—up to a point. Advertising mogul David Ogilvy discovered that super-celebs are actually *less* effective in selling products—because people assume, and usually correctly, that they've been paid vast sums of money for their endorsement. If you get a testimonial from a really big name, point out clearly that you haven't paid for it (assuming this is true, of course!).

However, some celebs can't be bought. If you have a product that seems right for a nationally syndicated columnist, be sure to send a review copy and press kit. A mention in something like Dear Abby or Ann Landers can move thousands of units (as can Oprah's endorsement, for instance). Of course, if someone important endorses you, that becomes another newsworthy event.

Many celebrities are more approachable than you'd think—probably not the most famous, but those who are extremely respected in their genre but not well known elsewhere. In these cases, be sure to identify them, that is, not "endorsed by Jane Smith," but "recommended by Jane Smith, CEO of Sirius, the number one European seller of canine kennels, who says . . ."

In tests conducted by sales consultant Bob Leduc <mailto:BobLeduc@aol.com>, direct-mail campaigns using testimonials outpulled the same letters without testimonials by up to 65 percent. This fabulous response is based in part on Leduc's focus on using testimonials that state the specific benefit of your product or service. (Note: Throughout this book, e-mail addresses are presented in angle brackets. This will enable most of those reading the book in electronic format to click and send an e-mail message easily.)

How does he obtain them? He explains:

Here's a simple procedure any business can use effectively. A short time after completing a transaction, send your customer or client a personal postcard asking what they liked best about your product or service. You'll be amazed at some of the glowing comments you'll get. When you receive comments you want to use in your advertising, simply ask the customer to sign a release giving you permission to quote those comments in your promotional material.

The release form I use includes the full text of the customer's comments. I request permission to use the comments "in complete or edited form" so I can shorten the text when it's too long. I also request permission to use the customer's name, city and state so it appears as "Ann Smith, Austin, TX" instead of "A.S., TX". The customer's privacy is protected by omitting the street address.

Even better: put your permission text and a check box right on the postcard.

Some of the best advice I've seen on testimonials comes from Dan Kennedy's book, *The Ultimate Marketing Plan* (Adams Media, 1991): Aim for testimonials that highlight a "before" and "after" comparison—how your product or service took away the negative qualities (obesity, loneliness, incompetence) and replaced them with positive ones (the right weight, popularity, success). Think of every claim or benefit you'd like to substantiate, and generate testimonials that specifically address that issue.

Kennedy also cites the importance of visual testimonials. His examples: a car dealer with pictures

*T*hink *of every claim or benefit you'd like to substantiate, and generate testimonials that specifically address that issue.*

of his smiling customers and their new cars—including the same folks several times over a period of years—and a diet products salesperson who carries a poster of herself, over fifty pounds heavier, as an instant credibility-builder for her program.

A word about permissions: Legally, if you are quoting a letter from a private individual, get written permission to use it. You also need permission to reprint an entire article or a major portion of it (unless you wrote it and did not sign a "work for hire" or "all rights" contract). You don't need permission to reprint a few sentences from a published article, as long as you don't change the context.

— Highlighting Your Benefits —

You don't have to reinvent the wheel each time you create a new marketing piece. Consider each time whether your copywriting should incorporate any of these aspects:

- Competitor comparison
- Case history
- Objections and their answers
- Qualifications and capabilities

Competitor Comparison

Do people automatically think of your largest competitor when they think of the product line you sell? In many industries, one firm has carved out such a large share of the market that it becomes identified with the product.

A few examples: What do you think of when someone describes a chocolate sandwich cookie with white filling? Yet Oreo is only one of several competing brands. Xerox copiers so dominate customer perception that in spite of Xerox corporation's trademark protection campaign, their brand has become a generic; many people talk of going downtown to Xerox something (the correct word is "photocopy").

If your competition is firmly associated in the public eye with getting that task done, you have a marketing challenge. You've got to prove to each prospect that you offer better value and/or do a better job.

A classic corporate example is Avis's "We're Number 2 but We Try Harder" campaign in the sixties. This campaign lasted many years and significantly eroded Hertz's market share.

Probably the easiest way to shift brand loyalty from Them to You is with a comparison chart, expressed in terms of benefits. Your product should demonstrate benefits your competitors don't offer: for instance, lower price, longer warranty, higher performance, expandability . . . The chart on page 18 is a fairly generic one I did for my own business.

If your competition is firmly associated in the public eye with getting that task done, you have a marketing challenge.

Case History

Sometimes your best marketing material might be a success story—an actual case history of a situation where you or your product solved a problem. Think of it as an expanded, third-person testimonial.

Essentially, you want to write a mini-article of say, two hundred to one thousand words. Begin by introducing the person and the problem. Then introduce your company, purveyor of the solution. Finally, show how you fixed things. Look for problems with wide applicability; avoid examples that are so specialized as to feel irrelevant to most of your prospects. If you sell products, be as specific as you can. But if you sell services rather than products, show what your company did, but not how. For the how—the specific step-by-step implementation of the solution—the prospect will have to come to you. For instance:

For Jane Franklin Associates, an industrial energy auditing firm, collections were becoming a major problem. Receivables were reaching 40 percent of gross revenues, and the company's cash flow and credit rating were beginning to suffer. Finally, after several attempts to solve the problem in-house, Jane Franklin Associates called in the experts: Accounting for Business Capital, Inc.

ABC's trained business managers and accountants began with an assessment of the problem. After

gathering data and observing procedures for one week, ABC created a detailed report outlining eight specific steps to improve receivables collection. These ranged from working out a discount for prompt payment to halting work on contracts where the client was in arrears.

ABC also provided a concrete implementation plan, including a one-month phase-in period with extensive training of the company's sales force.

The results: after sixty days, Jane Franklin Associates reported successful collection of nearly all of its debts. Receivables outstanding had fallen to only 8 percent of revenue, with further drops forecast as new clients came on board under the new procedures.

If you have a problem with accounting, cash flow, or business management, call in the experts. We can help you, just as we helped Jane Franklin Associates.

Objections and Their Answers

Successful selling involves meeting objections head-on, not trying to bury or trivialize them. Every objection a prospect presents should be treated not as a roadblock, but as an opportunity—because if you successfully answer the objection, you remove an obstacle to the sale. If you fail to answer the objection, the prospect is quite right to go elsewhere. But each answer creates momentum toward the sale.

So give your vocal cords a rest; answer objections before they're raised. Put together a sheet describing the most common points of resistance—and your best arguments why those objections aren't enough to block the sale. (See the example on page 19.)

Qualifications/Capabilities Summary

This is a sheet describing your credentials: why you, your firm, and your product are uniquely qualified to solve the prospect's problem.

At first glance, this may seem to contradict the principles of client-centered marketing; the emphasis here is on you, not your prospect. But a closer look reveals the qualifications sheet is not an exercise in egoism or horn blowing. Rather, you *use the document to demonstrate that you have the ability to solve the prospect's problem!* Here, you can list:

- Educational and other credentials
- Length of time in business
- Specific benefits of your product's features or your approach to providing a service
- Types of problems you have solved—and for whom

The tone of a capabilities statement should be professional but also soothing and reassuring. The example on page 20 is one we use in our business; notice how it takes a very small company—two full-time staff—and packages it in a confident, problem-solving way. It fits on one 8½ x 11-inch page.

With my training in journalism, I usually try to put the important stuff pretty close to the beginning—after all, newspapers and wire services cut from the bottom up. On the other hand, direct-mail copywriter Joseph Sugarman (a pioneer of the long-form, first-person ad) in his book, *Advertising Secrets of the Written Word,* says that the purpose of the

WHERE TO GO FOR THE BEST MARKETING MATERIALS

	Accurate Writing & More	Ad Agency	Public Relations Firm	In-House Writing/ Design Staff	Your Secretary
Professional Quality	X	X	X	X	
Experts in Low-Cost, Benefit-Driven, Client-Centered Marketing	X				
Principals Involved in All Writing Projects; Best Talents Working for You	X			X	
Fast Turnaround	X				X
Always a Focus on Helping You	X				
You Have Full Control over Creative Concepts	X			X	
Pay Only for What You Need; No Retainer or Salary	X	X			
Familiar with Internet Marketing	X	maybe	X	X	
International Reputation and Clients	X	maybe	maybe		
Editing Services Available	X			X	X

The Best Work at the Best Prices

ACCURATE WRITING & MORE

(413) 586–2388/(800) 683–WORD

http://www.accuratewritingandmore.com

headline is to get you to read the first sentence, the purpose of the first sentence is to draw you down to the second sentence, and so on. He tries to write copy that you can't stop reading—and often, he doesn't really describe his offer until close to the bottom of the ad. His anecdotal style aims at triggering psychological responses in his readers, among them a feeling of ownership of the product, a belief in the seller's honesty, credibility, and authority, and the intellectual ammunition to justify an essentially emotion-based purchase.

— Ogilvy's Principles —

David Ogilvy, founder of Ogilvy & Mather, one of the world's largest and most successful ad agencies, is a believer in research. Based on extensive testing, he developed guidelines for effective ads. He scattered them throughout his book, *Ogilvy on Advertising*, and I've gathered them together:

- If five times more people read headlines than body copy, your headline must sell—or you've wasted 80 percent of your ad dollars. Promise a benefit in your headline to attract four times as many readers.
- For the same reason, mention the brand name in your headline.

- Headlines below an illustration have 10 percent higher readership than headlines above the picture—but never put the headline under the body copy.
- Caption every illustration and use sales copy in the caption. Captions have much higher readership than body copy.
- In designing art, focus on one person, not a group—or focus on the product.
- Keep the language simple and the copy interesting (and that lets you use long copy, which Ogilvy favors).
- Use a great lead.
- Six times as many people read editorial copy than read ads. So consider making your ad look like a story. Ads that look like editorial content can get past the reader's automatic filter against advertising. Thus, full-page text-heavy ads with drop capitals, serif type, black ink on a white background, set in three- or four-column type, *without* the company logo, can work very well.
- Short lines increase readership.
- Devices such as bullets, asterisks, and arrows draw readers into your copy.
- Call attention to key points with bold or italic type, call-outs, bulleted or numbered lists, etc.
- If using long copy, break the page up graphically: use a two-line subhead between your headline

Why You Need a New Multifuel Furnace
Even If You're Happy with Your Existing Heater

OBJECTION	ANSWER
My old furnace works just fine.	Technology has come a long way in just a short while. If your furnace is over ten years old, the money you'll save in reduced heating costs will cover the cost of installation in only two years. After that, you'll save money free and clear every year.
Gas heat's gotten more expensive every year.	The beauty of our system is its multifuel capacity. You can heat with gas when that's cost-effective, switch to wood pellets when gas gets too high, even use bottled gas if you get a good deal on propane.
But I don't want to hassle with cutting and storing logs.	With our patented pellet system, you don't have to struggle with logs. You can burn scrap pellets available from us, or from your local lumberyard. You'll help preserve the environment by keeping wood scrap out of the landfills, too!

Accurate Writing & More

P.O. Box 1164
Northampton, MA 01061-1164, USA
(413) 586-2388 (voice) (617) 249-0153 (fax)
e-mail: info@frugalfun.com
http://www.accuratewritingandmore.com

Company Profile: How We Can Help You

Services Offered: Accurate Writing & More can assist you with all phases of any writing, editing, or marketing project: from initial conception to working with your design and printing team. Among the services we offer are:

- Writing/Research—Press releases, newsletters, brochures, business plans, annual reports, fliers, ad copy, Web content, direct-mail letters, even complete manuscripts. Particular expertise in media contact, résumés, sales/promotional writing, and articles.
- Marketing/Public Relations—Full range of techniques and materials. We create from scratch, revamp your material, and/or help you develop the strategy for your own promotional program.
- Consulting and Training—On marketing/advertising, career transitions, effective writing, public speaking, starting and running a small business, and the Internet.
- Manuscript Analysis and Content Editing—We evaluate manuscripts for structural logic, consistency, salability, and other factors. You'll receive a written critique.
- Line Editing—A sentence-by-sentence overhaul to eliminate turgid writing, clean up grammar and spelling errors, and flag areas that need content revision.

History: Founded in 1981 by Director Shel Horowitz and Codirector D. Dina Friedman, the firm benefits from the principals' experience in marketing, business, journalism, public relations, arts, human services, academia, and the public sector to serve a diversified international clientele.

Principals' Credentials: Shel Horowitz's third book, *Marketing Without Megabucks*, was published by Simon & Schuster in 1993. Author of over 800 articles (on marketing, business, computing, arts, etc.), he's been creating promotional materials since 1975. He is Webmaster at the award-winning http://www.frugalfun.com Web site, with over 350 money-saving, career-building articles. A frequent speaker and radio guest, he has a Communications degree from Antioch University.

D. Dina Friedman holds an M.S.W. from the University of Connecticut, and a degree in English from Cornell University. A former agency director and Oxford University Press staff member, she teaches classes on speaking and writing at Mount Holyoke College. Her work has been published in numerous journals, and she is the recipient of several creative writing awards. She has been creating marketing documents since 1979.

Fees and Turnaround Time: For most services, we charge an affordable hourly rate. Specific charges vary according to the nature of the job, time allotted, and special needs. We attempt to complete all projects as fast as reasonably possible. Rush service is often available for an additional charge.

Contact us to discuss how we can assist you on your next project.

and the body copy, start the body with a drop cap (13 percent increase in readership!), use no more than eleven words in the first paragraph, and use subheads every couple of inches. And use good leading—a fair amount of space between lines of type. According to Ogilvy, it increases readership by 12 percent.

— Grammar and Syntax —

Personally, I really like the rules of English. Our expressive language continues to evolve. It's no longer considered horrible to end a sentence with a preposition. Compound words have entered the language; string words into compounds when that makes sense—and coin new words when their meaning is unmistakable. And many words have modernized their spelling in the past few decades: "catalog" has replaced "catalogue."

Correct grammar is definitely preferable, if it works. But sometimes the 100 percent grammatically correct way to express something is a bit too stodgy to do the best marketing job. When you get frustrated with the limitations of perfect English, bend the rules a bit—*if* you know what you're doing. For instance, if you generally write in complete sentences, slip in a sentence fragment—vary the flow. But detours from schoolbook grammar should be deliberate, and should create the same tone you would use if you were speaking. Here's an example: Technically, "data" is the plural of "datum" (fact). But in speech, nobody refers to data in the plural; it's treated as singular.

Call me old-fashioned, but there are some rules you should never break:

- Never misspell, except in a pun ("Lite" can't substitute for "Light").
- Use punctuation properly; be particularly careful with apostrophes and semicolons.
- Except where common speech says otherwise, singulars and plurals, as well as pasts, presents, and futures, should be consistent; nouns and verbs should agree.

After all, if literacy goes out of fashion, who will read your marketing?

✍

I'd like to thank Dr. Jeffrey Lant for his help in crystallizing my copywriting ideas. His book, *Cash Copy,* makes a science of knowing why most copy doesn't work well—and how to change it.

4

By Design

Printing and graphics has its own language. Thus, a glossary:

Art: Any illustration, chart, or photo.

Balloon: Text coming out of someone's mouth, cartoon-style.

Bleed: Ink going all the way to the edge of the page.

Body Copy, or Body Text: The substance of your offer, the main text of your ad, flier, brochure, or letter.

Body Type: Typeface used for the body copy.

Border: A graphic element around the outside of an ad or separating one section from another.

Box: A border that completely encloses a section.

Bullet: A large dot or other graphic accent character, followed by a point you wish to make (I've used bullets extensively in this book).

Camera-Ready: All prepared for printing—fully typeset and laid out.

Clip Art: Art that has been removed from copyright protection, sold to be reused.

Copy: Words.

Dingbat: A non-alphanumeric character used for graphic accent.

Display Type: Decorative typeface used for headlines and graphics.

Drop Caps (Drop Capitals): The first letter of a paragraph is several sizes larger and hangs down to the left of the next few lines of type.

Fill: A percentage of color or gray added to shade an area.

Font: In computer lingo, the same as a typeface (i.e., Helvetica family). In typesetting jargon, a particular size, weight, and attribute of a typeface (i.e., 12-point Helvetica Bold Italic).

Four-Color: A printing process using four passes through a printing press to achieve a full range of colors.

Full-Size Page: A newspaper page roughly the size of *USA Today's*.

Graduated (Gradated) Fill: A fill that changes color or shade as it progresses.

Graphic Element: Anything other than straight text, used to add visual interest.

Graphic: A picture, whether drawn or photographed. See also *Art*.

Halftone: A photograph reshot with a photostat camera to make it reproduce better when printing.

Headline: Text in large letters, functioning as both a graphic and a quick summary of what follows.

Insert: A piece distributed with a publication but not bound inside it.

Layout: The way a piece looks on the page. Also used to describe the act of putting together a mechanical (see below).

Leading: The amount of space between lines of text.

Letterpress: A method of printing involving raised letters, typically used for high-quality, small-run jobs such as business cards.

Line Art: A high-contrast drawing suitable for inexpensive reproduction.

Magazine Page: Typically, 8½ X 11 inches or slightly larger, often supporting full color.

Mechanical: Camera-ready paste-up all set for the printer.

Offset (or Photo-Offset) Printing: The most common modern printing technology, in which a page is set from a photographic image, rather than from hot lead melted into letters. Allows infinite design freedom.

Pantone Matching System: Color selection and calibration based on standardized swatches of color (look them over at your print shop).

Paste-Up: Camera-ready layout, or the act of preparing one. Gets its name from the act of assembling and attaching all the elements on a page (the precomputer method).

Photostat: A high-quality photographic reproduction, suitable for use in camera-ready copy, made on a special camera called a stat camera.

Picas: Measurement of a typeset line's horizontal width. There are about six picas to an inch.

Points: Measurement of type size, representing the height of the letters. In most typefaces, an inch contains 72 points.

Pull Quote, Call-Out: A short excerpt from a longer piece, set apart in distinctive type, that functions as a graphic to generate reader interest. Can also refer to a testimonial quote, especially one taken from a media broadcast or printed article.

Reverse Type: White letters on a solid background.

RGB: A color matching system based on the colors output by a computer monitor's red, green, and blue electron guns.

Rule: A vertical or horizontal line within an ad, or between design elements on a page (for example, between two columns, or between the masthead and the articles).

Screen: Density of a halftone, in lines per inch. A 120-line screen looks better than an 80-line screen.

Secondary Headline (Kicker): A smaller headline that either reinforces the original message or adds a new one. It can be immediately under or above the main headline—that's when it's known as a kicker—or on a different part of the page.

Sidebar: A mini-article close to the main article, but usually separated by a box, shaded area, or other graphic device.

Spot Color: Use of one extra color to perk up visual interest.

Stat Camera: A specialized camera for making photostatic prints.

Subhead: A small headline within the body type, breaking up large sections of text.

Sunburst (or Starburst): Text surrounded by a series of radiating triangles in a starlike shape.

Tabloid: Larger than a magazine page but still not full size—say, 11 X 17 inches. Often, full-sized newspapers include tabloid sections or inserts.

Text: Words, body copy.

Text Effects, Special Effects: Bending, embellishing, and/or distorting type to create unusual effects.

Text Wrap: Shaping an area of text to fit around a graphic or white space. (Also refers to a computer's capability to move text to the next line without using a carriage return.)

Typeface: An alphabet, plus additional characters, all in a consistent style. There are thousands of typefaces available for both display and body type.

Typeface Family: A group of similar typefaces with different attributes. For example, a typeface family might include roman (regular letters), italic (slanted), bold (dark and thick), bold italic. Some typeface families also come in different weights (light, medium, demibold, extrabold).

White Space: Blank areas within an ad—a very important design element.

— Design Principles —

A good visual piece, whether it's a business card, flier, display ad, or even a direct-mail letter, should grab the reader and be easy to look at. Don't make it too busy and jumpy, unless you're selling heavy metal music or electroconvulsive therapy.

Remember, the visuals must support and reinforce your message:

- Lead with your most important point, in a large headline.
- Restate the point early in the body copy.
- Consider using a secondary headline, either immediately next to the main headline or in a different part of the ad.
- Use white space as a graphic element.
- Choose graphics (if the piece uses them) that your readers will want to look at, but that are also closely related to your message.
- Frame a partial page with a border (otherwise, your ad will float off visually into editorial matter—or worse, into someone else's ad!).
- Break up large areas of text with subheads or graphic elements.
- Use a slogan, logo, and/or typeface to project a unified image.

Extra Visual Impact

A flier has to draw attention on a crowded bulletin board. A small display ad may be packed in with a dozen others on the same page. Let yours jump out at the reader. Try a few of these tricks: borders and rules (thick or decorative ones will be more visible); sunbursts or balloons; reverse type; bold print; boxed pull quotes; fills and bleeds; boxed-off sections within the main text; sidebars; eye-catching display type; type manipulated and distorted with special effects; text wrapped around graphics; text used as a graphic; type set at an angle, around a curve, or in a vertical line (as long as it's still easy to read); spot color (in a single-color page such as most newspapers); a coupon with a thick border and noticeable type.

The larger your ad, the more subtle you can be—and thus the more attractive an ad you can create. But in a small ad, you don't have the space to be concerned with whether it's gorgeous; you just want to make sure it's read by almost every person who skims that page. The smaller the ad, the more it has to scream to be noticed in the crowd. So use several of these elements.

— Working with Specialists —

In every project, you have to make choices about whether to do your own work or bring in a professional for each component of the process. You might work with writers, editors, illustrators, photographers, paste-up/stat camera artists, designers, typesetters or computerized typesetting service bureaus, printers/xerographers, and/or Web programmers.

Many times it will make sense for you to do the whole job from start to finish (for instance, you can produce simple fliers with a computer and laser printer). At other times, you may want to do your own writing and design but reproduce the final document commercially. And sometimes you'll want to use a pro at some or all stages before your document is camera-ready.

Three important things to keep in mind: First, different people will be right for different projects, so keep a stable of associates. You may need different illustrators for original hand-drawn line art, computer-generated illustration, and photography. And that great direct-mail writer may not be best for an annual report or press release.

Second, the same person may offer a range of skills. You may find a skilled writer and editor with some desktop publishing and design ability (I'm an example). And your print shop may offer stat work and typesetting.

You may have some of these skills. However, sometimes it pays to collaborate. For example, if you're doing a classy brochure, and you are an adequate writer with no design skills, you might write a draft of the text, have a copywriter spruce it up, then turn it over to a designer.

Third, be clear about what you want and how the piece will be used. The better you communicate your needs at every stage, the more likely you'll be happy with the end product.

Important: Make sure to get the rights you need! In most countries, unless specifically granted in a written contract, the rights remain with the work's creator. If you contract out for a piece of writing, a photo, an illustration, even a layout, your written contract should specify that you have the unlimited right to use the piece in any medium, without additional compensation (or with a specified royalty for each use). Otherwise, you could invest time and effort into a marketing campaign and lose the right to use the image, slogan, or layout.

However, be fair to your creative people, too. In most cases, you shouldn't need an all-rights or work-for-hire contract (that would in effect give you ownership of the work)—but you might want a noncompete clause so that you don't see your competitors using the same work.

Following are some tips on selecting and working with these specialists.

Writers and Editors

Writing promotional material is both a science and an art. If you're going to spend a chunk of money doing a brochure or newsletter, make sure the copy is up to snuff. Before you set the type, try out the piece on people who will give you accurate and detailed feedback.

If you decide to call in outside help, you can either outline the project to a writer and wait for a draft, or write the first draft yourself and then let an editor or copywriter put the magic in it. Whether you or the consultant prepares the first draft, expect to play with it. Make sure each section uses strong sales language. Examine the different sections together, to see if they fit well and are in the right order.

Where do you find writers and editors? Get recommendations from other business owners whose marketing materials you respect. Look in the Yellow Pages under Editorial Services, Marketing Consultants, Public Relations, or Publicity. Or, of course, give us a call (you'll find complete contact information in Resources). Do make sure the writer or editor is expert with promotional material; a technical writer or journalist may not have a good handle on sales writing.

Illustrators and Photographers

If you want original art for a local marketing piece, ask instructors of commercial art classes for a recommendation. You may find a talented young artist willing to work for a low fee. These students are usually only too happy to build up their portfolios, and may remember your kindness later, when they are in demand. However, always look at an artist's portfolio before you make any agreements. Discuss the marketing focus and the reproduction technology of the final piece, and make sure the artist understands the limitations on what reproduces well in that process. Also, ask the artist how many hours of work it took to do some of the pieces in the portfolio. Sometimes inexperience shows itself in slow speed—and you may be better off paying an established pro three times as much per hour to do the work in a quarter of the time.

Photography is another matter. Don't diddle around with amateurs. Commercial photography involves many variables as well as specialized knowledge and equipment, and your uncle with his fifty-dollar camera is not going to be up to the task. Expect to pay hourly rates of anywhere from sixty to hundreds of dollars, and expect the photographer to shoot several rolls of film in order to get one or two perfect shots—and at those prices, don't settle for less than perfection!

Paste-up Artists/Computer Artists/ Stat Camera Operators

Most designers and commercial artists also have layout skills. Sometimes you might be able to lay out your own type, but have to "strip in" illustrations. (If the design will be repeated in another document, or the document will be revised, definitely use a computer—and get a copy on disk. That way, revision will be easy, and you're not tied to the original artist.)

If you're reproducing art that appeared somewhere else, you may need to have a scan or photostat made, to improve quality, alter the image, crop out extraneous material, or resize.

Designers

A good designer makes all the difference in the appearance of your finished piece. Skilled designers use color, type, special effects, layout, and paper selection to make your work stand out or to create a unified look for all your documents. The range of tricks is infinite and constantly expanding. Be firm, however, about your own aesthetics. If the designer shows you something in scrunchy type splayed unreadably around the edges of an irregular object, remind your expert that the purpose of the piece is to sell—not to be a showpiece for the latest in bizarre graphics.

Jeffrey Lant suggests getting your original version done by the best designer you can find, and doing later tune-ups with the least expensive, who can work from the world-class ideas of your original design.

Typesetters and Service Bureaus

These days, you'll have almost no occasion to create typesetting from scratch. It's far more efficient to enter the text on a computer and bring it to a service bureau for output directly from your disk onto high-quality typesetting systems. Most of the time, you will be bringing in the entire document: not just type, but graphics and layout incorporated electronically into a computer file. The typesetting system, called an imagesetter, will produce your finished page at anywhere from 1,200 to 4,800 lines per inch. Higher numbers mean better quality, but also more time and money. (Many service bureaus can also output color slides).

Set up text differently for typesetting than for straight typing: Use true typesetting characters such as curly ("smart") quotes—most word-processing software allows this automatically—and em dashes (solid dashes that look like this:—; not this: --). However, turn off the special characters if you'll be sending text by e-mail; it turns to garbage. Those of us who predate computers were taught to leave an extra space between sentences, an extra line between paragraphs, and to underline when we wanted emphasis. We were also taught to put in a carriage return at the end of each line. Unlearn these habits! Robin Williams's books *The Mac is Not a Typewriter* and *The PC is Not a Typewriter* will warn you of all the bugaboos.

Use these steps to save time, money, and trouble at the service bureau: (1) Prepare a laser-printed draft copy that shows exactly how you want the finished page to look; (2) list (and include on disk) every typeface you've used in the document; (3) consider leaving space for your art and pasting it in, rather than manipulating huge and awkward digital art files that can be painfully slow to set; (4) specify every shade of every color, using the Pantone system; (5) check the final copy before you leave.

Printers and Xerographers

You will be amazed at how much variety there is in printing cost, quality, and turnaround time. And different printers have different strengths; the shop that gives you the best deal on one hundred copies of a one-color offset flier may not even be competitive on a four-color job with a run of ten thousand.

Know the strengths and weaknesses of the printers you use regularly, and always get several bids for both price and turnaround time. Use printers and xerographers who guarantee the quality of their work. If at all possible, be present for a "press check" as your job is run.

For simple jobs, consider your local photocopy shop. Often, xerographers are skilled in doing simple paste-ups, shifting contrast, enlarging or reducing, and a host of other techniques that once were the exclusive domain of graphic artists and printers. Copy shops stock a wide range of papers and often have the best price on short runs.

Printers and copy shops may offer additional services to make your life easier. For instance, machine-folding may add almost nothing to the job price, but saves you hours while looking more professional than hand-folding. Also, if your material includes a tear-off return coupon, the printer may be able to score it for you so the coupon tears evenly and easily, or even supply you with prescored specialty paper.

5

Mastering Myriad Media

When planning marketing campaigns involving media, you must understand the difference between free publicity and advertising—because, no matter what the medium, you'll approach things differently if you're getting news coverage or paying for a sales message.

For publicity, someone else decides that you'd make a good story (or have a good story to share). In most cases, you have no control over the coverage, but you don't pay any money for it, either. Because you present yourself as news, your business might be featured in an article or endorsed on an Internet discussion group. You could be invited to be a talk show guest or give a speech. In seeking free publicity, your mission is to provide information and/or entertainment. An overt sales pitch will actually work against you.

Advertising is different: You pay for the space, and you control it. Your tone can range from screaming hard-sell to advertorials so subtle that most people don't even realize they're ads. You can use your thirty seconds, your quarter page, your 4 x 1-inch Web banner any way you want within the confines of acceptable standards. These standards vary—but media retain the right to reject ads they find objectionable.

But just because you've paid for the ad doesn't mean it'll do you any good. You don't have control over placement—where and when the ad appears—unless you've negotiated for it.

Of course, with direct mail fliers and your Web site, you make the rules. You're limited only by your budget and imagination.

Each medium has its own set of strengths and weaknesses, for both free and paid coverage. Consider audience targeting, immediacy, ease of changing the campaign. . . . We'll analyze a few generic categories in the table on the facing page.

Since each business is different, and has its own particular goals and budget, the appropriate mix will be different for every one of you. The important thing is that you take the time to evaluate any marketing tactic, make sure it fits into your overall strategy, and make your most educated guesses about the return you'll receive on your investment of time and money. In other words, don't assume something is a great bargain just because it has a low price. Be more concerned with the number of qualified prospects you're reaching, how receptive they'll be to your message, and the cost of converting each sale.

Keep that in mind as we go through the rest of the book. We'll start with free publicity in the media.

Medium	Strengths	Weaknesses	Approaches
Daily newspaper	Frequent publication Targeting by section of the paper, classified heading, and geography Excellent opportunities for finding news hooks for free publicity	Short shelf life General audience: pay to reach non-prospects Smaller reach than broadcast media	*Publicity* Active campaign of press releases, letters to the editor, building relationships with key staff, cosponsorships *Advertising* Classifieds; occasional section-specific display ads when tied to key events
Radio	Large audience Can reach prospects when other media can't get through (i.e., drive time) Low production costs Easy to create a mood	Intangible Ephemeral Requires continual repetition Expensive in major markets General audience	*Publicity* PSAs, guest appearances, cosponsorships *Advertising* Special interest shows, underwriting and premium donations for listener-sponsored stations
Your own Web site	Essentially unlimited information and sales opportunities Minimal start-up cost Reinforces and expands all marketing in every medium Enables you to capture a database for follow-up	Requires careful planning, considerable time, and thorough understanding of the medium Creates a need for continuous fresh content Can be frustrating to new users	*Publicity* Search engine placement of home page and subpages, cross-links, newsletter, e-mail "sig," mention in all other media, cyber-events *Advertising* E-zine sponsorships, banners, off-line media
Others' Web sites	Potentially large and very targeted audience Prospects can follow leads right to you Instant gratification Measurable results Trading ads keeps cost down	Server and browser problems Prospects may abandon slow-loading or poorly laid-out sites Traffic may or may not be prequalified	*Publicity* Your articles, cross-links, archives from discussion groups *Advertising* Banner ads, text links, promotional product giveaways

Also analyze every specific option before making any media buy or publicity campaign—for example:

Medium	Strengths	Weaknesses	Approaches
5-week sponsorship of "Car Crazy" on WKCZ	Reaches 4,000 hot-rodders who could patronize my muffler shop Will build recognition and market share rapidly $40 per insertion = $200 marketing cost	May interfere with market share among more conservative fleet owners Seasonal fluctuations; hot rod business only comes in during warm weather	*Projected Results* Estimated Return: 8 new customers, average first order ticket of $150 Total income $1,200. Total profit at 30% average markup (less cost of ad and products): $700 Additional benefits expected: more word-of-mouth, positioning as the muffler shop for hot rodders, back-end sales over several years We'll try it!

6

Media Publicity:
The Hidden Goldmine

Per prospect reached, there is not a more cost-effective way to market yourself than getting free publicity in the media. Newspapers, newsletters, magazines, Internet channels, radio and TV stations can give you thousands of dollars in free coverage—which enhances your reputation and makes your audience more receptive to your other marketing efforts. In fact, a well-orchestrated publicity campaign may be all the marketing some businesses ever need: Georg Schlomka of Germany built his company, A Conto GmbH, to a million-dollar business almost entirely through press coverage (you'll learn more about him later).

Let's look at the numbers: At this writing, a one-ounce first-class mailing costs 33 cents. Photocopying can cost as little as 3 cents per copy. An envelope costs a penny (in bulk). Thus, a one-page press release can cost as little as 37 cents. If you mail 20 releases, that's $7.40; 50 will cost you $18.50. (If you e-mail, hand-deliver, or fax the releases, you save the cost of postage and envelopes.)

If four small newspapers and a radio station decide to use your release, perhaps 100,000 people now know about your event, service, or product. From those 100,000 people, let's say 100 decide to attend your event or use your service. You have spent between zero and 19 cents to bring each person in.

Think about your own reading and viewing habits for a moment. When you see a feature story or hear an interview, how often do you want to do business with the person being profiled? How many books have you read because you saw the author on TV? Authors appear on talk shows to make their books stand out from the thousands of other titles published each year—to create demand for their product.

The Massachusetts-based natural-foods supermarket chain Bread & Circus has gotten excellent corporate-wide exposure through free media coverage, according to Hadley branch manager Dave Lannon: "When we opened the Brookline store, we got a three-page article in the *Boston Herald*. It would have cost thousands of dollars to buy a three-page ad, but [the story] didn't cost us anything."

Publicity also lends a lot to your credibility: A journalist wants to share your information with the public! That kind of independent validation can't be bought. If the press deems you important, you're important in the eyes of your prospects.

In fact, the whole reason people advertise is to get publicity. Advertisers pay for space in print or electronic media to say whatever they want. The advertisement creates publicity, which builds on an image to sell more goods, serve more clients, present ideas to new audiences, or be more effective in the community.

But by using the media effectively, you reap the same benefits without having to pay for it. Bob Wieler, a consultant with the National Association for the Self-Employed, puts it this way: "If you could, you would advertise in every possible place all the time—that way you'd reach everybody. The problem is, you can't afford to do that because it costs too much. Anytime you can get exposure for free, take it."

When you get free publicity rather than pay for advertising, you give up control over the content. But you have the added legitimacy of being chosen to represent your field. Because news coverage at least pretends to be unbiased, it is more valuable than advertising; you get, in a sense, a testimonial—a disinterested, credible party who thinks you're worthy of positive attention. Many people take news coverage more seriously than advertising—and may be more likely to be influenced by it than by a paid ad.

— Think Like an Editor —

In order to take advantage of this free publicity goldmine, you need to learn how to think like an editor. That's easy: *Make yourself newsworthy.*

News is anything that other people are interested in. And being newsworthy consists of letting editors and reporters know you're doing something of interest to other people—having an event; telling a story; creating or participating in any occurrence; supporting, opposing, or even merely observing a trend or activity.

Editors and producers have the tremendous challenge of coming up with new stories to fill their pages and air slots—day after day, week after week, month after month, year after year. It isn't always easy to fill all that space. Therefore, you become their ally. Your achievements—along with your ability to publicize them properly and work cooperatively with media people—will cause local editors to welcome

you with open arms. Not only will you have a very good shot at getting your press release printed (perhaps several times in different sections of the paper), but a reporter might even arrange a more in-depth story. And that's pure gold for you!

Stanley D. Friedman, retired public affairs producer for WWOR-TV (serving New York City and northern New Jersey), notes that—even in one of the top markets in the country—he had to seek out people to fill up his allotted airtime. Editors and producers, therefore, will be delighted to hear from you—but only if you are articulate and can present yourself as serving the community, rather than merely trying to seek publicity and make a profit.

Here are some events or situations that often lead almost effortlessly to lots of free publicity:

- Organizing an event open to the public
- Achieving significant recognition in your field
- Release of a book or record, opening of an exhibit, etc.
- Performing an important service to the community
- Running for office
- Writing legislation, testifying at hearings, etc.
- Inventing, manufacturing, or offering a new product or service
- Being present at—or, better still, involved in—major news events
- Joining or taking leadership in a professional or community service organization—especially one with membership standards
- Offering apprenticeships, training programs, classes, or opportunities to volunteer
- Teaching, lecturing, or presenting at a professional conference
- Winning a contest, sweepstakes, or lottery
- Offering franchises of your business

But you can also get some coverage of far more mundane events. You may not get followed around by a reporter, but you might well get your releases in the paper—and reap all the benefits we discussed earlier. Here are a few examples:

- Moving or opening a new branch
- Educational achievements (including attending work-related seminars) or other accomplishments by members of your staff
- Hosting an open house
- Hiring or promotion of employees
- Annual meetings
- Issuance of any publication available to the public

Use your imagination. You only risk a stamp, and may gain exposure to thousands of people. The media that promote you have something to gain as well; they need an endless supply of fresh material.

M*ost editors shy away from blatantly*
promotional pieces.

But don't expect the media to drop everything and report on you just so that you can get some free publicity. Remember their goals of reporting news and serving the community; you must blend with that agenda. Most editors shy away from blatantly promotional pieces.

— Make Life Easier for Journalists—

Present yourself as the kind of person editors want to deal with. In any oral or written communication with a media outlet, you should be friendly and approachable, articulate and concise. Be willing to answer reporters' questions, even if you have to research the answers and get back to them. (Don't be afraid to say you don't know but can find out, and *never give an answer you're not sure is accurate.*) If you're running an event or a tourist attraction, let the press in for free to cover it. Finally, know the deadlines and publication schedules of the media you deal with, and understand their importance.

A deadline is the day and time a reporter has to get a story in if it's going to be printed or broadcast in the next edition. Except for very hot last-minute news, those deadlines may as well be written in stone. Get your stuff in on time and don't try to wheedle a journalist into bending a deadline for you—the bad reputation you will get among the press is a far worse disease than being left out once. And don't forget that a reporter needs some time to work with your material and is balancing your story against many others.

Typically, morning daily newspapers close the edition around 10 P.M.; afternoon papers at around 10 A.M.; weeklies two to four days before publication. Some sections may close earlier than others. A large metropolitan Sunday newspaper may close the magazine, comics, arts, living, and classified sections as early as Monday and have them already printed and collated as early as the previous Thursday. This frees up the presses for news and sports sections that get printed Saturday night. TV stations tend to like to do the camera work several hours before the newscast. Give daily and broadcast journalists a minimum of a couple of hours before their deadline to write their story—several days if you're dealing with weeklies, and from three weeks to eight months for monthlies—and don't call any reporter or editor right at deadline, when he or she is frantically trying to get all the stories out.

Feature departments, including community calendars or letters to the editor, may have a deadline that applies to you rather than to the reporter. In my area, the newsweekly and the most popular commercial radio station both want calendar notices two to three weeks ahead! Again, respect the deadline and be on time.

— Events: Unlimited Publicity —

The easiest way to turn the press into your publicity bureau is by having an event. An event gives the press a handle; they understand how to treat events as news, and as promotable calendar items. Having any kind of event makes you automatically newsworthy. So a good trick for you as the publicist is to present your event as news. Yes, the same techniques apply to other promotable activities, but so many more doors are opened by linking your publicity agenda to some kind of event that I'd encourage you to do them whenever possible.

For instance, don't just have a sale; a sale is not a news event, but a commercial device to increase business. But a sale can be rolled into something more newsworthy, such as a charity dance-athon with reduced prices on dancing shoes and leotards; an appearance by a local person who is known for using your product, with a concurrent sale on the product; a craft demonstration by an artisan who uses materials that you sell, with price cuts in those supplies; a foot race from a central point to your food shop, with free refreshments for participants; old shoes trade-in: deduct 10 percent off the price of a new pair of shoes by bringing in an old but still usable pair for donation to charity; a food-sampling fair, with discounts on all the participating foods; a plain old party with a storewide clearance sale; a concert in a music store, with sales on the instruments the band plays; a downtown cleanup with free brooms to participants, as well as a sale on trash bags, rubber gloves, and so on.

Of course, it's not necessary to have a sale as part of your event. Many wonderful events can happen without a sale. But if you want a sale, you can get a lot more publicity if you focus on the event. Toward the bottom of your release, mention the sale: "To honor Emma Lazarus's reading and book signing, Great Books is having a sale on every book that contains any of her poems," or "In conjunction with the charity skate-athon, Alfredo's is offering reduced prices on all skates and skating wear."

— Community Service —

You will notice many promotable events involve charity or community service. This is not coincidence. It is always easier for a business to get free publicity if it's also promoting a cause. Food donations, community improvement projects, and raising and donating money all attract publicity—and help something you genuinely believe in. That last part is key:

If you try to do charity insincerely, it will boomerang back at you. But your firm can get commercial mileage out of its good deeds! The donation can be small or large, but it must be genuine and heartfelt.

Here's a large-scale example pioneered in my area by Stop & Shop supermarkets: They worked out a deal with a computer manufacturer to donate computers to elementary schools, then invited schools to participate. For every hundred thousand dollars or so in register receipts, the school got a new computer. It was a brilliant move; the promotion was much talked about in the community. Many people switched to Stop & Shop for the duration of the campaign. It cost the store nothing and also benefited the computer company. Not only did the manufacturer get goodwill, but it also trained a new generation of students in using its products—a classic win-win scheme.

Of course, nonprofit organizations can benefit by organizing their own charity events as well. Such events have a long list of benefits: they build visibility for the agency (as we discuss in chapter 39), raise money, provide an opportunity to receive many in-kind donations (something funders often look for), give volunteers a chance to get involved, and let the community enjoy a good time. Many agencies repeat the events year after year because—despite the significant organizing effort they require—they do so much for the agency and for the community.

In my city, some of the more successful annual charity fundraisers include:

- Books and Cooks: A major United Way fundraiser that teams famous cookbook authors with local restaurants. The authors prepare dishes from their latest publications.
- Transperformance: A concert series benefiting the local arts council, in which local musicians impersonate famous rock stars.
- Benefit Boogie: A rock concert by a well-known local band, with lots of business-donated door prizes, raising money and awareness for an agency that gives food and clothing to poor people.

- Tour de Sol: A multistate auto race of solar and hybrid-solar-powered cars, sponsored by an alternative energy clearinghouse.

— Get Sponsored by the Media —

For community service or entertainment events, enlist newspapers and broadcast stations as cosponsors. Typically, media cosponsorship means you do the work and spend whatever money is necessary; the station or publication gives you oodles of free publicity, reports on it, and/or broadcasts portions of the event.

Electronic media are required to provide public service programming as a condition of their license, and publications have a vested interest in maintaining their credibility as the eyes and ears of the community. Because cosponsorship demonstrates the media outlet's community interest and also lets the public hobnob with media personalities, a suggestion for cosponsorship will often be greeted quite enthusiastically.

What's the difference between the ordinary free publicity you can garner and bringing the station in as a cosponsor? Jordi Herold, talent booker for the Iron Horse Music Hall in Northampton, Massachusetts, uses cosponsorship several times a month. Asking for radio cosponsorship "is not asking for something for nothing, but raises the estimation of the station in [the eyes of] its audience—makes it possible to hear the same music live. It does a lot to contribute to the positive image of the station." Ideally, "it becomes a priority at the station. That's not measurable in times of mention, but it becomes part of the DJ's patter on the air—you can't log that, you can't buy that, you can't specify that."

Newer, smaller media are good bets, says Herold. "We have a station that's new in the area and is competing for market share. If I do a copromotion, I'm likely to get up to fifty free mentions in addition to my paid advertising. With a station . . . that doesn't have a relationship with the club, I may only get a one-to-one relationship between the spots I buy and promotional mentions. With a college radio station, you can be all over the map without any expenditure of money."

For live music, radio cosponsorship is an especially valuable endorsement, because the station's promotional spots will give listeners the chance to hear a little of an artist they may not know—and because the station's role as an arbiter of music carries over to readers who see the cosponsorship listed in the newspapers and on posters.

It's even okay to have several media cosponsoring an event—if they don't compete. For instance, I organized a candidate forum and got sponsorship—and publicity—from one newspaper, one radio station, and one cable TV station. If I'd wanted to get two radio stations, I would have needed to check with both stations that it was all right to have direct competitors cosponsor the event.

Consider cosponsorships for political candidate forums, live entertainment, fairs and festivals, auctions, and other special events.

— Damage Control —

Not all publicity is positive. Negative publicity has seriously injured many businesses.

So how can you protect yourself?

The best protection is not to do anything to get yourself in trouble in the first place. Run a clean, honest operation, treat your employees well, give customers more than they're expecting, and make your best effort to resolve problems directly with your clients and employees.

The second-best defense is an existing positive relationship with the press. At the very least, if there's negative news, your media contacts should call for your side of the story. At best, your strong credibility with the media may cause them to question—and thoroughly investigate—the truthfulness of, and motivations for, the accusations.

As large corporations have proven, even the worst publicity can be countered with a focused, long-term public relations campaign, using the same techniques you use in your other marketing. Remember the Tylenol poisoning scare some years back? The manufacturer immediately recalled the product and converted to tamper-proof packaging. But the company also used an aggressive publicity campaign to let the world know of the steps it was taking; this combination quickly brought back customers with many years of product loyalty.

Remember, being controversial is not in itself a bad thing. In fact, it's a great source of publicity. Don't be afraid to take positions that will raise an eyebrow (as long as you don't insult any class of people with slurs against their group). But being attacked for your opinions is a very different situation than being attacked as unethical, crooked, corrupt, or dangerous to people's health and safety. Those latter cases require careful handling.

If an attack is launched, first determine whether the impact is truly damaging. Sometimes, responding to a minor volley can actually bring more publicity to the original accusation, and the best response is ignoring the whole incident. If, however, the impact is serious, it's time for action. Get a bunch of people to write well-reasoned, moderate-toned, nonstrident letters to the editor in your defense. Look for some independent evidence—say, a favorable write-up in *Consumer Reports*—of your excellent quality, and do a press conference to distribute the positive claims. If at all possible, don't directly address the accusation, and don't say you're responding to it. Just put out as much trust-building as possible in press publicity, advertising, talk show appearances, and through every other means available.

Kathleen Buckley <mailto:Winenews@aol.com> points out that online tools can be crucial in countering damaging news:

If you represent a company that is suddenly in the news with "bad" press, don't ignore it online—your credibility is at stake. When I developed a curriculum for California postmasters on how to deal with the media, the objective was good news (new stamps, technology, etc.) but the reality was they also needed to know "damage control" tactics in the event of shootings, bombings and fraud. If you represent companies with the potential for breaking news (including financial), be sure the online component is part of the strategy. If I'm covering the story from a different time zone, it may be the only chance you have to get your word out. (Internet PR Discussion List, May 14, 1999)

— Okay, It's a Good Idea —

You don't have to hire a publicist to get the benefits of free media publicity. But most publicity doesn't just fall into your lap. Go out and work for it! Again, Jordi Herold: "We're engaged in publicity all the time. We're engaged in traditional press releases; we try to sway freelancers and editors to do feature pieces; we're continually looking for ongoing free listings. We work extensively with radio—college, public, as well as commercial, both mainstream and alternative. We're looking to affect the 'rotation' [how frequently an artist is played on the air] and to work up as many noncash ways as we can to get the artist mentioned on the air—promotional giveaways, contests of one sort or another."

✠

You may not have to work quite as hard as Herold, but the rewards of even a more limited publicity program can be great. The next several chapters will teach you how to garner your share of the free publicity that awaits you.

7

Who Needs to Know: Assembling Your Press List

Now you know why you want publicity. But how do you get it? Once in a while, media people may seek you out—usually because of some other publicity about you that the reporter found interesting—but don't count on it! If you want media coverage, court the media! Don't wait to be wooed by reporters.

It's easy to develop a media list; all the information is available with a little research. Do your homework, and you'll reap the rewards of free publicity that others have to pay for.

— What Media to Use? —

Start gathering your list by writing down every newspaper, magazine, or newsletter you read fairly regularly, every radio station you listen to, and every television channel you watch. If you use paid advertising, also include any publication or broadcast outlet where you already advertise.

Your media outlets break down into several types:

Geographical. Most radio stations, your hometown newspaper, a regional newsweekly, perhaps a neighborhood, urban ethnic, or regional business publication attract you primarily because you live in the area they serve. In the days before cable and satellite, this was also a criterion for TV, and may still be to some extent. You can also get publicity where you used to live. But only bother publicizing there if it will do you some good—if, for instance, what you sell is available by mail or nationally distributed.

Professional. Information is more widely and rapidly available to more people than at any time in human history, and nowhere is this more true than in work-related reading. You probably read several magazines, Internet discussion lists, and newsletters for work. Almost every field has at least one important trade journal. I average two hours a day of professional reading.

Association-Specific. Religious groups, college alumni associations, fraternal orders, civic groups, and membership-based issue focus groups (from Greenpeace to the American Association of Retired Persons) are a few of the many organizations that mail publications to everyone who sends in dues.

Special Interest. Everyone has at least one hobby. If you're serious about videos, environmental issues, coin and stamp collecting, bicycle riding, wrestling, fine arts, billiards, gourmet cooking, carpentry, handicrafts, or hundreds of other pursuits, you probably read at least one publication.

Current Events/Politics/Finance. The major news-weeklies, such as *Time* and *Newsweek,* cross many desks, as do national newspapers such as the *New York Times, Wall Street Journal,* and *USA Today.* Numerous smaller publications offer their own slant (for instance, *In These Times, The Progressive, Reason,* and *National Review* appeal to socialists, peace activists, libertarians, and conservatives, respectively).

General Interest/Entertainment. These publications include men's and women's magazines, pictorial publications such as *Life* and *National Geographic,* and the ubiquitous *TV Guide,* to name a few examples.

— What Your Prospects Read —

Ask clients, professors, and business owners what professional publications—including newsletters and Internet discussion groups—they read. If only 100 people read a publication, but 60–70 of them are seriously interested in what you're doing, your publicity will be more effective there than in a general interest magazine with 300,000 readers, virtually none of whom are your prospects.

— Research —

Now that you've exhausted the easy names, it's time to do some real work. The first stop should be an Internet research database such as <http://www.liszt.com> or <http://www.dejanews.com>, where you can find discussion groups on your topic, followed by one of the many directories of e-zines. Important: Please read the chapters on Internet discussion groups and e-zines *before* you send them

anything! Next, visit the largest newsstand in your area. Leaf through a few relevant magazines you might not have seen before. Do the same at the periodical room in your public library. Now, move over to the reference department for more in-depth research.

Reference librarians have valuable resources to help you put your list together. Ask for *Gale Directory of Publications, Bacon's Publicity Checker, Gale Encyclopedia of Associations,* and similar directories. Ask if your area has a specialized regional directory such as *Media Keys*—most major markets have them. Check all the Yellow Pages that serve your market territory, under these headings: Magazines; Newspapers; News Services; Radio Stations; Television—Cable; Television Stations. Also search the library's computer databases.

Be sure you've covered all the bases. Depending on your product/service mix, your list could include daily newspapers; newsweeklies; ethnic and special interest publications (your own and other ethnic groups', women's, those catering to a certain political bent, etc.); shoppers and calendars; regional and national trade magazines; business and general-interest regional magazines; major nationwide media and wire services; newsletters; directories; radio stations: commercial, listener-sponsored, and college; TV stations: network, local commercial, public, and cable; Internet forums of various types.

Copy down the following information about each media outlet you identify: publication/station name; frequency of publication; overall focus; deadline; address, including city, state, and zip code; voice and fax phone numbers; contact name (often the managing editor or editor-in-chief; with large, well-known publications it may be more effective to deal with an associate editor); departments; department editors.

Remember, when you do something noteworthy, your trade journal, alumni association bulletin, church or synagogue newsletter, national religious or ethnic magazine, and other associational publications will consider printing the information. And because people often like to patronize others who share an interest or affiliation, more readers may turn into prospects, and more prospects into clients.

Also, don't neglect names of corporations or human-services agencies that publish. Many will have both a house organ (distributed internally) and an outreach publication that goes to their clients and prospects.

For electronic media, establish the names and exact titles of the PSA (public service announcement) editor, the public affairs director, and the news bureau chief, as well as the producers of general-interest talk shows and any germane special-interest programming.

If you don't have the time, there are two alternatives: Either purchase an up-to-date media directory from a reputable company such as Paul Krupin's Direct Contact or Gebbie's All-In-One, or simply contract with a press release distribution service to send out your release for you (see Going National, below). But still, you'll want to supplement those lists with one that you develop, with strengths in your immediate local area and with specialty publications in your market niche.

— Going National —

Depending on what you offer, a media list based on your own geographic area and/or field of expertise may be too narrow. And, of course, you'll find that different media contacts will be appropriate for different releases.

So what do you do if you have a general-interest story and you want national or international press?

One option is to use media directories as you did when you created your local and niche lists. However, that will take enormous amounts of time, especially if—as you should—you verify the contacts before sending anything out.

An easier way: Use one of the many Internet-based press release distribution services that have presorted names into workable categories for you. In alphabetical order, some of these include:

http://www.bookflash.com
(for book authors and publishers)

http://www.daybooknews.com
http://www.e-wire.com
http://www.internetwire.com
http://www.m2presswire.net
http://www.mmgco.com.
http://www.newsbureau.com
http://www.newstarget.com
http://www.prnewswire.com
http://www.urlwire.com
http://www.xpresspress.com

Services will charge a fee based on distribution (i.e., so much for each release), number of recipients, or even unlimited service over a specified period of time. Though sometimes pricey, they'll save you enormous time over developing your own list.

One service with a twist is imediafax.com, where you can follow the categories to select your own custom list, and have a release distributed by fax and/or e-mail for 25 cents per recipient.

Other services offer Internet newsgroup posting and/or search engine submission. Eric Ward's Netpost and Steve O'Keefe's service are two reputable ones.

And then there are tools to put you in front of media people when they come looking. I've had very good luck, for example, with a Web site called GuestFinder.com, which promotes heavily to radio talk show producers and hosts. Through Guest-Finder, which charges a fairly low annual fee, I average thirty-five appearances per year on talk shows around the world.

Another service, ProfNet.com, sends out about fifteen e-mail bulletins every week, listing reporters who are looking for expert sources for their stories. ProfNet isn't cheap—$2,000 per year—but you're allowed to share a membership with up to four other people. Certain topics come up very regularly: computers, business management, health care, consumer issues. If you are an expert in one of these topics, it might be worth a look. I've generated significant media interest through ProfNet, but it's not for everyone. Most of its subscribers are full-time professional publicists, trolling for media where they can place stories about their clients.

— What Do You Do Now? —

This book assumes you have a computer that can:

- Manage media, customer, and contact databases
- Create and print documents with variable typefaces and sizes—and use mailmerge to address them individually
- Run a simple spreadsheet
- Send and receive e-mail
- Browse the World Wide Web

If you don't have one yet, get one. It will make almost every task in this book far easier. Decent used systems should start at around two hundred dollars or even less, and the time savings in this chapter alone will be enormous.

Let's define some terms. A "database" is a collection of information, broken into fields and records. A "field" is one set of information, which you can sort—for instance, last names, street addresses, or zip/postal codes. A "record" represents one set of entries in all the fields—in this case, one publisher or broadcast outlet. "Merging" is the process of combining information from a database into a form letter or other standardized document.

Now you have to turn your media list into something you can use. Set up a simple database file with a field for each piece of information. It's better to have too many fields than too few, because you can sort by any subset of the data if it's properly categorized.

Be thorough. Use separate fields for first names and last names, for street addresses, phone and fax numbers, e-mail addresses, cities, states, and zip/postal codes, and for the names and titles of different contact people at each outlet. Include fields to sort by categories, such as subject area, frequency of publication, and how far in advance you need to send information. If you know the contact's preference (postal, fax, e-mail), include a field for that.

— How to Use Your List —

You now have the definitive press list in your field and geographic territory. From this large list, you will develop a much smaller list of key media contacts—the people who generally print your material, and who reach the readers you want to focus on.

The key to effective marketing is targeting. You need to figure out exactly who needs to have your information, and put it in front of them as often as you can. There will be times when you want to send something to the entire list—generally when you release a new product nationally, or achieve a very high honor in your field. But for the most part, you will want to be selective.

Comb through your list and pick out the fifty who are most likely to use your material and put your information before your target audience. As you begin to send out press releases, track who's using your stuff and who isn't. Over time, you might refine your master list to twenty names or so, whom you contact every time you have something to say, reaching others from the wider list as appropriate.

— Pyramid Your Coverage —

Once you get any coverage, exploit it for its full marketing potential. Here are some ways to get the most out of your exposure.

An article or letter is a sales tool. In general, people are much more likely to buy from you if they've heard or seen your firm's name several times; Jeffrey Lant believes you should put your name before every prospect a minimum of seven times in eighteen months. Press coverage not only reinforces your name, but also provides independent confirmation that what you're doing is important.

Therefore, make sure people see it even if they missed its original appearance. Specifically, you want to make sure it is seen by two classes of people: those who want what you're selling, and those who will give you more publicity.

For print coverage, use "tearsheets"—photocopies of the article or letter (pasted up to fit on one page, if necessary), appearing underneath the publication's masthead, showing the publication name and date.

- Keep stacks of these tearsheets for distribution to your customers.
- Mail them along with other materials to prospective clients.
- Make a photocopied enlargement of the tearsheet, frame it, and post it prominently in your storefront window or on the wall.
- Assemble several different tearsheets—plus brochures, photos, and other materials—into a standard press kit.
- Do a poster combining a tearsheet with a special offer and put it up on bulletin boards.
- Put the article on your Web site (with the writer's or publisher's permission) and e-mail your con-tacts the URL and a line or two of description.

You can reap extra benefits from electronic coverage as well:

- Distribute audio or video cassettes to potential clients, media people, and groups that book speakers.
- Announce your appearance ahead of time in a flier or poster.

These final tips work for both print and broadcast coverage:

- Extract short favorable quotes from articles or tapes and use them as testimonials in a flier, brochure, or direct-mail piece (you don't need permission, but list the reporter and publication).
- Announce your appearance with a press release.
- Create and distribute a résumé of your media appearances.
- Include personal thank-you notes from reporters, talk show hosts/producers, and interviewees in your packet.

Now you're ready for a step-by-step course in print promotion.

<u>8</u>

Better Than the Grapevine:
Writing Your Media Releases

How do you get free publicity? Your most important tool is the media release (also called a news release or press release): a handout to journalists, letting them know about something you feel is newsworthy. The terms, "media release," "news release," and "press release" are interchangeable, except that some broadcast journalists feel the term "press release" applies only to print media.

What kind of impact can a media release have? Enormous, if it's picked up in the right place. One friend, a human-services worker, regularly sent out releases about her program. One ran toward the back of the *New York Daily News*. Even though the story was almost invisible, she got dozens of inquiries in the next few days.

In less urban areas, a release will usually have a greater chance of being used. In my own candidacies for political office, releases were the cornerstone of a strategy of going from a near-total unknown to a household name. Virtually all of these releases were picked up in both major daily papers in my area, and several resulted in extended news stories.

Releases can help businesses as well as nonprofit organizations. Stores can use them to promote new products, announce new branch locations, or pub-

licize events that will bring in customers. Concert promoters get write-ups about entertainers who might not be well known. My partner and I publicize the various for-profit classes we teach almost exclusively through releases and fliers. Businesses can also team up with charities to cosponsor events—both will get publicity.

And the right free publicity through media releases can even launch a national campaign.

— Writing Basic Releases —

A media release is nothing more than a way to convey information to the media and other organizations in your community. It's the usual way to let journalists know you have something that will interest them.

And if you follow the traditional format for writing releases, you're simply making it easier for newspeople to give you the publicity you deserve. Although trained to ferret out stories, newspeople can be as lazy as the rest of us; they are much more likely to use your material if it's handed to them. Thus, the easier to use and the more comprehensive your handouts, the more outlets will publicize you.

Cor van Heumen, a book publicist with Cate Cummings Publicity & Promotion Group in Kansas City (<mailto:Cor@BookPublicity.com>), offers a short checklist for writing an attention-grabbing release. While he's talking specifically about books, the principles hold true for promoting any product or event. Does the release . . .

- Have a strong opening?
- Show results?
- Give examples?
- Create pictures in the readers' heads rather than talking in abstractions?
- Give valuable information that hooks the reader—creates the incentive to go out and buy the product or to get more information?
- Focus on the central idea, not the product?
- Talk about experiences that readers can identify with?
- Raise emotion?
- Talk about real experiences with real people and make readers care about those people?

There are several types of press releases. General press releases, public service announcements, press advisories, calendar listings, and "People and Places" notices are most common. We'll look at each of these in detail later in the chapter.

In any case, there are a few things *any* release must include.

— What's Most Important —

The first and most important lesson a journalist learns is to get "the five Ws": *who, what, when, where, why* (and/or *how*).

So put them in your release!

Who are the important characters? *What* did they do, or *what* happened to them? *When* and *where* did it happen, or will it happen? *Why* is this occurring now? *Why* is it significant? *How* did it come about—what is the background information the news media need in order to see the value in your story?

Write the release clearly and simply, and stick to the point. Remember that your release may be used word for word as you write it, so make sure both the news staff and the public will have enough information to get interested and find out more.

And remember the lesson of targeting. Magazine editor Amy Zuckerman explains why that's important: "If you know your market, [you'll] shape your releases to the editors personally. People waste a lot of money and time sending me releases I will never use. We don't have a business sheet but we still get a tremendous amount of business releases that we throw out. Nobody bothers to see if we run this stuff."

The same principles apply when sending press releases to the electronic media. According to public affairs TV producer Stanley D. Friedman, who worked in the New York City market, "Very often, people who send press releases do not know anything about the show—it's a waste of money and time for them, and for us. There are media lists which list all the shows and exactly what kinds of guests they use. A lot of the releases end up in the wastebasket."

Paul Krupin <mailto:dircon@owt.com>, who runs a press release distribution service at http://www.imediafax.com, analyzed trends in his "hit rate." Here's what appears to be working the best:

- Human interest angles—particularly with heartwarming anecdotal stories
- Interpersonal relationships on difficult or controversial issues—focus on love, sex, money, communications between men and women, parents and children, companies and employees, government and individuals
- Tips articles—advice and tactics excerpted from books, ten commandments, ten tips, etc.
- Unusual events—unique personal accomplishments, unusual creative ideas
- Humor and wisdom, fun and tragedy
- Really new and unique products or innovations
- Politically and socially important editorial tie-in articles
- Holiday and event tie-in articles

The more thorough you make your material, the more likely it is to be used. But clear writing is vital. "What catches my attention," notes Amy Zuckerman, "is someone who knows how to present the facts as clearly and quickly as possible, up front, without a lot of gobbledygook."

Proper format is also important, because it makes it easier to use your release. While there are variations in acceptable formats, always:

- Have a contact name and information on the release
- Decide on a suitable release date
- Use proper format
- Keep it short!

We'll take these one at a time, and then look at some sample releases.

Contact

There are two kinds of contacts for a press release. First, a name, phone number, and e-mail at the top of the release for reporters to call if they need more information. Second, a contact in the text of the release, for the general public. Usually, one person can perform both functions, but if not, list both. For example, if a local daily paper does not print phone numbers, the public contact—who may not be the best press liaison—has to be listed in the phone book.

Both press and public contact people should be well informed about the event or issue, and at least reasonably articulate—enough so they don't freeze up when someone asks them a question. They should also have at their disposal a way to check spellings of names, logistical details, and so on.

Release Date

Your question here is one of timing. Readers should see the release early enough to make plans to go to your event, but not so early that they completely forget to attend. "Release date" refers to the earliest date you want your material in the hands of readers or the ears of listeners. It is not the publication's deadline, but the date of appearance in print.

A preliminary release might ideally be published ten to fifteen days before the event. Try a follow-up release with new information five to seven days beforehand, and perhaps a calendar listing in the days immediately before your event.

But these guides must be balanced against publication schedules. If you send your release to a magazine that appears on the first day of every month and your event is on the 22nd, obviously you have to compromise.

Both the public and the press generally have short attention spans and poor memory for details. Therefore, avoid too much early publicity for more or less routine events; save your publicity blitz for the month immediately preceding your activity.

However, there are some situations where you'll want to start much earlier and continue building the coverage. If you are organizing a major national conference or demonstration, for instance, you could send out an initial release three months ahead and follow up weekly for the final month; the new releases could list additional speakers, entertainers, or cosponsors, follow-up and supplementary activities, coordinated actions in other cities, and so forth.

Here's another situation requiring early planning: listing your event in the calendar of a national magazine or professional publication. Some of these outlets have lead times of six months to a year. If you've planned a major event that far ahead, send a preliminary release to those publications. (Don't forget that many magazines postdate their issues; a March issue might appear around January 15.)

Sometimes, release dates are quite crucial. If one of your suppliers introduces a new product, you want newspeople to know that you'll be carrying it—but you don't want the competition to get the jump on you. So choose a release date just a couple of days before you'd have the product in stock, and put that information right on the top of your release. If timing is important, type "DO NOT RELEASE BEFORE _____ [date]" or "EMBARGO UNTIL _____

[date]" in capital letters (although it won't always be observed).

If it's not time-sensitive, label it "For Release: On Receipt" or "For Immediate Release"—and don't include an actual date. Otherwise, people will think your release is stale and discard it once that date is past—and I've heard of releases that were picked up even a year or two after they were sent.

Format Properly

A proper release has contact information, release date, and perhaps an event summary single-spaced at the top. It drops down a couple of lines to a headline, and then begins with the text on the next line. If appropriate, begin your text with a newspaper-style "dateline": the city hosting the event or the location of your office, optionally followed with a date. The city name should be typed all in capital letters as the first word in the first full paragraph. Use your organization's letterhead. Proofread, spell-check, and fact-check before you send!

Even if you have a little single-spaced material in the heading, double-space the main text of your release—both because editors suffer from eyestrain, and also because double spacing leaves them room to edit (both for length and to conform with their own corporate style). For the same reason, try to use spacious margins: 1½ inches all around. (If it lets your release fit on one page instead of two, use narrower margins—but never less than three-quarters of an inch on any side.) Also, indent all paragraphs in the text, except the first paragraph if you're using a dateline.

Formatting rules are different for e-mailed releases, as we'll discuss shortly.

Never inflict handwriting on an editor. A typed copy, even if it's sloppy, is infinitely easier to read than handwriting. If your copy is handwritten, the editor—faced with deciphering important facts—may simply decide your release is not worth the bother. Even if it's used, the chance of printing your information accurately goes way downhill on a handwritten copy.

Both for the editor's convenience and to make sure vital information isn't left out, if your material absolutely has to run more than a page, *start a new sheet of paper. Don't use the back.* The editor and typesetter won't look for it there. If you have to go to additional pages, type "continued" or "more" at the bottom of the previous page.

Journalists handle a tremendous amount of paper. If your extra pages get mixed into a big pile, the editor will need to be able to reassemble them. So head each subsequent page with your organization, a one-to-three-word summary (called a slug), and a page number, like this:

Bart's Books/Shakespeare Reading/Page 2

Fasten the pages with a paper clip; don't staple (be careful that the pages can still be read and that they are easily separated). End the last page with "-30-" or "####" so that the editor knows that's the end. (-30- is a common newspaper symbol for "story ends here.")

Keep It Short

Your release should distill the essential facts into a form short enough to fill a small hole in the newspaper—and to be concise enough to stay in the reader's head and be remembered and acted upon. A well-prepared release can also act as a "teaser," inviting the editor to send a reporter to you for a more in-depth story.

WWOR's Stanley Friedman notes the importance of brevity: "Come to the point quickly in the first paragraph. Producers are very busy. You don't have time to read a three-page release to find out what it's about."

The ideal length for a typical press release is two hundred to three hundred words—even less if the event is pretty self-explanatory. While sometimes you may actually write a whole article, with quotes from participants, and submit it to the media, that's generally not the case in announcements of upcoming events, new products and services, and so on.

Unless you are introducing a product or service that no one knows how to use, filling in the media on an event after it happens, or covering someone famous, aim to fit the article on one typed page. In extreme cases, stretch it to two pages—but only after doing your best to try to squeeze it into one. If there's still too much, summarize in a press release and add supplementary sheets (see the section on press packets later in this chapter).

Paul Krupin, of imediafax.com, notes that if a two-hundred-word press release can stand alone as an interesting, punchy article, it may not only get printed but also lifted verbatim into electronic formats. "Good short articles in newspapers and magazines are often read on radio stations and on talk shows every day. . . . Wow—a force multiplier effect."

— Putting It into Practice —

Let's look at some sample basic releases.

VALLEY TRADE CONNECTION
324 Wells Street
Greenfield, MA 01301

For Release: On Receipt
Contact: Mary Jane Stuart, 555-0011

VTC Potluck to Feature 2nd Showing and Discussion of PBS Film "Affluenza"

EASTHAMPTON: With a turn-away crowd last month, Valley Trade Connection will once again offer a showing and discussion of the PBS film "Affluenza." The event will take place at Eastworks, 116 Pleasant Street, Easthampton, Friday, March 24, 2000. The movie will be shown at 7, and local frugality consultant Paula Ingold will moderate a discussion beginning at 8. The public is invited and there is no admission charge.

"Affluenza," narrated by National Public Radio's Scott Simon, examines an illness that is sweeping our country: rampant materialism. The film also interviews many people in the frugality/simplicity movement who show that a less stressful, more satisfying life is possible. "Affluenza" uses personal stories, expert commentary, hilarious old film clips, and "uncommercial" breaks to illuminate this serious social disease.

The Valley Trade Connection encourages economic resources to remain in the Valley by issuing local barter currency, Valley Dollars, that can only be used in the area. Currently, over 400 members exchange goods and services through Valley Dollars. For more information about VTC and its activities, contact Tim Carpenter, 555-0204, or Mary Jane Stuart, 555-0011.

####

This was almost a compressed news story. In addition to the usual items, I noted that this was a repeat of an event that generated a turn-away crowd, and got in a paragraph of information about the sponsoring organization and its mission.

Here's another one, announcing a concept rather than an event:

For Release: On Receipt
Contact: Carol Catalan
(413) 555-0123, x310

Shut-Ins Can Vote at Home

NORTHAMPTON: The Northampton Committee on Disability and the City Clerk's office remind you that it's your privilege to vote, even if you can't get to the polls.

Anyone with a doctor's letter that certifies a permanent disability can automatically receive absentee ballots from that point on, simply by notifying the City Clerk. These ballots do not have to be notarized and can be mailed back.

People with temporary disabilities who are unable to get to the polls can also request absentee ballots. These do have be notarized before being returned.

For more information, contact Christine Silver, City Clerk, at 555-0123, extension 219.

####

Now, some techniques for increasing the impact of your release and making the editor's job easier:

Customized Releases

One of the mistakes I see amateur publicists make repeatedly is not understanding their audience. A generic, "one size fits all" release can really be a mistake; it won't take into account the different needs of different editors.

Knowing this principle, when I announced the publication of one of my books, I sent releases to the newspapers in every city I'd ever lived in. Each of these releases had a local hook, for example, "Former Providence Resident Shel Horowitz, who was active in many community causes during his Providence years . . ." I even sent to press in my parents' communities, with headlines such as "Son of Montclair Resident . . ."

This is an issue I encounter constantly in my marketing consulting work. I create a lot of press releases for publishers, for instance. And a release announcing a new book to the book trade press is going to be quite different from one going either to the author's local area or to the trade press for the book's topic. And sometimes, a press release might be going to more than one set of journalists—a piece on youth sports may go both to the education and sports editors on the same paper, for instance.

An example: Here are two different leads I wrote for a new book on running a massage business. The first was aimed at health and wellness publications, the second at business markets:

It Takes More Than Healing Hands: Massage Therapists and Bodyworkers Need BUSINESS Help Too!

CARMEL, NY: Every year, thousands of people follow a dream of helping others and attend massage school. But once in the field, many flounder. Too many massage therapists and bodyworkers are unable to cope with the welter of business skills they need to know: licensing, marketing, office location, organizational structure, insurance, taxes, professional associations, and all the rest of it.

Success in the BUSINESS End of Massage and Bodywork: A New Resource Helps Take Away the Gamble

CARMEL, NY: The business of bodywork has grown phenomenally; it's now a multimillion dollar industry. Every year, thousands of people graduate from massage school and hang out their shingle. But every year, thousands of others close their doors, frustrated by the ins and outs of turning their dream into a successful business.

Some massage therapists make as much as $100 per hour. Others limp along, putting their heart and soul out for $10 an hour or less. Some develop a thriving practice, generating enough business to hire associates. Others flounder, unable to find a niche or differentiate from the competition.

The Event Summary—An Easy Shortcut

This is a good way to convey a lot of information in very few words. Simply list the answers to the five Ws we talked about earlier, in condensed form, at the top of the release. This does not replace their mention in the text, just reinforces it. But you know they've been listed and the editor can find them immediately.

Press Packets

When you need to convey more information than you can cram onto a short release, use a press packet (also called press kit or media kit). This might include:

- Performance or publication credits of an artist you're sponsoring
- A photograph of your subject and/or her or his work (which not only vastly increases the chances your release will be used, but also gives you more inches of coverage)
- Clippings of previous news coverage, with indication of where and when the story appeared (photocopy the clipping mounted under the publication's masthead, including date)
- A schedule of other related events during the season
- Background or historical information
- A copy of the product, or a reply postcard to request one (these are often called "bounce-back cards")

Collate the whole thing together in a presentation folder or 9 x 12-inch envelope and distribute it as you would a release.

Also, if you run an attraction, retail business, or agency, or promote a particular artist, product, or cause, keep some press packets around. Distribute them to reporters interested in what you do, and have them available for press conferences.

Incidentally, if you are promoting an event and there is a press packet already available (from the performer's record company, for example), you can save a lot of time by using material from the packet in your press releases, or even adding the local information onto a prepackaged release.

In sending anything to the media, remember that you are granting permission to use it, without compensation. Essentially, you have placed the material in the public domain (except for bylined stories, which belong to their author or to the newspaper that published them). If you want to maintain copyright on anything in your press packet, that item should be marked with the copyright symbol (©), the year, and the name of the copyright holder. However, in most cases, a copyright notice will drastically reduce the chances of your material being printed; reporters will hesitate to quote copyrighted material at length. So think carefully about how important it really is to retain your copyright, and generally save it for articles rather than press releases or press packets.

Remember, too, that once you create this material, you should make it accessible online. Any company with a Web site should have one page oriented to the press and another page oriented to potential advertisers. French journalist Kathleen Buckley <mailto:Winenews@aol.com>, writing in I-PR Discussion List on May 14, 1999, laid out a pretty good sketch of what you might include in your Web-based press kit:

1. Current and reliable promotions/press releases (ability to request samples, if pertinent)
2. Background on the product, the company, its directors, its focus or mission
3. Clearly identified e-mail address and fax and phone numbers (by expert or area of interest)
4. Reliable response
5. Downloadable magazine-quality photos in two or more formats; same with audio and video feeds
6. A "preview" section with digest of upcoming releases, events, promotions, and embargo dates
7. Language options (don't offer if you can't keep the sites current, though)

Buckley also reminds readers not to block journalist access through long, cumbersome registration forms.

Organize such a Web page as an invitation to the media, with links to each individual press release—giving the headline and a brief (two- to three-line) synopsis right on the link page—as well as links to company backgrounders, profiles of the major players in your company or agency, testimonials, review copy request forms, and so forth. If you're promoting several product lines, group each one's releases together.

— Specialized Releases —

In addition to the general, all-purpose release, there are specialized releases for particular situations. You may find yourself wanting to sharpen a release to cover only that specific medium. For example, it's common to rewrite a press release as a public service announcement for broadcast media. Here are a few of the more common types:

Public Service Announcements

A public service announcement, or PSA, is the radio and television equivalent of a press release. If you want to provide information for a station to use in another form (for instance, if you are trying to get on a talk show as a guest), standard press releases and press kits are perfectly appropriate. However, if you want to get something actually read over the airwaves, send a PSA instead.

What's the difference? First of all, many stations tend to choose relatively innocuous—and obviously nonprofit—PSAs. (However, college and other listener-supported radio stations may be much more willing to air controversial PSAs, so don't be discouraged.) Because a listener can't always tell the difference between a PSA and a commercial, stations are particularly chary about airing PSAs that benefit a particular business. However, if phrased as a news or human interest story, PSAs can often promote for-profit events.

Second, the format is different for PSAs and press releases. PSAs should be typed all in capital letters, using clear, easily pronounced language, and should state the event date and contact phone number twice. Remember, your message is being read on the air, often by an announcer who hasn't seen it before, and your listener has to grab the most important information in the space of a few fleeting seconds of airtime. If you must use a difficult word, include a pronunciation key right in the text (see the example).

Third, PSAs should be timed at fifteen to thirty seconds. Because reading PSAs takes time away from the business of playing records and hustling products in paid ads, and because announcers often read a bunch of PSAs at once in a "community calendar" format, the shorter and clearer your release, the more likely it will get read at all, and the more likely also that it will get read at a time when large numbers of people are listening. Read your draft aloud with a stopwatch. Time is the commodity that radio and TV stations sell; unless you're only sending to noncommercial stations, you've got to fit into the standard format.

If this seems alarmingly short, listen to the radio for a while and time the PSAs that you hear. Keep in mind that thirty seconds is also a common length for radio or TV advertising; obviously those advertisers believe they have ample time to get their message across. Besides, today's music-oriented radio listener or action-oriented TV viewer has a very short attention span for "talking heads"—just plain words. And generally, except for classy, high-tech, nationally aired PSAs prepared by the radio advertising

council and similar organizations, a talking head—an announcer reading your release—is all you get.

PUBLIC SERVICE ANNOUNCEMENT

EVENT SUMMARY	Contact:
PREVENTING LOW BACK PAIN	Jean Mayer, D.C.
LECTURE BY: Dr. Jean Mayer	(413) 555-0101

Director, Corporate Chiropractic Care
DATE/TIME: Monday, March 27, 7 P.M.
LOCATION: Corporate Chiropractic Care
17 Crooked Street, Northampton
ADMISSION: FREE

Back Pain is Curable

NO ONE HAS TO LIVE WITH BACK PAIN, ACCORDING TO DR. JEAN MAYER, DIRECTOR OF CORPORATE CHIROPRACTIC CARE. DR. MAYER WILL PRESENT A FREE LECTURE ON PREVENTING LOW BACK PAIN MONDAY EVENING, MARCH 27 AT 7:00 P.M. AT HER OFFICE, 17 CROOKED STREET IN NORTHAMPTON.

THE LECTURE WILL COVER SUCH COMMON AILMENTS AS SUBLUXATION (*sub-lucks-say-shun*) AND SCIATICA (*sigh-at-tick-uh*) AND WILL FOCUS ON PREVENTIVE CARE. COME TO THIS FREE EVENT, MONDAY, MARCH 27, 7 P.M.

REFRESHMENTS WILL BE SERVED.

####

Press Advisories

A press advisory invites the media to show up to your event but doesn't ask them to notify the public ahead of time. You use it when you want coverage of your event after the fact; you hope a reporter will cover you. Always use an event summary on a press advisory.

The advisory is a good tactic when you'll be having a press conference, an interaction with government or civic officials, street theater, a demonstration, or other colorful, newsworthy event—or you're hosting a visiting dignitary or celebrity who will be available for radio and TV appearances during his or her visit. Use the same advisory for print and broadcast media.

Calendar Listings

For calendar columns, a targeted, brief listing with
just the relevant facts is more likely to be used than
a longer release that the editor is forced to shorten.
Calendar announcements should be very short—
often just one paragraph plus a contact name and
number.

Include a copy of your longer version, so that if
the editor wants more information—or even wants
to feature your event as a highlight—it's at hand. If
the paper uses highlights, you're more likely to be
featured—and with far greater impact—if you include a good black-and-white photo.

Send it to "Listings Editor," or if the paper has
more than one set of listings, to the attention of the
appropriate editor for that department.

People and Places

A savvy publicist can use the "People and Places"
columns—they have different names in different
publications—to score media coverage even when
you don't really deserve it. These tidbits of hometown news or business briefs announce awards, promotions, transfers, births, publications, new employees, and other minor items. But they do get your
organization mentioned. Send them not only to your
standard media, but also to media where the person named lives now as well as where he or she
grew up. Don't spend a lot of energy doing these,
however.

This example was lifted directly from such a column in a regional business monthly (the names are
changed). Twenty-nine out of forty-four words promote the business, under the ruse of announcing a
new hire.

E-mail Releases

More and more editors welcome press releases by
e-mail. This is great for marketers, as it's even cheaper
than faxing, and less likely to end up on the wrong

side of the office. However, it is a different medium, and you ignore the differences at your peril.

Format e-mail releases single-spaced with an extra line between paragraphs. Turn off any nonstandard characters such as curly quotes and apostrophes, long dashes, and accent marks. If at all possible, include a hotlink to a URL (Web site address) with more information. Use a short, specific, attention-getting subject heading that truly describes what's inside and doesn't scream "sales!"—leave *out* the dollar signs and exclamation points.

Monique Harris <mailto:monique@onlinesalespower. com>, after polling members of the Internet Sales Discussion List, provided this summary of the advice she received:

1. Place the most important parts of your release within the first screen. This way when the journalist opens his or her e-mail they can quickly get the gist of your story, without having to scroll.
2. Choose your media list carefully. Don't send your release to any and every media person who has an e-mail address. It's just like spamming them. Make sure you know what topics they cover, and send accordingly.
3. I used to think that shorter releases were the best. But a few respondents have had good luck with releases that were up to 1.5 type-written pages. Tina Koenig of Xpress Press, <http://www.xpresspress.com>, sent me a few recent releases that were more than a few paragraphs, and did exceptionally well.
4. Tie your release into a recent news item. For instance, Jim and Audri Lanford of NETrageous, <www.netrageous.com>, sent out a news release in December titled "Furbies: Internet Myths and Scams Already?" It got picked up by a number of top name publications because many people were looking to purchase Furbies for Christmas.
5. Use a clear and concise Subject line, 5–6 words maximum.

6. Al Bredenberg, Editorial Director and Senior Consultant of Enterprise Interactive <http://www.enterprise1.com>, gave this helpful comment, which I feel is often one of the most neglected areas: "The biggest problem I see is just as much of a problem in hard-copy releases—poor copy. Failing to tell the story—the hard facts—the who, what, when, where, why, and how. Or not having a story to tell at all—no real news. Also, filling the release with product puffery and useless, self-serving, corporate-speak fake quotations." (Internet Sales Discussion List, January 13, 1999)

Janet Westergaard <mailto:janetw1@ix.netcom. com> of Avalon Communications elaborates on the advantages of e-press releases, in I-PR, May 14, 1999:

I've found that the Internet has done three things. First, we can communicate at the speed of light. Once a press release or query is approved, it can be in an editor's email box within seconds (or thousands of email boxes within seconds). Second (and along the same lines), we can have all our corporate information available at the speed of light. No more calls from editors requesting media kits—you can simply point them to the appropriate URL. And, the information is instant. Third, the PR cycle is greatly reduced (when dealing with e-pubs). You can distribute a press release in the morning and it can be all over the Internet by the afternoon. With traditional distribution/publication, this would NEVER happen. So in my mind, the Internet has opened up vast opportunities for efficiency in PR. But, PR is still PR.

Regarding distributing press releases via email, mail, or fax . . . what I've found is that email is far and away the MOST effective. BUT . . . the list needs to be pared down for each release (depending on topic). If you take the time to do this and really target the mailings, your results will be MUCH better—and editors will continue to read what you send. . . . Developing compelling subject lines for electronic distribution is an important factor in getting them read.

Another tip from Westergaard: Stick the contact info at the bottom of the release, so that only key content is visible in the first screen.

Before you e-mail releases, consider Peter Gill's <mailto:pr@thesurveyshop.com> findings:

While you and everyone you know may be online—don't assume the same about your target journalists. We conducted (in December '98) a survey of 167 UK print and broadcast journalists and found their personal preferences to be:

43%   *preferring to be mailed*
33%   *preferring to be faxed*
12%   *preferring to be e-mailed*
13%   *had no preference*

First set your sights—read who else is getting written or spoken about, where and why. Then make a list of your targets and what each of them tends to do for your field of interest.

Next, do more homework—get journalists' names, addresses and fax numbers. Make calls where required to fill in missing data (nobody said "free" publicity was easy publicity).

Then if you are new or have something different, pick up the phone and call your targets! You've got the best reason in the world to talk to them (you're new and/or different) and they are paid to find the new and different. Even when you're not successful, the feedback will be invaluable in shaping whatever you want to do next.

If you're beyond the new and different stage, then you have to find other reasons to make it relevant for journalists to tell their readers your story.

Our survey showed that this was how UK journalists evaluated (on average) 13 classic PR techniques where 10 = useful and 0 = waste of time:

6.9   *Results of a survey*
6.6   *Event organised for the media*
6.3   *Opportunity to profile a key person*
6.3   *Press release with warning or advice*
6.2   *Press release detailing a new product or service*

5.3   *Photo of a new product or service*
4.8   *Free samples*
4.5   *Reader competitions*
4.5   *National day or week linked to a cause or product*
4.5   *Reader offers*
4.3   *Glossy press pack*
3.7   *Novelty object or item intended to attract attention*
3.5   *Photograph of a PR stunt*

For more on e-mail press releases, I recommend Steve O'Keefe's book *Publicity on the Internet* (John Wiley & Sons, 1997). Though ancient by Internet standards, almost all of the advice on e-releases is still applicable at this writing.

Web Site Forms

Many sites will publicize your event if you just stop by and fill out a form. When I do any local public events, I always list my events on sites such as Noho.com, which covers my area of Northampton. I've also used the site to list merchandise for sale, attract interns, find contractors, and so on.

For online events such as chats, start with this list posted by Teri Gidwitz , Director of Marketing and Promotions for JAMtv Corporation <mailto: terig@jamtv.com>:

- On Now: http://www.onnow.com/ SubmitEvent.htmpl
- Yahoo: http://add.yahoo.com/fast/add?+Events
- Timecast: http://www.timecast.com
- EventZone: http://www.eventzone.com/ login.cfm
- NetGuide: http://www.netguide.com
- Yack: http://www.yack.com

— Getting Beyond the Basics —

Fancy Leads

Once you've mastered straightforward press releases and PSAs, get creative. Grab the reader's attention with an interesting, compelling lead (the first sentence or paragraph of an article).

Traditionally, news stories start their lead with a concise statement of the five Ws. But feature stories often begin with a question or a provocative statement. Even though your release is attempting to call attention to your news, you may find it has greater impact if you try to bring in the reader right away with an unusual lead, then go into your five Ws. Here are several feature-oriented leads:

Valentine's Day Massacre: An Evening of the Macabre

Vampires, monsters under the bed, and outlaw hermit crabs will be among the visitors to Brett Batcave's loft on Valentine's Day. The occasion: a reading of macabre poetry . . .

It's 10 O'Clock—Do You Know Where Your Credit History Is?

HIBBING, MN: It's 10 o'clock—Do you know where your credit history is? How about your employment records? Your confidential medical information?

How would you feel if you found out this sensitive and should-be-private material is "vacationing" in computer databanks around the world—accessible to corporate interests who can afford to track down and purchase it, but not necessarily open to your own inspection.

According to electronic privacy journalist and technology consultant Mortimer Gaines, this scenario is all too common. . . .

"Mythic Modernist" Yoshida Opens One-Man Show at Reddad

Stunning mythic and historical images from cultures around the world, combined in astonishingly fresh ways with natural and urban landscapes, fill Michihiro Yoshida's vibrant paintings. Huge faces stare out of totem poles. Pyramids, egg nests, and larger-than-life hands jump at the viewer in vivid crystal blues, deep greens, and flaming crimsons on these large and intense canvases.

This exciting artist makes his Greenwich Village debut with a one-man show at REDDAD Le Petit Musee, 498 Hudson Street, February 1–17.

New Puzzle/Trivia Book Is a Cat Lover's Dream

ATCO, NJ: Why did Charles Dickens change the name of his cat? What breed resulted from crossing an Asian Leopard cat and an American domestic? Which famous American naturalist commented, "She does not discover that her tail belongs to her until you tread upon it"?

Test your knowledge of cats with *The Original Cat Lover's Puzzle Book,* just released from Inmark Associates.

Each of these releases continues with the usual information. The electronic privacy release goes on to tout the expert's new book and his credentials, list a scary real-world example of privacy invasion, provide ordering information and the opportunity to interview him—all in 328 words that fit on a page in 12-point Times Roman type.

For the poetry reading, I listed the poets and their credits, then concluded: "A spine-chilling evening of wonderfully creepy poems is guaranteed. The reading will take place on Wednesday, the 14th of February, at _____ [location], on the faraway island of Manhattan. Ceremonies will begin at 8 P.M."

Use an Unusual Spin

Here's how I made a truly mundane event—an elementary school talent show—into a "must-see." This release was prominently featured in a local paper's weekly entertainment column, and we had a capacity crowd.

Benefit Performance Festival February 9 at Hilltown Cooperative Charter School

HAYDENVILLE: The old Brassworks complex on Route 9 will come alive with a vibrant mix of student performances Sunday, February 9, at 3 P.M., as students in the HCCS 3rd-4th-5th grade class showcase their artistic talents.

Classical music, comedy, original theater, dance, and more will be performed in an event that will:

- Provide a window on the unique educational philosophy of the school—mixed-age classes, a multidisciplinary curriculum influenced by the students' own interests, and a strong focus on the arts
- Raise money for a week-long class field trip to an environmental school in Maine
- Allow the community to enjoy an afternoon of entertainment completely conceived, organized and performed by children

Tickets are $2 for adults, $1 for children 3–12 years old. Children under 3 are free. Attendees will also have a chance to place bids on a silent goods and services auction, whose prizes include massage sessions, rototilling, a professional résumé, and many other bargains.

The talent show, auction, and various other fundraisers are all part of the class's campaign to raise $1,000 toward the cost of the Maine trip. Students have been involved in every aspect of the fundraising, from organizing a weekly school-wide pizza lunch to putting together a contra dance.

The public is welcome.

For information about the school and its educational mission, contact Ann Steeves at the above number.

####

Tie In with News or Feature Angles

I get hired to write marketing and publicity copy for a lot of publishers, and this can create a challenge: releasing a new book is not news—it happens more than fifty thousand times a year in the United States alone. (And neither is launching a Web site or opening a store newsworthy in itself.) If I can tell a story, or find or create a current events tie-in (as I did with the electronic privacy release on page 52) or a hook to an issue of interest to writers covering a beat, my material has a much better chance of being picked up. Third-party validation, especially from recognized names, is another part of my strategy.

Here are a couple of examples (I confess—the Mercator release went to two pages):

Missing for 400 Years, Mercator's Atlas Is Now Available in North America for the First Time

The year was 1570. Legendary mapmaker Gerardus Mercator, inventor of the Mercator Projection and the first to name his map collection for the Greek god Atlas, carefully separated his wall map of Europe to prepare a complete atlas of Europe for the Crown Prince of Cleves on a grand tour.

Then Mercator's crowning achievement—remarkable in its accuracy and exotic in its Latin names and period illustrations—disappeared from view, and languished for centuries. Only in 1967 did the tattered, priceless atlas resurface—purchased by a Dutch collector from an antiquarian bookstore in Brussels, Belgium. Among other treasures, it contains the only surviving copy of Mercator's 1554 map of Europe.

The original copy is on display at the British Library, which acquired it in 1997, for a reputed $1.2 million. A Belgian publisher assembled five scholarly essays and over one hundred illustrations (including numerous period maps by Mercator, his sons, and other cartographers) into a handsome volume to accompany the map folio, and released the book in French and Dutch in 1994. But until now, these commentaries have never been available in English, and the atlas itself was unavailable on this continent.

Now, a small Oregon publisher, Walking Tree Press, has released an edition of *The Mercator Atlas of Europe,* every bit as beautiful as the original. Lavishly presented in a gold-embossed linen portfolio and protected by a laminated slipcase, the large-format bound book and unbound map folios have received praise from *Mercator's World* and *Independent Publisher* magazines, as well as scholars and collectors everywhere.

"A valuable addition to the history of cartography . . . Exploring Europe through Mercator's atlas of 1570 is both a challenging and intriguing experience. . . . We owe the publishers of this atlas a debt of gratitude."

—PETER L. STARK, HEAD, MAP LIBRARY, UNIVERSITY OF OREGON

"Normally I don't hang anything but originals on my walls, but the reproductions of the maps are so fabulous, I will have some framed and display them proudly."

—GRAHAM R. BUTLER,
ANTIQUARIAN MAP COLLECTOR

The boxed set is available directly from the publisher, or through wholesalers Ingram and Baker & Taylor. Individual maps from the atlas are also available. For more information, call toll-free, 888-373-1570. Preview the Atlas on the Web at www.WalkingTree.com.

####

⚹

54 Million Americans "Swallowed by a Snake"

The snake is our grief, says author and psychologist Tom Golden. Nearly a quarter of all Americans are struggling to cope from inside the snake. And men and women often have big differences in the way they cut themselves out again.

In clear, straightforward language, Golden explains—using an old folk tale in which a man is swallowed by a huge snake and slowly cuts his way out—how men are likely to grieve. Grief, Golden says, is like the snake. It is all-consuming, must be dealt with a little at a time, and must be conquered from the inside out.

"A fresh look into the uniqueness of a man's grief in a way that both men and women will find extremely helpful."

—ELISABETH KÜBLER-ROSS, M.D.,
AUTHOR OF ON DEATH AND DYING
AND MANY OTHER BOOKS

Men's grief is typically focused on action: building or producing something, educating people, organizing events, and so forth. And though it's harder for outsiders to see, it's just as important as women's grief, which is more likely to be emotionally based. Golden's new book, *Swallowed by a Snake: The Gift of the Masculine Side of Healing* (ISBN 0-9654649-0-3, $13.95) will be released in April 1997.

"Tom Golden . . . will help both men and women understand the specific context and needs of grieving men. The path through grief is often a dark and lonely one. Tom's work will serve as compassionate and insightful beacons."

—HOPE EDELMAN, AUTHOR,
MOTHERLESS DAUGHTERS

Golden looks at other times and places where grief is more ritualized. He concludes with a strong call to honor the masculine way of grieving and to reclaim the death process from the medical establishment.

Golden has worked with bereavement clients for over twenty years. He created the popular "Crisis, Grief, and Healing" site on the World Wide Web <http://www.webhealing.com>. This interactive site won the Grohol "Best of the Web in Mental Health" award, and was rated a Top 5 Percent site by Pointcom. He has taught the masculine grieving approach to thousands of health care professionals throughout the U.S. and Canada and recently was the sole presenter at a two-day conference at Penn State University. His articles have appeared in *Bereavement* magazine and elsewhere, and he's been profiled in *The Washington Post*. He is available for interviews.

The book may be ordered directly from the publisher at 888-870-1785/301-942-9192, or through your favorite bookstore.

####

— Creating "News" —

What do you do if the media doesn't show at your event? Write up an article yourself, in the form of an extended press release (typically, two to three pages), and submit it *immediately*. Start with a tight lead describing the essence of the event. For example:

SPRINGDALE, June 30: Celebrated author Charles Dickens spoke on novel writing last night to over 150 people at Sinai Temple. Dickens, author of *A Tale of Two Cities* and almost twenty other novels, spoke both about his own process of self-discovery and his suggestions for budding writers.

That first sentence crams in four of the five Ws.

Your release would continue with themes and highlights from the talk, including a couple of good quotes from Dickens, and perhaps his response to a question. If the lecture was part of a series, end with a note about future events. And have it on the editor's desk before the close of business on the dateline day.

Sometimes you have to more or less invent the news hook. I was hired to promote a book that broke all the rules. As a dense philosophical work written by someone with no academic credentials, it didn't really fit into any standard categories. Here's what I did (yes, it did fit on one page, using carefully chosen type and a few formatting tricks):

The One Who Dies with the Most Toys— Is Just As Dead! Author Attacks Material Culture in Groundbreaking New Book

WASILLA, ALASKA: Every once in a while, a book comes along that can change the entire way society thinks. From Martin Luther to Harriet Beecher Stowe to Rachel Carson, and more recently, Christopher Lasch (*Culture of Narcissism*), John Naisbitt (*Megatrends*), and Alvin Toffler (*Future Shock*), certain authors have had a deep and lasting impact. Every thinking person needs to be familiar with the work of these writers.

Into this select group, from a small town in remote and rugged Alaska, comes a new contender: Charles D. Hayes and his new book, *Beyond the American Dream*.

Exhaustively researched—the 24-page bibliography cites authors as diverse as Einstein, Kant, Stephen Covey, Mario Cuomo, Deborah Tannen, Peter Drucker, Will Durant, Erich Fromm, Al Gore, Cornel West, Abraham Maslow, Jack London, and Gail Sheehy—this new and dramatic work explodes myth after myth of American society. Hayes is thoroughly unconventional and also unabashedly liberal; he makes the case that the materialist era is ending and a new era is dawning in America: the era of multicultural accommodation and lifelong learning.

> "It is an inspiration to hear from someone who both cherishes and exemplifies independent thinking. A brilliant and moving work."
> —PHILIP SLATER, AUTHOR,
> *THE PURSUIT OF LONELINESS*

Beyond the American Dream is not a quick and easy read. Rather, it's a probing, intense examination of the entire American society; race relations and affirmative action (he's a strong proponent), environmental issues, fallacies of the New Age movement. It's a book that will be talked about for years to come.

> "In a world of flabby, fragmentary, and postmodernist thinking, Hayes offers a glowing tribute to old-fashioned curiosity and reason."
> —BARBARA EHRENREICH, AUTHOR,
> *FEAR OF FALLING, BLOOD RITES*

Journalists: to get your review copy of *Beyond the American Dream,* which will be released during Self-University Week, September 1–7, 1998, or to arrange an interview with Hayes, please contact the publisher at 907-376-2932 or by e-mail at autpress@alaska.net.

####

Using this release and several follow-up releases, the publisher was able to scoop up a number of excellent reviews and awards, which he then parlayed into sales success.

Even the right testimonial can be worthy of a news release. The document on page 56 is one I did to promote my previous marketing book.

This testimonial came originally as a phone call; Georg wanted to know if the book was available in German for a bulk purchase. I asked him if he would e-mail a note with his comments, and it was on my desk in less than an hour. I sent out this release in a few different versions—so that Massachusetts media, for instance, knew of the local connection.

After a trade magazine ran a negative article, Georg called the writer "and told him about our Noise-Control technology. We supplied the magazine with a sample computer built with our technology." A full-page feature resulted.

Eventually, he got his products featured in thirteen other publications. To get the same result without the free coverage, "We would have needed something between $200,000 and $400,000 . . . but without achieving the believability that comes from the praise of journalists."

Schlomka tries "to anticipate journalists' needs and provide for them. Telling them about our Noise Control is fine, but giving them a neutral piece on the problems and technologies . . . is much better!"

Accurate Writing & More

P.O. Box 1164, Northampton, MA 01061-1164, USA
(413) 586-2388 (voice) (617) 249-0153 (fax)
e-mail: info@frugalfun.com; Web: http://www.frugalfun.com
ISBN Prefix: 0-9614666; SAN #692-4786

For Release: On Receipt   Contact: Alan Friedman

German Business Owner Builds Million-Dollar Business
with ZERO Advertising Expenditure
by Reading Low-Cost Marketing Book

NORTHAMPTON, MA, USA: A very unusual testimonial from Germany came into the offices of Accurate Writing & More, distributors of Shel Horowitz's book, *Marketing Without Megabucks: How to Sell Anything on a Shoestring*:

"Thank you for your wonderful book *Marketing Without Megabucks*. It is the single most profitable investment I've ever made. With its superb advice, I managed to build a small company turning over close to 1,000,000 US Dollars a year within 2 years and I have not spent a single penny on paid advertising! With our special computer-noise reduction products we have obtained front-page coverage with the most important German computer magazine, and have been featured in 13 other magazines and newspapers. We (rather the product) even have been featured twice on TV. . . .

"Starting this year, we employ 5 people, and estimated turnover for 1999 is 1,400,000 US Dollars. Most helpful were the chapters on working the media, and on customer service/referrals. (20% of our new business comes from referrals.)"

—Georg Schlomka, A Conto GmbH, Germany,
e-mail < aconto-nord@noisecontrol.de >

The book, written by AWM's director, Shel Horowitz, is a 384-page comprehensive guide to inexpensive, effective marketing and publicity, including major sections on press coverage, advertising, direct mail, and self-made marketing. Originally published in 1993 by Simon & Schuster, it is now available exclusively through the author's firm, with an extensive update. Including shipping and the e-mail update, the book is $20 US in the US or Canada. A Korean-language edition has also been published.

Horowitz founded Accurate Writing & More in 1981, and has used the techniques in this book to turn his company into the largest firm of its type in a three-county service area. AWM now serves clients on three continents

Horowitz is available for press interviews. Journalists may request a review copy of the book. For more information, call (413) 586-2388, visit http://www.frugalfun.com, or e-mail < info@frugalfun.com >.

####

9

In-Depth Print Coverage:
The Best Publicity Money Can't Buy

Sure, it's great when your three-paragraph press release appears under a tiny, one-column headline, on page 46. But it's a lot better to get a major feature story with a large, visible headline going across several columns. A feature article can provide all the benefits of a press release, multiplied several times. Similarly, you will make a far more powerful impression as the featured guest on a half-hour talk show than by having your PSA read for a few seconds five times a week.

Features and broadcast guest appearances are only two of the marketing techniques we'll examine in these two chapters. There are many ways to exploit the media publicity machine to its fullest potential. All of them will help you be remembered in your community, and keep your product, service, or ideas in the public eye—at virtually no cost to you.

Believe it or not, it isn't all that hard to get this kind of coverage. You probably won't get on *Oprah* right away, but local newspapers, magazines, and radio and TV stations will be receptive to you if you have something worth saying. (And after a couple of years at the local level, you'd have a much better shot if you did want to go for national coverage; successful publicity builds on itself.)

— Feature Articles —

A feature article can be a goldmine for your business or organization. Lois Barber, founder and director of 20/20 Vision, a national peace and environmental lobbying group, notes that one feature story in *The Washington Post* netted three hundred inquiries from readers—not to mention about thirty stories that appeared in other media as a result of the initial article. "They read each other's papers and magazines. People who are looking for stories say, 'This would be a good story for us,' and they call—that's very frequent." Barber says press coverage has been instrumental in the group's growth; from the original chapter founded in 1986 with 300 members, the group grew to 75 chapters and 11,000 participants within five years.

Features, also called "human interest stories," "personality pieces," or "profiles," are full-length articles, perhaps four to eight double-spaced typed pages, focusing on one subject. That subject could be one business, one personality, or a broader topic that covers not just you but other people with similar products and expertise.

For the most part, features (unlike hard-hitting,

Who's Hot

by Judith Solomon

Dorothy Benjamin and Peggy LaKind are living the sweet life these days. Since they started their own candy-making company, Platinum Treats, three years ago, word-of-mouth has made local sales boom.

Fifty-two-year-old LaKind has always had her fingers in a lot of pies. A wife and mother of four grown children, LaKind has taught school, owned a boutique, and has a master's degree in marriage and family counseling.

"I always loved to cook," she says. "And I had a big family who loved to eat. I always wanted to do something in the food area and was interested in the chemistry of food. So I decided to enroll at the Schoolcraft College Culinary Arts Department. I wanted to find out what the mystique was all about, what was different from what I did at home. And I thought maybe I would write a book about it."

After a year at the cooking school, LaKind did a one-year internship with Chef Steve Romanik at Romanik's Restaurant in West Bloomfield.

"One day Steve asked me to roast some nuts," she says. "He liked the way I did them and started using them in some of his dishes.

"Once back in my own kitchen I started thinking what else could I do with nuts to make them more interesting. After playing around and listening to the comments of family and friends, I ended up with my hand-roasted dipped pecans."

Using large, fancy southern pecans, LaKind dips them first in creamy caramel, then in dark Swiss chocolate. Lastly, they are topped with either chopped roasted nuts, chocolate brickle, coconut-flavored chocolate crunch, or chocolate sprills.

"The thing I love most is the nuts," she says. "They're totally mine. I created them. There are 20,000 truffles out there done 20 different ways, but no one has ever taken a pecan before and treated it the way I did."

LaKind met Benjamin when they were both working at a boutique in Franklin. "We were both kitchen people," she says, "and we had talked about going into business together."

Sixty-two-year-old Benjamin, a former medical technician, had come from Indiana to Michigan with a wonderful family recipe for chocolate bark candy.

The two women began experimenting with the bark recipe, ending up with a delicious white-chocolate candy that incorporates pecans, chocolate cookies, and tiny pretzel sticks.

Then, with bark and nuts in hand, they went into business in November 1986.

Steve Romanik was their first customer. "He really launched us when he decided to use the candy in his catering business," Peggy says.

Today, the candy is still made by hand, but the product line has expanded. And the women make up party trays and wicker baskets for special occasions.

Some of the Platinum Treats products can be purchased at the Merchant of Vino in Southfield, the Golden Unicorn in Rochester, and Marmel Gifts in Farmington Hills.

Or, you can receive a mail-order catalog plus a sample of the bark and four different types of nuts by sending $2 to Platinum Treats, P.O. Box 8082, West Bloomfield, MI 48304.

fact-digging investigative reports) are "puff pieces"—uncritical, highly favorable publicity about you, your accomplishments, and your organization. Reporters and freelance writers like them because they are easy to write and lead to useful community contacts; editors like them because they present a positive community image and tell interesting stories. And the subjects—that means you—love them because they generate attention. So everybody wins!

The article on page 58 is an example, from *Michigan: The Magazine of the Detroit News*. Though there's not too much copy, the article fills an entire magazine page, thanks to a creative, luscious photo, which not only shows the tantalizing product and its two designers, but also prominently displays the firm's logo. Sources and contact information are included.

This is important: When you or your firm is profiled in a feature story, you have absolutely *no control* over any editorial or artistic decisions. If there are points you want to make sure are included, stress them in your interview. But don't make a pest of yourself, and don't be too upset if your article leaves out points you'd like included, or even misquotes or misrepresents you. You can ask to look over the manuscript *for factual accuracy only,* but most writers won't grant that wish.

W*hen you or your firm is profiled in a feature story, you have absolutely no control over any editorial or artistic decisions.*

With photos, there's a bit more latitude. You can suggest creative, promotional shots and can make available any publicity photos you already have. You can also work with the photographer to provide the editor with a range of photos that highlight your best advantages.

Note that like writing, photographic images belong to their creator. If you contract with a photog-

rapher for a publicity shot, make sure your contract gives you the unlimited right to use the photos for promotional and informational purposes in any medium. Let a lawyer review the agreement before the photographer sees it.

— Product or Event Highlights —

Many publications have a department that prominently displays products or announces events. Typically, you get a good-sized headline, two to five paragraphs of text, ordering information, and often a photo. These fall into a couple of different types:

New Product Introductions

Many magazines—especially trade magazines catering to a clearly defined interest group—have a column featuring new items of interest to their readers. Traditionally, the focus is usually on products. But a savvy service provider ought to be able to get in here as well. Think of a visual, concrete representation of your service, write a press release that describes it as a product, and hope for the best. For instance, if you are a consultant and you offer a written report in a spiffy binder, and a photograph of one of your reports, along with a caption describing the results—the benefit to the client in increased sales, lower costs, and so forth—you might have a shot at this coverage.

Best Bets, Editor's Choice

These are short roundups of places, products, or events that feature some combination of low prices, high quality, particular interest, and excitement. In a calendar, these might be set aside as highlights. In other columns, they stand together without other editorial matter and comprise an entire article.

If you have a product you feel is worthy, send it along to the appropriate editor. If it's too expensive to mail out unsolicited, send a press release with a notation that free copies or trials are available to the press—and follow up in a month by telephone.

A variant on the editor's pick is the reader's choice; the magazine conducts a survey of its readers, asking their preferences on various products and services.

In either case, many publications feature an award ceremony, allow the winners to use the publication's award logo in their advertising and in-store displays, and use the awards as an excuse to try to sell the selected businesses display ads.

— Reviews and Previews —

Reviews inform the reader about an event or an available product (or, less often, a service). When possible, editors often have a preference for reviewing something that their readers can still experience— for instance, a movie or play at the beginning of its run. Previews are "coming attractions," which the reporter writes without actually seeing the performance—the article is written on the basis of press kits, interviews, and/or the reporter's expertise. Previews are pretty much limited to the performing arts and special events (such as a balloon fair or restaurant festival). But commonplace subjects for reviews include books, publications, and record albums (especially by local people); musical events; theater, film, and dance; art exhibits; restaurants; any kind of live entertainment (especially for a charity); retail shopping and bargains.

Always enclose your news release when sending a product for review, and put news releases in your press packet along with clippings. Some lazy reviewers will often quote directly from the release, or even run the whole thing as a review. So if you want something said, say it first.

Advance coverage is obviously more helpful in bringing people to your event. But reviews after the fact are good follow-up publicity, too. If you run several events a year, and your events get frequent and generally favorable reviews, they will help attract people to future events. And if the event or performer has appeared elsewhere, use reviews that appeared in other cities.

When you want an event reviewed, your advance press work should indicate to the editor or reporter why it's important. If you have frequent events, you should begin to cultivate the press people who cover

you. But even if you're only doing a one-shot promotion or event, be sure to help the reporters do their job. And don't scrimp on free tickets—for each reporter and his or her guest.

If you run a tourist attraction, you may get visiting travel writers dropping in on you without advance notice. So keep press kits on hand and let them in for free. Ask them to send you tearsheets of anything they publish about you. Take their names and addresses to add to your press/publicity mailing list. And make sure all writers have full contact information and know what you and your staff can do to help them.

If you supply photos, keep on hand a selection of professional-quality, high-contrast 8 x 10 or 5 x 7 black-and-white prints and color slides. Include both horizontal and vertical shots. Ask—but don't expect—the reporter to return your photos after use. Caption them, either on the margin or on the back (with a typed label or felt-tip pen, *never* a ball point pen), with both a description and the photographer's credit line.

Most reporters will be relatively cautious with negative reviews. But if the event or attraction is horrible, they have an obligation to report it.

Allow Access to "Stars"

If writers want to interview your celebrity, try to facilitate it. If several press people want to talk with the same person, an informal press conference will be the least strain for your star. Allow enough time for everybody to ask their most important questions. Finally, any rules restricting photographs should not apply to media people unless there's an extremely compelling reason—and if so, you must provide photos.

— Letters to the Editor —

Don't forget the most obvious way to get into the newspaper! Politicians, human-services people, educators, and business operators use the letters column all the time. It keeps their message in the public eye and identifies them as spokespeople for their beliefs. Letters are a perfect opportunity to provide clarification or additional information about a topic covered in a recent article; list your firm as a resource for or provider of an activity or service discussed in the publication; refute points you disagree with, or that portray your activities in a bad light; publicize events, products, services, and ideas; make a public thank-you or acknowledgment; and comment on local, national, or international events.

A Marketing Miracle

Gene Kroupa is perhaps the ultimate letter column success story. In just the first six weeks after publishing the following letter in *The Mother Earth News* (January/February 1985), he received over six hundred written inquiries about his expensive product:

Back in your January/February 1981 issue, you did an article on a multipurpose wood stove that I invented. Four years later, I'm still surviving in the business you helped me start. As a result of that story, I received a great many letters from like-minded people, who encouraged me, offered helpful criticism and better ideas, and revived my hope for the future of this planet.

We've all worked together by mail and telephone, and the result is, I believe, a very practical, functional, and beautiful new stove. Kroupa Two is designed to be the furnace, fireplace, cookstove, and water heater for the new breed of housing . . . or to fill a prominent place in any country kitchen.

If interested readers will write to me at the address below, I'll be happy to send further information.

> *Gene Kroupa*
> *R.R. 2, Oliver, B.C.*
> *Canada V0H 1T0*

Let's analyze this clever and effective letter: It uses a casual tone and simple language; starts with a reference to a previously published article in the magazine—a profile of the author's earlier invention; follows up with thanks for helping his business; cites community input that improved the product; announces the new version in seductive, futuristic phrases; ties the new product both to innovative new homes and to existing country kitchens, thus

appealing to two huge potential markets; and concludes with an action step for the reader, complete with full address.

Gene Kroupa is either a marketing genius who carefully crafted this letter, or just a sincere guy who wrote a quick, lucky note in a language his readers could relate to. Either way, it cost him roughly one-twentieth of a cent to get each prospect. Six-hundred-plus responses is a pretty good return on his investment of one first-class stamp!

Obviously, the range of topics and ideas suitable for the letters column is broad. Almost anything other than libel, obscenity, or naked self-promotion can be phrased as a letter to the editor—even thinly disguised self-promotion such as the above example. Some papers will print virtually everything they receive, except outright slander or blatantly commercial messages. Others, such as *The New York Times*, are far more selective, printing only a small fraction of the vast contents of their mailbag. But for the cost of a stamp, it doesn't hurt to try.

Public Relations/Social Policy Instruments

People involved in any facet of politics have often used the letters column as a soapbox, or as a forum for public relations. Here's how a state legislator used the letters page of the Binghamton, New York, *Press and Sun Bulletin* to rally his constituents against the governor (a member of the other party). Notice how he uses empathy with voter frustration both to duck any responsibility for the delay and at the same time to propose a five-point reform program that embarrasses the opposite party.

Like most New Yorkers, I was frustrated by the lengthy delay in adopting a new state budget.

Valid reasons for the delay were little discussed—primarily Gov. Mario M. Cuomo's failure to submit all the bills to the Legislature at the same time. By submitting his proposals late, he left less time for the Legislature to do a thorough job. . . . Be that as it may, Senate Republicans have proposed a comprehensive budget reform plan.

The centerpiece . . . is an automatic austerity budget that . . . would carry forward the previous year's spending levels, adjusted to meet expected revenues. This process would guarantee . . . state aid. . . .

Other components . . . include public meetings held by the financial committees . . . and making agencies' budget requests public. I also support setting aside a portion of each day's session for debate on the budget.

Last, our proposal requires that the governor submit the entire proposed budget at the same time. . . .

Our proposals would restore some integrity to the budget process and ensure that school districts and local governments wouldn't have to borrow when the Legislature disagrees with the governor's proposals and attempts to fashion a fair budget.

> James L. Seward
> New York State Senate
> R-Milford

Even the stately *New York Times*, whose influential letters page is probably the hardest to get into in the country, runs large numbers of letters advancing a commercial interest or cause, attempting to influence public policy, boosting the author's credentials, or commenting in a professional capacity.

Let's look at just one day's letters column: All nine letters that day respond to published articles. Of those nine, six are in some way self-aggrandizing or advance a pointed social agenda. Not coincidentally, all six writers list an organizational affiliation. Here's a bank lobbyist:

> Donald J. Cohen and Kenneth A. Guenther both address important public policy issues in "Save Bankers From Themselves by Regulation" (letters, Aug. 4), and so does Representative Charles E. Schumer in his July 19 Op-Ed article.
> Mr. Cohen warns that "deregulation, however diligent, is not the answer to lower risk; it's better bankers." Maybe so. But even our best bankers find it difficult to cope with a protectionist system of financial services regulation from the 1930's. . . .
> Mr. Guenther expresses concern over a proposal . . . that would permit commercial ownership of banks. . . . Our economy is filled with examples of commercial organizations that conduct . . . banking. General Electric owns some of the largest lenders in the country. . . . Subsidiaries of Ford, General Motors, Sears, American Express, Prudential, John Hancock, I.T.T., and

Merrill Lynch offer financial services, including Federal Deposit Insurance Corporation–insured deposits. The public is well served by these arrangements.
> Representative Schumer identifies the Federal deposit insurance system as [a problem]. But instead of limiting the number of insured accounts . . . or calling for an end to de facto coverage of uninsured . . . deposits, Mr. Schumer proposes to dismantle our system for a new regulatory structure . . . an expansion of taxpayer liability without real change in the system . . . that hurts the performance of our economy.

> Thomas Ludlow Ashley
> President, Association of
> Bank Holding Companies

Also, that day's *Times* printed letters from the Consul General of Panama, defending his government against charges of allowing drug exports; the state chapter director of the National Alliance of Families for the Return of America's Missing Servicemen, criticizing an article that disputed claims of live prisoners still being held in Southeast Asia; a Thailand-based American businessman praising that disputation (he has much to gain by thawing U.S./ Vietnam relations); a professor of Slavic languages, outlining the ethnic differences between Prussians and Slavs; and a medical school instructor, responding to an article on restaurant inspection with a proposal to reduce infectious disease through stricter standards for food service workers.

Letters can directly promote for-profit enterprises, as long as you have that news peg. Here's another one from *The New York Times* that generates interest in two of the author's cookbooks—a wonderful example of seizing the moment:

> I was astonished that your obituary article on I. B. Singer gave short shrift to his vegetarianism. Mr. Singer contributed interviews and recipes to two of my books, The New Vegetarians *and* Famous Vegetarians and Their Favorite Recipes. *I can assure you vegetarianism was essential to his vision as an artist.*
> When I asked him how it was that vegetarian leitmotifs and themes appeared in his novels long before he formally became vegetarian, he said:
> " . . . [T]hese things came out through my pen almost

automatically. Yes, I always thought about eating meat. These things bothered me all the time."

After giving me two of his favorite recipes . . . for Famous Vegetarians, he said I could have them if I also included the following quotation:

"I think that everything connected with vegetarianism is of the highest importance because there will never be any peace in the world so long as we eat animals. This also applies to fish. I do not eat any fish. I had felt guilty and ashamed about the fact that I had eaten the flesh of an animal. I think that animals are as much God's creatures as men are. And we have to respect and love them, not slaughter them."

This makes a fitting epitaph for a man who was a vegetarian—not because he loved kasha, potatoes and rice pudding (for which he had an inordinate craving)—but because he loved humanity.

Rynn Berry
Brooklyn

The author commented to me that the letter's publication "sparked a good deal of interest in my books. Bookstores that hadn't been aware of my books hitherto, suddenly started carrying them. Moreover, I'm still receiving inquiries more than two months after publication."

Type letters single-spaced with an extra blank line between paragraphs. Send them out on your letterhead if you're speaking in your organizational role, and on plain paper if you're acting as an individual. Expect to be edited down if you run longer than two hundred words or so.

Letters Online

Letters can be very effective in online publications, too, where they're called "posts." Here's an example:

I have to respond to James Lamb's assertions regarding the latency in third party ad serving. AdKnowledge, and Focalink before it, has been doing third party ad serving since August 1995. Let me assure everyone that third party ad serving is NOT inherently slower than when ads are served from the server where the rest of the page content resides. . . .

Several factors DO affect delivery speeds, including the:

- design of the ad server
- hardware running the ad serving software
- bandwidth purchased for delivering the ads
- geographic proximity of the ad server to the browser requesting an ad
- congestion on the Internet between the ad server and the browser

In the case of AdKnowledge, ad serving is our business, and we tend to deliver ads more quickly than most sites. We have optimized our servers to deliver ads quickly (they do nothing else). We also have invested in completely redundant, fault-tolerant systems. With over $1.5 million invested in hardware alone, I dare say we deliver ads about as quickly as they can be.

Thanks for giving me the space to clarify this issue. Since it is a core part of our business, when people spread the perception that third party ad serving is somehow slower, it requires a response from us.

****

David Zinman, Founder, Dir of Product Mgmt
AdKnowledge, Inc.
2191 East Bayshore Rd., Palo Alto, CA 94303
Phone: (650) 842-6508 / Fax: (650) 842-0665
mailto:dzinman@adknowledge.com
http://www.adknowledge.com

AdKnowledge. We make web advertising work.

****

Now, as it happens, this letter ran in the *Internet Advertising Digest* (September 17, 1998). Of the eleven thousand subscribers to this list, it's a safe bet that at least eight thousand of them buy or sell Internet advertising. With just a few keystrokes, Zinman put himself in front of his best prospects.

We'll talk about getting maximum marketing impact through participation in Internet discussion groups and magazines in much more detail in part 4.

Letters Written by Others

It may sometimes make sense to arrange for letters by others, in addition to or instead of letters you write yourself. This is particularly important if there's a controversy surrounding you and you want loud, staunch defenders. Third-party validation always means more in those cases than you tooting your own horn.

However, don't neglect this tool for ordinary marketing as well. Testimonial or thank-you letters by others will carry a great deal of weight with readers, especially if the letter's author is a person of importance in the community; these work because they show others benefiting from their interaction with you. One magazine I know even has a department in each issue called Service Heroes, featuring one letter that highlights a customer-service success story. Letters by others can also be an effective tool in any kind of win-lose contest, such as a closely contested political battle.

— Features and Talk Shows —

If you've been doing a thorough press campaign all along, reporters and talk show hosts may contact you to arrange a profile or guest appearance. After all, they need continuous streams of subjects to fill up their allotted airtime or column inches. WWOR-TV's Stanley Friedman was responsible for a guest editorial department called Viewpoint. "If people don't invite themselves—a very small percentage invite themselves—I just get it from the news. I read the papers and see what issue would make a good Viewpoint. I call them and say 'I read your view in the newspaper.' Most people are delighted."

So even in one of the largest markets in the country (the New York metropolitan area), some producers have to seek people out. But don't sit around waiting for that to happen. Send out a release on a carefully focused topic, announce at the end of the release that you are available for interviews, and do the appropriate follow-up work. If you do this three or four times a year, eventually it will pay off.

Once you've started to get this kind of coverage, include a summary of your media appearances and other public talks in your release as part of a biographical note. For example: "Annie Johnson has discussed Bolivian culture on National Public Radio and was the subject of a recent feature in *Latin America* magazine. She owns and operates Andean Heights, a boutique in Smith Village." As your credits accumulate, include a media summary in your press packets. Here's the heading from mine, which currently fills two columns in small type and is broken down into nationally syndicated radio shows, major and medium radio markets in the United States, major international markets, TV, and national print media:

Shel Horowitz—
Selected Media Appearances
Notes: Shel does over 50 shows a year.
Starred entries (*) were 30 minutes or longer,
% = repeat appearance.

Cultivate the friendship of reporters and working freelancers. Send appreciative notes when you like a story—and when you're quoted (writers love getting fan mail). Call up your contacts with advance notice of a new development. Be cooperative when interviewed: be flexible about scheduling interviews, provide your reporter with lots of background information, and answer questions as fully and articulately as you can. Be generous with perks such as free passes. Forward information about possible stories, even if they don't directly involve you. Eventually, gently suggest that you think your operation would make a good subject for a profile. Or have a mutual friend or business acquaintance make the suggestion. Don't be afraid to ask, but don't push it if the reporter says no. Ask again a year later, after another dozen press contacts.

Coverage generates more coverage. Aim first for features in small-town dailies and community weeklies. Then mail off a packet of photocopied articles to more prominent media, with a note on the order of "As you can see, odorless toothpaste has become a very timely subject of late. If you would like more information on any part of this phenomenon, please feel free to contact me." Include coverage of other people doing similar things. With our toothpaste example, you might include an article interviewing a dentist who recommends your product, or a pharmacist who tracked its sales growth.

— Write Your Own —

Not everyone can write well. But if you can, article writing can add significantly to your prestige, create very favorable publicity, and perhaps put some dollars directly in your pocket. Think for a moment about the types of articles you can write *and use as marketing tools*—and who would read them.

Proper article format is almost the same as for a multipage press release. Include a word count and your social security number on the front page. Margins should be at least an inch all around; start the headline and text of your first page about a third of the way down.

Problem-Solving Feature Articles

If you provide any kind of service, think about generalized problem-solving articles that steer the reader in the right direction, but are not too specific; then the reader can call you in to consult when he or she needs more concrete suggestions. For example, an accountant could write an article on the importance of keeping accurate records, with some general tips about how to set up a record-keeping system. The same accountant could also write about financial planning services, tax breaks for his or her target audience, and so on.

A caterer could do an article on successful party planning. An office supply wholesaler could discuss the latest equipment. A landscaper could put forth theories about the perfect plants for different growing conditions. Use your imagination.

Marketing—and not additional income from freelancing—is your primary reason for writing articles. Your goal is to appear to prospective clients as a sophisticated expert *who can solve their prob-*

lems. Thus, fight hard to get information included on how to contact you. Consultant and author Jeffrey Lant, whose syndicated column appears in over 250 different publications, barters his column for a resource box with full contact information.

The article on page 66 was written by an attorney specializing in collection law, providing advice and also presenting himself as an expert for those who want to hire someone else to clean up their accounts receivable.

In the writing trade, these are called service pieces, because they provide a service—useful, concrete information—to the reader. They can be structured in many different ways. Here are a few of the many possibilities:

- Straight how-to: this is the task, and these are the steps to accomplish it
- Success profile: the people of this organization experienced a problem, and this is how they solved it
- Ask our experts—or a variant, Ask the readers: I'm having a problem; how would each of your regular panelists suggest surmounting it?
- Five or ten points to solve a problem
- Broad-brush analysis: this is a problem facing many of your peers, and this is how to deal with it
- Roundup: these several companies used these approaches to deal with the problem

Format and Submissions

Some publicists prepare "canned" features and send them off to noncompeting newspapers. However, expect a very low placement rate.

For magazines, send a one-page query outlining an article you'd like to write, and your credentials. You can send the same query out to several people at once, with individualized addresses. Don't send the article itself simultaneously to competing markets, but you can send queries. If an editor perceives an article as written just for his or her magazine (in response to a go-ahead on your initial query), the publication will be much more likely to accept it. Once your material begins to appear in print, send

When the Check Isn't in the Mail
by Jerome S. Gold

There's no time like the present." Teachers, parents, coaches, and other mentors have chimed these words to their charges since time immemorial, in areas ranging from organizing term papers to memorizing play books. For those of us who own and operate a business today, these are challenging times. Few, if any, businesses have escaped an increase in bad debt during the current economic downturn. A solid "game plan" is needed to curtail further losses and to establish a proper foundation for the future. And there truly is no time like the present!

In my 26 years of collection experience, I can reflect upon a variety of business practices that directly contributed to losses and could have been avoided, or at least minimized, by an established credit and collections policy. space does not permit an examination of every area, but I will highlight a few specifics.

First and foremost, do not scrimp on the expense of establishing and sustaining effective credit and collections personnel, policies, and procedures. Whether your business is the sale of goods or of services, it is likely that the key emphasis is sales. Much time, effort, and expense are devoted to promoting your product or service, training and inspiring your staff, and closing the deal. However, consider this: If your profit margin on sales is 5%, a bad debt of $500 requires future sales of $10,000 to offset the loss.

Credit and collections cannot be relegated to poor stepchild status.

Whether your business allows for only a one-person credit department or a cast of thousands, attention must be given not only to hiring qualified credit personnel, but also to their continuing education. A variety of local resources offer training manuals and seminars.

"Credit Applications." Salespeople cringe at the words. "The competition doesn't require it and we'll lose sales," they plead. I could say, "Better you should lose the sale now than lose the receivable later," but that is entirely too simplistic. Clearly, every business needs to establish its own guidelines as to if, when, and how to use credit applications. I suggest sales limits be established and adhered to, and sales exceeding a specified dollar amount would require a credit application.

Whether an application is used or not, every effort should be made to know who is responsible for payment. Are you dealing with a sole proprietorship, a partnership, or a corporation? Is a trade name being used? Should a personal guarantee be required? My clients who obtain signed credit applications have receivables with a higher degree of collectability in nearly every instance than those who do not. And, if properly written, a credit application can help to defer the costs of collection by assessing collection fees.

Small Claims Court is available to you for pursuing receivables up to $1,500. While personnel reductions in all of the state's courts have resulted in considerable delays in obtaining Small Claims Court

hearings, your attorney will experience similar delays if the case is referred out for legal action. Small Claims Court provides you with a means of acquiring judgments, of examining a debtor's ability to pay through Show Cause hearings and, if successful, of obtaining court-ordered payments. Court personnel or your attorney can assist you in understanding how to effectively take advantage of this low-cost collection remedy.

If all self-help collection remedies have been exhausted, it is advisable to seek outside collection assistance. Collection agencies may be able to assist you when a balance is not enough to warrant a lawsuit, or when your customer base is spread over a multi-state area and you desire to centralize your collection accounts.

In seeking legal counsel for your collection work, I urge you to find an attorney or firm concentrating in creditor representation. Your general counsel or others in your business are a good source for recommending the firm that can best suit your needs.

Whatever your chosen course, do not delay striking while the iron is hot. Collectability is greatly enhanced when appropriate action is taken as soon as a collection problem is discovered. There is no time like the present.

Jerome S. Gold is an attorney concentrating in collection law with Gold & Vanaria P.C. in Springfield, and is co-author of the "Massachusetts Collections Manual."

tear-sheets of your published work with your pitches.

Submit articles freely to noncompeting markets, as long as you don't sign a contract that says "all rights" or "work for hire." For instance, publish the same article in journals serving Baptists, Lutherans, and Congregationalists. And a how-to article aimed at business owners in Florida could easily be modified for business publications elsewhere.

However, even if the market isn't as clearly segmented, you can multiply your audience. I once proposed the same story (on a computerized solar-assisted bicycle) to computer, safe-energy, back-to-the-land, regional, and bicycling magazines. If one market rejects your idea, query a competitor. Finally, you can even query different editors at the same publication with the same idea (wait two years or so).

A business consultant applied one thesis to three different target markets: real estate professionals, businesspeople, and the general public. Here are excerpts:

Americans Get Bitten by
Their Bank Watchdogs
Donald Todrin
[Boston Business Journal]

The watchdogs of the banking industry, in an ill-conceived attempt to repair the economic hole we're in, are burying the small-business person, destroying the banking system and wreaking havoc with the economy. . . .The regulators are overcompensating for having allowed the banks to run amok. . . . If for no other reason than the protection of a bank's profitability, it is a bad decision to automatically liquidate viable loans. . . .

Cooperation Profits Banks
and Borrowers
Donald Todrin
[New England Real Estate Journal]

Consider the profit in solving borrowers' business problems . . . profitability, performance on the loan, stimulation of the local economy and loyal, lifelong clients. . . .

Why do [bankers] put their resources into demolition rather than preventive maintenance? . . . What I most frequently hear is "We never find out until it's too late. . . ." Fear of the bank prevents the businessperson from seeking the bank's aid. And the fear is well-founded, based on the liquidation mentality. . . . If people thought the bank would help them rather than put them out of business, they would be grateful for the advice. . . .

Another Way to Treat Debtors
Donald Todrin
[Daily Hampshire Gazette]

It's today's reality and tomorrow's nightmare.

A borrower has defaulted on a loan, the bank has foreclosed . . . and attempts to sell them at auction. . . .

Most businesses and real estate have inherent value. As going concerns, they are actively operated and promoted and, as such, are valuable. When they are privately sold as a going concern, a significant return can be realized. . . .

On the foreclosure auction block, the intrinsic value of potential profitability disappears and the asset viewed is the value of salvage. . . .

All three articles closed with a variant on "Donald Todrin is vice president of Visioneering Corp., a Northampton business consulting and communications firm."

Op-Ed Columns

One department in virtually any daily newspaper and many weeklies and magazines actively encourages contributions from the community: the opinion, or Op-Ed, page.

Like a letter to the editor, an Op-Ed is a sounding board, but formatted as an article and carefully focused. An Op-Ed can't ramble and is usually longer than most letters—six hundred to one thousand words is typical. Op-Eds run with a byline and often a one- or two-line biography. They're ideal for commenting about a current issue that's relevant to your business.

Op-Eds should be sent to noncompeting papers simultaneously. Most papers print very few one-time Op-Eds, so the chance of publishing an Op-Ed in any particular paper is much smaller than the chance of publishing a letter. Therefore, multiple submissions will improve the odds. Often, an Op-Ed writer will target major newspapers throughout the country. However, if you send a piece to one national newspaper—*The New York Times, The Wall Street Journal,* or *USA Today*—don't send the same article anywhere else in the United States until it's been accepted or rejected.

If a national newspaper or magazine accepts your piece, you can still send it out elsewhere, but only with a clear notation that you're offering "second rights." Mention where and when the article appeared. If you've published in a paper that only circulates locally, you can still offer first rights within a new circulation area, for example, "First Texas Serial Rights."

In most, but not all cases, expect to get paid between $10 and $300 for an Op-Ed. If you get something into *Newsweek's* "My Turn" column, you'll earn a cool $1,000.

Regular Columns

Once you have a track record, a regular ongoing column certifies you as an expert in that field. In a small town, you and your business may become quite well known; people may stop by your store or office to let you know how much they enjoyed a piece you did. My local small-town daily and weekly magazine insert have had columns on the following subjects, among others: cooking, rock music, home repair, town history, social security, the changing seasons, local sports commentary, stress reduction, entertainment picks for the week, TV and TV movies (separate columns with separate authors), and gardening.

The rock music column was started by the owner of a record store; when he gave it up it was taken over by a local disk jockey. An employee of the cooperative extension service prepares the gardening column. A psychologist writes about stress.

As long as the publication has nobody else already covering your field, just convince the editor that (1) you can write and are reliable, and (2) people will be interested. If it already has a columnist on your topic but this seems like a good technique, try another publication.

Say you have a hardware store—try a question-and-answer home repair column. Are you an environmental activist? Explore easy, low-cost conservation and waste-reduction techniques.

The only caution is that you have to maintain your credibility. Answer honestly, and don't actively pitch your own product or agency. Your business or number of clients served will increase with the growth in your stature as an expert, not because you're directly hawking your product or service.

Of course, you must be willing to make a commitment to turn in your five hundred, eight hundred, or one thousand words regularly. Be sure you have enough ideas to keep the column going for at least a year.

Once you have a track record, a regular ongoing column certifies you as an expert in that field.

This isn't as difficult as it sounds. You work in the field and thus can spot trends in trade journals, in the mainstream press, and in conversations with vendors and customers. Every time you read or hear about a new development in your field, it could spark a column: Is it the beginning of a trend? What economic or social impact does it have? Do you have a commonsense way out of the problem? Ideas show up in ads and articles, in natural disasters, in political events—absolutely everywhere. In fact, I'm planning to write a booklet called "How to Find Your Next 10,000 Ideas." If you'd like to be notified when this is available, please send me e-mail at <mailto: shel@frugalfun.com>, subject line: "Notify Me about 10,000 Ideas."

— If You Can't Write —

There are several options open if you don't want to write, but want the benefits: work with a collaborator, ghostwriter, or editor; subscribe to a newsletter service; or take courses in writing.

In the first case, you work with a writer who interviews you, drafts the article, and then checks back with you for input and revisions before submitting the piece.

Newsletter services prepare the same newsletter for many different firms; you add your company identity and address and distribute to your clients and prospects. In this case, you are on ethical high ground, since you don't claim to write the problem-solving articles, just distribute them. But avoid services that mass-market the same articles to different "original authors."

Other Kinds of Creativity

Similar self-promotion techniques work well in other media: visual arts, performance, landscaping, cooking. . . . A photographer or illustrator could work with print media in much the same ways as a writer, while a musician might do better as the host of a show on radio or cable TV.

10

Let Fingers Do the Walking
—and Find You

The Yellow Pages are the marketer's blessing—or worst curse. The way you set up your Yellow Pages advertising campaign may prove the most important of all your marketing decisions.

With every business phone line, you get one free, no-frills listing in one heading: your business name in small, light, upper- and lower-case print, along with your address and phone number. Beyond that, you have to buy advertising space.

The standard Yellow Pages directory is distributed free to every home, company, and agency within its circulation area; many households and businesses request several copies. Nothing can equal that market coverage—not even physically visiting every home and business in your area. Each book stays near a telephone for a year, and in the course of that year, the book's owner will probably turn to the directory many times. Many businesses—particularly service providers—achieve a stronger return from Yellow Pages advertising than from any other medium. And every person who opens up the directory to your category is a targeted, motivated prospect who wants what you offer. In other words, Yellow Pages advertising combines total market saturation, long shelf life, and selectivity.

Simon Zylph <mailto:szylph@cwix.com>, a former Yellow Pages sales representative, identifies five types of buyers who use the Yellow Pages: newcomers, people with an emergency, those who are dissatisfied with their current supplier, those who buy very infrequently, and prospects seeking competitive bids (I-Sales HelpDesk, November 30, 1998).

Since the prospect hasn't chosen a firm to supply the need yet, you want your ad to jump out and say, "This is what you're looking for."

— Choose Your Headings —

Defining your category headings carefully is essential—even more so than in other classified media, because the publisher may try to list you under obscure, unintuitive headings. For instance, to hire a temporary worker, you'd have to know to look under "Employment Contractors—Temporary Help." Sometimes there will be cross-references; sometimes the reader just has to guess.

Make a list of the full range of your products and services with a local clientele. Which are primary, which are ancillary? What's your strongest suit—

and what do you enjoy the most? Where are you competent for basic work but not the reigning expert? Where do your customers look for you—and what else are they looking for? And where in the book will your ads stand out next to the ones that are already there? Finally, how much business do you want?

Let's look at my business as an example of this process. We build our local marketing around our individually crafted résumés. We draw on about a forty-mile radius for 90 percent of our résumé work, while our marketing and editing clientele is worldwide.

How do we advertise in the Yellow Pages? Since résumés and related services are our strongest local draw, we've chosen a strong presence in that heading. But because the competition is limited, it doesn't have to be too strong. Only six businesses list under Résumé Service in our local directory. One has a two-inch color display ad. Along with Kinko's, which doesn't actually write résumés but rents do-it-yourself workstations, we have a one-inch classified. The rest are all simple listings.

There were eleven listings when I researched my last marketing book, back in 1991. We survived the shakeout because our ad emphasizes our USP—affordable, professional résumés while you wait; our A name puts us first; and we mention a prestigious award.

▶ **Resume Svce.**

ACCURATE WRITING & MORE
Resume Specialists Since 1981
- Affordable professional resumes while you wait
- Writing, editing, cover letters, updates, copies
- In-person or by phone / Fax / e-mail
- 10 minutes from Northhampton, Amherst
- Advocate "Best of the Valley"
CALL NOW FOR YOUR APPOINTMENT
Hadley MA --------------------------------**586-2388**

This ad in our local directory brings in about 50 percent of our career services business. We also advertise résumé services in four other directories, but since they're farther away, we don't get the same kind of return. Another big chunk is repeat and referral

business, and our other marketing brings in a tiny fraction of this work.

One client per month more than pays for the cost of the insertion.

Though the vast majority of our marketing clients find us from outside the area, we have our free ad under marketing consultants—and pay for an extra line listing my marketing book.

We know from experience that people don't look for writers or editors in the Yellow Pages, so we have no presence in those headings.

One danger with Yellow Pages advertising is that you can put together such a good ad that the response will put you out of business if you can't meet the workload. Let's say a service business has 100 client slots a month, and fills 50 of them with a one-inch ad. Repeat and referral clients might account for 30 more. Going up to a quarter-page ad would oversaturate; most of the people who called would have to be turned away, and the return per dollar invested would decrease sharply. Better, perhaps, to put another small ad in a neighboring book, which would bring the business up near capacity without turning clients away or wasting ad dollars.

In general, I would suspect most businesses are better off with large classified ads rather than display ads; you can still dominate your category with the right one-inch ad, and you won't pay the dramatically higher costs of display ads. Plus, you're assured that your ad will be located in the category listings, whereas a display ad may end up on another page, invisible.

— Increase Visibility —

At a fairly minimal cost, you can spruce up your ad, thereby increasing its visibility—and its pulling power. Consider some of the following:

- A boldface and/or all-uppercase name listing
- An extra line
- A box around your ad (usually standard with a half-inch or larger ad; sometimes available even in a smaller insertion)

- A list of the services you provide, with each item separated by bullets (•) or dashes (—)
- Inclusion of Web and e-mail addresses, and fax and/or TTY numbers

Beyond these visual frills, of course, are larger classified ads, and beyond those are display ads.

Choose the ad sizes that will be most effective in light of the competition's ads. The ads will change from year to year, but the current directory will help you make educated guesses about the next edition. If a category has two pages of display and large classified ads, it doesn't make sense to put in a tiny ad that will be ignored. Go in with something noticeable or leave that category alone. By contrast, if a category has only a few small entries, it might be the place to put your free listing (and possibly an extra line). Alternatively, you could put in a larger entry to dominate the underserved category. Then try your freebie in a category where you wouldn't list if you had to pay for it, and see what happens.

Although display ads are available in increments as small as a quarter column (one-sixteenth of a page), those ads really aren't any more eye-catching than a classified would be—especially since they're often stacked so densely that if you're on the bottom, you'll get lost in the shuffle. Worse, the display ads are often separated from the classified list-

Sample ads in different sizes—where does your eye go first?

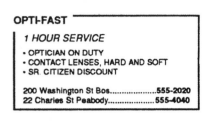

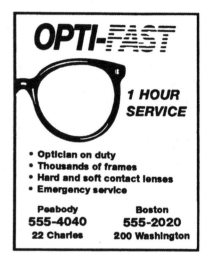

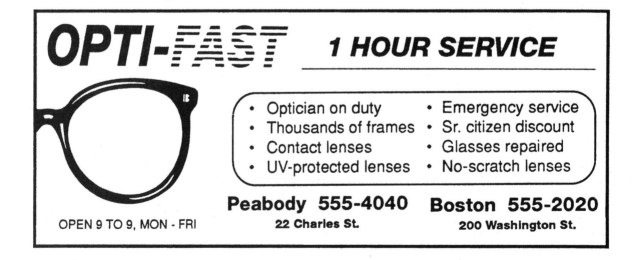

ings—sometimes even on a different page. Thus, a small ad might not be seen, and the advantage of targeting by category can be negated. Therefore, keep to classifieds, unless you're willing to pay for a quarter page or half page—and can handle the business such a large ad would bring in.

Consider spot color—just a couple of words or a graphic in the midst of black copy. Don't let the rep try to sell you on doing the whole ad in color; a solid sea of red is just as lost as a solid sea of black—especially if the ad reps have pushed a lot of red ads that year. Two colors have many times the visual impact of one. Similarly, reverse type (yellow on black) can also draw in the eye, if used judiciously to highlight a portion of an ad. Most directory publishers will design an ad for you for free. Take a look at what they can do for you, but be prepared to do something better on your own, since their approach is often formulaic or unattractive.

— Geography —

Although in most situations, the largest portion of your Yellow Pages budget should go toward your strongest categories in the book that serves your own community, consider neighboring directories.

There are often many choices. What's right for your company will depend on numerous factors: Are you in a rural community, small town, medium-sized city, or major metropolitan area? How far are you from the bulk of your client/customer base? How much competition is there outside your immediate area—will people travel some distance to do business with you, or find someone closer? Are there specialized directories, such as university campus or business-to-business? Do you have to consider privately published directories (i.e., those not distributed by your local former Bell division)? Finally, how much will it cost to have a significant presence in these books—do you have to set priorities?

In a major metropolitan area, the number of books may be staggering. Boston, for instance, has separate White and Yellow Pages for the inner core as well as for two immediately adjoining areas, plus a Business-to-Business book; each of these seven books is at least an inch and a half thick. But even that doesn't cover the entire Greater Boston area; there are over a dozen smaller books covering communities within a half hour's drive. Even in smaller cities, full coverage may require a presence in numerous books.

How do you choose? Again, examine your competitors' listings. If a category is full of half-page ads with local addresses and telephone numbers, a distant location won't succeed. On the other hand, as you go toward more sparsely populated areas, you may find that a nearby region is wide open or severely underserved. If you go in with an ad that will be noticed—and there's enough population to create a reasonable demand—you may do very well in that book.

Some businesses draw only from a narrow radius; no one is going to drive forty miles to a laundromat if there's one around the block. Others, such as a BMW repair specialist, may draw from a much larger area. And some businesses, such as my own, draw differently for different services.

Do your market research carefully. Are any of your current customers coming from the area you want to break into? How do they hear about you? How often do you go to their area for business? What services seem in short supply? How can you make it worth a trip and possibly a long-distance phone call?

Most importantly, what can you list in an ad that will convince that potential buyer to go to you instead of someone closer? Low prices? Free delivery? Brand-name products? Convenient parking? Easy access to a major highway? Extraordinary service? Lifetime guarantee? You've got to make it strong enough to overcome the psychological barrier—especially if your target is across a state or county line. So look for ways to turn that to your advantage. For instance, if you sell computers, stereos, or other expensive items, a customer from another state usually won't have to pay sales tax.

Where are your prospects oriented? If they are used to going to your city, you have a much easier shot than if they usually think about going in the other direction. Look for patterns of commuting; pick up a local newspaper and see where the advertisers are from.

Start small with new directories. If your ad works, increase its size the following year. If it doesn't work—as has happened to us several times—your loss is minimal.

— Account Executive —

Once you expand beyond the basic free listing, you will be assigned an account executive (sales representative), who will work with you to finalize all your ads.

Of course, your rep will try to sell you a fatter advertising package than you had intended to buy. Be firm; the account exec will respect you—or else you can request a different rep and someone else will get the commission. Ask about any promotions or special offers, such as a low-cost upgrade to the next size ad, or adding an extra line to a plain listing; even the Yellow Pages sometimes has sales and incentives. In fact, it's always a good idea to find out how much it costs, say, for a full-inch classified as opposed to a half-inch. The difference may be surprisingly little. Do this every year, because prices and special offers change—and so do your needs.

Here are some wise procedures to follow in dealing with your account exec:

First, before your appointment, skim the whole directory and look for categories that suit your business. Note how many other businesses are in each category, and how big their ads are. And note categories that you offer but that aren't listed.

At your meeting, be clear on your needs. The consequences of a bad ad are severe. In a daily, weekly, or even monthly publication, you can change an ad that isn't working. But once you've placed a Yellow Pages ad, you're stuck for the entire year. Improve your chances of getting what you want by working closely with the publisher.

Listen to information about options to increase your visibility, but don't buy anything you don't re-

ally want. Once you've made your decision, the rep will write up a contract for each book in which you place ads. Look over the contract carefully. Triple-check all spelling, as well as every word, punctuation mark, dingbat, and border. Make sure the punctuation you've chosen is available; my local book won't give commas in a classified, for instance. Verify the sizes and prices of all your entries. *Write "Page proofs required" on the contract; both you and the rep should initial the amendment.* (Some publishers reserve this privilege only for display ad purchases, so you might have to make some noise about this.) File your contracts, proofs, and your rep's business card in a safe place.

— If You Have a Problem —

In an ideal world, Yellow Pages would be the perfect medium. Unfortunately, it often doesn't work out that way. There are two major areas where you might run into a problem: (1) before the ad appears, and (2) when you first see the book in print. In both cases, the first person you should call is your ad rep—and then just keep asking for supervisors until you find someone who can help you.

Before the ad appears, you obviously have more recourse. If you offer services in a category outside the standard list of Yellow Pages headings, the company may resist creating new headings. Sometimes a substitute category does just as well; if you bake specialty pastries, list under Bakeries. I had to list under Editorial Services, when I would have rather listed under Editing.

Other times, you may be a pioneer in your field, and you can negotiate. Point out that categories are added all the time, and that in smaller books, many category headings only have one listing. All personal-computer related industries have been added since 1978, and several—such as Web Designers—were added only in the past few years. There is no good reason why if you're offering something no one has offered before, the company can't create a category for you—but you may have to go high up the chain of command to convince them.

If the issue has to do with punctuation or wording, be willing to sit down and hash out something that meets your needs, but is also acceptable to the publisher. Be flexible; consider bullets or dashes if you can't get commas or semicolons.

After publication, things get trickier. You've done your best to keep things smooth and get what you want, but sooner or later it happens: a wrong phone number, incorrect category listing, grammatical error, reversed graphic, or other major blooper in one of your ads. After publication, the problem is harder to straighten out; directory publishers all limit their liability to the cost of the ad. It's an insult and aggravation to all business owners, but without expensive and time-consuming litigation, there isn't much we can do other than accept the terms.

*B*e *your own best advocate, negotiate reasonably, keep going up the hierarchy as far as you need to go, and try to avoid problems in the first place by being careful with your ad rep.*

However, that doesn't mean you can't make some noise. Remember, you required page proofs on the contract. Obviously, if you did see the page proof and didn't catch the error, you're out of luck. If they didn't keep their end of the bargain, or if the page proof—you kept a copy, right?—differs from the final appearance, call up your rep and discuss the error, pointing out the contract language you added. Ask what the publisher can do for you. Because of the clause you added, you may have recourse in small claims court if you can show real damage. But check with a lawyer, because the directory's limitation of liability is very carefully worded.

If a major error clearly interferes with the ad's effectiveness, get a refund on that insertion. Get the name of anyone at the publisher's office who grants you any credit; document it with a letter stating the date of the agreement, the name of the directory's representative, and what exactly the company is promising. Check your bill and make sure the credit was applied.

The good news is sometimes an error that appears major to you won't really change the ad response. One year, the directory changed my résumé ad copy from "While You Wait" to "While-U-Wait." I successfully argued that because my business involved careful writing, the ad's destruction of my grammar was harmful. I got credit for the ad, but it drew inquiries all year long.

Other times, the ad is completely wasted. My father is a chiropractor in another state; his phone number was printed wrong in two successive years. In that situation, the first thing to do is to contact the person who has that number and ask that your callers receive your number. But that relies on his or her goodwill and patience, and your prospects' willingness to go through a runaround. Otherwise, all you can do is publicize your correct number, and try (probably unsuccessfully) to get the publisher to pay your costs. If you're lucky and the number is not in service, demand that the publisher pay for that number to be given to you in addition to your existing number, at least for the life of the ad.

Again, be your own best advocate, negotiate reasonably, keep going up the hierarchy as far as you need to go, and try to avoid problems in the first place by being careful with your ad rep.

— White Pages —

Too many companies make the mistake of cross-advertising the Yellow Pages in their display or radio ads—that is, using other media to tell consumers to look them up in the Yellow Pages. But that opens up a firm prospect to seduction by your competitors in their ads. Better to tell prospects to look for you in the White Pages—a straight alphabetical listing where you aren't necessarily near your competitors. Even better: Give out your Web address.

Many White Pages directories will allow bold or extra-bold listings, and sometimes even an extra line. Few firms take advantage of these tricks, so you may have the only enhanced listing on the page.

— Phone Service Options —

Although it's not strictly related to directory advertising, let's talk for a moment about your telephone service. Many very small businesses with only one phone line never know how much business they lose because customers can't get through. Don't let your customers get a busy signal; instead, add voice mail service and/or an additional phone line with "hunting"—calls roll over to the first available line. If you work from your home, use your residence line to call out and a business number to receive calls. This will often save you money, since many parts of the country offer unlimited local or expanded calling only for residence lines. Having two lines also gives you conferencing capability, and the two lines can even serve as an intercom system if your office is spread out.

Consider a separate line for fax, modem, and/or TTY—without call waiting, which can disrupt the electronic signal for your equipment. If your use of these machines is light, you can share a line with voice calls. Buy a call director that automatically sends the call to the appropriate machine or person. (Or get your faxes as e-mail through efax.com, jfax.com [the one I use], or a similar service—see chapter 20.)

Everyone should have an answering system—with a message that markets for you in your absence. Ours actively markets our services, books, and Web site.

If you advertise in books that reach outside your local calling area, make your business a free call for those customers. Many people, when faced with the choice of a free or toll call, will choose the one that costs less—even though it might cost more to actually conduct business. Any time a potential customer has to dial long-distance, it's one more psychological barrier to overcome.

Use either a toll-free number—ours covers forty-eight states and Canada, has no monthly fee, and costs under nine cents per minute—or a "tie line" that gives you a local number in the distant calling area.

Thoroughly test the new number at least a month before the closing date for the book you're entering. That way, if there are any glitches with the number or the service, you'll get them straightened out in time. But if you pay monthly charges, don't go too far in advance.

The way some phone companies work, every unique business phone number (with or without extra lines) is eligible for one free listing in any company phone book (other companies restrict your free listing to your own area code). By manipulating this offer, you might get a big reduction in the cost of penetrating a large city. Adding an extra line or bold listing is less expensive than starting from scratch. So instead of squandering that listing on a nearby small-town phone book, buy a cheap ad in the local book and use your free listing plus an extra line to save substantially over the cost of advertising in the bigger book. Consider one extra line for a marketing point and another for your Web site (but compare this cost with a half-inch in-column ad).

Other phone options include "500" numbers that can follow you all around the country if your business moves often, local or nationwide toll-free numbers, caller ID that can hook into your database and give you an instant customer profile as soon as you answer a call from a previous customer, and, in some places, a business listing on a residence phone (important for home-based consultants). It's also possible to get "rollover" lines, so if your main number is busy, the call bounces to the next available line (be sure you have enough staff to handle this without keeping people on hold forever).

We got rid of call waiting—and our venerable answering machine—in favor of the phone company's own voice mail. We're not interrupting our callers to answer another call in the middle. It will take a message when our line is busy, whereas call waiting only accommodates two callers at a time. And it avoids keeping people on hold for long periods.

Of course, it's not perfect either. It holds only forty calls—not enough if I'm promoting a book on a national TV show, for instance (I have a fulfillment service for that situation). And it costs us $12 per month, as opposed to $50 or so for an answering machine that lasts several years. Plus some people will only talk to a human being. We do warn people on our outgoing message that if it picked up immediately, it means we're on the phone, but some can't be bothered to call back.

— Toll-Free Number Directory —

Toll-free Directory Assistance is owned by AT&T. If you have phone service from someone else, you'll have to pay for a listing. Worse, most people don't know this—so if you are not listed, they don't find you. Many competing directory numbers have sprung up—but I'd avoid any that charge for a listing.

Incidentally, if you do have AT&T toll-free service, you also get to list your phone number on AT&T's Web page. Call 800-562-2255.

Also, there's a surcharge if someone calls your toll-free number from a pay phone. Let your congressperson hear from you on both issues: There should be one centralized, *complete* toll-free directory, and no surcharge to call from a pay phone (phrase the arguments in terms of customer convenience).

Another issue—or opportunity—is that the supply of 800 numbers is almost exhausted. New toll-free numbers will start with an 888 or 877 prefix. Here's the opportunity: If you couldn't get a letter or number combination with 800, lock in your preferred 888 or 877 number now.

Long-distance rates continue to plunge. Good plans charge 7.5–13 cents per minute, in six-second increments—inbound or outbound, twenty-four hours a day. For volume users, I've seen ads for rates as low as 4.9 cents per minute.

By the way, toll-free numbers are now transportable. You can keep the same number and change providers, as you can with outbound long-distance service. So get a good deal! Change your service if you're paying more than 10 cents per minute.

— The Numbers Game —

If incoming calls represent a major way your customers find you, think about the phone number itself. A number that's easily remembered, or whose numbers can form a word that's relevant to your business, can be a big plus. This is particularly useful if you do a lot of radio and TV advertising, where you have to rely on people remembering your phone number.

If 413-737-8637 had been available, I'd have grabbed it for a Springfield tie-line; it spells R-E-S-U-M-E-S. A friend of mine in a health food mail-order business acquired 1-800-G-R-A-N-O-L-A. It doesn't have to be the entire number, either. Our toll-free numbers are 800-683-W-O-R-D, and 877-F-R-U-G-A-L-F-U-N. Notice that 877-F-R-U-G-A-L-F-U-N is longer than ten digits. When you dial a telephone number, any digits after the number connects are ignored. This provides more flexibility as your choose your letter combination.

Other businesses aim for numbers that stand out as numbers. While they have less sales value than a word or slogan phone number, they are still easy to remember—and a good deal easier to dial than translating words back into numbers. Thus, it's not uncommon to see large firms whose numbers end in three zeroes. Several cab companies in Miami have managed to get all seven digits the same, so a client can dial something as easy as 555-5555.

✍

Put together an effective Yellow Pages campaign, have the right White Pages and phone service for your business, and make sure the phone is answered with a professional tone, and the phone book will do a lot of your selling for you. See chapter 31 to learn how to transform those telephone inquiries into booked appointments and confirmed sales. Meanwhile, read on for advice on applying what you've learned about Yellow Pages to other classified advertising.

11

Unlock the Secrets of the
Classified Page

The classified section is often one of the most carefully read parts of any publication, yet costs very little compared to display ads. Classifieds, therefore, can be effective low-cost marketing tools for many businesses—but only if they're carefully chosen, placed, and worded.

To some degree, classified advertising allows you to target a specific audience within a publication's more general readership—or to fine-tune your readers within a special-interest subscribership. A classified section groups ads under various headings. Different groups of people will read certain groups of headings and not others, but when someone is interested in a category, he or she is likely to read all the entries under that heading.

Still, reading and action are two very different things. Ideally, your ad will be:

- Noticed by people who weren't necessarily reading that category
- Read thoroughly by anyone interested
- Followed with an action step

If you don't get that action step, you may as well not run the ad.

Although classifieds sell an amazing variety of products, the ads themselves are usually very small. This makes sense, since the merchant is charged by the size of the ad: either per character, per word, per line, or per column inch. You will see some "display classified" ads, running one to five inches deep and surrounded by a border of some sort. These are eye-catching, to be sure, but they will cost significantly more than a short, simple classified. We'll come back to display classifieds later, but for now, let's concentrate on the smaller ads. Give people enough information to respond appropriately—and don't assume your reader is clued in. Twenty words or less is a good goal. That may seem awfully short, but it's enough to pack a mailbox with inquiries—if you use those words for maximum effect.

How can classifieds help you in your business? People looking in the classifieds for merchandise, by and large, are expecting secondhand products at low prices. Let's say you're a retailer. First of all, do you sell a category of merchandise that's frequently advertised in the classifieds, such as stereos, sporting equipment, or cameras? Do you discount the list price? Put an ad in under the appropriate category, perhaps like this:

STEREO AND ELECTRONICS

Brand New Bargains. 20% off Sony, Yamaha, Kenwood. Custom installation. Electric Boogie, 255 Main St, 555-0011, www.electricboogie.com. 11–6; Thursdays 11–9. [20 words]

Because people reading ads in this category will go through the entire list of stereo ads, looking for an inexpensive system, the ad leads with the information that new name-brand equipment is available at a low price, including installation. The store name, hours, and contact info finish off the ad. And because the ad copy is early in the alphabet, even if there are numerous ads, this one will get noticed.

Once you've taken all the trouble to set up a Web site, it should be your best selling tool. In any ad, in any medium, mention your Web site.

Notice the inclusion of a Web site address. Once you've taken all the trouble to set up a Web site, it should be your best selling tool. In every ad, in any medium, mention your Web site. Surely, five or fifty or five hundred carefully organized Web pages convert more prospects than a twenty-word ad—or at least provide you with addresses for a newsletter that puts your offer in the foreground with every issue.

— Dollars and Cents —

Typically, classifieds cost somewhere between five cents and ten dollars per word. So a twenty-word ad will cost somewhere between a dollar and two hundred dollars. And although in display advertising there is often room for negotiation, very little discounting occurs in the classified section, other than for frequency. Even the discount to ad agencies often doesn't apply to classifieds.

It's also often possible to barter any advertising purchase—if you have something the publication wants. If you write an article, for instance, you can sometimes get the editor to throw in a free ad. Barter might also work if you sell a product the magazine needs, such as office supplies or health insurance.

Obviously, cost per word, expected rate of return, and profit margins are going to influence your placement decisions. Say you can expect to pull in $500 from a $100 ad (20 words at $5 per word). If you're selling a $10 item that costs you $7 dollars, 50 orders will net you only $50 after the cost of your product and advertising. Your first 10 orders will only pay for the ad, so it's probably not a good buy, unless you can convert those buyers to long-term customers.

But if you're paying 5 or 10 cents a word to advertise the same $10 item, you'd make the cost of the ad on your first order. If your copy is clear and to the point, and you're advertising in the right publication, there's no reason to hesitate. Even up to a dollar a word, well-targeted and well-written classifieds are almost always a good value. Beyond that, you just have to use your judgment and test extensively. If you have an ad that's a proven winner in a less targeted, less expensive market, don't be afraid to gamble—the higher per-word rate may pay off in drastically increased response.

Needless to say, don't neglect free classifieds. Often, you can get an ad for free in the publication of an association—as long as you're a member. Occasionally, too, publications may offer a free ad as a subscription incentive. Also, many newspapers offer free classifieds for individuals selling a very inexpensive item.

— One- or Two-Step Selling —

There isn't a lot of room for a sales pitch in a twenty-word ad. Therefore, the first decision to make is whether to sell the product from the ad alone, or to use the ad to collect a mailing list of serious prospects to whom you then mail a full-fledged offer packet (and/or draw traffic to your Web site). In other words, do you make the sale in one step, or in two?

One Step: Sell From Your Ad

In general, one-step selling works well for products with a very low cost (say under ten dollars), or a very high recognition factor—something you don't have to explain. Don't list the price of a three hundred dollar item in a small classified aimed at a general audience and expect to get anywhere with it.

Written reports are ideal for the one-step approach. They can be produced and shipped very cheaply, provide real value to the customer, and—if the writer did a reasonable job—open up the door to selling future products to the same customer through direct mail and/or telemarketing. Thus, it's common to see one-step classifieds selling recipe collections, how-to booklets, information on buying surplus property, and the like.

Modified one-step selling also works well for individuals unloading used merchandise. However, this is a special situation, for two reasons: (1) the vendor has the opportunity to describe—and sell—the product over the phone, and again in person; (2) the buyer is already interested in buying a product and only needs to make a selection. There's no need to do follow-up by mail. Typically, people buying through local classifieds expect to do a lot of phone shopping before making a choice.

Two-Step Selling: Using the Ad to Generate and Follow Up on Leads

For most products, the goal of the ad is not an immediate sale, but a prospect: a person coming to your store or Web site, a phone inquiry, or a name and address. The prospect takes the first step by contacting you for more information; you take the second step of giving the prospect what he or she needs to become a buyer.

The two-step classified allows you to screen out all but serious prospects. However, because two-step ads often don't have pricing information, you don't know if your prospects are still serious at your price point. A way around this is to mail your main offer, but also include offers for other products, priced lower but of interest to the same people.

You can recognize two-step ads by phrases such as "free details," "send stamped self-addressed envelope to . . . ," or "call for more information." For computer-literate audiences, two-step selling also lends itself well to selling through e-mail autoresponders—thus eliminating postage costs.

Yes, you will be spending a bit on postage, following up false leads. But ultimately, you'll make more money on high-ticket items than by using one-step selling. Your prices should be high enough to support the cost of the ad, the mailing, and telephone follow-up. If you can sell a product with a list price of thirty dollars or less for four times what you've paid for it, you'll probably do all right in mail order. On a product that costs several hundred dollars, a 25 percent markup ought to be sufficient to cover your costs and provide a nice profit. Between those price points, you'll have to factor in your costs and profits to determine appropriate markup. But if you're only making 25 percent on a twenty dollar item, small classifieds are not the right venue for you; you'll probably lose money filling every order.

— Qualify Your Prospects —

Especially if you're using a two-step ad, you want to make sure that as many of your respondents as possible are actually serious customers—not just wasting your time and postage window-shopping for a bargain they don't really want. But how do you do this? By forcing them to make a commitment to you.

One way is to ask them for their phone number—they won't want to be called if they're not really interested. Or you can list a phone number instead of an address; you can quickly qualify prospects over the phone, and mail more information to the serious ones.

Similarly, you can ask your prospect to send you a stamped self-addressed envelope. However, don't assume people will know that *SASE* means "stamped self-addressed envelope"; I once used that abbreviation in an ad and most of my responses were addressed to "SASE"—and I had to pay the postage!

Another alternative is to ask for a small sum of money—one to three dollars—for a sample or demonstration copy. If you feel generous, you can even apply this initial fee to their first order.

— Write and Design Your Ad —

How can you say enough to draw customers and clients in, but not enough to cost very much? What do you want to offer? A specific service? Location? Brand-name quality? A special sale? Reputation? Pick the key element and open your ad with it.

First Lines

The first few words of your classified—the ones in bold and/or capitals—will determine whether the rest of the ad is read. So they should be showstoppers.

For your ad to be effective, those words must attract and inspire your reader—in one to five words. Use benefit-oriented action words such as "Free," "Now," "Save," "Earn," or direct-benefit statements such as "20% Off." Throw in an exclamation point or two (but please, only one per word).

Capsulize your offer as briefly as possible. Stress results, not features; in the old advertising adage, sell the sizzle, not the steak. Don't be afraid to use questions and surprises—"Why buy used?" (your brand-new product is just as affordable); "Need $10,000 extra this year?" (who wouldn't answer yes?); "You too can be a TV star" (reader: really?).

Once again, though, always make sure you focus on the prospect, not on the product you're selling. A headline such as "Want to Know More about Crinkle-Foam?" is going to flop. There's no indication even of what Crinkle-Foam is or does, or what's in it for the reader. Better (for a targeted audience, anyway): "Can Crinkle-Foam Cut Your Dry-Cleaning Bills in Half?"

When you ask a question in a headline, it should be so specific that every one of your serious prospects can answer the way you need them to. If I were selling publicity and marketing consulting with a headline such as "Getting Enough Free Publicity?" I'd be opening myself to the reader who answers,

"Yes, I already am." In that situation, I failed to change that person from a reader to a motivated prospect. But if I asked, "How Much Would Your Company Benefit from Free National TV Exposure?" my chances of getting the reader to follow through would be much higher.

Sometimes, a headline may do the whole job; you may not need body copy at all. Here, for example, is an ad from a Philadelphia ethnic weekly paper:

LOCKSMITHS
KEYS MADE AT AL'S PLACE.

The body copy is just an address and phone; Al is gambling on ethnic loyalty to bring him business. Even so, he could have done better in the same number of words with:

KEYS, LOCKS, REPAIRS—AL'S PLACE.

Body Copy

Unless your headline is self-explanatory and unmistakable, follow the initial words with a brief follow-up pitch.

Here in western New England, people take going to yard sales very seriously. They go through the ads in the paper, group them along a driving route, and pick the ones with the most appeal. Here are two approaches, exactly the same length. Which one works for you?

YARD SALES
Center Village: 84 Goodbar Street (off Main), Sat. 10–4. Furniture, books, kitchenware, golf cart, much more. [16 words]

Yard Sale: lots of interesting stuff because we're moving. 84 Goodbar Street in Center Village, Saturday. [16 words]

The first ad is specific, direct, and to the point. The first thing it lists is the town, which enables yard-sale-goers to decide immediately if it will be convenient for them. Next is a street address, and because it's an obscure street, instructions on how to find it. Then the date and the hours. All of this information will help customers put this sale into their itinerary. Then there's a list of the most important items for sale, allowing customers to know it will be worth their while to find Goodbar Street. And all this information is conveyed in sixteen words.

But of the sixteen words in the second ad, only the five that locate it provide any useful information at all. It's obvious that there's a yard sale or it wouldn't be advertised under that category. What's interesting to the seller may be very boring to potential customers—and since nothing is listed, it may not be worth it to even check. Furthermore, most readers have probably never heard of the street, and in any case it's listed under the Ys while all the other sales in Center Village are grouped together under C. The ad is essentially worthless.

In twenty words or less, you ought to be able to convey an appealing message and provide contact information. There are many ways to shorten your word count:

- Use contractions and abbreviations—but only if they can't be misunderstood.
- Replace words with punctuation.
- Create compound words (in our yard sale example, "kitchenware" instead of "kitchen items").
- Roll your tracking code into another word (for example, I might list my address in an ad as POB1164B, rather than Post Office Box 1164, Department B—one word instead of six).

Examine each word to make sure it's necessary—but don't leave out really crucial information; an ad that says nothing is worse than no ad at all.

Sometimes you need more than the matter-of-fact, straightforward approach. Even a short ad can be crammed with sizzling prose. Needless to say, such an ad will probably pull more, as long as you don't neglect the basic information. Here's one listed under Catering in a specialized service directory for party and function planners. It pulls me (an unabashed chocaholic) right in:

CHOCOLATE baskets and chocolate boxes filled with dipped cashews, chocolates and mints. Elegant Endings, Inc. _____ [phone]

All that yumminess in only sixteen words! This ad is almost perfect: The repetition of the word "chocolate" three times reinforces the message. The listing sets them off from others in the category, who emphasize full-service catering rather than desserts. Elegant Endings is a catchy name that reinforces the dessert specialty. In only sixteen words, they could even afford to "waste" a couple on transitions such as "filled with" (which serves a mouth-watering purpose here).

There's really only one improvement I would suggest: change the ending from "chocolates and mints." to "chocolates, mints . . ." The sense of finality is a mistake in the actual ad; my version implies that the list of wonderful things runs right off the page and keeps on going.

I do have to wonder, though, if the ad is under the right heading. If it were my ad, I would experiment with placement under Chocolate Desserts or Dessert Specialties, as well as under Catering. After all, this is not a full-service caterer but an after-dinner-treat specialist.

Sizzling prose can apply to far more mundane goods and services than chocolate. Here are some examples:

HOUSEPAINTING

WALLS GLEAM BETTER THAN NEW! Interior, exterior, even rough surfaces. 10 yrs exp. _____ [phone] [14 words]

BOOKKEEPING

FASTER THAN A SPEEDING BULLET computerized bookkeeping/payroll/tax prep. Free parking. _____ [phone, Web site] [13 words]

LANGUAGE INSTRUCTION

MADRID! ACAPULCO! MAJORCA! Learn Spanish—World at your doorstep! 6 wk intensive starts 5/17. International Language Academy. _____ [phone, Web site] [19 words]

Note how some of these ads bend language to mirror speech patterns. To be 100 percent grammatical, the first ad would have to read, "WALLS GLEAM MORE BRIGHTLY THAN WHEN THEY WERE NEW." But not only is that expensively verbose, it also sounds awkward and pompous: nobody talks that way in everyday speech.

Format Tricks

The more your ad stands out from others in the category, the more easily each reader skimming that category will be drawn to it. Many publications will jazz up your ad for a small fee, using some of these methods:

- Larger headlines (also, all-bold headlines if that's not the publication's usual style)
- Larger headlines on a separate line (or one word per line)
- Boxes around the ad, or rules—horizontal or vertical lines—separating your ad from others
- Shading the ad in gray
- Reverse type (white words on black—most effective when used just for the headline)
- Boldface type in unusual places, for instance your firm's name
- Logos

— Place Your Ads Effectively —

What publications will you use?

- Daily newspapers
- Weekly newspapers and magazines—either general interest or targeted
- Monthly, quarterly, and annual publications
- Special directories
- Newsletters and house organs (magazines distributed within one company, to clients and employees)
- Ad sheets (publications consisting largely or totally of advertising)

If you're advertising anything of a limited duration—a sale, a seasonal service, and so forth—concentrate on the dailies and weeklies.

Again, pick the market that serves your prospects. If you edit term papers, the local college newspaper or entertainment guide might be suitable. For a garden store, the daily paper or a garden-and-farm publication makes more sense.

If mail order is an important part of your sales, try a niche-based monthly magazine. While daily and weekly ads rely on someone calling immediately or stopping in on the next trip downtown, mail-order ads place their hopes on the long shelf life of the carrier medium. Since people rarely drop what they're doing to mail in a request, you rely on the ad attracting the customer's attention several times during the course of the month—and several months in the year—eventually resulting in an inquiry or order.

If you offer house inspections, advertise in a guide to homes for sale. A therapist could try a guide to alternative healing. Ethnic craft or food items are a natural for ethnic newspapers. But avoid generalized ad sheets that have not identified their market (and that includes the thousands of untargeted, uncategorized classified sites on the Internet).

— Frequency and Readership —

It takes a while for an ad to sink in; readers often want to see it several times before responding. This makes the purchase decision a bit tricky, particularly for a monthly magazine. You'll need to put the ad in at least three times before you know if it's working—but if you wait until the ad has run three months before you renew, you'll miss a few issues. So start with three months—but if the ad seems to be pulling after one month, renew the ad early so that you don't miss an issue.

There are also seasonal considerations: Different products will be more successfully marketed in ads at different times of the year.

Remember, too, that different magazines will turn over their readership faster than others. You want the ad to be seen by the same people several times, but not so much that they get sick of it. A bridal magazine is going to have almost no carryover of readers from one year to the next, while a publication targeted to parents of school-age children might keep 80 percent of its readership. A computer-specific trade journal will gain new readers every year, but also keep the majority of its existing readers. So factor the circulation demographics into your insertion schedule. If the magazine's readership is stable, rotate several different ads. However, if the readership shifts constantly, you can keep a successful insertion running much longer.

Keep in mind, too, that you can design your own insertion schedule. If you feel you get the best combination of exposure and economy by appearing three months in a row, twice a year (i.e., March, April, and May; September, October, and November), go ahead and do it that way—or any other way that makes sense for you. Track every insertion in every medium (see chapter 38).

— Choosing Headings —

What categories will work for you? The same rules apply as in picking out Yellow Pages categories, except that you have more control. Choose the most specific heading you can; if the right category isn't offered, create the one you like. Magazines and newspapers are generally far more willing than telephone directory publishers to create new headings for you, so don't settle for an inaccurate or vague heading. You'll often find headings such as: Books and Publications; Business Opportunities; Crafts; Items for Sale; Real Estate; Services; Wanted (some of these will offer various subcategories).

Creative Placement

Sometimes the best heading for your ad may not be the most obvious one. Suppose you offer career counseling for disadvantaged youth. Your prospects would assume that they can't afford you; they won't

find you under Career Counseling—because they won't look there. But they probably do read the Help Wanted listings. So you could put in an ad like the first one that follows.

If you retail a new technology, try the second approach. When your customers really want full service, check out the "up-selling" third sample. The fourth ad sells new products to people who thought they wanted secondhand merchandise:

HELP WANTED

JOB HUNTING? FREE HELP for unemployed, ages 16–21. Mayor's Youth Job Core, Rm. 367 City Hall, ____ [phone]. [17 words]

BOOKS/PUBLICATIONS

READ IN THE DARK! READ STANDING IN A RUSH-HOUR TRAIN! Amazing e-reader lets you read books **anywhere**! www.ereader.com. Toll-free 877-555-1000. [21 words]

BEAUTY AIDS

MORE THAN COSMETICS! Expert hair, skin, nail consultation. 10 years experience. _____ [phone] [12 words]

FURNITURE

WHY BUY USED? New futons and frames, 50% savings. Futons To Go, 358 Elm Street. _____ [phone, Web site] [17 words]

Think outside the box. If I were running ads for this book, I'd list under Marketing Assistance or Marketing Services. I'd list under Books only if the publication targeted small entrepreneurs.

— Service/Business Directories —

Many newspapers and magazines offer a separate area in the classifieds for business and service listings. These ads are perfect for small businesses or human-services agencies that rely on attracting new clients at the time they actually need the service.

The following categories were offered by one newspaper on one day: Animals, Appliance Repair, Auto Rentals, Auto Upholstering, Builders, Building and Renovating, Carpentry, Carpet Cleaning, Chimney Repairing, Chimney Sweeps, Cleaning, Dance Instruction, Driveway Sealing, Driveways, Drywall, Electrical Services, Energy Management, Entertainment, Excavating, Firewood, Floor Sanding, Flooring, Food Preparation, Furniture Refinishing, Glass, House Cleaning, House Inspection, Household Accounts, Interior Wood Finishing, Kennels, Knitting Machines, Landscaping, Lawn Care, Lawn Mower Service, Lawn Mowing, Luggage Repair, Masonry, Massage Therapy, Moving-Hauling, Odd Jobs, Office Services, Painting, Paperhanging, Photography, Piano Service, Plumbing Service, Propane Gas, Remodeling, Restoration, Roofing, Sewing, Siding & Roofing, Television Service, Therapy, Tree Service, Typewriter Service, Typing, Upholstery, Vacuum Cleaner Service, Windows.

The ads were sold only in orders of five weeks at a time, but the paper's minimum price was under a dollar a day. Thus, one sale can pay for the entire month of ads. In all, the service directory filled a little over half a tabloid page.

The two best times to advertise in a business and service directory are: (1) if you have a seasonal service and you don't want to advertise all year in the Yellow Pages (for example, snow removal, lawn care), and (2) if your service business is aimed at homeowners and business is slow. Experienced homeowners know how frustrating it is to call twenty plumbers or electricians out of the phone book in order to find one who's interested in the job. But if people put ads in the service directory, they are actively looking for work—or at least they were within the last month. I've consistently located sources for electrical work, masonry, tree removal, emergency plumbing repair, carpentry, and similar services in these directories.

However, a general-interest service directory isn't likely to do much for a consultant or other professional office. My own experience bears this out. During a slow time, I noticed a competitor's ad under Résumé Service. I put in an ad of my own, although I didn't expect much. I got three inquiries, only one of whom became a client. Since I figured I'd need three sales to make it worthwhile, I didn't repeat the experiment—and neither did my competitor.

Specialized Service Directories

Some papers may have more carefully targeted business and service directories. I'm looking at a Philadelphia specialty weekly that includes these two subdirectories:

- Pet Directory, with headings for Dog Obedience Training; Pet Services; Pet Shops; Pets for Sale; Veterinarians
- Party Guide, listing the following categories: Bridal Services; Catering; Entertainment (including clowns, magicians, disc jockeys, and even computer-portrait-makers, as well as musicians); Florists; Party Planners; Party Supplies; Photography and Video; Printing

— Display Classifieds —

Some advertisers find it useful to put a very large ad in the classified sections—even half a column or more. Some may look like an expanded classified ad, but if you're buying that much space, you may as well use it to create eye appeal with a small display ad in the classified section. The ads stand out visually, with white space, graphics, large headlines, and the like. Plus, they are big enough to sell much more expensive items in one step. Yet they have all the benefits of classifieds: targeted placement and a lower rate than regular display ads.

Smaller ads can use similar tricks. Many ad designers supply their own camera-ready ads, typeset with smaller body copy and a larger headline than the magazine's own classified-ad style. Two such ads; shown on page 86; each fits into a one-inch space.

Even in a densely crowded classified page, the eye will jump to bold ads such as these. The books-by-mail ad is from Melvin Powers and his Wilshire Book Company. The ad has run for many years without changes—because it works. Notice the use of

Small-space display classifieds

reverse type and several visual elements (including a thin border, a clear line between the reversed headline and the subhead, the book graphic, and the arrow graphic). The interested prospect has absolutely nothing to lose, but has enough information to know whether it's worth responding. The real-food ad uses display-size headline type, crammed into a space one inch high and half a column wide. Two words fit nicely there, and because the prospect is interested, the designer can afford to use very small type to convey something about the product, including ordering information.

Many mail-order fortunes have been made on small-space display classifieds; flip through the back pages of any supermarket tabloid to see examples. These ads are often quite ugly, but they are visually distinctive—the eye seeks them out on a crowded page. As a result, though they are unattractive, they do a good sales job. If you want to experiment with small-space ads of this type, I strongly suggest that you read up on them and work with a proven copywriter and designer, at least until you get the hang of them.

Since display classifieds may cost several hundred dollars per insertion, I suggest trying one only after you've experimented successfully with a smaller ad in the same publication.

Resist the temptation to go wider than one column, and never go a full column high. Otherwise, you might be shunted out of your category to the bottom of the page, or all alone under the category heading but away from everything else. You want to make sure the reader finds you within the category—preferably right at the beginning. So the biggest display classified you should use would be one column wide by three-fourths of a column high.

⚹

So, when would you use regular display ads instead of display classifieds? Read on!

12

On Display

Display advertising is a tricky beast for the low-cost marketer. It's all too easy to blow a huge wad of money and have very little to show for it.

If you have money to burn for a very large campaign, display advertising will be effective. But for most of you, display advertising should be used cautiously, in circumstances that warrant it, and in a well-thought-out, consistent program.

A private study by marketing/PR consultant Cliff Allen of full-page color ads in magazines with approximately 100,000 circulation found response rates of 100–300 (0.1% to 0.3%), and a cost per inquiry of $100–$200. There are better ways to market!

Still, some of you are going to be using display ads extensively, so if you're going to do it, do it right—particularly if you're paying full price. (See chapter 13 to learn how to save substantially over the published rate sheets.) Here are some pointers:

— Once Again, Targeting Is Key —

Target as closely as you can. The publication's demographics should exactly match your prospects. Never buy advertising space solely on the basis of cost per column inch, or even cost per thousand readers; you must evaluate cost to reach *your* market.

If you're advertising in a special-interest publication, you're ahead of the game—particularly if your ad can be located near an article about your product—or at least your niche. If you're advertising in a general-interest publication, fight for placement in the section your prospects will be reading.

Michael Corbett, in his book *The 33 Ruthless Rules of Local Advertising,* advises you not to worry about the prospects you can't afford to reach yet. Instead, do your best to sell the ones you can reach. You will convert more prospects into customers by reaching fewer people more often than by reaching many people only once.

Charity Advertising

Charity and arts organizations will ask you to buy ads in their program guides. These are marvelous ways to make charitable contributions that are deductible as advertising expense. But as you can guess, if it doesn't target your audience it won't bring results. Don't try to make these ads serve any real marketing purpose; they're just public relations, community visibility, and charity. And don't let yourself be shaken down by organizations you don't support; you won't even recoup your investment.

Use these as serious ads only if:

- You advertise a product that's so general everyone can use it
- You offer an immediately redeemable discount coupon (for instance, a nearby dessert parlor might offer a two-for-one after-show special)
- The audience is carefully targeted and matches the profile of your ideal prospects

Otherwise, don't get your hopes up.

— Attracting Attention —

When does a display ad make an impact on the reader? When it reemphasizes points made in the publication's articles, is repeated several times, is part of a series, and/or when it dominates the page through its size, shape, and/or design.

Reinforcement of Editorial Matter

Obviously, you don't have any control over where your ads will be placed. But often, you can negotiate (or pay for) favorable placement, in the section that's most germane to what you're advertising. Publishers may cultivate this kind of placement by creating special theme sections (wedding, garden, winter holiday, auto, home, etc.) and actively soliciting ads for these special editions. After all, it's in the publisher's interest to give you good placement, because that makes your ad more effective—and you're more likely to come back again to advertise regularly. Never try to negotiate with the editor on this; placement is a matter for the art department, and you should work through the ad sales and layout people.

Even *The New York Times* is willing to peg ads to specific editorial departments. To mention a prominent example, Mobil promotes its corporate agenda with a regular all-text ad on the Op-Ed page.

Given the principle of editorial reinforcement, one good time to use display ads is when you've secured coverage in a news or feature story. Try to find out when the piece will run, and put in a midsized display ad in the same or the next edition.

Repetition

In a daily newspaper, you might put an ad in every Tuesday and Friday for a month, then evaluate it. (Track display ads easily by asking people to bring the ad in or mention it to get a bonus: something free, 10 percent off, etc.) It takes a lot to get through to people these days; one insertion is never enough. Furthermore, people may miss your ad on certain days—they skip that page, don't finish the section, or they are engrossed in an article and don't notice your message. So never give up after only one insertion, because one insertion will almost never work, except for something like a three-fourths-page signature ad supporting an issue or candidate. Remember Jeffrey Lant's Rule of Seven: A prospect should encounter your messages at least seven times in various contexts before you become familiar enough to do business together. As people become familiar with your ad and expect to see it, they will be more ready to do business with you. Obviously, with the right offer it will take fewer times to reach the most motivated prospects. But you want the lazy and less motivated ones, too.

Series Ads

A series is better than the same ad repeated constantly. It's a sequential collection of ads that carries a common visual image and corporate identity, but changes its content from one insertion to the next; each builds on the ads that have come before it. Each ad is clearly recognizable as belonging with the previous and subsequent ones, but focuses on a different sales message—stresses a different benefit—and each ad contributes to the seven required exposures. Volkswagen used series ads very effectively, back in the sixties. More recently, Apple Computer continues to use this technique.

Series ads often seem to get away with a much higher ratio of text to white space than the general run of display ads; if you make the copy interesting, people will read them much as they read their favorite columnists. David and Carol Majercik, owners of a general store in Williamburg, Massachusetts, run a weekly one-column ad (at right). They use a folksy tone, headline the ad "Stop A Moment," and often feature townsfolk news. This series has run every week since 1979 and has a loyal following.

Shape and Size Considerations

Ads come in two basic shapes: horizontal and vertical. Most ads are horizontal (including square ads) and are sold either in blocks such as an eighth of a page, quarter page, half page, and whole page, or by the column inch.

There are no technical reasons why you couldn't buy an ad in some other shape—say a circle or triangle. However, an odd-shaped ad would present production challenges: It would be hard to figure out the price, and it would make it a bit tougher to design the page. Still, nothing prevents you from buying a square or rectangular insertion space and filling it with a slightly smaller ad of a different shape. With a big, bold border, this could really make your ad come alive.

An ad can be virtually any size; I've seen them as small as one column inch (one column wide by one inch high), and as large as seventy pages—a complete catalog, bound in as part of the magazine (and probably a huge waste of money).

If you want to do a truly humongous ad, you would probably save a fortune by doing it as a separate insert, folded into the publication, rather than an actual display ad taking up multiple pages in a magazine.

For our purposes, we will only consider ads up to two pages. Two pages is the visual unit that the reader sees at once. You can buy a small chunk, a column on the outside of each half of the spread, a full page, a full two pages, the inside halves of both pages, an ad running across the bottom of both pages

Stop A Moment
By DAVID & CAROL MAJERCIK

Culinary herbs are easy to grow. Just stick them in the ground, add water, and stand back. **Parsley, sage, rosemary and thyme** are favorites. If you'd like to try something new this year, plant **broad-leaf garlic, chives** or **borage,** or **chamomile.** You'll find these and a couple dozen more herbs at the General Store.

Most of our herbs are raised from seed with loving care and attention by the Tobin Family of Westhampton. Cindy Tobin, who also happens to be our expert bookkeeper, starts planting herbs in the Tobin greenhouses while there's still snow on the ground. In early spring they're moved out to the cold frames where they toughen up a little. Around the first of May she loads up the trunk of her big car and delivers us a goodly number of vigorous herbs that are raring to grow in your garden.

A Fuchsia for your mother. Or gorgeous **double petunias** in a hanging pot. Once again, the Tobin Family shows off their horticultural know-how. With a little care (water and weekly feeding) these plants should bloom all summer long. They're really beautiful.

We enjoy offering you a good value with herbs and flowers. You'll often find me outside fussing with them (Our Michelle Dufresne suspects I just like being outside in nice weather!) We carry all kinds of interesting plants during May, so come on over and check them out.

Speaking of good value ... I figured I'd give my ancient lawnmower one more chance. So I brought it to Ed Garvulenski, the small engine doctor at the VA hospital. It works like new!!

Ed heads up the Small Engine Repair Therapy Program at the VA. He's like the master surgeon, while the hospital patients stand by for his commands of "wrench" ..."screwdriver,"... "gasket" etc. If you mower needs resuscitating, call Ed at 584-4040 (X2109). The cost is very reasonable, the work is fully gauranteed and some wonderful men will feel appreciated. (Also ask about their lawn-care services and senior citizens discounts.)

♥♥♥♥♥♥♥♥♥♥♥♥

Last call to order one of those stoneware pitchers with your town's name and incorporation date on it. These are handmade for us by Pennsylvania craftspeople. We place a large order about twice a year. These are excellent gifts — very attractive and useful. Call us to see if we can get one made for your town. (Come in and see the ones we have on display.)

SPRING HOURS
Mon.-Thurs   9-6
Fri.-Sun.   9-7

We ship every day.
VISA /Mastercard taken.

Williamsburg General Store
Main St. (Rte. 9), Williamsburg
268-3687

Stop A Moment
By DAVID & CAROL MAJERCIK

PARIS COMES TO WILLIAMSBURG. The Williamsburg & Haydenville Business Association has contracted with Marlin Art Auctioneers of New York to bring some of the world's finest works of art to our town. If you've always wanted to own a fine oil painting, lithograph, watercolor or etching please join the art lovers who'll be at the Williamsburg Grange Hall on Sunday, October 20. Preview is at 1:00 P.M.; the auction is from 2:00-4:00. Tickets are $5.00, either at the door or in advance from many of our businesses.

This is an extraordinary opportunity to acquire a work of art by an internationally known artist at a price that's far below what you'd pay at a gallery. In fact, a great many will likely sell for under $100.00! Please call me at 268-3036 for more information.

Foliage the best in years! In fact I can't recall a more brilliant fall. Recent cool nights and sunny days have brought out a riot of reds and oranges. Nature herself is quite an artist and I urge you to drive out and see her handiwork. Williamsburg is the Gateway to the Berkshires, so drive out Route 9 and you'll soon be in the heart of the magnificent Massachusetts hills. Stop at the Williamsburg General Store on the way. Get a Wrapple or two for the ride, or a raspberry-peach Roll-up or maybe a bag of penny candy.

We serve 32 flavors of real ice cream all day every day. We brew up our own blend of coffee; we also make hot, mulled cider for you to enjoy. The General Store can be a fun part of a fall foliage trip, so please stop by.

It was a joy and an honor to talk to Bill McCarty's Marketing class at Greenfield Community College. Eighteen adults gave me their attention as I explained a little about retail marketing and about our store. Bill McCarty, who lives in Worthington, is an adjunct instructor at four area colleges in addition to owning his own industrial packaging business. He was one of my instructors some years back, one of the best I can remember.

CINNAMON BROOMS "What's in the oven?" There's nothing like the sweet aroma of cinnamon to remind you of mom's apple pie. A cinnamon-scented broom fills your kitchen with that same, wonderful aroma. We have them for you right now.

FALL HOURS
Mon.-Thurs.: 9-6
Fri., Sat., Sun.: 9-8

We ship every day.
VISA /Mastercard taken.

Williamsburg General Store
Main St. (Rt.9) Williamsburg
268-3036

. . . the permutations are limited only by your imagination.

There's also the question of page size: a 10-inch ad will take two-thirds of a column in a tabloid, a full column in an 8½ X 11-inch magazine, and about half a column in a full-sized newspaper.

Large Ads. According to a study by Professors Sidney P. Feldman and Jean C. Hallerman, an eighth-of-a-page ad on a four-column page, two columns wide by a quarter-column high, will outpull a one-column-wide quarter-column ad by five times. Going up to a quarter-page ad (two columns wide and a half-column high) will produce an ad that pulls fifteen times as well as the quarter-column, even though it's only four times as large. The quarter-page ad quite effectively dominates the page, while the quarter-column (one-sixteenth of a page) is much less noticeable.

*M*any people will skip a page that's nothing but ads, but if they're reading an article on the same page, your message will be staring at them when they've finished the piece.

These principles apply to any display ad. The larger your ad, the more people will see it. On a page with editorial matter, a quarter page is usually enough to draw the reader's eye directly to the ad.

However, avoid full-page or full two-page ads; make sure there is some editorial content on your page. Many people will skip a page that's nothing but ads, but if they're reading an article on the same page, your message will be staring at them when they've finished the piece. Many full-size daily newspapers use this format: open up to the middle of a section and you'll often see a column of text on the outside with an ad taking up the rest of the page, or

an article going across the top of the page for a few inches with an ad below it.

Although it's not overly common in publications with other formats, you could shape an ad that way in a tabloid or magazine. In fact, your message will be stronger in a smaller-page format, because an ad that fills almost an entire full-size daily newspaper page—which measures 22½ X 14 inches in my town—is too big to be taken in all at once while reading an article alongside it. (Thus, an ad in a full-size paper that runs three-fourths of a page deep would be both cheaper and more effective than a full-page ad.)

Midsized Ads. Probably the best values in display advertising are for ads between one-quarter and three-quarters of a page. These are big enough to be eye-catching, but small enough to stretch the budget. If possible, get your ad placed above the fold (if you're advertising in a full-size newspaper), and on the right-hand page; this is the area where visibility is highest as a reader is turning pages. Your ad message is also much stronger if it's adjacent to a relevant article.

Small-Space Ads. As we discussed last chapter, there is a school of thought that supports the idea of very small, very bold display ads. However, I'm not of that school. I believe there are only three situations where small-space ads are cost-effective: in the classified section, in a "merchandise mart" section devoted entirely to small ads, and in a catalog. In other words, use small-space ads when they put you on an equal or better footing with everyone else advertising in the section. But avoid, desperately, any situation in which your tiny ad is competing against display ads several inches longer and higher than yours; your ad simply won't be noticed.

In my view, any ad less than two-thirds of a column vertical in a full-size page, a half column vertical in a tabloid, slightly less than a full column vertical on a magazine page, or a quarter page horizontal in pretty much any publication, relies on luck to be effective in the general-interest pages. If there are no other ads around it, such an ad might work. But if it's surrounded by other ads, it will be too small to attract much attention. Go for something big enough to be seen no matter what else is on the page.

This may mean you can only afford to put the ad in once a week (or once every second issue, in a monthly publication). But since frequency is a major factor in a display ad's effectiveness, this may be shooting yourself in the foot.

Think about ways to do it differently. For example, in a daily paper, run a large ad with frequent insertions—for example, two or three times a week for a month—and then take three months off before doing it again.

There are exceptions to that rule, but so much of a small ad's impact depends on placement. Ad pages are often designed as a series of stacking boxes, usually forming a staircase going down from the edge of the left-hand page to the center, and back up on the right-hand page; the larger ads are blocked out first and the smaller ads are squeezed in where they fit. Below is a sketch of a typical two-page ad layout.

If you have an eighth-of-a-page ad, it may be on the bottom of the page, separated from the editorial matter by two or three other ads. Therefore, most of your prospects won't notice your ad, and you won't get the return you're paying for.

If you really want to use a small-space ad, think about inserting the same ad or a series of ads in several locations throughout the same issue of the publication. And in small-space ads even more than large ones, be sure to make your ad as visually striking as possible.

Design

Remember, the most important thing about your ad's appearance is that it can be noticed on a crowded page—not that it win awards for attractiveness, subtlety, or cleverness. Yes, your ad should be attractive. And yes, your message should reflect the tone of the publication. You wouldn't, for instance, put in a screaming, hard-sell, bargain-basement type of ad in *The New Yorker*, whereas you would *need* that kind of ad in the *National Enquirer*. But most of

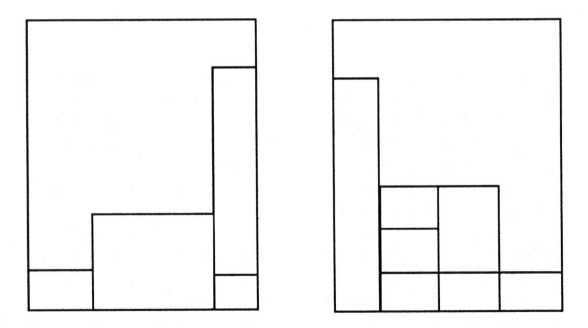

A typical newspaper or magazine layout showing news blocks on the inside top and ads stacked in staircase formation under the story.

all, your ad must be *seen!* Go back to chapter 4, and incorporate some of those visual techniques into every display ad. Remember, too, that the smaller the ad, the harder you need to work to catch the reader's eye.

— Costs —

Each insertion of a display ad will have a cost. Perhaps for a small ad in a small weekly paper, it might be as little as $30. But a single full-page ad in a major national publication could run tens of thousands of dollars. However, as we've noted, single insertions are a waste of money. So let's do some budgeting.

Say a decent-sized ad in your target publication costs $200 per insertion, after you've figured out all the applicable discounts. If it publishes daily, you might decide to run three ads per week for two three-week periods during your traditional slow seasons. That works out to an annual expenditure of $3,600.

A $200 ad running in eight out of twelve annual issues of a monthly would only cost $1,600—and

have the benefits of longer shelf life and higher readership targeting. But $200 might only buy a smaller ad, so you'd have to spend, say, $400 per insertion, or $3,200, to get the same impact.

If you want to splurge and take an $800 ad out in a midcirculation regional daily paper, five days a week, fifty weeks a year, you're spending a hefty $200,000, just on this one publication. This is the approach that all too many merchants take. Supermarkets, for instance, often engage in saturation advertising in daily newspapers, including a weekly insert and several smaller ads every week. Now you know why the same item costs a lot more in a supermarket than in a food co-op that doesn't advertise heavily. Surely there are more effective ways to spend that money.

⊠

Don't despair, however. There are many ways to bring down the cost of paid advertising, and we'll examine a number of them in chapter 13.

13

Ask for a Bargain

An advertising rate schedule is something like the listed sale price on a house—a starting point for negotiation. But you can't just say, "That's too high; let's negotiate." Instead, you have to play the game: Use the accepted methods of getting a discount.

Many of these methods are applicable in any paid advertising medium: print ads, Yellow Pages, radio, TV, even such media as your community weather telephone hotline. However, individual media outlets may or may not be interested—and virtually none will inform you of most of these tricks. If the ad sales people at a particular broadcast or print outlet believe they can sell so much at full price that they don't need to negotiate, it'll be take it or leave it.

But start talking; you might save hundreds or thousands of dollars.

If ad sales are down, you'll have a better shot than if the ad seller has all the business he or she can handle. But also, many of these bargains are easier to arrange if you have a good relationship with the seller; your account executive will be more likely to be flexible if you've worked together for a while. And if your account rep won't talk about any of these things, try talking to the advertising manager. Some

places will have rigid policies eliminating most of these budget stretchers—but you have absolutely nothing to lose by asking about them! At the very least, you will be treated as an informed consumer who deserves some respect, or even preferential treatment. At best, you'll save oodles of money.

We'll start with three methods you might hear about from your account executive, and move on to the ad industry's insider secrets.

— Free Sales Aids —

Many media outlets will provide sales aids to reinforce your advertising or get more people to see it—thus giving you more for your money. For instance, you might get a mounted reproduction of your ad, with the magazine's logo or masthead. You can then use this as a poster in your storefront window. If you're using electronic media, play your ads on a continuous-loop video—or do up a sign that says something like "Guaranteed to use 30% less water. As seen on Channel 52." Again, the station will often have materials for you, with their logo, since you are promoting them as well as reinforcing your own message.

— Co-op Advertising —

If you mention a manufacturer's name or product line in your ad or use their logo, you may be eligible for co-op advertising funds. The manufacturer shares the cost of the ad in exchange for your public endorsement. If you can mention several different brands, the ad's actual cost to you may be little or nothing. (Some manufacturers restrict your ability to mention competitors, but others are more lenient.)

Many media outlets have a co-op specialist who can help you meet the manufacturer's requirements to participate. Why will they help you? So you can afford to advertise more often—and the sales reps still make their full commission. If the print or broadcast outlet you're working with doesn't do this, contact the manufacturer directly. Call and ask for the co-op advertising manager, and find out what you need to do and how much they are willing to pay. Find out about any restrictions or guidelines (for example, is participation limited only to their brands? Do you need to guarantee a certain number of insertions?), and whether they will pay the media outlet directly or whether you have to front the money. Also find out how much time elapses before they pay. Once you're ready, protect yourself with a written contract.

If you distribute a name brand, also see whether the company will take out Yellow Pages ads in your areas of coverage and list you as an authorized distributor. Manufacturers will also often provide you with professionally designed in-store displays and various other sales aids that would have been expensive to produce on your own. Use these as you would use the free sales aids from the media.

Self-Organized Co-ops

You can have greater impact with lower cost in any advertising program if you join forces with others. Here are a few of the many ways to do this:

Geographical. Band together with stores in your shopping center, on your block, or in your neigh-borhood, and chip in for a large ad purchase. Run a promotion involving validated parking; offer a card that participating merchants stamp in order for customers to qualify for a drawing; or provide discounts for patronizing a certain number of businesses on the same day.

Our local Chamber does this annually. Some forty stores list themselves on a shopping bag, and anyone bringing in the bag on the appointed day gets a 20 percent discount on any one item. Main Street is mobbed that day.

Product-Specific. Join up with the other outlets for one manufacturer's product, and advertise together in a large regional paper that covers all your locations. Car dealers do this all the time.

Trade Association Members. It's to your advantage to tout your group as the certified experts, the qualified problem-solvers. So create visibility—advertise the organization and list all the participating members. This could include general organizations, such as the Chamber of Commerce or Better Business Bureau, as well as groups that are tied to one kind of product or service.

Here's a terrific variation on that theme: This quarter-page ad (opposite) appeared in my local newspaper the week before Mother's Day; it includes about half the florists in the area. Spot color for the words "florist" and "grocer" helps make the point, there's plenty of white space to let the message come through, and it's targeted to everyone who has a mother.

Tag On to Others' Ads with Testimonials

Here's a terrific win-win idea! If you're satisfied with a product or service, offer a testimonial for that company's ads. Jim McCann's wildly successful 800-FLOWERS was plugged in national TV and print ads by AT&T—because McCann praised the telecommunications giant's toll-free service. It would have cost him hundreds of thousands of dollars to get the exposure if he'd paid for it himself.

You wouldn't buy your groceries from a *florist!*

So, why buy your plants from a *grocer!*

For the healthiest plants and flowers, it makes sense to buy from a grower or florist... not a grocer! We can tell you how to expertly care for everything you purchase. Our commitment to our customers doesn't end when we make a sale. It just begins. And we're proud that our reputation for quality and service grows stronger every year. Come check-out our selection!

Always in Bloom
220 No. Pleasant St.
Amherst
253-5545

Child's Flower Shop
80 Maple Street
Florence
584-6689

Main Street Florist
89 Main Street
Easthampton
527-9536

Mt. View Greenhouse
26 Strong Street
Easthampton

Dwyer Florist
202 Main Street
Northampton
584-3784

Wildflowers of Williamsburg
Colonial Shoppes, Rt. 9
Williamsburg
268-9330

Spuds & Buds
Rts. 5 & 10
South Deerfield
665-8371

Florence Village Flower Shoppe
29 Keyes Street
Florence
584-9595

Nuttelman's Florist
Corner of Woodlawn
Ave. & Prospect St.
Northampton
584-2272

Truehart's Garden Center & Florist
25 College Highway
Southampton
527-5047

Luci's Country Greenery
100 Elm Street
South Deerfield Center
665-2997

Remember Mom with flowers! Mother's Day — Sunday, May 10th

On a much smaller scale, I offered a local telephone book publisher this plug:

I track my sources of clients, and Yellow Pages advertising brings in about 70% of them. Right now, I'm in the Pioneer Valley book and three Nynex books. Amazingly enough, Pioneer Valley is outpulling all three Nynex books combined. Keep up the good work!

—Shel Horowitz, Author,
Marketing Without Megabucks: How to Sell
Anything on a Shoestring;
Director, Accurate Writing & More,
Northampton, MA

Not only did the company run this testimonial in local papers—and yes, I heard from several people who saw it—but it also showed its gratitude by throwing in a few hundred dollars in upgrades to my own ads in its book.

Not a bad deal for something that took about three minutes to write and maybe thirty minutes to negotiate.

Look for other kinds of cross-promotions, too—anything that adds value and either costs you nothing or gains you exposure. The Snowy Owl Inn in Waterville Valley, New Hampshire, cross-promotes with an airline, a rental car company, and ski, golf, and tennis operators to add value for its customers and gain from its colleagues' marketing.

— Frequency/Volume Discounts —

One discount your media outlet almost certainly *will* tell you about is volume or frequency. If you purchase a certain number of inches or insertions within a specified period of time, the rate usually goes down. As we discussed earlier, however, *never* place a long-term insertion in an untested medium just to qualify for a frequency discount. Instead, test the ad on a short run, and try to negotiate application of your initial purchase toward a frequency discount later, if your total annual purchase qualifies you. If the outlet balks, phrase it as a long-term contract with a no-penalty cancellation option.

— Deduct 15 Percent —

If you set yourself up as an ad agency, you can place your own display and broadcast ads at a 15 percent savings. Ad agencies work much the same as travel agencies: They fund themselves partially out of agency discounts—placement commissions of 15 percent. When you buy an ad through an agency, it doesn't cost you any more than if you buy the same ad as an individual. (Ad agencies do charge their clients for creative work, however.)

If you set yourself up as an ad agency, you can place your own display and broadcast ads at a 15 percent savings.

If you are recognized as a legitimate ad agency, you not only save 15 percent on your own ad orders (except sometimes on classifieds, which may be noncommissionable), but you can also make some money purchasing ads for other businesses and taking the commission.

Here's how to do it: Create a name for your ad agency that's different from the name of your business (and get a company checkbook under that name). Prepare an insertion order form under your ad agency letterhead listing the following information:

- Client (your regular business name)
- Client's product or service
- Media outlet
- Size (length, for an electronic ad) and frequency of insertion (or "till forbid" if you want it to keep running until you tell them not to)
- Specific insertion dates, if applicable
- Specific insertion locations (or shows), if applicable
- Ad copy, or "see attached camera-ready art" (if the latter, don't staple)

- Price per insertion and total price
- Your discount (generally 15 percent, sometimes with 1–2 percent additional for payment at the time of insertion)
- Net amount due
- Number of your credit card (with expiration date and the name on the card) or check

— Pay Only for Your Prospects —

Instead of paying a flat fee for advertising, wouldn't you rather turn the newspaper, magazine, or broadcast station into your commissioned sales agent? You can! It's called per-order (P.O.) or per-inquiry (P.I.) advertising, and it means you pay only for your prospects' responses.

On a per-order ad, you pay a fairly high commission for orders actually received; per-inquiry ads pay out a lower figure for every response, whether or not the prospect purchases anything. You then have the job of taking these very hot leads and selling them through direct mail, telephone, or whatever else you've got up your sleeve.

This is how it works: your ad contains a mailbox address at the newspaper or station, and responses go to the media outlet—which forwards responses to you and bills you for each one. If your ad is wildly successful, you may actually pay more than the magazine's base rate—in which case you would want to switch over to the standard rate structure for your next ad. You might even want to negotiate a contract that caps the amount you would pay on a P.I. or P.O. ad at what you would have paid to run it at standard rates.

More likely, however, you will get fewer inquiries than that—and you'll save money every time the ad runs.

— Remnants and Remainders —

Can you move fast when an opportunity arises? Do you keep camera-ready ads available in various sizes, or can you generate them within a couple of hours? If the answer is yes, you can avail yourself of one of the greatest bargains in the advertising world: remnant space.

Just as it's often possible to pick up remaindered books or discontinued car models at huge savings, it's also possible to make great deals on leftover ad space as press time approaches.

This is particularly true for magazines, which have less production flexibility than newspapers. Magazines are generally printed in "signatures"—groups of pages. The number of pages in a signature will depend on the magazine's printing and binding processes. One typical format is a four-page signature, formed from the back and front of a single 11 x 17-inch piece of paper, folded in half. Partially used signatures cause wasted press capacity as well as binding problems. Magazines figure their editorial content based on the amount of ad space they've sold—but because editors have to plan in four-page segments, it can be hard to fine-tune the exact amount of editorial matter relative to ad space.

So here's your opportunity: Let's say ad sales were a little short, and instead of a full four pages, a signature only has 3⅓ pages of material. The staff needs to fill up that extra two-thirds of a page. They can do this in one of several ways:

1. Enlarge an illustration, or run an extra one
2. Fill the space with public service ads or little filler articles
3. Run—and pay for—a short article from their backlog of timeless articles
4. Cut out enough stories to shrink to one less signature
5. Sell the space at a deep discount and get some revenue rather than none

When a publisher chooses the fifth alternative, you may get the chance to fill that space at 50 to 80 percent off the regular price.

Needless to say, you can't sit around and wait for publishers to contact you to see if you want to do a remnant ad; they have to know ahead of time that you're available. So tell them! Call up the advertising coordinator of a magazine you're interested in, and explain that you'd like to be notified if any remnant space is available. They will probably try to talk you into a regular-rate ad, or even an ad at an introductory sale price of 20 percent off or so. Just sit tight and repeat your availability.

Eventually, you might get a frantic call offering a remnant ad if you can supply camera-ready copy by express courier within twenty-four hours. Now you're in a position of power. Negotiate your best price, fax the magazine a rough of your layout and a confirmation of the order, and send the actual art via e-mail or through one of the guaranteed next-day-delivery courier services.

— Regional Editions —

Many national publications have separate editions for different parts of the country. An ad in one or two regional editions should be substantially cheaper than buying space in the entire print run.

Using a regional edition ad makes sense in two situations:

- You want to test an ad's effectiveness, or
- Your target market is concentrated geographically.

— Tricks of Trade —

I've saved the very best bargain for last: Whether you call it a barter, swap, horse trade, or exchange, everybody wins on a good trade deal. If you're trading your own products and services, you're getting the deal for your wholesale cost. Better still, if you can barter something you bought but don't need anymore, you're trading your junk for someone else's treasure.

Jeffrey Lant gets all his ads through barter. "The last time I bought an ad was a long time ago. You do a lot of creative swapping. Most people do not have a swap track in their brains—they expect to pay cash for everything. I'll try to get something on a swap first before I ever pay cash for it. I've gotten art, gems, foreign travel, air tickets, liquor, lots of books, [as well as] an enormous amount of media space."

What does he trade? His marketing advice column, space in his direct-mail postcard deck and/or his catalog, books, consulting time, and, of course, his mailing list. "Names are a kind of currency. As you develop a mailing list, a lot of people want those names. Names will get you free cards, ad space, a better spot in a [post]card deck, other names."

What can you supply to a publication or broadcast station? Among many possibilities: computer equipment or software; food or lodging; office equipment; travel; temporary office staff; video production; Web site design and maintenance; landscaping; furnishings, decorations, and houseplants; pest control; bookkeeping; professional services (from accounting to zebra-striping); writing and illustration; messenger services; indexing; subscription processing; circulation and distribution (either of a publication or of promotional materials); premiums and advertising specialties; books and records; free tickets to events; contracting; office cleaning and maintenance.

You can probably find three or four things you can offer in trade. When you hear of a new ad venue, be particularly assertive in suggesting barter; new media outlets are frequently undercapitalized and often have long wish lists. Newsletters of nonprofit organizations are also usually quite receptive to the idea, for the same reason.

Complex Barters

A one-for-one trade is simple to arrange, but sometimes you need to go an extra step. For example, say you paint houses and you want to barter painting for advertising slots on a radio station. The station doesn't want painting, but the ad manager is complaining about high dental bills. You paint a dentist's office, the dentist fixes the ad manager's teeth, and the radio station gives you airtime.

Finally, consider a formal barter exchange network. You pay an annual fee, plus a percentage on everything you "buy" through the network. You accumulate credits as people use your service or acquire your product, and you subtract them as you patronize others. National barter associations always have plenty of advertising available for trade dollars; evaluate each offer as you would any other media buy.

14

Squeeze the Most from the Post, Part I

Direct mail is the art and science of getting your offer directly to your prospect's mailbox.

There are five major advantages to direct mail:

- Direct mail can be carefully targeted.
- It provides wide distribution for relatively low cost.
- You can get far more information into an envelope than through ads or press releases.
- You can personalize your appeal to readers.
- You can lower your costs through a wide range of tricks.

While Internet marketing offers many of these benefits, and at a generally lower price, there's still a place for direct mail. Millions of people have a postal address but aren't on the Internet, and there's more flexibility as to what you can mail—in terms of both technical issues and cultural acceptability.

Careful Targeting

Mailing lists let you go directly to your best prospects. In the classifieds or Yellow Pages, you pay to reach every person who receives the publication, but only the ones who are interested will look under your heading. But in direct mail, you send only to people who are already identified as interested; you don't have to pay to mail to the wrong people.

Direct mail is the largest source of new business for the Professional Association of Résumé Writers (PARW). Director Frank Fox explains: "We have people all over the country. We can identify our prospects through mailing lists and customize our appeal to them."

Lists from commercial mailing-list brokers are broken down into such specific categories as Automotive Wear Guard Mail-Order Buyers, College and University Directors of Audiovisual Media, Finance and Accounting Seminar Attendees, Mattress and Bedding Stores, Oxygen Therapy Equipment Services, Purchasing Agents of Leading U.S. Corporations, *Pizza Today* Magazine Subscribers, and Waterproofing Contractors.

A commercial-list house prescreens your prospects. Someone who has already purchased an auto wear guard through the mail is a prime prospect for anything else that extends the life of a car. And if you've developed a nonstick pizza pan, you'd want to reach the pizza shop owners who read *Pizza Today*.

Not only can you target previous customers or contributors (or even those who inquired), but you can also select users of similar products and services, donors sympathetic to similar causes, or find prospects according to various geographic and demographic criteria.

Wide Distribution at Reasonable Cost

Mail can take you beyond any geographical base; the cost is the same to mail in your own building or two thousand miles away. The cost per prospect is very small—although the actual cost per sale is often quite high.

More Information

A one-ounce mailing in a number 9 or 10 envelope holds four 8½ x 11-inch sheets of bond paper plus a return envelope, or five sheets without a return envelope. So you have up to ten pages (front and back) to convey your message, and each page can have as many as one thousand words. Even a more graphically appealing, less dense page can easily fit six hundred words.

Personalized Appeal

If you desire, you can merge information from a list of names and addresses into your sales letter to provide a personal touch. (This is referred to as a "mail merge.") Certainly, most people would rather read a letter addressed to their own name than to "Dear Friend" or "Dear Purchasing Agent." However, personalization is offensive if poorly done—as in those awful sweepstakes mailings that misspell your name three times in the body of the letter and don't even try to hide their computer-generated origins.

When you use a personalized salutation, first make sure your list is clean and accurate. Get the names right and sort carefully for duplication. Second, be discrete. Don't say ridiculous things such as "You will get a call on your <<name of town>> phone," or "Watch the letter carrier bring your package down the driveway at <<street address>>. People know this stuff for the load of horse manure it is. Furthermore, it gives you that many more opportu-

nities to be wrong. After the address and salutation, keep it to a maximum of one additional personalization in your letter.

Third, use software that makes the personalization look like part of the letter—in the same typeface, without unsightly gaps around it. It should look individually prepared, even if it obviously isn't. If you can see the difference between the personalization and the letter, so can your reader. Therefore, the goal of treating the reader as special becomes an insult. The reader thinks, "They don't even care enough to get my name right or make it look hand-typed."

Fourth, allow plenty of extra lead time in your preparation. It takes far longer to print a merged letter than to duplicate one unpersonalized master copy on high-speed equipment. Also, you have to be much more careful to match the right letter with its envelope; that's much slower than just grabbing letters and envelopes out of a pile.

Even without a mail merge, you can still achieve a semipersonalized effect by using a superspecific salutation (i.e., "Dear Fellow Hospital Cost-Control Professional"), and *focusing your letter tightly* on the needs, problems, and aspirations of the person you're targeting—and the benefits you have to offer that person. Don't try to make the same letter serve more than one population; it will either degenerate into blandness or feel irrelevant to its readers.

However you set it up, be totally honest in your claims. If you say that the mailing is only going out to a carefully selected group of executives but the recipient gets three copies each at the office, home, and post office box and notices that the janitor also got one, any other claim you make is suspect; you've lost credibility.

— List Development and Screening —

The best list, obviously, comprises your customers; your existing inquiries are a close second. These are people who have already established a business relationship with you, and you have complete control over targeting.

As you create your own database, be even more specific than the list brokerage firms. Data to track include purchase dates and frequency, dollar amount per sale, type of items, brands and model numbers; demographic information, and how the client found you. Now you can do pinpoint marketing: a special mailing, for instance, to Yellow Pages customers who purchased at least one hundred dollars worth of your product since February.

That kind of list is going to bring a very high response. Since these folks already know you, they're predisposed to do business with you.

Still, although you won't have the level of information or the personal contact, you may want to use others' lists to find new prospects. Here are four methods:

Commercial List Brokers

Brokers will be happy to accommodate you—for a price. The large houses cater to mass mailers. Edith Roman, for instance, has a minimum order of 5,000 names. At a base price of $50 per thousand, the minimum cost would be $250, plus shipping. If you have your own ad agency, deduct the 15 percent commission. Another broker, Hugo Dunhill, has a $150 minimum, plus minimum shipping of $15, but doesn't mention an agency discount.

Few people will get the base price, however. The same 5,000 names from Edith Roman on pressure-sensitive labels with a tracking code, within a particular zip code range, and with telephone numbers by job function, cost $26.50 per thousand extra, or $382.50 for the 5,000. But at over a million names a year, the base cost is down to $20 per thousand ($20,000 per million).

Clearly, at these prices plus postage, you only want to use a thoroughly tested mailing. To test on a smaller list, look at ads in the various entrepreneurial magazines; you'll often find brokers willing to provide small quantities at $6–$12 per hundred. Make sure they are guaranteed to be clean. If more than 5 percent come back as undeliverable, you should get at least the same percentage of your money back (better would be the cost of the bad names, plus the cost of third-class postage to those names).

When dealing with any list broker, it's important to understand the difference between compiled lists and direct-response lists. A direct-response list is made up exclusively of people who subscribed to a magazine, purchased a product, sent in an inquiry, or even responded "no" to an offer that asked for a yes-or-no reply. These names are worth much more, because they're receptive to mailed offers.

Compiled lists, on the other hand, were assembled from public information. They include both customers and those who are resistant. Thus, compiled lists will typically be far less successful.

Be aware that when you rent a list from a list broker, you don't own the list. You only buy the right to use the list once, unless you've made other arrangements. List brokers invariably sneak in a few checking names, so if you go beyond your agreement, you'll get caught—and face severe penalties. However, once a prospect responds to your mailing, you own that name and can use it as often as you like.

Compile Your Own Lists

Sometimes it may be worth it to develop a customized list from public information (telephone directories, the Encyclopedia of Associations, membership lists, etc.), just as you put together your press list. Aside from the obvious cost savings, you get precise control over recipients.

For instance, I once put together a list of some ninety-six independently owned résumé writing specialists in Massachusetts. I didn't want to talk to the chain stores or to secretarial services with a small résumé sideline, so I sorted through every telephone directory in the state. A commercial list would not have met my needs; the only way to prepare this specialized list was to compile it myself.

Other Businesses

Anyone who offers a service or product that complements yours might be interested in a collaborative effort. If the other business maintains a list, swap names one-for-one. Now you've got a fresh list of prospects who've bought something similar—and it didn't cost you a penny. Try to get them supplied on diskette—or at least on typed labels.

Include someone else's flier in your mailing; in exchange, they'll do the same for you.

Bypass Lists Entirely

Finally, you can let someone else do all the grunt work. Usually, you'd do this in one of two ways: list your product in someone else's catalog, or insert a mailer into a postcard deck or coupon envelope.

The former is an excellent avenue: Any mileage you get out of other people's catalogs is pure gravy. But commercial card decks and coupon mailers require a substantial investment: several hundred dollars for a few thousand copies of a coupon mailer—an envelope stuffed with one-third-page fliers, usually mailed to every household in a certain zip code range. Use them only if your product has broad appeal: pizza delivery, lube-oil-filter specials, banking or drugstore specials, and so on.

Postcard decks are much more carefully targeted, using standard mailing lists. But they also have a much higher cost of participation—around three thousand dollars for most decks, and over one thousand dollars for cheap ones. Another disadvantage: Many people throw the whole deck out unopened. Card decks also have larger circulation and national distribution.

Although you have no expense in getting a list, you also give up control over who's getting your offer—unless you start your own coupon or card deck mailing (see chapter 15).

— Database Marketing —

A database is nothing more than a collection of information, organized by fields. The term "database marketing" was coined by software companies to sell products such as D&B's Lotus Marketplace—database directories providing detailed information on businesses. Typically, these offer not just names and addresses, but officers, titles, annual revenues, and so forth—and sometimes demographic and purchasing-pattern information. Such programs are a useful, time-efficient tool for generating new prospects on a massive scale, and if direct-mail or telephone prospecting of new customers is an important piece of your marketing mix, it might be a good investment. Contact Dun & Bradstreet to get invited to one of their Marketplace seminars; you'll not only learn about their product but get a substantial discount if you make the purchase.

It's not a bad idea. But, of course, there are cheaper ways of doing the same thing. For example, a compilation of all U.S. telephone directories, for all businesses and residences in the country, can now be obtained easily and cheaply on CD-ROM (or for free on the Internet). These CDs, naturally, allow you to go through and generate your own list, although without the depth of information. Either way, prepackaged or do-your-own, creating a targeted list of appropriate prospects obviously makes sense for any kind of direct-mail or telemarketing campaign.

In fact, as computer power continues to become more affordable, the cost of tracking several million customers is the same as the cost of tracking *just one* customer was in 1950 (*Marketing Tools*, March/April, 1995).

Also, John Miglautsch points out in the same magazine that a huge database by itself is not enough—better to have a 100,000-name list from which useful information can be extracted than to have millions of names without enough data.

— Your Offer —

Okay, now you're ready to prepare a mailing. Be aware of the pitfalls that snare so many would-be direct-mail millionaires. You'll save on overhead and be more successful if you do it right—and that's true for nonprofits as well as businesses.

Simple Is Beautiful

Forget about glitzy, complicated sweepstakes offers, with seemingly dozens of different-sized papers, foils, stickers, and scratch-off cards; your production cost will be enormous before you even start.

Besides, they cost you tons of money mailing to and following up on false prospects.

A simple, straightforward approach is far better. Use ordinary paper sizes and stocks, and win the prospect over through the strength of your offer—not gimmicks or packaging. You'll stay within your budget, and target serious prospects, not a bunch of chiselers hoping for a million dollars from you, Ed McMahon, or the tooth fairy.

However, a little hand-added personalization on the envelope may make a difference. Marketing consultant Dr. Kevin Nunley <mailto:DrNunley @aol. com> cites an example:

> *Business presentation expert Tom Antion recently sent me a copy of his new book Wake 'Em Up! I could tell Tom knows what he's talking about as soon as I saw the package. It practically jumped out of the pile of mail.*
>
> *Tom adorns his mailer with brightly colored stickers. His mailing label features a red logo along with his photo. How many mailers come with a photo of the person who sent it? It's a real attention getter.*
>
> *Tom also puts several orange stickers with his Web site address on the package.*
>
> *Stickers and labels are a great way to make letters and packages stand out and get opened. Printers specializing in stickers are everywhere (think of all the items produced in your area that require professionally done labels). The strength of the glue can be varied from easy-to-remove to almost permanent.*
>
> *Copy shops can usually handle small runs. For just a few stickers, use your laser printer on colored labels available at any office supply store.*

A recent trend is 6 x 9-inch or 9 x 12-inch envelopes that appear as if the sender spent a huge amount of money overnighting it, but it in fact went out through regular first-class delivery.

These are very effective if you happen to be the first person sending one to your recipient. Unfortunately, however, it doesn't take long before savvy customers know what's going on, and then your advantage is lost.

So far, I have seen them only on business-to-business mailings. So when mailing to a less sophisticated, residential audience, it may still have quite a bit of impact. But when mailing to businesses, the effectiveness will drop off rapidly as recipients get more and more of these. And just as no one pays attention to all the obvious junk mail marked "Extremely Urgent," so these envelopes that scream loudly for attention become just another bit of noise in the background. An envelope with a more personalized message will probably be cheaper and more effective, in the long run.

The exception: Priority Mail flat-rate envelopes, available free from the post office. You can mail as much as you can cram into them for $3.20, and most of the time, they arrive within a few days. Pickup is free, too.

Respect Your Reader's Intelligence

Treat your reader like a friend, not a fool. Don't bombard the reader with high-pressure tactics or screeching type. Just state the problem you intend to solve, show the reader the benefits, *then* make your offer.

Don't make unbelievable or unrealistic claims. Credibility is your most important selling tool in direct mail to new prospects; don't blow it with an avalanche of self-serving, obviously false marketing verbiage. And don't think anyone will be fooled for a moment if you use blue ink and a handwriting font to write a note at the edge of the letter.

And provide a strong offer. If it's some worthless *chatchka*, few people will respond. Direct mail is not the place to get rid of your overstock of junk; use a yard sale for that! If you don't think your offer or your premium is attractive, your readers won't think so either.

Make Responding as Easy as Possible

Here's another place where sweepstakes offers fall down: They make the reader go through so many hoops. I'll answer sweepstakes that allow a single yes-or-no response: peel the appropriate sticker and throw it on the reply card. Yet many mailings require ten to twenty steps. Why bother?

In any direct-mail piece, make it easy for the reader to respond. The moment your prospect opens your envelope is your best shot at selling. If he or she stuffs it in a file to deal with later, the prospect's initial enthusiasm will cool—and he or she may not even find it again until the offer has expired.

So provide for the easiest possible responses, and the most incentives to act quickly. Include full information on price, quantities, shipping charges, and so on, along with your firm name, tracking code, address, and phone number. A toll-free number may be a real sales booster; many people haven't realized how much long-distance prices have fallen.

But don't get suckered into offering a 900 (pay-per-minute) number; you're asking for customer complaints, a bad reputation, and, potentially, prospects' inability to call you from work. If you're not able to staff a telephone without charging for it, change your marketing!

If you're serious about direct mail, you must accept credit cards. Otherwise, you can't accept phone or Web orders, and much of that initial momentum will be lost.

Be Honest

Deceptive trade practices are not only immoral, they could put you out of business; selling by mail is strictly regulated. If you offer anything free with no purchase necessary, then really make it available. Needless to say, if you promise and don't deliver, you're never going to get the person's business again. At worst, you could get into serious legal trouble.

— Components of a Mailing —

A mailing can range from a single postcard on up to whole boxes of material—but try to keep it to one ounce. Which components will help you reach your goal?

Postcard

Use a postcard to make a quick "hit" in a two-step sale, get an existing client to schedule a repeat appointment, or announce an event. Postcards have two major advantages: They can't be thrown away unopened, and the postage cost is lower. But they also have two major disadvantages: It's easy to lose them, and they can't hold much information.

Get around the first problem by using brightly colored (goldenrod, purple, or any neon color) or specialty-design card stock. Triple your selling space with oversized postcards such as 5 x 8 inches or 6 x 9 inches (warning: these take a letter stamp instead of the cheaper postcard stamp). Provide your Web address, a phone number, and/or a coupon to request more information. Also consider double postcards; they mail as a single postcard, but then open up into a marketing message and a tear-off return postcard. You get two extra panels working for you, though printing costs more.

Another way to set yourself apart with postcards: Print up some that match your business card and include your photo. Use them for thank-you notes, problem resolution, and other follow-up mailings. People like the personalization in our increasingly impersonal world.

If you have a Web site or sell information—books, videos, audiotapes, special reports—do up postcards with the cover—or your Web site home page—on one side, and a small selling blurb with ordering info in the upper left corner of the reverse side. Some publishers even put several covers on a single postcard.

Envelope

The envelope is the client's first chance to evaluate you, so make sure it counts. If you're following up on an inquiry, say, "Here is the information you requested." If it's the letter equivalent of a cold sales call, give the reader a reason to open the envelope. It could be a teaser question, such as "Do you really need a weatherman to tell which way the wind blows?" Or state your leading sales point: "Recover up to 80% of your 'uncollectable' debts," "Get your next car for $200 over dealer invoice," "Work part-time, earn full-time." If you're enclosing a premium—a reward for opening your envelope—say "Free _____ Enclosed." But make it worthwhile—not a silly decal with your logo.

Your message should be big enough to read easily, but not so big that it interferes with the post office's ability to handle your mail. And you have both the front and the back to work with—although recipients may not notice the back.

If you're worried about getting stuck with large numbers of obsolete preprinted envelopes, attach your message with stickers, or use a low-cost self-inking or rubber stamp. Voilà! No wasted envelope inventory!

For low volume, even though it slows delivery, I'm a big fan of actually hand-addressing an envelope (and no, you can't cheat and use a handwriting font in order to get the bar code discount. If your audience is at all sophisticated, they'll recognize this trick for the fraud it is.) Hand-addressed mail has a much higher chance of being opened, because it's from a human being and not a computer.

Letter

A letter, whether or not you address the recipient by name, is personal. It should combine an emotional and intellectual appeal. Your recipient uses the letter to decide if it's worth reading the rest. Sometimes a letter is the only component of your mailing, and it has to sell all by itself.

Effective letters talk to the reader's self-interest: what he or she has to gain from acting on your offer, or what he or she has to lose by failing to act. Include a deadline—a firm expiration date or impending price increase—to encourage a fast response.

- State the benefits clearly, concretely, and right at the beginning.
- Use bullets and other graphic call-outs.
- Long copy sells better—but only if it's compelling; if you really need four pages, or even more, go ahead and use them.
- Use an informal, friendly, personable tone; avoid bureaucratese.
- Always focus on the reader, not yourself.
- Include a P.S. and make sure there are captions for all illustrations—they're the most read parts of the letter after the headline.

- Include the order information in case your letter and order form get separated.

Flier or Brochure

This contains your strongest product-specific sales pitch—the reasons to buy this item, get it from you, and act soon. Chapters 16 and 17 will cover fliers and brochures in detail. In a mailing, a flier doesn't compete for attention with many others; you can put in a lot more text and use both sides. Finally, your response form can be a separate piece.

Order/Response Form

Include as many ways to place an order (or request more information) as possible: phone, fax, e-mail, postal mail, Web site. Include space for name, address, and phone/fax numbers. Ask respondents to type or block print, for legibility. Use check-offs for the order, and space to write in other items from your regular catalog. Also indicate the method of payment, including space for a credit card number, expiration date, and signature.

Don't forget to restate the offer! You want your order card to sell for you even if it's separated from the other components, so include the key benefit: "Yes! I want to learn 15 no-fail ways I can insulate my house even with no carpentry skills."

If another step follows before you close the sale, let the prospect call or e-mail you. Then determine just what kind of information they're looking for, and answer their questions immediately, while the desire to order is still fresh.

An order/response form can be printed as a postcard, appear on its own sheet of paper, be bound into a catalog, or be designed to be torn off from a flier. . . . If your order form is not a self-mailer, make sure to include a return envelope.

You can set up Business Reply Mail for your return envelopes; you pay postage on the ones that are mailed back to you. But only do this for orders, not inquiries, for they cost more than first-class postage. According to the United States Postal Service Web site <http://www.usps.com> as of July 1999, Business Reply Mail costs $400 in annual fees, plus 5 cents per envelope above the cost of postage—or $100 in fees and either 8 or 30 cents per envelope (the cheaper rate kicks in if you pay in advance). The $400 rate also gives you a 3-cent discount on the first ounce of a letter, or 2 cents off postcards, so the real saving is 6 cents per envelope. Thus, if you expect to receive more than 6,667 returned business-reply envelopes per calendar year, it's cheaper to pay the higher fee.

Some mailers believe in the psychology of attaching your own first-class stamp to the return envelope, so the recipient feels guilty if he or she doesn't return it. Don't! People will cover your address with a blank label and reuse your postage and envelope someplace else. Besides, even if your mailing pulls 5 percent, you'll spend $6.60 just to get each envelope back. If your offer is interesting enough, your best prospects will gladly put on their own stamp.

Memo

A memo is a short additional letter. Often, it might contain a third-party endorsement. Other times, it might be labeled on the outside, "Don't open this unless you're not going to order" (these are called lift letters, because the prospect is asked to lift the fold).

Personally, I'm not a big fan of lift letters. I have never seen a "don't open unless" memo that convinced me to order anything I hadn't already decided on. Third-party endorsements, on the other hand, are another matter—particularly if the name carries some weight in your field, but is not so well known that people think you've bought the endorsement. If you have a well-written note from someone else saying how much the reader needs your product, it will probably increase your return. Use it freely, and consider it one way to do . . .

Testimonials

Again, you're selling trust: Prospects must feel safe enough to buy without ever meeting you or handling your product. So let people say great things about you. But get the right kind of testimonials: attributed by name, city, and occupation; strong and

to the point; reinforcing of your sales message—emphasizing specific benefits received.

In charitable organizations' appeal letters, a variant on the testimonial explains how the writer was helped by the organization—the concrete differences the agency's intervention made in people's lives. You aren't asking people to buy anything, just to help you help others.

Guarantee

Another excellent trust-builder is a guarantee. The prospect hasn't seen, heard, touched, tasted, smelled, and tested your product—and most of us have been burned on overpriced, shoddy mail-order goods that weren't nearly as seductive as the ad copy that sold them. So assure the prospect that he or she:

- Will get what he or she has paid for
- Can return it if he or she doesn't like it
- Will get a product that performs as claimed
- Will receive a reasonable degree of mechanical reliability—and recourse if there are mechanical problems

On products sold by mail, a multipart guarantee is a good idea. Offer, for instance, a twenty- or thirty-day free trial period, plus free repairs for a specified time (typically, anywhere from ninety days to lifetime). Long warranties go a long way toward proving your own faith in your product. My Cuisinart came with a twenty-eight-year warranty; that helps explain why people buy two-hundred-dollar Cuisinarts instead of thirty-dollar food processors that only last a year. If you offer a subscription or membership package, let people get a full refund if they don't like their initial selection, and allow them to cancel at any time, with—at the least—a refund on unmailed issues.

Want to know a secret? Only a tiny percentage of people will take you up on your promise. Even those who really ought to return the product because it doesn't suit them often won't, out of laziness or carelessness, loss of original packaging materials, and so forth. But your willingness to stand behind the product will soothe a lot of fears.

The few people who do take you up on your offer should be treated with respect, courtesy, and a prompt refund—even if they no longer have the original packaging. Your name will be spread as an honorable company. But if you blow it with these people, the word to stay away will get around very fast.

Yes, a few exploiters will take advantage of your initial bargain offer and leave you hanging, but these will be very few. The vast majority of those asking for refunds will be people who bought the wrong product for their needs, double-checked the budget of their impulse purchase, or otherwise made a genuine mistake—or were misled by your marketing into thinking they were getting something else. Returns will probably average only one in a few hundred sales. See them as an opportunity, rather than a burden: a chance to find out what didn't work, refine your products, and sharpen your future marketing—possibly even find another product that does meet the customer's need.

—Wrap It Up Together—

Think of all these mailing elements as items on a menu. Pick and choose what's appropriate, and for whom. Save postage and printing by combining some of these on one sheet of paper: for instance, a flier with an order form at the bottom, a guarantee and testimonials included in your flier and/or letter, or an envelope that opens out into a flier.

Does the sample direct-mail letter on page 108 work for you? Why or why not?

The envelope had this teaser copy on the front: First line, in headline-sized red letters: "Isn't it time someone held the media accountable?" Second line, still oversize, all-caps italic: *FREE ISSUE—DETAILS INSIDE.* On the back: the name Steven Brill and a logo and address for *Brill's Content*—a magazine I'd never heard of before this letter showed up.

I don't know what list they bought, but it was a good fit for me. I'm a writer, an avid reader, and a politics junkie. Even though I already get too many magazines, I opened the envelope. They had targeted the right person.

The letter starts with eight separate teasers, in blue and typeset for high visual impact.

Then the body copy: a tricky, somewhat sarcastic opening that speaks to my own high skepticism of the media and my own progressive politics. The writing is compelling and I keep reading.

Then there's the indented paragraph, making the point that though the media's role is crucial, it escapes scrutiny. Then there's a very familiar phrase: "Pay No Attention to the Man Behind the Curtain." We know that the phony wizard is about to be unmasked.

The next paragraph shows several reasons why the media need more scrutiny. Notice that the page ends in midsentence, and there's a jump line to remind you to continue. These are both effective devices to keep the reader reading.

The second and third pages talk about what the magazine will do for me, and why this unknown stranger is the right person to do this for me. The copywriter made the mistake of ending page 2 at the close of a paragraph, but I keep reading, because by now I'm totally hooked. Page 4 lists some of the stories the magazine has covered—including several that hit my hot buttons. Page 5 is crammed with testimonials from some of the brightest, most respected names in journalism—and the appeal crosses generations: Baker is an icon of my parents' generation, Rather speaks to Boomers, and *Wired* magazine resonates with Generation X. Then there's a historical claim; *Brill's* wants to follow in the footsteps of George Orwell.

Finally, on the bottom of page 5 and on to page 6, the offer: a free trial. There is a P.S., though it fails to move me. However, the rest of the letter did the trick. On this, the first contact from a publication I'd never heard of, going to a battle-worn skeptic who already has too much to read, I sent in my reply card (something I do about once a year with a company I'm not familiar with).

BRILL'S CONTENT™

Whom can you trust?

What should you believe?

Where has good journalism gone?

Which media moguls kill stories to protect their interests?

Why is the message still more important than the medium?

Introducing BRILL'S CONTENT, the monthly magazine that's your survival guide to the new information age!

Intelligent, irreverent, and undaunted by icons, BRILL'S CONTENT digs into TV, websites, newspapers, magazines, and more — to report from the front lines of our exploding media age!

May we send you the next issue of BRILL'S CONTENT? FREE?

Dear Friend:

Welcome to the Age of Information. An age when dollars are digital. Virtue is virtual. The most valuable property is intellectual. And -- more than ever before -- knowledge is power.

There's only one problem: in this brave new world of information, there are no road maps. No way to know who and what's behind what we're reading, watching, and logging on to.

Ironic, isn't it?

At a time when the media are playing a more important role in our personal lives, in our careers, in our society and in our culture, the single most under-reported aspect of American life is the media.

More and more, the media shape our world, and shape us -- as citizens, as consumers, as content creators, as investors.

Yet, enthralled, we watch the show...and studiously obey our orders to Pay No Attention to the Man Behind the Curtain.

Pay no attention?

Even in a year when The Boston Globe fired two columnists for inventing stories? When The New Republic fessed up to running false stories by a hot-shot young reporter? When Time and CNN were forced to retract a report that the U.S. used nerve gas against defectors in Vietnam? In a year when the Washington press corps became addicted to leaks -- and

over please...

---

to the two most unforgivable words in journalism: "Sources say..."

But attention must be paid. The Romans asked: "Who will guard the guards?" In today's world, the question is: "Who will report on the reporters?"

Tough-minded journalist Steve Brill is doing just that with his new magazine -- BRILL'S CONTENT. And he'd like YOU as a Charter Subscriber.

In years past Steve parted the curtains on America's legal system with The American Lawyer magazine and the COURT TV cable channel.

Now he has brought the same refreshing jolt of honesty, clarity and unbiased, lively reporting to the world of American media.

And he's succeeded!

The cover story of BRILL'S CONTENT's very first issue caused a sensation, as we reported on how the press covered the Monica Lewinsky scandal -- how reporters rushed on the air, online, or into print with any and all leaks, and how the pundits became drunk on their own predictions.

Get the picture? BRILL'S CONTENT is an outspoken voice that covers the media world in a way it has never been covered before.

With independence. Authority. Insight. A firm belief in standards. And an edginess that's based on staying informed -- not on peddling attitude.

BRILL'S CONTENT is vigorous -- and rigorous. It's entertaining -- and challenging. It's surprising, informative, provocative, and amusing.

BRILL'S CONTENT...

- Reports on the media in all their manifestations. As a business. As a cultural force. As an evolving technology. And as a fascinating gallery of brilliant artists, driven journalists, gifted hucksters, and outsized egos.

- Analyzes how the news is made. Which book authors get picked for "Oprah" -- and why? Which media people suck up to get on Imus -- and whether they succeed. Who chooses the books that Barnes & Noble pushes? Who decides what channels your cable system will carry?

- Criticizes the way the news is made. In an age where an online magazine can "out" a congressman for adultery and force the rest of the press to follow its lead, and where Richard Jewell can go from hero to villain to victim in less than 24 hours, BRILL'S CONTENT sets out to identify the standards of good reporting...and names the magazines, TV shows, newspapers and websites that adhere to those standards, as well as those that don't.

3

- Applauds the most creative minds out there. In a world where many traditional newspapers are going toe-to-toe with the tabloids, what are the best local newspapers in America -- and why? The best radio talk-show hosts? The most informative Sunday Beltway gabfest? The best newspaper pundits? Which journalists are "keeping the faith" in the profession ...and which are just becoming celebrity entertainers?

- Guides you, as an engaged consumer, to the finest work being done in today's media world -- from breakthrough websites to the wittiest editorial cartoonists.

- Updates you on the developments in the evolving media industry ...from next year's prime-time schedule to why CBS News may be split off from CBS.

- Introduces you to the people who make the news. In a world where media moguls are carving up territories and airwaves, BRILL'S CONTENT brings you face to face with the off-camera gatekeepers -- the players who control which voices you hear on talk radio, what you see on the Web, which guests you'll hear on Today -- tomorrow.

And yes, there are some things BRILL'S CONTENT doesn't do.

- We don't take cheap shots at easy targets -- though we do report on those who do.

- We don't run puff pieces on executives, journalists, and websites -- though we do report on those who do.

- We don't parade attitude in the guise of journalism -- though we do report on those who do.

- We don't clear our stories in advance with our advertisers -- though we do report on those who do.

- We don't run "analysis" of tabloid stories as an excuse to rehash the stories -- though we do report on those who do.

BRILL'S CONTENT is dedicated to the idea -- dare I say it? -- that the message is, in fact, more important than the medium.

Is it any wonder that BRILL'S CONTENT is the sworn foe of Information Pollution?

In a world of "docudramas" and "edutainment," in a world where ad executives vet magazine stories, BRILL'S CONTENT tells us what's true and what's not. What's honest and what's fake. Which players to respect, and which to ignore.

Need proof? Here are some feature stories from our first five issues.

- CONSUMER ALERT. BRILL'S CONTENT investigated 20 stories aired by

over please...

three TV newsmagazine shows. We rated them: fair or unfair. And we reported on some tricks of the trade -- common techniques the shows use to scare viewers, and keep them glued to their sets.

- AN ANCHOR SPEAKS. Steve Brill interviewed Dan Rather on "Fear, Money, and the News." Rather to Brill: "The companion to 'if it bleeds, it leads,' is 'If you lead [with a] foreign story, you lose.' The Hollywoodization of the news is deep and abiding."

- ENTERTAINMENT. How Hollywood's leading trade papers -- Variety and The Hollywood Reporter -- strong-arm the same movie studios they report on every day to ante up for special editorial supplements.

- MOUSE-KE-FEAR. Or how the dread of a scandal too close to home prompted ABC News to ruin its credibility by killing a tough story about Disney, its corporate parent.

- ALTERNATE REALITIES. How, at any given hour of the day, what's news depends very much on which all-news network you are watching -- CNN, MSNBC, or Fox.

And every month, you'll find regular departments in BRILL'S CONTENT that will keep you ahead of the spin on media news:

- Credentials. How much experience do TV analysts and press reporters really have about their subjects? Should Jonathan Turley really be analyzing impeachment issues? And which business reporters really know business?

- Lynched. We identify a person, corporation or cause most unfairly maligned by the press.

- Payday. An illuminating table that reports the salaries, speaking fees and outside income of journalists major and minor. Are you listening, Cokie Roberts?

- Next. Believe it or not -- a hype-free, flack-free report on how the digital revolution is really affecting content.

- The Culture Elite. Who are the most powerful people when it comes to criticism of the theatre, movies, and the arts -- and what's the story behind their work?

- Unsung Heroes. A look at the best reporting and creative work being done in smaller media markets.

- Unhyped Books. A different kind of book review section -- one that celebrates challenging works you otherwise might never find, because they don't have celebrity authors or big-bucks PR machines behind them.

PLUS -- In each month's BRILL'S CONTENT, you'll find columnists such as

5

Calvin Trillin, who dissects the media from an insider's perspective -- and flays it with humor.

BRILL'S CONTENT's goal is simple: to raise the bar for American journalism. And we already have the support of some of the most media-savvy among them!

- "One of the most powerful institutions in our society is the press. We need a check [on that power] and this publication is definitely that."

    -- Ken Auletta, The New Yorker

- "I expect that [Brill] may publish stories about me, about us, that we won't be comfortable with. ...But he's a solid journalist and he's got a very good idea here. I think he may pull it off."

    -- Dan Rather, CBS Evening News

- "Competition's devastating effect on careful journalism is brutally and embarrassingly illustrated by Steven Brill's article, 'Pressgate,' in the first issue of...[BRILL'S CONTENT]."

    -- Russell Baker, The New York Times

- "Brill's brutal dissection of the bizarre process by which a literary agent, a disgruntled federal employee, and a handful of Washington reporters have led the United States to the brink of constitutional crisis is riveting reading for anyone interested in modern media and how it has come to ruin."

    -- Jon Katz, Wired News

Who should be reading BRILL'S CONTENT?

You should -- if you care as much about the information you ingest as the food you eat!

George Orwell's brilliant essay on "Politics and the English Language" founded the modern study of the media.

And his depiction of the world of Big Brother in 1984 gave us a chilling view of a world dominated by false information.

Orwell, unfortunately, will never see our pages. But others -- including you -- absolutely must.

Hence, our offer.

You're risking absolutely NOTHING when you accept this FREE ISSUE offer. Because, plain and simple, you must experience BRILL'S CONTENT.

over please...

6

Please -- send no money.

Simply return the FREE-ISSUE RESERVATION CARD enclosed, in the postpaid envelope provided. If you should decide to stay with us, fine. You'll become a Charter Subscriber to BRILL'S CONTENT at significant savings.

If you choose to bail out after examining the FREE ISSUE, we part friends.

Either way, though, we strongly urge you to join us in our quest for superior quality from our media -- and in our determination to understand and appreciate our new media world. It's one we inhabit together.

Cordially,

Margaret E. Samson
President

P.S. You're going to be blown away by the way BRILL'S CONTENT names names and lays it on the line. Not for the dubious "fun" of savaging individuals...but in the interest of raising standards. Don't miss the next issue!

BRILL'S
CONTENT

521 Fifth Avenue
New York, NY 10175

The rest of the package is also compelling. The lift letter repeats the question from the envelope, and adds, in the same red headline type, "Now someone does. BRILL'S CONTENT." Signed by Steven Brill, it outlines his qualifications (founder of *The American Lawyer* magazine and *Court TV* cable TV show), restates the benefits of subscribing, and concludes with an action step (before the P.S.): "So, may I look forward to hearing from you by return mail?" And the P.S. on the lift letter worked better for me: "P.S. Remember, BRILL'S CONTENT is for everyone who believes the most under-reported subject in American media . . . is American media!"

Also in the envelope: a brief, glitzy four-color brochure that opens up as a poster. It targets three distinct audiences, includes four sample covers and four sample magazine pages. And, of course, an order form that restates the guarantee.

Although four-page letters are standard, I think it's hard for inexperienced copywriters to sustain that much momentum. A tight, fast-paced one-to-two-page letter will do better; people don't have all that much time for you. I make up my mind within the first two or three paragraphs whether I'm going to read all the way through a letter. Better to keep the letter short and add supplementary material. The successful one-pager on the next page is several years old, but I haven't seen a better one.

This good letter could have been even better with stress on the primary benefit: that in an unlicensed field with wide variation on price and quality, membership and certification assure customers that you know what you're doing. By marketing this benefit, the PARW could have shown how the cost of membership pays for itself many times over in bigger market share.

Let's look at an example from the nonprofit fundraising world shown on page 113.

This letter is done on a letterhead befitting a famous person—but she's an unknown. I think that actually incites curiosity and is a pleasantly sneaky way of getting the reader to begin reading.

Right away, we know something big is going to be discussed: "I thought it couldn't happen in America." We're going to be hearing about some fundamental issue that many people take for granted in this country. The next two paragraphs define the issue: censorship of school reading lists, and a subordinate concern of apathy in the surrounding community—and by extension, the country at large.

Then the letter lists some of the banned books: works of literature that almost anyone would recognize as having merit.

Next, a reiteration that this is not some militia fortress in the middle of nowhere, but an ordinary American town. The implication: This could happen to you! Then she describes the opposition's tactics: the Big Lie technique popularized by Hitler, a forged signature campaign, even arson and death threats. The plot is starting to sound like a novel.

On page 2, the hero is introduced: National Coalition Against Censorship—battling the right-wing censors all around the country. The bottom of page 2 and the top of page 3 show even more outrageous examples of censorship in the classroom, and then more about what NCAC does to prevent these abuses, including its campaign to bring national attention to censorship battles. Finally, page 4 gives the money pitch, and closes with a note about the victory. Underneath, a list of prominent advisors, including some that are household names and another large number that are well known in liberal circles.

Was this effective? Well, I received this letter sometime around 1990 and have been donating to the group consistently since then. From me, at least, they got a good return on their investment.

— Speed Your Way —

Mail does get lost or delayed. But you up the chances of safe, prompt delivery if you follow post office guidelines. As the mail system relies more and more on automation, machine-readable addresses become crucial. Use standard-sized rather than odd-sized envelopes, and put the information where the post office expects to see it. For regular mail, put the return address in the upper left-hand corner or on

PARW Professional
Association of
Résumé Writers

October, 1991

Dear Résumé Professional:

We invite you to start 1992 with a new profit center, increased client bookings, professional credentials, and a wealth of successful ideas and information from over 500 professional résumé writers who already belong to PARW.

Reasons To Join Your Industry's Professional Association:

- To include the "Member of PARW" logo in your Yellow Page ad and all of your promotional literature. It's an important credential that clients use to choose a professional résumé service.

- To test for the "Certified Professional Résumé Writer" designation in 1992. The PARW Certification Committee is developing standards and testing procedures that will allow the true professionals of our industry to add "CPRW" after their name, and promote this distinction when soliciting new clients.

- PARW has established the National Résumé Bank, an on-line computer résumé service that can add additional profits to your business on every résumé you prepare. Access to posting client résumés on the National Résumé Bank is exclusively available through PARW Member résumé companies.

- To be included in the 1992 PARW Membership Directory issued in January.

- Plus...you receive the monthly PARW Newsletter packed with articles and information on promoting your business to new clients, pricing strategies, adding new services, etc. You receive a PARW Membership Certificate and a PARW Code of Business Ethics for display in your reception area or office, "Member of PARW" logo sheets, promotional advertising layouts you can use as your own, and information on books, one-day seminars, the annual PARW convention, access to the toll-free consulting line, and other programs developed specifically for résumé writers and business owners.

A membership application form is enclosed. Join today to start your membership benefits immediately.

GLORIA T. PIPKIN

Dear Friend,

<u>I thought it couldn't happen in America.</u>

I thought that my students and I would never have to face down a horde of extremists who were out to "clean up" the school curriculum—and remove from it dozens of the greatest works of world literature.

Even after the book-burners appeared, I thought that the entire town would unite to save an English program which had won national recognition for its success in motivating young people to read.

<u>But I was wrong.</u>

Recently, in the town where I teach—Panama City, Florida—64 works of literature were banned from school reading lists.

The blacklisted books included <u>Wuthering Heights</u> and <u>Hamlet</u> . . . <u>The Red Badge of Courage</u> and <u>The Autobiography of Benjamin Franklin</u> . . . <u>Oedipus Rex</u> and <u>The Old Man and the Sea.</u>

Also banned were some of the finest examples of contemporary fiction for young adults—books which had stimulated the minds and the interest of my students, and introduced them to the pleasures of reading.

All of this came about in a <u>perfectly ordinary American community</u>—a place where you'd never dream that ignorant self-appointed censors could take over the schools.

It happened because a group of extremists managed to impose their narrow views on a school system that serves more than 125,000 people!

You've probably seen such people on TV. They're the ones who hint darkly that "secular humanism" is destroying our country . . . who try to weed references to evolution out of biology textbooks . . . <u>who treat new ideas as diseases which might infect a child, instead of challenges which can teach a youngster to think.</u>

They'd be the first to tell you how "moral" they are. But the tactics they used in Panama City were anything <u>but</u> moral.

First came the big lie—the assertion, repeated over and over, that our students were reading "dirty" books, "dangerous" books, books that attacked so-called "traditional values."

Next the organizers circulated petitions demanding that such books be banned. They claimed to have gathered over 9,000 signatures. You can imagine the strong impression those petitions made on school officials. It wasn't until a reporter examined the petitions that the truth came out. There were only 3,000 signatures—and pages and pages of them were forgeries or the signatures of children!

And when the reporter went on TV with her findings, <u>her apartment was set on fire</u>—and a crude anonymous letter threatened her life! <u>The same letter threatened me—and two other teachers—with death.</u>

Suddenly, freedom to read wasn't the only issue at stake in Panama City. Some good people were afraid to speak their minds, for fear of what might happen to them.

I have to admit that I was a little frightened, too. but I was determined that a small band of fanatics would not deprive the kids I teach of their right to read and discuss good books.

So with my fellow-teacher Alyne Farrell and 41 other teachers, parents and teenagers, I went to court—and filed a lawsuit demanding that the school superintendent and the school board lift the ban on every one of the books prohibited from our classrooms.

In fighting back against the book-burners, we've discovered a valuable ally—an extraordinary organization called the NATIONAL COALITION AGAINST CENSORSHIP.

NCAC is the national nerve center of the fight against bigots, book-burners and would-be censors. It's a cross-section of Americans of many professions, religions and races—all of whom are dedicated to the fundamental American principle of free expression.

From the enclosed list, you'll see that NCAC includes writers and actors, civil libertarians and union members, publishers and educators, religious leaders and students.

Through NCAC, they work to help defeat the people who try to force their beliefs on schoolchildren and other readers—in Panama City or any other American city or town. Even in your community.

For all across America—in big cities as well as small towns—the right to read is threatened far more often than you might imagine.

In the months since NCAC began helping us, I've learned about dozens of places in which the self-appointed censors have managed to suppress books with which they disagreed.

- In Carlsbad, New Mexico, the school board ordered removal of the Merriam-Webster Collegiate Dictionary from classrooms because it contains "the most obscene words imaginable"!
- The Alabama State Textbook commission stigmatized high-school English anthologies on the extremists' "hit list." Joyce, Fitzgerald, Ibsen, Virginia Woolf, Wallace Stevens, James Baldwin, Anne Frank, and Langston Hughes were among the authors whom the book-burners found to be "to bitter," "bizarre," and "poor writers."
- The Winnetka, Illinois, school board removed Huckleberry Finn from a high school's required reading list because of complaints that Mark Twain's satirical dissection of the attitudes behind slavery was itself racist.

Thanks to NCAC, a strong national network of support and action is ready to help fight the censors in each and every one of those embattled communities.

NCAC provides vital information which local teachers and parents need to organize against the book-burners. From NCAC, local citizen groups can find the answers they need to hundreds of questions, from help in filing a lawsuit to such nuts-and-bolts concerns as how to organize an effective public meeting or local press conference.

NCAC's extensive media network can focus the attention of a state, a region, or even the whole nation on the fight against censorship in any city or town.

For if there's one thing the book-burners hate, it's the glare of truthful publicity. Just remember what happened to the reporter in my home town! Such publicity can make school board members more willing to say "No" to censorship—and make local citizens understand the importance of their children's, and their own, freedom to read.

Through its contacts with TV, radio and newspaper reporters across America, NCAC brings national attention to individual censorship battles. For when censorship is imposed in any school district or town, it's not merely a "local matter"—it's a threat to the rights that every American holds dear!

We in Panama City who are fighting the censors have found NCAC to be important in another way, as well. You remember I told you that many people were frightened to stand up against the book-burners. It's hard to do what you know is right, when you know you'll become the target of abusive, hysterical attacks.

NCAC let us know that we're not alone—and that all across America, millions of intelligent, decent people are four-square behind us. It's hard to express how very much courage and consolation that knowledge has given us.

The struggle in Panama City is not yet over. but I cannot imagine how we could have gotten as far as we have without the help of NCAC.

I'd like to think that no other teacher, in no other town, will ever again have to go to court to protect her students' right to read. But I know that's just wishful thinking. For all over our country, the censors are busily trying to remove "dangerous" books from the schools.

I want to be sure that NCAC will be able to give parents and educators in beleaguered communities vital assistance, information and advice.

That's why I'm writing you this letter . . . to ask you to help fight the book-burners—not just in Panama City, but in every town and city where they try to bully teachers, librarians and school boards—by becoming a supporter of the NATIONAL COALITION AGAINST CENSORSHIP.

You see, NCAC is supported by the tax-deductible gifts of individuals—people like you and me who are determined that the extremists will not "protect" us or our children from books and ideas they don't like.

Your gift will help to defend your family's freedom to read—and provide vital assistance to local groups who suddenly find themselves on the front lines of the fight against censorship.

Please send your tax-deductible gift of $25, $50, $100, $250, $500—as much as you can—to the NATIONAL COALITION AGAINST CENSORSHIP. I have enclosed a reply envelope for your convenience.

On behalf of all of us fighting the book-burners in Panama City—and people fighting censorship in other towns and cities across America—thank you for your prompt and generous response.

Sincerely,
Gloria T. Pipkin

P.S. After all the negative publicity about censorship in Panama City school, you'll be glad to learn the school board has restored classics like Shakespeare, Franklin and Hemingway to the curriculum. But important works of contemporary literature for young people are still banned from the classroom. Your gift to NCAC will help to fully restore our young people's freedom to read.

National Coalition Against Censorship

2 West 64th Street • New York, NY 10023 • 212-724-1500

Rev. Carl Flemister	Jo Levinson	Harriet Pilpel	John Sucke
Co-Chair	Co-Chair	Co-Chair	Vice Chair

Marvin Rich	Jeremiah Gutman	Leanne Katz
Secretary-Treasurer	Counsel	Executive Director

Council of Advisors

Shana Alexander, *author* • Isaac Asimov, *author* • Judy Blume, *author* • John Harris Burt, *Episcopal Bisop of Ohio* • Alice Childress, *author* • Adrian W. DeWind, *partner, Paul Weis, Rifkind, Wharton & Garrison* • Robert F. Drinan, *S.J., professor of law, Georgetown University* • W. W. Finlator, *retired minister, Pullan Memorial Baptist Church, North Carolina* • Frances Fitzgerald, *journalist, historian* • Victor Gotbaum, *former executive director, District Council 37, American Federation of State, County, and Municipal Employees* • Franklin S. Haiman, *professor of communication studies, Northwestern University* • Ed Handman, *public relations director, District Council 37, AFSCME* • Mildred Jeffrey, *member, board of governors, Wayne State University* • Rhoda H. Karpatkin, *executive director, Consumers Union* • Sylvia A. Law, *professor of law, New York University* • Robert E. Lee, *playwright* • S. Jay Levi, *partner, Levi Economic Forecasts* • Jay Mazur, *president, International Ladies Garment Union* • Eve Mirriam, *poet, stage director* • Joyce D. Miller, *national president, Coalition of Labor Union Women, member, AFL-CIO Executive Council* • Victor Navasky, *editor, the Nation* • Aryeh Neier, *vice chairman, Helsinki Watch/Americas Watch* • Robert M. O'Neil, *president, University of Virginia* • Gerald Piel, *chairman Emeritus, Scientific American* • Irwin H. Polishook, *president, Professional Staff Congress, City University of New York* • Barbara Scott Preskel, *former vice president, Motion Picture Association of America* • Betty Ruder, *communications consultant, former vice president for public affairs, New York University* • Stanley K. Sheinbaum, *regent, University of California* • Piri Thomas, *author* • Robert Wise, *film producer and director*

Organizational affiliations for identification only

the back of the envelope, centered at the top. The addressee's information should be about halfway between the left and right margins, and the bottom line should be about an inch above the bottom edge of the envelope. A stamp, Postal Service–approved bulk mail indicia, or postage meter printout should be on the upper right.

The post office prefers addresses all in capital letters, unpunctuated. When you mail to someone's attention, use the first line in the address, never the last. If you're mailing abroad, put the country name as your last line. (While your mail will get through if you put the "attention" address on the bottom left corner, use punctuation, etc., it may need to be hand-sorted and lose some time.)

Postal Classifications: A Quick Primer

The United States Postal Service (U.S.P.S.) provides several different kinds of basic service:

- Express Mail: Guaranteed next-day delivery, with flat-rate prices up to eight ounces, and again up to two pounds.
- First-Class/Priority Mail: Typically, delivery within one to three business days, but no guarantees (I once waited six weeks for a Priority package from the opposite coast).
- Periodical: Slower, cheaper bulk periodicals rate.
- Standard Mail: For a minimum of two hundred identical pieces—very slow and very cheap.
- Special Book and Music Rates—no minimum. There are various subdivisions. You'll probably deal with Special Standard (SS, formerly called Book Rate) and perhaps Bound Printed Matter (BPM). BPM costs a lot more for larger distances, but not much more for extra weight. SS cost increases rapidly with weight, but stays the same across distance. Thus, a five-pound book shipment to a nearby city will be cheaper with BPM, while SS will save you money on a two-pound shipment halfway across the country.

Also, consider these extras:

- Insurance: Provides replacement cost if item is damaged or lost.
- Return Receipt or Delivery confirmation: Options start at 35¢ extra
- Registration: Must be signed for by the recipient and is carefully handled throughout its time in the postal system—best for mailing notices of legal action and similar very important papers
- Certified: Must be signed for, but is not handled as strictly. Available with or without receipt.
- Special Handling (formerly called Special Delivery): Package is delivered in person to the addressee (a waste of money; it can significantly delay mail).

Postal Discounts

As automation increases and rates change, the various options for saving money on mailing shift like sand grains in an hourglass. But the more work you do, the less you pay.

As of this writing, nonprofit mailers can pay as little as 7.2 cents to mail one letter weighing an ounce or less, in drops of at least two hundred pieces. To qualify for that deep discount, you must use machine-addressed zip+4 codes, postal bar codes, and carrier-route-level sorting and meet qualifications based on geographic density. For-profit businesses meeting the same criteria can mail for as little as 16.2 cents apiece. Bulk mailers pay an annual fee of one hundred dollars, and another one-time one-hundred-dollar fee to set up an account and get a permit number (waived for stamped or metered mail). Various discounts also apply for sorting by zip code to nine, five, or three digits; sorting by carrier route; attaching bar codes; and bundling large batches with common zip codes.

If bulk mail is too slow, use presorted first-class to mail at least five hundred pieces at a time (23.8 cents with bar codes).

Full details on all the various discounts are available from the post office, on Postal Ratefold 123. Postal employees will work with you to hold your cost down, since every step you do for them reduces their burden.

Amazingly enough, the post office will even insert carrier routes and nine-digit zip codes into your database on an IBM-PC compatible diskette—for free! (If you work with a different computer system, convert your data to the IBM-PC format, let the post office process it, and convert the data back.) Do this every six months or so, both to process your new additions and to keep your information current as the post office switches carrier routes around.

Let Your Mail Take Shortcuts

Delivery time can be greatly enhanced if you reduce the number of postal employees who handle your mail. The farther along the system you put it in, the faster it will go.

Never throw your mass mailing into the corner mailbox. A small postal substation is only a slight improvement. In ascending order, you're better off taking it to a full-service branch post office; the main post office for your town; the central post office for your three-digit zip code region; or your regional Airport Mail Facility (for nonlocal mail only).

Take a bulk mailing—with all the proper paperwork—around back to the bulk mail drop or the loading dock, rather than bringing it through the stamp line. Some post offices even require this.

— Alternatives to the — Postal Service

The U.S. Postal Service is not the only game in town. For each mailing task, consider:

Package and Courier Services

Federal Express, Airborne Express, Purolator Courier, and others offer next-day delivery. However, U.S.P.S. Express Mail is the only courier that can deliver to a P.O. box. Express Mail will also pick up from you without extra charge—but only if the package is ready when your letter carrier delivers your mail. If you mail out many packages, negotiate a better price—shop around. For instance, many computer software distribution companies—which ship out hundreds of packages every day—offer next-day delivery for only five dollars per package. Professional associations and third-party resellers may also offer discounts.

Don't neglect United Parcel Service and its major competitor, Roadway Package System (RPS). UPS offers various plans, including guaranteed next-day and second-day delivery. Sometimes, it may even be worth delivering a letter via UPS; it will have more impact than regular mail, but cost less than a courier service. RPS partners with many professional organizations to offer discounts as a member benefit.

If there's no UPS depot near you, UPS will pick up packages at your door anywhere in the United States. There is a small charge for this, but it covers any pickups in the same week. So if you ship on Monday, Wednesday, and Thursday one week, you only pay the pickup fee for the first visit.

Private or franchised storefront mailing services make their money by adding a hefty percentage to the shipping cost. If you ship often, you'll spend hundreds of unnecessary dollars on these commissions. But they may be best for occasional single shipments.

Messenger Services

Although their popularity is waning as fax machines become almost omnipresent, there is still a place for private messenger services. Small packages, in particular, lend themselves to bicycle delivery across two miles of crowded inner-city commercial center.

Western Union

For a high-impact, cost-no-object splash, telegram delivery by messenger will run you $31.90 for fifteen words, delivered in the continental United States within five hours of your call.

Why spend that kind of money to send 15 words? Consider this scenario: You're in a community action group that's been seeking a meeting with a government official for months. Embarrass your target by sending a telegram requesting a meeting, with the press present when the messenger shows up. Thirty bucks is not a bad investment if three nightly newscasts cover your group's frustration.

Electronic Delivery via Modem

When used correctly, e-mail is the marketer's truest friend. It rates its own chapter (chapter 23), in the Internet section.

Fax

Since faxes don't come in an envelope, they are always at least glanced at before being thrown away. And on deliveries within your free local calling area—or single pages anywhere in the country—faxing is cheaper and faster than postal mail.

However, junk faxes are a nuisance for many companies and are deeply resented. They're also illegal. So be appropriate: Fax people more information if they request it during a telephone sales call. Fax old customers a special offer that's relevant to their past purchases. Fax press releases to media. Fax ad layouts back and forth for input. You can probably list a dozen other ways to increase productivity and cut costs by faxing.

Hand Delivery

Within a small geographic area, hand delivery may make sense. You can deliver materials yourself, hire a high school student, or—if you're promoting a cause or candidate—draw on volunteers.

If you pay a worker $7.00 an hour, and in that hour, he or she can distribute 200 fliers in an apartment building, your delivery cost per prospect is 3.5 cents. However, speed will vary greatly depending on the density of the neighborhood—and worker efficiency. In a wealthy suburban neighborhood, it may take an hour to do only 20 fliers, and your cost is comparable to mailing.

Caution: Never put your flier inside a mailbox! It is illegal to deliver mail to a mailbox without paying for it, and if the Postal Service catches you, you will be charged for postage. Acceptable locations include in or under the door, attached to the outside of the mailbox with a clothespin, or squeezed between the mailbox and its extender bars (the rungs on the bottoms of some mailboxes designed to hold news-

papers and such). But it's okay to use a nonregulation, open box such as a wicker basket, or a mail slot.

Appropriate uses for a hand-delivered flier might include restaurant promotions, office supply discounts, introduction of new services, promotion of neighborhood-oriented businesses, and community meeting notices.

— Will Direct Mail Work? —

To succeed, you should make money if 0.5 percent to 1 percent of your recipients become customers. These rates of return may sound low, but mail actually draws better than many other media. Consider a display ad in a publication with a circulation of 80,000 or a radio ad that reaches 100,000 listeners; you'd be ecstatic if you got 400 to 1,000 new customers (0.5 percent of 80,000 to 1 percent of 100,000).

Let's assume a fairly expensive route: a one-color, two-sided, five-sheet package sent via first-class mail. Your printing and mailing cost per prospect to deliver this sizable chunk of information is 60 cents or less for photocopying, a penny for the envelope, and 33 cents for mailing—94 cents for the whole thing. (In chapter 15, you'll learn to drastically reduce this figure.) If you rent a mailing list, add 4–15 cents per name.

I've ignored them because they vary too much, but include your other costs: labor to stuff the envelopes, cost of product and inventory, and, of course, advertising. Do this kind of analysis for any marketing method, but it's crucial in direct mail.

If the 0.5–1 percent range holds, that same 94 cents in mailing cost per prospect translates into a cost per sale of $94–$188 (ouch!). On the low end, if you're mailing a single-sided postcard, your cost per piece will only be 23 cents (20 cents to mail, plus 3 to print)—or cost per sale of $46 at 0.5 percent. You won't make as many sales, since it's hard to provide enough information on a postcard to get people motivated to buy. But you could inspire a visit to your Web site.

Obviously, you can play with the per-piece cost by varying the mailing. But any way you look at it, the cost per sale to reach first-time customers with a private first-class mailing is objectionably high.

A clever idea from Alexsandralyn Stevenson of Cattails Publishing, writing in the June 1999 Publishers Marketing Association newsletter: target retail outlets! If, say, you offer better terms with a ten-piece minimum order, and those outlets become regular sales channels for you, direct mail suddenly makes a lot more sense.

Thus, view the initial direct-mail contact as only the first step in a long-term relationship; it may be worth $94 to grab a customer who'll spend $5,000 over the next three years. But it won't be worth it to sell one $100 product, once.

In fact, this is the logic that many of the biggest direct-mail marketers use. They mail hundreds of thousands of pieces a year, test offers and lists in batches of five thousand, and are content to break even on acquiring a customer. They expect to make up the acquisition cost many times over in a long-term selling relationship, and they provide excellent products and service to ensure that relationship.

Also, many direct mailers pour money down a hole with bad marketing, inappropriate offers, and poor-quality list management. You're going to do it right; consequently, aim for a 2–5 percent new-customer response rate. The Professional Association of Résumé Writers (PARW), for instance, consistently maintains a response rate in this range. Still, base your projections upon the lowest responses you can safely count on; then you won't get burned if you're wrong. If a mailing starts to pull a 2–3 percent response, it's clearly a winner. If you achieve a 5 percent response from people who haven't dealt with you before, consider yourself a certified marketing genius and hang out your shingle as a consultant.

From existing customers (or donors), expect a much higher return—in rare instances, up to 50 percent. But 5–10 percent is more believable, and is a reasonable goal. At 10 percent, the same 94-cent packet costs $9.40 per sale—a much more viable figure.

Knowing typical response rates also helps you figure out how much to mail. For instance, 100 names is too small to accurately judge a mailing. One sale could represent anywhere from 0.5 percent on up to 1.9 percent.

Five hundred pieces is a reasonable minimum test mailing. In an initial mailing of 500 full-ounce pieces, at 94 cents per piece, your cost is $470 for the entire test. If your offer pulls fewer than 3 responses out of 500, it's not working. At 3 to 5 responses, you're in the ball game but you'll want to strengthen either your offer or your marketing piece before testing another 500 names. If you get more than 5 responses, it's a winner—and if more than 15 responses come in, mail immediately to the entire list.

Boost Your Return with Follow-Up

Of course, one mailing by itself is generally not enough to get your message across. Remember, you need to reach people several times with different marketing tools. You can drastically increase the pulling power of your mailing by reinforcing it. Listen to PARW's Frank Fox: "It takes more than one contact—it takes five or six or eight. Maybe we don't get them that first time, but later they get a sample newsletter announcing a new product or service, and at some point, someone says yes."

From your test list of 500 best prospects, you still have 490 to 497 who didn't buy from the first mailing. Choose 100 at random—say, every fifth name—and follow up by telephone. (*Important:* Track whom you've called, and don't try telephone sales until you've read chapter 31!) Ask if they've seen your offer and if they have any questions. Provide an inducement to act quickly, but don't be pushy about selling right now. And if they ask you to send more material in writing, do so immediately (and mark the envelope, by hand, that you're sending in response to your conversation); they've expressed serious interest in evaluating your offer and want to see it again. Believe me, they aren't doing this just to get rid of you, but because they think they might genuinely be interested. If you add 10 more solid customers by follow-up calling, call all the others; if your percentage holds, you will turn 39 of them into customers. In all, then, with 500 mailings and 490 to 497 follow-up phone calls, you've turned your original 3 to 10 sales into 53 to 59.

Do you think it's worth the effort? Consider a real-life example: The Vermont chapter of 20/20 Vision, the peace lobbying group, uses telephone reminders to achieve a 90 percent membership renewal rate.

Telephone follow-up allows you to draw the prospect's attention to your mailing—to separate it out from a growing pile of unsolicited mail. At the very least, they'll be looking for the second mailing you send out if the telephone call reveals ignorance of your original mailing.

You can also follow up through the mail, but your batting average will be lower, and you'll quickly reach a point of diminishing returns. Don't just send out the identical mailing again—the prospect will wonder why you don't check for duplicates. At the very least, put in a cover note that says something like, "Three weeks ago, I mailed you the enclosed offer. I still haven't heard from you even though I know this information will help you [restate major benefit]. Please give it another look, and feel free to call me at [phone number] if you have any questions."

Better still, modify the offer: "I've been waiting eagerly for you to take advantage of my offer to help you make $5,000 in the next six months by growing and marketing Oriental vegetables. It's been three weeks and I still haven't heard from you. But since you're just the kind of person who would really do well with this information, if you order within ten days, deduct another 10% off our already low price."

Still, the interplay between mail and telephone is far superior to reliance on mail alone. Before deciding on mail follow-up, try it by phone.

Mail to Your Best Customers

If you've provided quality products and service at affordable prices, customers will probably think of you the next time. But why wait? Refresh their memory with a carefully targeted mailing. This works particularly well if you have a mix of related products. For instance, if your camera store sells someone a zoom lens, they might want a wide angle lens, carrying case, tripod, or flash attachment. Track your customers by brand name, and mail a flier of specials on accessories for a different brand each month.

A specialty music warehouse could announce an artist's new releases and offer a small discount to buyers of the previous albums who bring in the flier. A bookstore—or better yet, book club—can group ten new titles on the same subject and send a mailing to people who've bought three or more books in that category. Be creative:

- "We've missed you these six months; 10% off to get reacquainted."
- "Thanks for referring customers; take 10% off any purchase in May."
- "Become a member and save on every product we offer."
- "Animal lovers' veterinary clinic special: Bring in your cat for shots and receive a free pound of cat food."
- "It's been a year since we cleaned your teeth; please call for your appointment."
- "Bonus sale for preferred customers: Only those who've bought above this dollar volume."
- "Thanks for your generous donation; here's how we've used your money to make a difference in someone's life. Now, could you give again so we can help others?" (Don't overdo this.)

Next, learn how to spend less, increase your rates of return, and lick fewer envelopes—in other words, how to do better at direct mail.

15

Squeeze the Most from the Post, Part II

The previous chapter showed a worst-case direct-mail scenario: a return of 1 percent or even less, and a cost per sale of up to $188. Now here's how to increase productivity, lower your cost per piece, and boost your response.

— Make Sure Your Mailings Work —

To use direct mail effectively, you've got to use accurate lists, screen out duplicates, match your offer to your targeted list, and create an effective marketing package.

Accurate Lists

Unfortunately, the only sure test is to mail out and wait for undeliverable pieces. Put your return address on the outside of your envelope; for bulk mail, include the phrase "forwarding and return postage guaranteed." You will pay to send mail on to the new address or back to you, but you'll know which names are still good.

Still, the more cleaning you can do *before* you mail, the better off you'll be. Remove any obsolete names and enter any address changes.

For high-volume mailing, consider using National Change of Address: a clearinghouse that matches the Postal Service's list of forwarding orders against your computerized list, for a fee. Ask your postmaster for Notice 47, National Change of Address.

If you rented a list, you deserve 95 percent deliverability or better. If undeliverables exceed this figure, ask for reimbursement for those names. If you get more than 10 percent back, get your money back on the entire purchase and switch to another mailing-list house next time. Not all brokers will guarantee this level of performance, so choose accordingly.

If you mail primarily to existing clients, be vigilant about getting the names right. Your reputation for personal service will be seriously impaired if you mangle clients' names.

Purge Duplicates

Repeating the identical offer to the same client in the same mailing costs you needless money and presents you as a nuisance. Particularly when combining names from more than one list, weed out duplicates.

Computer mailing-list software can do this to some extent, but don't leave it up to the computer. It will either miss close matches or eliminate some unduplicated names (for instance, two households in the same building, or two branch offices at different addresses). So go over the list visually. If you see an uncommon name at both a street address and a P.O. box with the same first three zip code digits, it may be the same person.

Look, too, for variant but close names at the same address. For example, I legitimately get mail for Shel Horowitz, S. Horowitz, and Horowitz/Friedman (my wife's name is Friedman), at both my home address and my business P.O. box. Sloppy copying yields Morowitz, Horowicz, Hortwiz, and so on. And my street and business name get equally mangled. I've been known to get ten copies of an offer—what a waste!

Match Your List to Your Offer

By now, you should know this well enough to tell it back to me: Sell to the people who want to buy. Identify the problem you can solve, and mail only to those who need that benefit.

Infomercial guru Bill Myers proposes an interesting twist: do it backward. Find the best list you can, for instance, buyers of expensive gold coins within the past thirty days. Then identify the perfect product for this audience, write an offer that engages all their hot buttons, and laugh all the way to the bank.

Make Your Mailing Piece the Best It Can Be

There's no secret here. Experiment and monitor the results closely. Mail out versions with different headlines, illustrations, body copy, and the like. Test different price points. But test only one or two variables at a time. Code each version separately, and mail them at the same time, to different people on the same list. As results shift in favor of one version, vary another element. Test-market and refine over and over, until you know your mailing is a winner. And continue monitoring the results. Any marketing material will lose its punch eventually; when yours stops working—whether it's six months or sixty years after you introduced it—be ready to replace it.

— Creative Ways to Save Money —

All the techniques in this section are variations on two themes: (1) share the cost with someone else, and (2) include additional pieces whenever you mail. Either way, you come out far ahead.

Traditional Co-op Advertising

Just as in display and Yellow Pages advertising, co-op mailing money is available from manufacturers. They may supply you with promotional materials, including glossy four-color fliers you couldn't afford to produce yourself. But evaluate their marketing materials before using them. Make sure they focus on benefits to the user. Otherwise, either replace or augment the manufacturer's materials with customer-centered marketing—and if adding your own flier, make sure yours is seen first.

Since many firms have little experience with co-operative direct mail, you get to educate them—and you propose the terms. Try offering prominent mention of their product in return for 30 percent of the mailing cost.

Bundling

Enhance the value of your product—and thus its direct-mail marketability—by combining complementary products that add value, for less money than buying them all separately. Bundle your own products together, or items from different producers. In the latter case, all the manufacturers share the marketing cost.

Here's a real-life example: To compete with integrated software that includes all these functions, four different software companies bundled together a word processor, spreadsheet, database, and graphics package. One company coordinated marketing. The same company also sold the word processor separately—but offered a free grammar-checker.

Big companies do this all the time; you've undoubtedly seen ads that offer bundled goods—for instance, "Buy a picnic cooler and get a free bag of charcoal briquettes." In these cases, the second manufacturer helps defray the promotional costs while adding value and sales to both products. Bundling can also provide incentive for a fast order: The bundled product becomes a premium if the customer acts soon enough.

Do add real value, though. You won't get much extra sales if you throw in a pencil with every purchase of a car.

Do Your Own Coupon Mailer

The whole premise of coupon mailers and postcard decks is lowering the cost of mailing by sharing postage and printing. Why not take this a step further and cut out the coupon broker?

You and other mailers with complementary products can prepare mailing inserts from all your businesses, share the labor and/or cost of addressing and stuffing the envelopes, and split the postage. For instance, a photographer, florist, caterer, dress designer, musician, jeweler, and printer could mail together to future bridal couples. The co-op could even add a bundling component, by providing discounts if several of the services are selected, or even organizing a "we will plan your entire wedding" package for one-stop convenience.

Many businesses can share in a venture. If each business makes up a one-third-page flier, up to 30 businesses can share first-class postage of 1.1 cents each per piece. A trial mailing of 100 packets will then cost each business $1.10 for postage, another 3.33 cents for envelopes (at 1 cent each), and (at $3.00 per hundred per side) about $1 for printing—or a total of $2.13 per business, inclusive of all costs. That's a mere 2 cents per envelope! If you can get even one new customer, you've made money. If only 10 businesses participate, each business would still only pay $6.42 per hundred-piece mailing, or 6.5 cents per prospect. (Because the added value may significantly increase your rate of return, and because different offers will appeal to different recipi-

> *The key to success with a very small mailing is pinpoint-accurate targeting; the people reading your message must want what you have to sell.*

ents, you can test out a sample of 100 instead of the 500 I recommended earlier. When everyone reports their results, you'll know the total effectiveness of the mailing—hopefully in the 10 percent range or better—as well as the results from each individual coupon.)

A private mailing of a one-sided flier would cost 37 cents per envelope; the one to two resultant orders must yield at least $18.50 to $37 each just to break even on mailing—not counting other costs. But in a 30-member co-op, the same two $18.50 orders leave $34.87 for those other costs. If your product doesn't cost much to manufacture or ship, you're already making a profit.

The key to success with a very small mailing is pinpoint-accurate targeting; the people reading your message must want what you have to sell. If that same group offering bridal services sent a mailing to 100 homeowners, they'd be lucky if any of them got one response.

How do you get such a targeted list? Let's use the bridal example again. Many communities have annual bridal fairs. One company could gather names at the show, or names could be rented from the show organizers. Alternatively, one person in the co-op could read the engagement notices in the paper. The co-op could prepare the mailing and the designated member would address envelopes as needed.

Generate Follow-up Sales

If you only sell one product once, direct mail is the wrong venue; the return will not be worth the expense. Direct mail works best when your product line is diversified. Therefore, the sooner you can compile a catalog, the better. You invested time, energy, and money converting prospects into customers—so sell them other products! We'll cover catalogs further in the next chapter.

Since postage is the most expensive part of direct mail, every time anything goes from your office to the customer, include a relevant, targeted offer. Enclose marketing materials when answering an inquiry, shipping a product, mailing an invoice (though you'll save money if you include your invoice with your product shipment), replying to a customer service request . . . Let your products work together so each one increases the desirability of all the others.

This technique is especially useful for those who sell information. If every response to a query about a product listed in a classified ad goes out with a typed list of other products available, you may well get orders without having to advertise; the prospect may be interested in other products you didn't list.

Don't limit yourself to your own mailings, though. Exchange fliers with other companies so that you can both mail to each other's customers. Or pay a complementary firm to include your offer in their mailings. And once again, always try to list in others' catalogs.

Let Your Names Earn Their Keep

Your mailing list itself can defray costs. If you've done the methodical targeting and coding I've suggested, you have an intensely marketable commodity once it gets up above a few hundred names. Keep it thoroughly current and mail out often; your list will be especially valuable.

You'll command a premium price if you handle and market your own list rental. Still, a regular list broker can generate additional income without any hassles. Plus, you can barter your names for another list.

Make sure any agreement with a list broker specifies a fixed percentage of the rental fee every time your list is used (either in money or credit), and the right to continue using your own list without restriction or charge. Also negotiate approval rights; you want to see who's mailing what to your list. If it's a direct competitor or an offensive offer, refuse it.

Be aware of the negative effects on your customers; they probably won't be happy when you begin to rent their names. And *never* rent out your in-house e-mail list; the backlash will be strong and the damage permanent.

— Explore Two-Level Selling —

Just as in classified advertising, you may sell in one step or two. A preliminary postcard to entice a request for more information is less expensive than a letter, and your follow-up mailings will go only to people who've already *identified themselves* as serious prospects. Properly handled, this method has several advantages:

- The additional information is requested, thus more carefully read.
- The prospect feels in control of the process.
- Repeat contact makes the reader feel familiar with your company and your offer, and reinforces your image.
- You've established the potential for further contact; thus, you have the beginning of a long-term selling relationship.

Here's an example of someone who did it right. Just after my traveling notebook computer suddenly fried its video circuitry and main memory, I received a teaser mailing about an extremely lightweight, low-cost notebook computer. It included a picture, a price, and a phone number—not much else. I called and gave my name and address; within two days I had a packet of information and a complete price list. The business owner also included a handwritten note with his name and an 800 number to call if I had more questions.

— Avoid Calluses —

The actual work of preparing a mass mailing is not pleasant. Presorting involves not just stuffing envelopes in the right order, but meeting complex and precise Postal Service regulations.

Metered mail is certainly a time saver, and some postage meters will even seal your envelopes for you. Also, if you do regular mass mailings, a Postal Service–approved permit box (called an indicia) can either be preprinted on your envelopes or applied with a rubber stamp. Indicias are less personal than a hand-applied stamp. For specific mailings where tone is important—such as to a donor's list of people who've contributed $100,000 or more—use hand-applied first-class stamps.

There's no need to destroy your tongue licking stamps and envelopes, though. Try this: stack up eight or ten envelopes so that their gummed flaps are all showing. Drag a wet sponge across all the glue at once, and then rapidly close each flap. Press down hard on the completed stack, and voilà, sealed envelopes! Use the sponge for stamps, too. Fold eight or ten stamps at a time along the perforations, run them over the sponge, tear off, and press (or just use the peel-and-stick stamps). Unless you're Superman, ten is about the maximum you can do at a time before the glue dries out.

If you don't want to lick your own stamps, consider six ways to get help (provide adequate supervision for the last three):

Lettershops

Businesses exist to serve your mailing needs. A lettershop will take your mailing, acquire the list, stuff it, and send it out. Some lettershops may also write copy and coordinate printing for you. They have specialized equipment such as Cheshire label applicators, which enable them to work closely with mailing-list houses. Sometimes they will even deliver it to the nearest regional mail depot, thus saving several steps over mailing from your local post office. And, because they qualify for the complete line of postal discounts, some lettershops may actually be cheaper than doing the mailing yourself.

Order Fulfillment

You can also farm out filling the orders. If you've ever wondered why a magazine that is based in California is shipped from Colorado or Ohio, it's because the magazine uses a subscription fulfillment house. These companies will warehouse your merchandise, pack it, and ship it out.

Or leave order fulfillment in the hands of the manufacturer. You deduct your commission, then provide the names, addresses, and items and quantities ordered; the company "drop-ships" it directly to the customer.

Temporary Help

If you're doing a ten-thousand-piece mailing, hire four or five people for a day or two (students will be less expensive, but less reliable, than using a temp agency).

Mailing Party

Many hands make light work, as the cliché goes, so invite a few friends over to have a good time. It's fine to serve pizza, but keep the food away from the mailing! (Pretzels might be a better idea.)

Sheltered Workshops

Provide a community service: Hire your mail fulfillment out to a sheltered workshop. These are community agencies that provide simple jobs for people with mental or physical disabilities. You help them learn skills and discipline and enjoy gainful employment.

✦

As a copywriter, I tend to focus on the written word. But graphic presentation is just as important. Read on!

16

Visual Marketing

There must be a hundred different types of self-created media that rely on visual impact to attract attention. Many of these can be quite cost-effective.

You already know the principles of effective display advertising, which we discussed in chapters 4 and 12. Designing a flier, table tent, sign, package, or other visual marketing aid is similar, except that you have to adjust the amount of information according to the medium you're using—people have more time to absorb a table tent than a bumper sticker, for instance. What you learn about producing effective fliers and signs will apply as easily to almost all types of visual marketing. Thus, we'll focus in detail on posters, fliers, and signs.

— Posters and Fliers —

A flier is a piece of paper that you hand to someone, post for people to see, insert in a newspaper, or deliver to someone's mailbox or fax machine. It can be any size and any range of slickness. It has a headline, body copy, and possibly graphics. It may include tear-offs or an order form.

A poster is a large flier, usually at least tabloid size and often much larger, designed especially to be put up on a wall or in a store window. Often, posters are on thicker stock (sometimes even on cardboard). And they tend, by and large, to be professionally designed and polished in appearance.

— Making Effective Fliers —

The most important decision you will make about a flier is whether or not you will post it on walls, in windows, and/or on bulletin boards. If the answer is yes, your flier must be clearly visible on a crowded bulletin board and able to attract attention from people walking by on their way to something else.

If you're not sure whether you'll be posting your flier, it may make sense to do two different versions: one for bulletin boards and another to distribute individually. That way, you'll be able to design each version with the strengths of its distribution medium in mind.

Posted Fliers

Typically, a posted flier will be seen only briefly, as people walk past. And if you live in an area similar to mine, with a large number of fliers and a small number of bulletin boards, your flier will be posted on a busy stairway in a shopping mall or in a crowded corridor of a university building, jammed up against a dozen other fliers—and papered over within a few days.

A successful posted flier stops passersby in their tracks, but doesn't keep them very long. A large, bold headline is essential, and a graphic is helpful in getting someone to stop and look. The main text should be restricted to just a few points, and again, the type should be pretty large.

Tear-offs and Other Take-Aways

A final consideration in putting together a posted flier is what kind of response you want from the flier's reader. You may just want to bring the reader to an event or announce the availability of a product at your store. In those cases, you may not need to leave the reader with a concrete action step.

But many fliers incorporate a next step for the reader: something to take away. If you're trying to sell a product, it's nearly essential. That way, someone can grab your number while walking past and call you later, when they aren't in such a rush.

Keep your take-away useful. A phone number by itself is not enough; you need a couple of words to remind your prospect of your offer. Otherwise, when your prospects empty their bags, wallets, and pockets days or weeks later, they'll come across a scrap of paper with your number, and say, "What's this doing in my pocket? I don't remember anything about it." It goes into the trash and you've lost your chance to hook an interested prospect.

There are several ways to provide this action step: tear-offs at the bottom of or all the way around the flier; a stack of cards or order forms in a pocket or attached by a nail, stacking several fliers together with an invitation to take one, providing space for passersby to sign their names, to name a few possibilities.

Don't paper the walls with your flier or cover up others—it's rude; take down expired ones to make room. But if you have thirty feet of bulletin board in a corridor, you can safely put up three to five copies of your flier. Run it off on several different colors of paper. That way, when you come across a bulletin board dominated by yellow and pink fliers, you can put up a blue or green one for extra visibility. Vary your placement—put some high, some low, and some in the middle, so people of different heights can easily find your flier. Also vary the fliers they're next to.

Nonposted Fliers

A flier that you design to hand to someone, or to appear as the reader opens an envelope, doesn't need to scream so loudly for attention; you don't have to worry so much about making it eye-catching and can concentrate on giving a more detailed, informative sales pitch.

You also don't need any kind of tear-off or response form right on the flier. Include an address and/or phone number in the body of the flier, but enclose your response form as a separate piece of paper.

Thus, you have a lot more room for your real message, and can have a smaller headline and considerably more body copy. Instead of three or four points in a bulleted list, you might include three paragraphs of your strongest sales message.

Design and Cost Considerations

You can pay three cents per flier for high-volume photocopies—or fifty dollars per poster for a small-run, four-color job that cost several hundred dollars for design work and an equal amount for printing.

In general, with any visual material, I suggest you make the product look professional. But don't spend a lot of money on the design if you can do it for less. You probably don't need four-color printing, halftone photos, ink bleeds, die-cuts, foil embossing, or a lot of the other fancy tricks that jack up the price. But attractively designed type done on a laser printer is cheap, professional, and effective; in most situations, it's an excellent way to go.

Of course, you have to match your product to your audience. If you're putting something up on bulletin boards in an elementary school, and your message is aimed at the students rather than the teachers, you may actually want to scrawl something out by hand with a wide-point marker—you'll be meeting your prospects on their own design level, and it will look familiar and feel like it was created by one of their peers. But if you're marketing a luxury product to the very wealthy, you'll want to pull out all the stops, using full color, a professional designer, and the highest-resolution typesetting you can find (2,400 dots per inch or more).

Usually, a laser-printed flier provides a comfortable and affordable middle ground. But in some industries, professionally designed one-sheets—four-color fliers on slick paper—have become an art form. See the flier on the next page as an example.

If your competitors' materials look like this, a simple one-color laser copy isn't going to make it. In large quantities, the extra cost per piece for the fancy design work diminishes; you're amortizing the cost of the designer and the extra press work across the entire run. Listen to Lois Barber of 20/20 Vision: "If you print 50,000 copies of a two-color trifold brochure, it can get down to 4 cents a copy, whereas if you're printing 10,000, the cost is 15 cents apiece."

There are five principal design elements in any visual piece: type, graphics, color, texture, and size/shape.

Type

Type is the character of the letters you use: their shape, intensity, and quality. We'll look first at quality.

In our technological age, there's no excuse for a sloppy product. While even a few years ago you could get away with handwritten fliers, or a mixture of handwriting, typing, and rub-on headlines, the computer revolution has raised people's standards. It's also made it absurdly easy to produce professional work in a matter of minutes, and at almost no cost.

Note, though, that the computer revolution has also made it easy to generate incredible ugliness. Don't use more than two—or, at the very most, three—typeface families in any one flier. And make sure your typefaces complement each other; it's all too easy for them to clash. Also, avoid the currently popular "ran-

som note" style, where every letter is a different size and weight; it's almost impossible to read.

In nearly all cases, I recommend that you do your fliers on a 600 dpi (dots-per-inch) or better PostScript laser printer—or, at the least, a top-of-the-line color inkjet. When you want your flier to look even better, bring your disk to a service bureau and get it typeset.

Graphics

Your choices in graphics run the gamut. Many successful fliers don't use graphics at all—just an eye-catching headline.

Remember that the text itself can work graphically. Use elements such as italic and bold, as well as various sizes and weights of type, to create a graphic effect; or arrange the type into a visual shape. Specialty fonts can also incorporate graphic elements.

Of course, if you have a logo, it should be on your fliers. But a small logo down at the bottom may not be enough graphic impact for the task at hand. So either use a large version of your logo, or else incorporate a large graphic to catch attention and a small logo to reinforce your unified image.

The next step up in complexity is to plug clip art—camera-ready art in the public domain (in other words, unhindered by copyright restrictions)—into your fliers. Clip art is available either in printed scrapbooks or on computer disks; the latter allow you to manipulate an image if it's close but not quite right. If photocopying, look for high contrast and avoid pictures with lots of detail.

For original art, your best bet is a line drawing. Make the lines thick enough to be seen easily.

Finally, there are more complex graphics, including photos and professional illustrations. Complex illustrations will require more care in printing. For instance, a photograph requires halftones and offset printing for best reproduction.

Color

Black ink on white paper may be fine, but always consider whether your piece can benefit from color. What are the advantages of color?

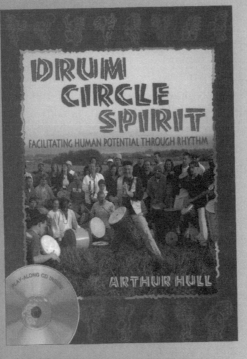

- Your flier stands out and is more attractive on a crowded bulletin board.
- You can highlight benefits.
- Color can clarify and help explain—for instance, in a chart of sales revenues, different colors can show the relative strengths of different items at a glance, or an exploded parts diagram can be much clearer if different kinds of parts are in different colors.
- For some items, full color is the only way to demonstrate the product—if, for instance, you design packaging for retail merchandise.

There are two ways to get color into a document: with ink and with paper. In both cases, the range of options is immense.

The three most common reproduction techniques are (1) offset printing, (2) photocopying, and (3) multiple originals from a computer and laser printer.

For simple documents—black ink, simple graphics that reproduce well—high-speed photocopying is fine. You can do as many or as few as you need. If you have your own equipment, black-and-white copying may be cost-competitive with printing services at surprisingly large quantities.

With photocopying, until a few years ago, color had been pretty much restricted to the choice of paper stock. Color copying does exist, but it is expensive—typically around one dollar per page, at this writing—and generally practical only for very small runs.

However, some high-end copiers can actually add spot color, making it practical and economical, even on short runs. These machines can manipulate images in many ways:

- Change the color of a black- or red-ink original—or even change different sections of the same original into different colors
- Highlight or black out any elements of the page, by circling the area with a marker
- Fill in an outline to generate shaded areas or reverse type
- Pump out high-quality copies rapidly

- Add a notation as if you were using yellow sticky-pads

If you can find a copy shop with this capacity, your fliers will certainly stand out! Few people know about these features, even though they've been around for almost a decade.

Printing originals from a laser printer makes sense up to about one hundred copies; quality is higher than from photocopies, and shaded art will reproduce well. High-quality "dye-sublimation" color output from computers has improved dramatically of late, though purchase and per-page costs can still be daunting.

That leaves offset printing as the only real choice for generating large amounts of a document with color ink. In offset printing, a mask is made from a photographic image of the page, and the mask is used to press the ink onto paper. Ink colors are made up of blends from four primary colors: blue, yellow, red, and black. Printers and graphic artists often define colors either by where they fall on the CMYK (cyan, magenta, yellow, black) scale, or by their Pantone number. Pantone is a widely used system for shading inks; go into any offset print shop and ask to see swatches.

Each of the four colors requires a separate mask and a separate run through the presses. Each run must be precisely aligned with all the others, or else both the colors and the graphics will be skewed. It calls for skill and precision, as well as extra labor to clean the press between colors. As a result, four-color magazine- or brochure-quality printing can be quite expensive.

Reminder: Printing quality, prices, and turnaround times vary widely. Get at least four estimates on any print job, and ask for work samples and references before making your decision.

You can gain some of the benefits of color while keeping expense down by opting for one of these four techniques:

Colored Paper. You can get solid colors in almost any imaginable hue: somber brown, fluorescent pink, deep red . . . Most copy shops keep a good selection on hand. If you do choose to use colored paper, select a color that's both appropriate to your message and easy to read with your flier on it. You can also get specialty paper, with borders, subliminal graphics, full-blown abstract or landscape designs, preprinted spot color, color blends, graduated fills, and various other special effects. I've found the best values in Quill's Laser and Inkjet catalog, 800-789-1331, and, believe it or not, at Kinko's retail outlets. The latter is an especially good choice if you need only a handful of copies, since you can buy one sheet at a time.

Specialty papers have become a booming business in the past few years, with over a dozen companies jumping into the act. Prices and quality vary widely, and sometimes the catalog picture varies from the actual stock. These papers are usually cost-effective only for short runs. If you're doing several thousand, it's probably much cheaper to let your printer or designer add a spot color or border as a design element—or use a company that will print in bulk on their specialty paper, such as Beaver Prints, 814-742-6070. They'll even mail for you.

Note, though, that certain styles are showing up everywhere, and their impact decreases from overuse (for instance, Paper Direct's purple-green). If you've seen more than two or three other companies' promotions on a particular stock, leave it aside and choose something more individualistic.

Also, make sure that your preprinted paper enhances, rather than interferes with, your message. I once received an unfortunate choice on speckled recycled stock, offering laser cartridge recharges. Unfortunately, the effect reminded me of smeared, defective cartridges, and that vendor didn't get my business! There are, of course, many excellent recycled papers. Use environmentally friendly papers and soy inks to great effect, especially if you're reinforcing a "green" message. But use a grade that's good enough that you have to point it out, for example, "Printed with soy ink on recycled paper."

An interesting new product idea available from several of these paper houses is the photo-preprinted brochure. You buy a paper that already has a color photo on it and is set up for three-column brochure printing. If they happen to have the right picture for you, this will be a winner. (Another alternative: find a CD-ROM photo clip art collection with the right picture—but this means expensive four-color printing.)

Most of the reputable companies will send you a sample sheet to try out, so I suggest picking three or four styles you're interested in on a short-run project, and then printing a sample of each before ordering several boxes.

Another way to do short-run spot color is through laser foils. You run off your document on a laser printer, then cut out a piece of colored foil, plop it on the part you want colorized, reinsert the page into your printer, and run a blank page. It looks gorgeous, but since each page has to be done individually, it's quite labor intensive.

Of course, as decent-quality color copiers and color laser printers continue to drop in price, more and more copy shops and service bureaus will provide them. You can get absolutely stunning output at relatively reasonable prices. Or work out an attractive design using several shades of gray, black, and white—and print it out on a laser printer with at least 600 dpi resolution. There's no easier or cheaper way to get high-impact visuals and ultra-crisp text.

Single-Color Ink. While it does cost more than black ink, using a different ink color is not costly. Using a different color may add ten to thirty dollars to the cost of the same job in black ink, but if you're doing hundreds or thousands of fliers, the extra charge will add only a few cents per sheet. Choose an ink that has high contrast against the color of paper you're using; bright reds and blues are often good choices for visibility. Avoid mushy colors such as brown or pink.

Spot Color. Better still is spot color—using a colored ink for just a few graphic elements, while keeping the rest in black. This technique dramatically increases visibility, but only requires two runs through the printing press. A bright red or blue might be effective: on a headline, to emphasize a word such as "Free," to highlight an offer's expiration date, or to provide a visually interesting break between sections with a horizontal or vertical rule.

Gang Runs. If you're patient, save on color printing by asking your printer to gang your job with another one of the same color. The press doesn't have to be cleaned again between the other customer's order and yours, so you save the cleaning charge. But before you commit to this, get some sense of how long the wait will be. Or bring several jobs in the same colors in at once; you'll pay less than if you bring them in one at a time.

Texture

Texture also adds interest, and reinforces your image. The simplest way to change texture is by switching paper stocks. Papers are available with fine and coarse, smooth and bumpy textures. Formal documents are often created on paper with a "laid," linen, or parchment finish. You can get glossy paper that shines, flat paper that absorbs light, a thick stock with flecks in it that looks unprocessed or recycled.

You can also create textures through printing tricks, but of course they do add to the cost. Diecuts allow part of the following page to show through, provide a nice tear-off edge for a coupon, or create an unusual shape. Foil or acetate overlays give texture to a small part of your document. Large sweepstakes mailings often use foil stickers. Embossing raises letters in a part of the text. In general, however, I'd stay away from all this kind of thing. It's overkill, and you'd spend the money more effectively by putting out more copies of a flier that's simple and to the point.

Size/Shape

The final element in making a flier distinctive is the size and shape. Paper is usually sold in standard sizes: 8½ x 11, 8½ x 14, and 11 x 17 inches (or their British equivalents). Your flier can stand out by trimming from one of these standard sizes to something unusual—if you plan to mail your flier, be certain you can get envelopes to fit! Trimming also allows you to get a "bleed" effect—ink running off the edge of the paper—without having to limit yourself to a printer who can do bleeds on full-sized paper. Simply trim off the uninked margin and you have your bleed. For added distinction, trim your paper at an angle; since virtually every flier is a rectangle, yours will stand out with its odd shape, particularly if you're using a striking and uncommon paper color. For instance, with one cut you can do two fliers: one on a triangle pointing up, and one on a triangle pointing down (or print one half upside down, so after cutting they're all identical).

— Bumper Stickers and Decals —

A bumper sticker is just a very small flier with adhesive backing. Since the people who read it are usually driving, the letters must be big enough to read at highway speeds. With space at a premium, its message has to be short and concise: no more than eight words, and one to two is best. Bumper stickers make sense for slogans, political campaigns, and name recognition of a business. Decals can be used on a wall—to denote membership in a professional organization, for instance.

— Signs, Banners, and Flags —

We're all familiar with storefront signs and movie marquees, but that's just the beginning. There's a whole world of signs out there.

For any sign that is displayed outside of your office or store, zoning ordinances probably apply. Check on what you need before you pay to have any sign created or installed. There may be restrictions on size, placement, and even—in historic districts—color or typeface. Conform to the regulations, and apply for a permit if you need one. Otherwise, your sign might be confiscated or destroyed. Generally, sign permit fees are fairly nominal.

Many signs can be enhanced with lighting—or ruined, if you go for the gaudy look. Consult with a lighting designer to get an effect that matches your business image. As for specific types of signs . . .

Stationary Sandwich Boards

A pair of signs on two sides of an easel, placed on the sidewalk during business hours and folded up in the store at night. Great for businesses that don't have street-level storefronts or that are on a side street close to a busy corner.

Walking Sandwich Boards

A person wears a sign on the front and back, and either walks up and down the street or stays in one place. The sign holder can attract more attention by dressing in costume—particularly if the costume is related to the message—and add effectiveness by handing out fliers. Ideal for a very short-term offer, such as today's restaurant lunch special.

Other Sidewalk Signs

Many stores use signboards with moveable letters, which work on much the same principle as a movie marquee. However, they stand on the sidewalk instead of being overhead. Like a movie sign, they allow you to make one permanent investment in a sign with a message that keeps changing. Unfortunately, these signs are usually very ugly—especially the kind with a row of light bulbs flickering on and off. They are also vulnerable to vandalism; you may find letters stolen, or words rearranged to a very different message, or someone may just punch a hole in your sign one night.

In short, the principle is sound but the execution is tacky. But sooner or later, someone will come up with an attractive version, using quality, interesting lettering and a lockable clear cover, perhaps on a wooden frame instead of the plastic and metal eyesores. Then businesses will be able to enjoy the flexibility of a changing message without sacrificing the appearance of quality.

Store Window Signs

If you have a store window, or even an upper-floor office visible from the street, use your window as a sales tool. Window signs can be permanent or temporary, and can take many forms. Hang a computer banner, use stencils or rub-on lettering, or display a poster.

Good uses for window signs include announcing sales or special promotions; calling attention to new product lines or personnel (hair salons use this technique constantly); highlighting a product you might not expect to find—for example, I once saw a safety equipment store with two window signs announcing cellular phones. Without these signs, it would not have occurred to me to look for a mobile phone among the oxygen tanks and stretchers. (It does make sense, though: Emergency services need reliable two-way communication between the base and a rescue vehicle.)

Pickets

Get a group of theater students to stage an event in front of your business. Coach one of them to be a press spokesperson, and let them carry picket signs with sales messages such as "Best Prices in Town," "Thank You, George, You Run a Great Store," "Can't Beat Your Service." Then have a friend report it to the media (make sure your picketers will be there long enough to be photographed). In this situation, you wouldn't want to notify the media in advance yourself—although your pickets could—because you don't want to appear as the instigator of the picket. (Thanks to author and business consultant Barbara Lambesis for this idea.)

"Mini-Billboards"/Point-of-Purchase Aids

I've coined the term "mini-billboards" to refer to any marketing material at the point of purchase that grabs the reader's attention—for instance, table tents (those little folded cards on restaurant tables promoting drink and dessert specials). Once the customer's menu is taken away, it's the only thing to read until the food comes, so it gets lots of attention.

Other types include countertop stands—such as those coin-collecting displays for various medical research charities—literature dispensers, and good old-fashioned on-the-shelf labels announcing new products or low prices. See chapter 34 for more on in-store point-of-purchase aids.

Banners

A banner is a long, narrow sign stretching across a building, over a street, above a doorway, and so on. Banners are used very successfully to promote large-scale events. If there is some charitable interest, or the ability to promote the entire business community at once, the town itself may be willing to hang a banner. In my own town, City Hall has flown banners announcing, among other things:

- Tour de Trump (a national bicycle race)
- A Taste of Northampton (restaurant street festival)
- Annual Crafts Gallery Walk
- Button Up Northampton (a weatherization program)
- First Night (a nonalcoholic New Year's Eve festival of live entertainment)

It's even sometimes possible to hang a more controversial banner in a public space. An abortion rights group used a banner in a college town near my home. And, strung across 125th Street in New York, I once saw two banners several blocks apart, proclaiming "Jesus Is Lord in Harlem" and promoting a particular church—despite numerous other churches and a large Islamic community.

While it's great to have a banner attached to City Hall or flying across the main shopping street, don't neglect this tool even without municipal sponsorship. There's a bank in town that hangs a banner welcoming students every fall, and another congratulating graduates in the spring. Other businesses use banners hung over their own doorways to announce sales, vacation giveaways, or other special offers. Once again, double-check on your town's rules *before* you commission your banner!

Flags

Flags are small banners, supported at only one end. A few years ago, red, white, and blue flags that say "Open" or "Sale" became popular. Personally, I think the Open banners are fairly silly, unless this isn't obvious. For instance, if you've been closed for a while, have just opened a new location, or are operating behind someone else's construction site, it could make sense to use a flag such as this for the short term. A sale flag is a much better idea, because it says something unusual and implies a need to act quickly. But better than those mass-produced ones would be one you did up yourself, featuring your business name. Examples: "During Construction, Enter Joe's on State Street"; "Office Products 20% Off Through August 15"; "Two-for-One Lunch—Ann's Emporium."

Lawn Signs

Lawn signs are either permanent or temporary. Permanent signs are often used at corporate headquarters, housing complexes, and colleges, where buildings are frequently set back from the road on a campus. If your building is set back from the street—even if it's only thirty feet from the road—consider a permanent lawn sign if you want people to find you easily.

Temporary lawn signs are most commonly used in political campaigns. But they could do so much more even in that context. Too often, a sign just has the name of the candidate and the office he or she is seeking. The sign creates visibility, but doesn't provide any useful information. Consider the impact of these two signs:

> **JONES**
> CITY COUNCIL

> **SMITH**
> HOUSING-JOBS-ENVIRONMENT

Only the second one gives me a reason to vote.

The same principle applies to issue referenda:

```
SAVE UNION JOBS

NO ON 4
```

has much more impact than

```
VOTE NO ON

QUESTION 4
```

For businesses, temporary lawn signs can be used much like flags and banners—to draw attention to a short-term attraction. All it takes is some oaktag, three pieces of wood (one each across the top and bottom of the back of the sign, and one tall one from the top crosspiece to the ground), and some nails and staples. If you don't want it to look too crude, buy some large stencils and paint through them for nicely formed, even lettering. If you employ lawn signs frequently, buy the oaktag in bulk and save the slats for reuse.

A variant, which I'm not too thrilled about because it creates a lot of clutter, is the old Burma Shave style of sign, where you drive past a series of small signs, each one with only part of the message—one word, or even one letter. But in this environmentally and aesthetically conscious age, I'd be cautious.

There's one more kind of lawn sign—the landscaped one. Bushes and plantings form words, logos, and borders. It provides an attractive, eye-catching result, and can be very large (I've seen them billboard size and larger). However, this is obviously a lot of work to set up and even more work to maintain over the years. To fit in the rest of your work, you'd have to hire a gardener.

Of course, if you sell anything related to gardening, landscaping, horticulture, and so forth, this is

a perfect vehicle for you, because it emphasizes your product and expertise both subliminally and overtly. If you can work with plants to benefit yourself, you're the one to assist your customers with their gardening needs.

Vanity Plates

Can you condense your message to six to eight alphanumeric characters? Get a vanity license plate. For about fifty dollars, you put a very short advertising message in front of every person who sees your car, day in and day out. Use them in conjunction with bumper stickers and auto sunshades (or, if you have a commercial vehicle, painted or magnetic lettering) to provide contact information. And if your business is hard to find, mention your car as a landmark when giving directions.

This is one area where creative phonetic spelling is just fine. Some examples: FLWRS-4U, RENOV8, FIX CAR, TEETH, COPIES, BASBAL.

Navigational Signs

A growing number of states and communities are restricting outdoor signage, particularly along scenic and secondary roads. Billboards are outlawed entirely in several states. Instead, the state provides standardized signs, clearly visible from the road but small enough that you have to slow down a bit to read them. The signs name an attraction or a business and may include a directional arrow and/or a mileage figure. These are actually a boon to the smallest businesses; they put even a one-person operation on the same footing as a huge tourist attraction with a staff of two hundred. If your community already uses these signs, find out how to get some to promote your business. If your state doesn't restrict billboards, get involved in a movement to adopt the standardized-small-sign model used in Vermont and Maine. You'll be seen as a blessing to your community, working to eliminate roadside eyesores. Meanwhile, you're creating a level playing field for your own business to prosper.

A variant: If you run an educational institution, major business, or tourist attraction—or a roadside restaurant, gas station, or lodging house—talk to your highway department about attaching a small sign to the appropriate highway exits.

— Outdoor Advertising —

Large, stationary outdoor ads—on billboards, in and around sports and convention arenas, or on the walls of bus and train stations—are common. But are they effective? They're a great revenue source for the operator of the billboard or transit authority, but they serve primarily as reminder advertising—a luxury most small businesses can't afford. Reminder advertising is a great bonus if you don't have to keep paying for it; see the discussion of vanity plates above, or clothing later in the chapter. But in general, these signs can only reinforce other marketing—they serve merely to build name and image recognition, not move a prospect toward a purchase. Other forms of outdoor advertising—signs on the outsides of buses and taxis, skywriting, banners towed by planes—suffer from the same problems.

There are, however, four situations where this type of ad can be useful:

1. You rely on tourists or passersby finding you from a nearby highway, and you can trumpet those magic words, "This Exit." This works well for gas stations, motels, restaurants, factory outlets, and tourist attractions; it wouldn't be effective for anything geared primarily to the locals.
2. You're using geographical proximity in a more urban area, particularly if your business doesn't have a storefront on a main street with resultant high visibility. For instance, during tax season, the sign above would be a good ad at a nearby bus shelter. But it's often hard to contract for just a couple of specific bus shelters and train stations. Don't be talked into advertising throughout your city if you're trying to attract clients on the basis of your convenient, immediate location. If the agency won't cooperate, reach your prospects another way.

3. If you own a blank wall, you could paint a permanent billboard—especially if it adjoins your business and thus also serves as a storefront sign.
4. Finally, if you can get outdoor advertising donated to promote a charitable event, it will reinforce your message at no cost to you.

— Car and Truck Signs —

A sign on your own vehicle can be quite effective, and you don't have to keep paying a fee to an advertising agency or transit company. You have a lot of freedom in design, and you can get dramatic impact and high visibility. Friends of mine have a window treatment business. It's very small, with two workers and two vans. But they have a superb, professionally designed logo and their company name on both vans. They use these vehicles not just to install window treatments, but also to pick their kids up at the YMCA, go to the beach, and drive around town; people see their vans, and their logo, all over the place. They have created the illusion of a large, professional operation.

Co-owner Heather McLaughlin commented, "Several people have said to me, 'Oh, you've been doing a lot of advertising lately.' But we haven't done any advertising at all recently; we've just had a lot of errands."

In some locations, you need to register your car or truck as a commercial vehicle in order to use permanent vehicle signs. Check your local laws before going ahead.

Driveable Billboards

Technology now exists to paint an entire vehicle with an advertising message—windows and all—and still have it safe to drive. From inside, it's like looking out the window, yet the coating appears opaque from the outside.

In my area, one local bus service offers these high-visibility advertising vehicles, and they've proven popular with several companies. Believe me, they get noticed!

Of course, you have to rent space on the bus. But nothing should prevent you from using the same technology on a private vehicle. You'll still have to pay to design and paint it, but that's only a one-time cost—and you have control over where and how your message is displayed. Think of the impact if you park a large painted truck at an appropriate trade show, with the picture carrying right over onto the windows!

The only contact I know about is P&C Media, P.O. Box 779, West Springfield, MA, 01090, telephone 413-746-1626. But also check with your own local public transit companies or with shops that cater to industrial artists.

And speaking of trucks, have you noticed in the past few years how people have started using the sides of their delivery fleet to carry a big, bold, attractive marketing message? It seems to have started in the beer industry: a row of 15-foot-high frosty beer bottles on the side of a truck. It's beginning to spread to other industries—and frankly, as a driver, I kind of like it. They're a lot prettier to look at than the drab side of a plain (and usually dirty) truck, and make being stuck in traffic slightly more palatable.

Again, the start-up cost is likely to be significant—though cheaper if you can spread the design and labor costs over a whole fleet. Be sure to keep a line item in your budget for cleaning and touch-up, be-cause if these get tawdry, they'll reflect really badly on your company.

A probably cheaper alternative, though an annoying one: vehicles whose only purpose is to display an ad message. In New York City, for instance, I've seen large billboards on wheels, in a skinny frame that can move through dense traffic like a bicyclist. There could be a backlash from those who resent the extra traffic on those already overcrowded streets, but they might be useful to promote short-term events.

— Interior Bus and Train Placards —

Inside a mass transit vehicle, the situation is quite different than outside. First of all, you have a captive audience. People will be staring at your message for the entire length of their trip (especially if it's crowded and they are standing). And second, you can provide tear-off coupons with follow-up information, so you don't have to rely on the reader to remember your offer or contact info. Might be worth an experiment.

— Packaging —

Any product that you sell is packaged somehow; even no package at all is a statement about packaging. If you sell strictly through the mail or to people who are already buying services from you, packaging has relatively little marketing impact on a first-time purchase. But when you sell your own brand of items through any retail channel, packaging becomes crucial. Your item must stand out visually on the shelf next to a dozen similar items. Also, packaging can be informative in its own right—particularly on an item that will stare at the buyer for a long time. Think of the Wheaties cereal boxes and how much sports trivia they've imparted over the years. Or go to a health food store and look at a bottle of Dr. Bronner's soap; Bronner's complex and eccentric philosophy is outlined in detail, in tiny print that covers the entire label. Information can be combined with a sales pitch: This is why our product is good for you. Food manufacturers do this constantly.

Think of packages as three-dimensional fliers; all the rules of good design and cost-effectiveness apply. Packaging can be as simple as a label attached to a bag, or as complex as a nested Chinese box. But also consider these additional factors:

- Product visibility—can people see the product itself through the packaging?
- Environmental considerations—avoid the backlash against plastic blister packs, foam peanuts, nonrecyclable mixed materials, and excessive trash by keeping your packaging environmentally sound. Keeping packing simple—or, in some situations, eliminating it entirely—is not only better for the environment, but also cheaper. (You could even send out a press release describing your environmentally friendly packaging and its cost savings to the consumer—especially since you may be reducing or eliminating your ability to use the packaging for a marketing message.)
- Shape—a nontraditional shape costs more than a bag or rectangular box and is harder to display, but stands out more.
- In-store display stands (known as "dumps," for some reason)—will you be supplying them, and will the stores use them?

Advertising Specialties

There's a whole industry devoted to producing gifts to give your customers; these gifts are known as advertising specialties or premiums. They have become quite a bit more sophisticated in recent years, and the ability to gain some benefit has increased considerably.

Even the timeworn giveaways such as calendars and writing implements have improved. For instance, you can now get premium calendars with interesting, unusual art instead of the same old country scenes. You can also buy pens whose barrels are a nontraditional shape—one that can emphasize your message. (Chiropractors were early adopters of crooked-barrel pens. I have a Texas-shaped pen from Texas Instruments.) And quality is higher—goodbye to those dreadful hexagonal-barrel pens that stopped writing the third time someone used them!

Then there are also many, many new and interesting premium ideas. I've seen chocolate business cards (not cheap, but certainly memorable for a caterer or similar merchant), golf and fishing accessories, desk sets, custom-printed books . . . and one of my favorites, refrigerator magnets (they're very inexpensive, easy to customize, and really get used, although relatively few people see each one). Also consider products that allow the recipient to choose what to get—for instance, a real credit card with a fixed credit line.

How should you evaluate a potential premium purchase? With the same criteria as any other advertising buy. Examine:

- How well and often it will be used
- How many people will see it
- Whether those people include your target market
- The price per item, overall cost, and quality (cheap, chintzy premiums that feel shoddy and wear out quickly may do your image more harm than good)
- If additional customizations will be effective (for instance, the back of a two-sided T-shirt might often be hidden under an overshirt or sweater. A tote bag or an auto sunshade, on the other hand, benefits strongly from two-sided printing because the message can't be hidden.)

The ideal premium is something your prospect will use constantly and will expose the advertising message to as many people as possible. This is why apparel and canvas bags are so popular, even though the price per item can be significant. (Plastic bags, by contrast, have a very low price point in quantity, but they wear out quickly. Still, they can be used very effectively at trade shows, for instance. Use them to make an offer that brings people to your booth.)

The message itself should be easy to read and understand. Thus, don't expect much mileage out of sunglasses. The recipient will wear them, but the advertising message is too small to attract attention from passersby.

A recent arrival in the premium scene is the prepaid telephone debit card. They're a nice idea, but relatively expensive as outright gifts. Still, give them some consideration. Like apparel, they can be sold as well as given away. So if you only want to spend $1 per client, buy a bunch of imprinted $5 cards (ask about wholesale discounts, of course) and sell them for $4. Every time the recipient pulls out the card, he or she sees your name and remembers the 20 percent savings. Shop carefully; look not only at how much phone time you get for the money, but also whether you get six-second or full-minute billing, minimum charge per call, and so on.

Plan your premiums creatively. Think of an item that will be used frequently and actually remind users of how you help them. Examples: A solar-heating contractor could remind people of cost-free solar energy with a solar calculator, printed with a marketing message on the back; a jar opener could promote a kitchenware store or gourmet food shop; a computer dust cover keeps the dealer in the buyer's eye. Try premiums only if you can get the item produced at high quality and low price.

Auto Sunshades

Auto sunshades are one of the best values in specialty advertising. For a nominal cost, you get publicity from mobile billboards all over town. Give them away to your clients or sell them inexpensively. There's room for a fairly large, bold message, they provide a clear benefit to the user (who will therefore actually display it), and they are exempt from zoning or auto registration restrictions on signage. A client of mine used sunshades very effectively in

a political campaign. Using 8-inch-high letters in a penetrating blue ink, she did up a batch that just read "Mary Ford for Mayor" and sold them as campaign fundraisers. You could read them from three blocks away. She won the election by four hundred votes.

Try premiums only if you can get the item produced at high quality and low price.

Keep the design simple enough so you can use very large, bold lettering. Print a sales message on both sides, so that the user can't put it blank side out.

Calendars

If you've been thinking about calendars, consider not just the preprinted kind but also a custom design that you could produce in-house. A calendar doesn't have to have expensive four-color photographs to be used. Graphic elements can include original computer or hand-drawn images, clip art, or just an attractive mix of text and borders. Color ink can add dramatic impact, even if everything is shades of the same color. And software can automate the layout and day numbering. Find a copy of the April 1995 issue of *Technique* magazine for a great article on calendar making.

The possibilities for information content are endless. A few examples:

- Provide a timeline for seasonal activities related to your products (e.g., a garden store could offer guidelines on when to plant, prune, or harvest various products)
- List your own or your profession's upcoming events: speakers, entertainment, charity fundraisers, and so forth.
- Introduce the reader to interesting historical information (a great fundraiser for schools, museums, cause-related groups, and others; for

a good example, get a calendar from the War Resisters League, 339 Lafayette Street, New York, NY 10003).

- Highlight the graphics and printing capabilities of an artist or print shop.

Clothing and Tote Bags

Apparel is a great promotional item. Everybody loves new clothes, and a stylish T-shirt, hat, sweatshirt, jacket, or bag with your name, service, and logo can bring you visibility at times you can never predict. I regularly volunteer at a folk festival about three hours from my home, and whenever I wear my festival volunteer shirt, people stop me and ask me about the event. This is also a way to build an image in your community. For example, you could sponsor a high school or Little League sports team and create uniforms with your firm name.

Give attractive shirts or bags with your logo, slogan, and contact information as presents, use them as premiums, or even sell them to your customers. Some custom-print companies will do orders as small as two dozen.

In 1997, before my first time attending a giant national trade show for books, I made three shirts with the cover of my book, *The Penny-Pinching Hedonist: How to Live Like Royalty with a Peasant's Pocketbook*. Text above the cover: "The King of Frugal Fun." Below the cover, it had the name of my marketing book, my phone number, and my Web site address. The total cost was just under fifty dollars.

These shirts stayed usable through one regional and four national trade shows, and opened doors to many intriguing business possibilities. Various foreign publishers, literary agents, distributors, and vendors who could make my material available in new formats (audio, video, e-books) stopped me to discuss my books. In fact, the shirt made getting the contract to do the book you're holding much easier: Stephen Morris, Chelsea Green's publisher, was in his booth promoting the theme of Sustainable Hedonism. I pointed to my shirt and suggested we talk.

In short, I got my fifty dollars' worth many times over, and I wore them around town after I retired them from trade-show duty—and generated both interest in the books and press coverage.

Some other advertising specialties, such as mugs, can have similar impact. However, they won't be seen by the general public, whereas apparel will be.

Balloons

While balloons can have a logo, and serve some limited degree of direct promotion before they go flat, their best use is to help people find something: a grand-opening party, for instance. Three or four balloons tied to your mailbox or lamppost will let people know they've come to the right place, and attract the attention of passersby who hadn't known about your event.

✄

Beyond the visual stands content. If your marketing materials themselves provided valuable information to your prospects, do you think it would help business? Turn the page and find out.

17

A Substantial Impression: Publicity Materials Your Prospects Will Hold On To

Sometimes you want your marketing to hit the prospect right away as he or she walks by. But other times, you'll want to give the prospect something to hold on to: a constant reminder of what you can do for them, so when they're ready to act, they know how to find you.

Permanent marketing materials take many forms. We'll concentrate on five here: business cards, helpful hints, brochures, catalogs, and newsletters. These should provide a somewhat more lasting impression—and more depth—than a flier or poster, because the prospect will take it home and study it.

— Business Cards —

Hand out business cards to practically everyone: Pass them out whenever you're networking with someone or when you just need to tell a friend how to reach you. Drop them in fishbowls at trade shows. Give them to any customers or clients with whom you've had a decent experience. Tack them up on bulletin boards. Attach them to mailings. They're easy to file, easy to keep, and, if properly designed, can pack a marketing wallop. And their cost can be just pennies.

Business cards accomplish several marketing objectives. They:

- Increase your appearance of legitimacy (and therefore should be among the first investments a new business makes)
- List all your contact info in one convenient place
- Facilitate referrals from clients, community organizations, and others
- Provide an ongoing reminder of your service

The range of business card possibilities is broad. Consider some of these options:

Basic

Conventionally, a business card presents your name and title, your company logo, name, contact points, and possibly a slogan—not necessarily in that order. Give something more: a benefit. Remember, the paper size is small; use it efficiently. Your card should represent you as concisely but completely as possible—the essence of you or your agency.

Business cards are usually printed in multiples of 500, and you can pay anywhere from about $18 to $70 or more per 500 (a larger order will lower the cost per card).

Simple business cards usually are all in one color ink—black, more often than not. The traditional, conservative business-card formats are still fashionable, although more and more people are trying to put some visual impact into their cards—with eye-catching logos and designs, ink colors other than black, paper colors other than white, large type, and similar devices. I believe this is a good trend. It's not hard to create a memorable business card, and the cost doesn't increase much. The same visual tricks that work in a flier, such as spot or full color, reverses, and display type, can add a lot of life to a business card.

Ultra-Basic

Here's a rock-bottom approach for small quantities: Type a master, copy and paste it until it fills out the page, and print out your 12-copy master on a laser printer (if you don't own one, rent time at a copy shop).

If your software permits it, this trick will make the final copy look almost as good as typesetting: Type it twice as big as you actually want it on your computer screen, and then print it out at a 50 percent reduction. This firms up the letters and doubles resolution. Your image is far sharper, and no one will believe you did it on a laser printer.

Copy the master sheet with the 12 cards on card stock in the colors of your choice (it should be about 2 cents per sheet more than the standard photocopy cost); then separate them with a paper cutter. Forty-two sheets will produce 504 business cards. If your cost is 6 cents per sheet, that's $2.52 for the bunch—only half a cent apiece! At 8 cents a sheet it's still only $3.36.

Two great times for this technique are:

1. When you know some information on the card will change soon. An acquaintance who runs a car repair service out of his home and moves frequently runs his cards off in small batches to avoid being stuck with large quantities of obsolete cards.

2. If you're experimenting with several different business card styles. Pass several different ones out to your clients and ask for their feedback!

Still, remember that professionally printed business cards can often be found for less than $30 per thousand—and they look a whole lot better.

"Mini-Fliers"

An eye-catching, attention-grabbing business card can serve as a very small flier, displayed on bulletin boards. Use large, dark type, and perhaps a high-contrast graphic. Consider all the tricks we discussed for spicing up fliers, too.

The two cards below are done in one color, but they use various tricks to stand out on the page.

Two standard-sized business cards.

Two-Sided

Any piece of paper has both a front and a back, but most people use only one side. Jeffrey Lant is a firm advocate of using the second side of a business card for an additional marketing message. Lately, this seems to be a growing trend—but include a message on each side to turn the card over!

Fold-Outs

Take the concept of a mini-flier even further with a double business card that folds into the standard size. Sometimes, one flap will be slightly smaller than the other, so it's obvious to the reader to lift the flap and see what's inside. Since standard-sized business cards are 3¼ inches long by 2 inches wide, a horizontal fold-out gives you an area almost 4 inches deep on the inside—enough for a reduced-size version of a full-page flier—plus the outside flaps. In all, you have four times the area of the standard one-sided business card. However, with two-sided printing, folding, and larger paper area, the card will cost substantially more to produce. By shopping around, I got 1,000 of these for under $60, from my own camera-ready copy, through Quill Corporation, 800-789-1331. Other estimates were as much as $200. By comparison, my last run of standard-sized cards cost $23 from a local supplier.

You can also use all four flaps, as on page 145. This also shows how to get the most out of a second color by using different screens and fills.

The fourth panel costs nothing more to print, since the third panel already forces you to print both sides.

Rolodex

Funny thing about Rolodex cards: they're just a wee bit bigger than the standard business card. Take advantage of this and do business cards that fit on a Rolodex, complete with holes for mounting inserts and a tab that sticks up to allow people to find your card instantly. These are attractive and practical, and they will be used.

Here's a suggestion: Print your Rolodex and standard business cards together, on the same piece of paper. Together, they will fill approximately a third of a letter-size page. Print them on card stock or durable plastic, with die-cuts or perforations so the recipient can easily detach them. Also perforate each third-of-the-page section. If you run off 200 full pages of these, you end up with 600 each of the standard and Rolodex cards, which your client can detach and file in both places. This format has the added advantage of not letting the client forget he or she has your card, because before it's detached, it's too big to get lost in a pocket or wallet.

You will be somewhat restricted in your choice of print shop—not everyone will be set up to handle this—but it may still be very much worth your while. The Rolodex cards really do have tremendous impact, and it surprises me that more people don't use them.

Alternatively, Paper Direct (800-272-7377) sells Rolodex card stock, already scored. Use your laser printer to do your cards in-house.

Oversize

Some people have tried to get more on a business card, or to stand out in a pile of others' cards, by using larger paper sizes. But any advantage in extra information is negated by the extra hoops people will have to go through to store your card. If it won't fit in a standard-sized business card file, it'll probably end up in a desk drawer at best, or a wastebasket at worst. Or your card will be stuffed into the standard file and will crumple, fade, and generally age a lot more rapidly than the cards around it. The last thing you want is a really ratty-looking card staring at the client after a few months have gone by.

Picture and Hologram Cards

Photographs certainly get noticed, but the cost is high. Will a photo on the card really help your marketing or just stroke your own ego? Consider using a picture card to highlight your product's effectiveness as a problem solver, rather than show off your brilliant white smile. For instance, a home inspection service could show a jumpsuited consultant poking a hand into some piping. A portable-computer dealer could use a picture of the product being used in a relaxed, outdoor setting. A woodstove manufacturer could photograph a happy family sitting around the stove in shirtsleeves, while a bitter winter day is visible outside.

Principals:
Shel Horowitz, D. Dina Friedman

Services:
Affordable résumés, marketing/PR, writing/editing, book and publishing consulting, manuscript analysis, developmental editing, creative writing workshops

Books:
Marketing Without Megabucks:
How to Sell Anything on a Shoestring;

The Penny-Pinching Hedonist:
How to Live Like Royalty w/ a Peasant's Pocketbook

Website:
Over 200 articles to save you money and help you live better …
Monthly Frugal Fun and Frugal Marketing Tips Archives
Arts, Travel, and Business Magazines
http://www.frugalfun.com

Advocate "Best of the Valley"

Assisting job seekers, business owners, writers, and publishers since 1981.

ACCURATE WRITING & MORE
ideas into words…words onto paper
✢

P.O. Box 1164, Northampton, MA 01061, USA

(800) 683-WORD/(413) 586-2388

Fax: (617) 249-0153 • info@frugalfun.com

Two examples of double-sided fold-out business cards. Health Claims Advocates uses both blue and black ink.

info@healthclaimsadvocates.com
413-467-2799 fax
800-787-0417 phone

6 University Drive, #228
Amherst, MA 01004-6000

Angela Barth, *Director*

Health Claims Advocates

TAKE CHARGE OF YOUR
HEALTH INSURANCE CLAIMS!

Health
Claims
Advocates

GET YOUR MONEY
KNOW YOUR RIGHTS

We will:

Educate   Advocate   Negotiate

Potential Benefits

Collect much more money from your health insurance company

Negotiate a price saving of hundreds of dollars on your coinsurance

Settle outstanding claims and bills

Appeal claims possibly denied in error

Learn to be an effective advocate for yourself and your family members

CONTACT
1-800-787-0417
www.healthclaimsadvocates.com

As for holograms—those changing designs we see on credit cards, that shift depending on the angle of the light—I can't see any situation where using them on a business card is worth the expense, unless of course you design holograms as part of your business services.

Magnetic

Business cards with a magnetic backing combine the visibility of a premium item with the content of a business card. They could be worth a try.

Multiple Cards

Just as you wouldn't use only one press release, you may need more than one version of your business card. Over the years, we've used fairly standard cards in both one- and two-color formats, a fold-out card, a standard-sized card designed specifically for bulletin boards, and a Rolodex card. Presently, we're using the fold-out as our main card, and a standard-sized card on elegant rose-colored paper for our publishing ventures.

— Helpful Hints Checklist —

An often effective variant on brochures is a sheet designed to both provide useful general information and point the prospect back to you in order to carry out the specifics. Typically, it might have a couple of opening paragraphs setting the tone, followed by several bulleted points, the last of which explains how you can do all this for them. You want to provide something genuinely useful, but also you want to show your own expertise—and lead the client naturally to the action step of contacting you. The idea is to create a marketing piece that will be kept, rather than thrown out. It's a long-range marketing document; the client may keep it for several months, until a relevant situation arises. Then, as he or she attempts to follow the checklist, the prospect will call you in to do it right. For example, the document on page 147 fits on an 8½ x 14-inch sheet and promotes my entrepreneurial consulting service.

The wonderful thing about a marketing tool such as this is that it's perfect as a premium. You can offer people a "free report" or "free checklist" in return for their prompt order or inquiry. Be specific, for example, "Order within ten days and get a free checklist to help plan your estate," "Free with your order—ten steps to better home-buying," "Just for filling out this questionnaire, we'll send you an eight-point checklist on what to look for in a home audio system."

— Brochures —

Almost any business or organization—performing-arts ensembles, human-services agencies, tourist attractions, consultants, motels, retail and service operations, craftspeople, charities, diversified corporations, politicians—can use a brochure—or several.

Brochures use many different formats. The easiest setup is an 8½ x 11 or 8½ x 14-inch piece of paper, held so the long side is horizontal, with vertical folds dividing the paper into two, three, or four panels on each side. A three-fold, for instance, provides for one introductory panel and four or five of information (depending on whether you use one panel for a return coupon). But a brochure can also be a forty-four-page magazine on glossy paper, with lavish illustrations, such as a corporate annual report . . . a twenty-page stapled plain-paper booklet, as in the typical community event program guide . . . a tabloid piece of paper folded map-style, with each half or quarter page subdivided into three or four panels . . . a pair of circles hinged at the top . . . or any other format you can work out with your graphic designer and your printer.

Since prospects often collect and compare competing brochures, keep these rules in mind when writing and designing your brochure:

- Know your objectives, and focus the brochure appropriately.
- Point out what makes you special: what differentiates your offering (including both product and the service level) from others

Are You Ready to Start a Business Yet?

Copyright 1992, 1999 by Shel Horowitz

I. Are you ready in your heart?

Do you have a marketable skill?

Have you determined if there is a market for your skill?

Are you willing to commit the necessary time, energy, and money to try to make a go of it?

Can you be disciplined enough to get the work done, but also disciplined enough to get the rest you need?

Do you have the support of family and friends?

How willing and competent are you to: Market through direct selling? Market through the media, Internet, mail, and bulletin boards? Set up a workable system of accounting and record keeping? Build and maintain equipment? Deal with suppliers and clients? Establish checks and balances for payables and receivables? Supervise other workers? Set up efficient and orderly systems for your business? Modify those systems as your needs change or you discover what does and doesn't work?

Are you really ready to give up a regular paycheck and the network of office acquaintances gathering around the water cooler?

II. Are you ready in your pocket?

Do you have the financial resources to survive the first three to six months? If not, what options do you have (loans, research grants, part-time employment, full-time job with moonlighting, selling assets . . .)?

Can you carry over health insurance from your previous employer, parent, or your spouse?

How much start-up capital do you need for a bare-bones beginning?

Do you need any additional training?

What equipment do you need? Can you lease with option to buy? Purchase used or deeply discounted equipment? Use someone else's at first on a fee-for-use basis?

What will you be doing yourself? For what will you be relying on other people (experts, employees, and subcontractors)? Where will you find these people?

How will you obtain your first clients?

Where, physically, will you work? If other than a space in your home, will the extra rent and utilities cause too high a burden? If in your home, do you have adequate separation between workplace and living space? How much privacy are you willing to give up?

III. Do you have expert advisors in place?

You'll need an accountant to set up your books . . . a business license . . . a lawyer to review your contracts . . . and marketing assistance and entrepreneurial advice. We at Accurate Writing & More will be happy to provide affordable marketing and entrepreneurial consulting, as well as write all your marketing materials. We serve an international clientele, emphasize cost-effective solutions at affordable prices, and have been helping small businesses get started for over twenty years. Give us a call at (800) 683-WORD or (413) 586-2388, or visit our Web site at http://www.frugalfun.com to find a treasure trove of information to run your business better—including excerpts from our book, *Grassroots Marketing: Getting Noticed in a Noisy World.*

on the market—in other words, your USP.

- Identify and highlight both the problems you can solve and the continuance or exacerbation of the problem if the client doesn't act.
- Transform all features into benefits.
- List the important specifications of the product, each accompanied by the resultant benefit, spelled out in full detail.
- Never assume your reader can extrapolate the benefits for him- or herself.
- Put enough useful advice into the brochure that it has value in and of itself. Thus, it will be more likely that your prospects will keep the piece, even if they aren't ready to buy (for instance, include checklists, product comparison charts, or specific suggestions on how your target audience can solve a problem).

Define Your Focus

Since most organizations have more than one product, service, benefit, or idea to promote, the fundamental choice is whether to take a catalog approach, listing various products and services with a small blurb about each, or to do separate pieces for each aspect of your product line. I'd suggest doing both. An overview piece, plus specific and detailed literature on every product, is a very strong combination—as long as it addresses the reader's concerns and not the marketer's ego.

Our main brochure is eight 8½ x 5½-inch pages (two 2-sided 8½ x 11 sheets, folded and stapled). The outer covers summarize the contents and provide contact information and a slogan. Inside, three two-page spreads address the benefits of working with us on marketing, writing/editing, and career services. With minor modifications, these two-page spreads exist as separate documents on my Web site.

An inexpensive brochure can still present a class act. The brochure to the right achieves an upscale effect achieved with thick paper stock, silver ink filling the outside, and lavish but cost-effective black-and-white photography—all built around an elegant logo and typeface combination.

TREAT YOURSELF DELICIOUSLY

ONE TASTE IS WORTH 1,000 WORDS

To some people, candy is candy. To Dorothy Benjamin and Peggy LaKind, candy is a treat, lovingly prepared by hand each time it is given. ◆ For years only their families and friends delighted in their confections. The word however, started to spread, and they began making candy for others. When Monthly Detroit Magazine sought them out, and honored their creations with the designation: "Best Detroit Candy Secret of 1988", they decided to launch into full-scale business. Today their families are involved in almost every step of the business, and their friends still volunteer as "creative consultants". And now, as then, only Dorothy and Peggy do the actual candy making. ◆ Each confection is made when it is ordered. Not before.

Having searched out the finest ingredients, they use the best Swiss chocolate, the most succulent caramel, and the largest, fanciest southern pecans. Once an order is made, it is carefully, not to mention attractively, packaged and immediately sent out. ◆ There is candy and there is candy. And then there is Platinum Treats, a name which richly and aptly describes the confections. But it is the taste that really says it all.

ENJOY!

Dorothy Benjamin
Peggy LaKind

CHOICE CONFECTIONS

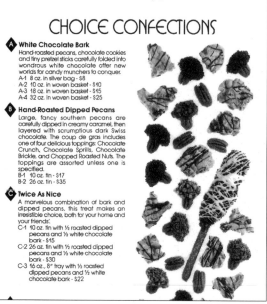

A White Chocolate Bark
Hand-roasted pecans, chocolate cookies and tiny pretzel sticks carefully folded into wondrous white chocolate offer new worlds for candy munchers to conquer.
A-1 8 oz. in silver bag - $8
A-2 10 oz. in woven basket - $10
A-3 18 oz. in woven basket - $15
A-4 32 oz. in woven basket - $25

B Hand-Roasted Dipped Pecans
Large, fancy southern pecans are carefully dipped in creamy caramel, then layered with scrumptious dark Swiss chocolate. The coup de gras includes one of four delicious toppings: Chocolate Crunch, Chocolate Sprills, Chocolate Brickle, and Chopped Roasted Nuts. The toppings are assorted unless one is specified.
B-1 10 oz. tin - $17
B-2 26 oz. tin - $35

C Twice As Nice
A marvelous combination of bark and dipped pecans, this treat makes an irresistible choice, both for your home and your friends.
C-1 10 oz. tin with ½ roasted dipped pecans and ½ white chocolate bark - $15
C-2 26 oz. tin with ½ roasted dipped pecans and ½ white chocolate bark - $30
C-3 16 oz., 8" tray with ½ roasted dipped pecans and ½ white chocolate bark - $22

Unfortunately, this format is going to have problems if prices change. They wouldn't want to ruin the high-quality image with handwritten price increases! I would suggest that when they redo the brochure, they drop prices from the body copy and do up an order/price form, on the same stock, as a short-run insert. Then, as prices fluctuate, they can reprint just the insert in a suitable quantity.

— Catalogs —

Think of a catalog as an expanded brochure—as simple as a typed sheet, or as fancy as a five-hundred-page, full-color, glossy showcase. When possible, try for something in the middle: a product list with sizzling, benefit-oriented copy and illustrations, three to eight items per page, color if you can afford it. No matter how slick or raw it is, the catalog can highlight numerous products together, at a much lower cost than individually. Enclose it with every order, and distribute it as well through other means: put piles in stores, hand it out to other prospects, and so forth.

Catalogs, especially the well-written, problem-solving ones focused on benefits to the user (but including product features, too) are hard to resist. Think of what happens to your favorite gardener when a seed catalog arrives on a cold winter day—he or she disappears for a couple of hours and emerges wiping the drool away and reaching for a credit card and the nearest telephone.

You can use catalogs in a variety of formats:

- Monthly or weekly sale offer, listing current specials
- Full product listing, showing everything available and highlighting those on sale
- New product announcement, with detailed pages on every benefit from its features
- Discontinued merchandise, available in limited quantities at great bargains—for example, Damark for electronics or Publisher's Central Bureau for books

Catalog Frequency

What follows is direct-mail heresy.

It seems like most direct-mail marketers think they should saturate their readers with catalogs every three to four weeks. I disagree. As I get busier, I have less and less time to go through my mail; catalogs are low priority and often get thrown away unread—especially if I've just read one from the same company. And I'm sure I'm not alone. (Exception: supermarket specials that change weekly—but even there, I'm more likely to cruise the supermarket aisle looking for marked bargains than to actually read the flier.)

The worst offenders are those with expensive fully illustrated color catalogs. It's costing them a fortune to keep me drowning in paper—not to mention the waste of trees and pollution risk from metallic inks.

I suggest that you'll have considerably more impact mailing every four to six months—especially if you clearly highlight what's new and on sale. Or if you're going to mail frequently, just focus on those specials—mail a complete catalog less often. Quill, a prominent mail-order office supply company, has been doing this for years. And they also segment their mailings: They have separate catalogs (on newsprint) for office furniture, specialty papers, computer supplies, and so forth, and then a huge twice-a-year master catalog, printed on more durable paper and perfect-bound.

If you raise money for charity, be even more cautious: once or twice a year, with extras only for a genuine emergency. I've removed a number of charities from my list because they spent my entire contribution asking for more money.

— Newsletters and Magazines —

With modern desktop-publishing technology, it's easy to be a publisher—and even easier online. Consultants, retailers, and product manufacturers have all used newsletters and magazines to keep their existing and potential client base up to date. They:

- Provide ongoing certification of your expertise
- Clearly demonstrate your problem-solving ability
- Easily inform clients about new or updated products and services
- Answer common questions without having to spend time on one-to-one customer support
- Increase customer loyalty and satisfaction by demonstrating new uses for the product
- Build on the perception that you care about your clients and customers enough to go the extra mile
- Communicate contact information in each issue
- Keep your name in front of the customers, with a silent reminder that you're ready the next time they need to order
- Have intrinsic value, therefore will be shared with friends and colleagues who may become your customers
- Can include a catalog, as well as sales-oriented fliers and inserts that would otherwise have to be mailed separately

Sounds pretty good. But be aware of the downside. Regular mailings to all your customers, or even all recent customers, will cost a considerable amount. So will producing a fancy newsletter or magazine, especially if you have to pay freelance writers. Production will either take away a big chunk of your own time from other products or force you to hire out the work at additional expense. Electronic newsletters have no production expense, but may not be as versatile.

Still, you don't have to do a full-color, glossy monthly magazine: A simply printed but useful newsletter appearing three or four times a year will provide all these benefits.

In many fields, you don't even have to write or produce your newsletter. You can recruit articles from recognized experts in your field; offer them publicity (including full contact information) rather than payment. Or subscribe to a newsletter service that will prepare a rather general, often bland, but still useful newsletter under your logo and address. You get the credit; they do the work. Of course, it won't be nearly as relevant to your clients, or as personal, as something you produce in-house. But particularly for consultants whose strong suit is not the written word, it's plausible. If you go this route, include one of your own marketing pieces when you mail the newsletter to your own client list.

Some tips on writing newsletter articles: By and large, the process is similar to writing any other kind of article, except that you distribute it yourself. Keep in mind, though, the particular audience you're dealing with. Try as much as possible to be:

Consultants, retailers, and product manufacturers have all used newsletters and magazines to keep their existing and potential client base up to date.

- Up to the minute with the latest breaking news in your field
- Upbeat about the ability to solve the problems your audience faces
- For consultants, specific enough to point in the direction of the appropriate solution, but general enough so the client still has to come back to you to actually deal with the situation (in other words, tell *what* to do to solve the problem, but don't explain *how* to do it)
- For product sellers, focused on showing how further purchases can solve a problem

— Distribute! —

You can do the best business card or brochure or catalog or newsletter in the world, and it won't do you a bit of good if you don't get it out of its box and into your prospects' hot little hands. Consider these avenues, among others:

- Tourist information and Chamber of Commerce visitors booths
- Targeted mailings to new prospects
- Fairs, block parties, trade shows, concerts, and other events
- Responses to inquiries
- Mailings to your existing clients (especially for newsletters and catalogs)
- Your Web site
- Providers of complementary services

For a general product, distribution may be quite far-reaching. Honoré David distributes sixty-five thousand catalogs describing continuing-education offerings at the University of Massachusetts at Amherst, several times a year. Distribution is con-centrated within fifty miles of the campus, but stretches a tentacle here and there as far as one hundred miles away. "We put them in grocery stores, drugstores, liquor stores, banks, laundro-mats—that's a place where people sit down and want something to read." David also evaluates the distribution channel. "If [the delivery runner] leaves ten and they're all still there, we'll switch to another location."

✄

Whatever printed materials you use, they will surely play an important part in your marketing. But marketing isn't just ink on paper. Electrons have a vital role, too, as we will see in parts 3 and 4.

18

Free Publicity over the Airwaves

Every trick of print media exposure has an electronic analogy. If you can manage a microphone, you can reach more people at any one instant than through any other technique. Although you sacrifice depth for volume, thousands to millions of people will hear you at the same instant.

You don't need to speak in perfect sentences—just make sure people can understand you. You should be able to make points clearly, without undue rambling. You must also be able to think quickly on your feet in response to unexpected questions.

Listen to your speaking voice on tape. Learn to speak clearly, project your voice, vary your tone, and smooth out your accent. Not only will a good voice serve you well in broadcast media, it will also help you present yourself as a pro over the telephone and in person.

Just as writing isn't for everyone, neither is speaking on air. However, if your goal is effective low cost promotion of a product, service, or idea, you can't afford not to use electronic media. If the microphone and camera give you the jitters, pretend you're just in the living room talking to a close friend.

Since many amateur publicists are far less familiar with using broadcast media than working with print, I'll go into some detail here. Television, especially, has a distant and surreal quality about it, as well as an awesome power to reach people. It's hard to believe, but we ordinary people can harness radio and TV for our own purposes.

Audio versus Video

Television relies primarily on the visual impact on the screen to hold its audience. That's why even commercials—especially commercials—are full of fast movement and dramatic action. Television is also far more expensive than radio to produce, so the ratings pressure, sensationalism, and avoidance of meaningful discourse are greater.

With radio, the visual effect is irrelevant. Words and sounds alone conjure up images and streams of thought. Radio often plays a background role; something else is going on as the main activity. But when TV exists only in the background, much of its impact is lost. People can listen to the radio, and absorb your message, in situations where a TV will have no impact at all.

Aside from the obvious difference of including video, be aware of other differences between radio and TV:

- Most TV segments are very short (sometimes under a minute), and the questions tend to be more shallow. However, good visuals may prolong your exposure.
- TV producers may want exclusivity within a certain time period (if you think there might be a conflict, *ask* the show producer how he or she feels about you appearing elsewhere).
- Radio interviews can be done over the phone, while TV usually requires a trip to the studio (generally at your expense, unless you're a member of the right union).
- It's much harder to get your ordering information displayed on TV than announced on radio.

Community Access versus Closed-Format

For the publicist, this is the most important differentiation. In cable TV, community access refers specifically to channels that are reserved for the public. However, I'm referring to any program or piece of airtime that is open to residents of the community (and for which the studio allows its production facilities to be used). Along with the traditional cable formats, this can include audience call-in shows and shows with guests.

A closed show has no space for on-air audience response. For the most part, you will be concerned with public access. If you really want to crack a closed show that doesn't take guests, your only options are luckily placed PSAs and paid advertising.

— Short News Interviews —

If you're the contact person on a press release or PSA, you may get interviewed for a news or public affairs broadcast. This will be very concise, typically under five minutes, of which perhaps ten to fifty seconds will be used on the air. Know what you will say before the phone rings. Make your points as quickly and clearly as possible. In this situation, unlike a full-length talk show, the interviewer's question will almost invariably not be broadcast—only your response. Therefore, if you're asked an inappropriate or unimportant question, ignore it, and answer as if you were responding to the question you want asked.

— Call-Ins —

An on-the-air call-in is a live letter to the editor. The host and/or guests take questions or comments over the air. Sometimes they are prescreened by the station's receptionist; in other instances the announcer answers directly. Some keep their callers anonymous; others demand the caller's identity. This type of talk show may be either local or national.

There are two main differences between letters to the editor and radio call-ins. First, "publication" is determined by whose phone call gets to the switchboard first. Second, in a letter you have the time to write and revise—but radio is spontaneous.

If you listen regularly to a particular show, program the station's live call-in number into your phone's speed-dialing memory. Should you get ringing instead of a busy signal, don't hang up! Be prepared to wait several minutes until the disc jockey finishes an extended conversation with the person or people ahead of you.

In the United States, some stations still use a seven-second delay on live call-ins to allow the engineer to cut off any obscenities before they go over the airwaves. Sit where you can listen to the radio. But because of the delay, you'll hear the announcer's voice in your ear while the previous caller is finishing. Turn down your radio (so you don't generate feedback or become confused by the delay) and go for it. Ditto if you're listening over the Internet.

Some announcers will allow a fairly lengthy call, with questions and answers back and forth. Others will cut callers off after only a sentence or two. So be prepared to get your point across quickly.

Some hosts, particularly on afternoon AM commercial radio, rely almost exclusively on callers, plus their own banter and an occasional piece of music, to glue a show together. Sometimes they will have a topic; other times it's a free-for-all.

Here's how this can work for you as a publicist:

"This is WOOF Radio and you're on the air!"

"Oh, hi. I heard you talking about Brazilian dancing just now."

"That's right. Who is this and where are you calling from, please?"

"My name's Nancy Evans and I live in Queens. I think people might want to know there's a Brazilian dance festival happening a week from Saturday."

"Well, that's just great. Where's it happening, Nancy?"

"It's a benefit for the Muscular Dystrophy, and it'll be at the skating rink in Flushing, starting at noon."

"Nancy, thanks so much for that information. So, folks, you can watch some Brazilian dancing and give to a good cause. Hold the line and I'll have James take down the details so if people didn't catch it, they can call the station. Thanks and call again!"

"Good morning, WXYZ, may I help you?"

"Yes, I'd like to be put through to the studio please."

"And what did you want to talk about?"

"I want to comment on the question Bob just asked about unwed mothers."

"Okay, I'll put you through. He's got one more call ahead of you so it might be a minute. Just hold on."

"This is Bob Jones and you're on the air."

"Hi, Bob. You were talking about unwed mothers, and one thing I didn't hear anyone mention was that their education usually gets cut off. So many of them drop out of school and never go back. I only know of one program that provides day care so teenage mothers can go on with their schooling, and that's out of the Congregational Church on South Street. How come nobody else is addressing that issue?"

"That's a very good question. Why aren't there more programs to get these kids back in school?"

"I've got an idea about that."

"Okay."

"A lot of people just aren't willing to look the issue in the face. They think that if they hand these women a welfare check and let them disappear into the woodwork, they met their obligation. That because jobs are scarce, why provide training for

them? But actually, not only does an uneducated woman have difficulty finding work, she also wastes her life. Plus, once someone gets training and has marketable skills and motivation, she doesn't need a handout. The Congregational Church program I was talking about also provides counseling for the mothers, both about how to raise their kids and how to find meaningful work. Anyone who wants to know more can call the minister there."

"Okay, thanks. Let's see if the next caller has any more ideas on the subject."

"KCAR-FM, you're on the air."

"Jane, you were talking yesterday about the shortage of repair people."

"Right."

"Well, this is Steve Edwards from Steve's Electronics Repair in Tudor Hills, and I want to do something about it. I'm now offering to train six apprentices, starting on Monday night. I need all the help I can get right now, and I'll give these kids a job, too."

"Okay, thanks. That's all the time we have today. Want to learn to fix sound systems, call Steve. Tune in again at two o'clock tomorrow."

One Key Trick

If possible, try to connect your point, *however tenuously,* to something that was discussed—especially if it was discussed within the past few minutes.

— Talk Show Appearances —

Famous authors and film celebrities aren't the only ones who appear as guests on talk shows. Every area has its own broadcast stations, and virtually all of them use guests at least occasionally.

Talk show producers need to fill an awful lot of airtime—and that's your opportunity to get your message across. I've heard these and other folks as radio or TV guests: owners of newly expanded businesses; candidates for—and holders of—public office; real estate developers; community activists; collectors of obscure 1950s doo-wop records; directors of social service agencies; visiting speakers from other countries; assorted musicians, poets, authors, and theater directors; organizers from a rural peace center; recently returned travelers; Ralph Nader's mother, promoting her Lebanese cookbook (on *Donahue*!); energy lobbyists and policy makers; small-press publishers.

National Association for the Self-Employed's Bob Wieler tries to appear as a guest every month to six weeks. "I couldn't pay for that kind of advertising. And instead of a thirty-second spot five times a day for several thousand dollars, I get two hours of exposure for free." I average more like one a week, from five to sixty minutes each time.

Ways to Get Booked on Shows

Just as in soliciting features, make contacts with talk show hosts and producers. Emphasize what you can offer their audiences. And if you have other credits—clippings by or about your operation, a list and/or a tape of other on-air or live speaking engagements, a thank-you from another host—share them with your contact.

Alvin Donovan, a well-known motivational speaker, uses a faxed "hook sheet" to book over a thousand radio gigs a year. Donovan also includes a confirmation form, a fact sheet with a bio and sample questions, and an overview of the techniques he'll be discussing on the show.

Here's one of his hook sheets:

As featured on national radio and TV including Howard Stern

Alvin Donovan

"Unlike Any Romance Expert You've Ever Interviewed! Alvin is the best guest I have had in my over 20 years of radio, he melted the phones, they would not stop ringing!"

—ED SHAW, HOST,
RUTH AND ED SHAW NATIONAL RADIO SHOW,
TALKAMERICA RADIO NETWORK

How to Get Someone to *instantly* Fall in Love with You!

There are tons of "romance experts" but only Alvin Donovan guarantees he can teach you how to make someone fall for you in 30 seconds or less! Bring him on your show to learn exactly how it's done.

Your audience will learn . . .

- How to persuade any woman or man to unconsciously do what you want.
- The 15 words that set hearts aflutter.
- How to read a prospective date's thoughts by following their eyes.
- Why attractive strangers love it when you share confidences or confess something to them.
- Why using words like "might," "if," and "why" will brand you a loser by your prospective date.

"I received more calls about Alvin than I did about Garth Brooks, President Ford and Mike Wallace!"

—RHETT PALMER, HOST,
RHETT PALMER FLORIDA SHOW

A popular media guest, Alvin Donovan is a recognized master persuader who has taught his techniques to many of the world's top Fortune 500 companies. His secrets for getting anyone to instantly like you can also dramatically increase your income. He is author of the best selling book *How to Get Anyone to Instantly Fall in Love with You,* and the audiocassette series "The Power of Love."

AVAILABLE 7 DAYS A WEEK
Contact: Meg Northcroft at 1-561-794-1025 or e-mail alvindonovan@compuserve.com

NOTE: See some amazing interview material at www.MyAlvin.com

If you get frustrated approaching producers on your own—and you probably will, especially if you're trying the bigger markets—there are a number of services that put potential guests in front of broadcast producers. Most of these use a magazine or newsletter format, and the price can get pretty steep if you want constant penetration. For instance, a full-page ad in the best-known publication, *Radio-TV Interview Report (RTIR)*, is well over five hundred dollars.

A cheaper—and in my personal experience, more effective—alternative is to list at a Web site called GuestFinder <http://www.guestfinder.com>. You get a whole year's listing for less than the price of one insertion in *RTIR* or *Broadcast Interview Source*. In its first two years, GuestFinder brought me about sixty show bookings—all over the United States and Canada, and as far away as Europe and Taiwan.

If you want to crack a major show or, for that matter, any major media outlet, persistence—real persistence—can really make the difference. Book author Velty Bautista courted "Bottom Line—Personal" for many months before being featured not once but several times. And here's how Tim McCormick, publisher of Greentree Press, got one of his authors on TV with Barbara Walters. He:

- Acquired the names of three different producers, from six different referral sources (including print mentions in trade publications, word of mouth from another producer he'd worked with, and a past guest)
- Sent a total of thirty review copies over a two-month period, including seven FedEx packages
- Made seventy-five phone calls—if he got voice mail, he hung up and called again later
- Faxed fourteen separate follow-ups—and for both the phone and fax contacts, followed the show's lead and did not make a pest of himself
- Asked each contact when to follow up (not only how far in the future, but at what time of day)—and followed through at the appointed time
- Treated initial rejections not as a blow-off, but as an objection to be overcome

On-Air Tips

In a perfect world, interviewers would submit questions in advance so that guests could prepare answers, they'd ask useful, intelligent questions, and you would have time to answer each articulately and smoothly. Unfortunately, it doesn't always work that way. Broadcast media can make you look ridiculous if you're not careful. Don't assume the interviewer has researched you at all. Many don't adequately do their homework, and some of the questions may be downright stupid. I'm pleasantly surprised by about five interviewers per year who've obviously read my book ahead of time; the rest either use my press packet or just wing it. Fortunately, I can take control of an interview and get my message across without making the interviewer look like a jerk.

Try to anticipate. Give the interviewer a list of questions you'd like to be asked—do this a couple of days before your segment is taped (or broadcast live), and bring another copy with you when you show up at the studio. (Incidentally, always show up at least half an hour before air time.)

When that microphone is on, avoid long pauses; "dead air" will drive listeners away in droves. If you start to freeze up, just pretend you're talking to a good friend in the center of the audience.

Don't be afraid to elaborate—that's what the audience is waiting for. The interviewer will cut you off if you get too technical or ramble too far.

If you are asked a really dumb question, probably the best thing to do is answer quickly and divert the subject to a related, but more interesting matter. Let's say I'm promoting my online marketing consulting:

Announcer: "Aren't you afraid that computers will take over the world?"
Me: "That's bad science fiction, but the Internet, properly used, can be a business's lowest cost and most effective marketing tool. And those who understand the right way to market online, not the computers they use, will 'take over the world.'"

— Host Your Own Show —

The qualifications for becoming a talk show host are similar to those for writing a regular newspaper column. However, because broadcast media are so focused on the present tense, you must be comfortable on the air and able to think quickly on your feet. Several formats suggest themselves: answering questions received by mail; answering call-in questions; interviewing guests (with or without audience questions); or just you, talking for a few minutes on your field of expertise. Your range of topics is as broad as your imagination.

A few examples: In my area, at least two stations present Wall Street reports by local brokers. A restaurant manager has a program of short tips on cooking, gardening, and pets. And a member of a town housing authority hosts a public affairs talk show.

Famous people do this, too. Franklin Roosevelt, Abbie Hoffman, and Mario Cuomo used their fame to host a talk show and then used the show to promote themselves and their ideas; Dr. Ruth became famous through her shows.

A show can be quite short. Stock market and gold reports may be only a minute or two. General-store owner David Majercik airs two different original mini-show series modeled after ski reports:

WHYN Foliage Report
9/27/91

Fall foliage has about peaked in far northern New England. It's colder there and the nights are longer, so the leaves turn color there first. Peak color is moving slowly southward—it'll be in central Vermont next weekend and it should arrive in western Massachusetts around Columbus Day.

But there's no need to wait that long to drive into our beautiful hills and see the color that's already here. In fact, the higher Berkshire Hills are already quite beautiful, with about 35 percent of the leaves already turned.

It's the harvest season and a stop at a farm stand or a country store will reward you with apples, cider, pumpkins, Indian corn, and the many other good things that make western Massachusetts such a wonderful place to visit.

To help you find your way around the hilltowns, you may have a free fall foliage guide and map when you stop at the Williamsburg General Store. Williamsburg is on Route 9, a few miles west of Northampton.

I urge you to find an hour or two this weekend to drive out and see the foliage. For foliage information, call 1-800-632-8038. For the WHYN Foliage Report, I'm David Majercik.

WHYN Maple Report
3/22/91

The best weather for making maple syrup is frosty-cold nights and sunny, warm days. That's when the sap runs best. Years ago, maple producers would drill a hole in a sugar maple tree, hammer a metal spigot into the hole, then hang a bucket from the spigot to catch the sweet, dripping sap.

Quite a chore back then, going around to all those buckets and emptying them one at a time into a tank setting on a wagon, probably drawn by a team of horses. When that job was done the sap was poured into a large pan set over a roaring fire. The sap boiled vigorously until it turned into maple syrup. Sugarmen often worked more than twenty hours a day reaping their sweet harvest of spring. Today, many producers use plastic tubing in place of the metal buckets, but the boiling is done the same way as always.

Even though this weekend's weather is damp and dreary, many sugar houses are offering pancakes served with syrup made just this past week. For a free guide and map to Massachusetts sugar houses, stop at the general store in Williamsburg. The Williamsburg General Store is on Route 9, a few miles west of Northampton—right in the heart of Massachusetts maple country.

For the WHYN Maple Report, I'm David Majercik.

The maple report was Majercik's idea. In return, the station mentions a free maple guide and map available at his store. "It's aired ten times each weekend in March. The store is mentioned 160 times; it costs me about two hours' time."

After the second year, the station requested one on fall foliage. This airs for six weekends and earns Majercik's store 240 mentions. Preparing those spots takes him about three hours—or thirty minutes a week.

19

And Now a Word from Our Sponsor: Advertising in the Electronic Media

The same principles of effective advertising hold true in the electronic media as in print: Use the right message to the right audience. Although this chapter will focus largely on radio, the lessons here are applicable in any electronic communication.

— Radio —

Radio is a diverse, thriving medium that reaches all types of listeners. It is the most accessible, widest-reaching, and usually most cost-effective electronic approach, other than the Internet.

Both commercial and noncommercial stations offer specific demographics, often shifting at different times of the day.

Saturation versus Targeting

Listen to commercial radio for a while. You'll become familiar with the current ads from major corporations—some are aired several times an hour, often on every station in the broadcast area. It's called saturation advertising.

But while it seems to work for Coca-Cola and McDonald's, it won't work for you. Remember—the products that benefit from saturation advertising are universally available and nearly universally in demand. Saturation won't work for the average small business or community organization, which is limited in scope, range of products or services, and geography.

Also, because a radio commercial is so transient, a saturation strategy needs numerous airings to hammer in the message. The price of each insertion will vary with listenership. It might be just a few dollars on a small station serving a rural area, or it might be as much as $2,500 for a minute on the morning block on WCBS-AM in New York. Let's say you average $25 per insertion and you want to cover 8 stations with 15 ads per day, 5 days a week. Your annual budget for radio advertising will be $780,000; you're spending $3,000 every weekday. And you'll waste a lot of energy speaking to people who are not your customers—or others who get sick and tired of your commercials.

Now, let's compare the costs of a targeted campaign. Perhaps there are four shows per week that seem appropriate for your product. If the average cost is still $25 per insertion, and you run one ad on each program, you spend only $100 per week, or $5,200 for the year. If you run 30 weeks instead of 52, you're down to $3,000.

That still may seem like a lot of money, but compared with other forms of electronic advertising, it's a real bargain. If each ad reaches 5,000 good prospects and brings in $600 in sales, you would make $72,000 on your $3,000 annual investment—not a bad return! Also, your cost per insertion may be much lower, particularly if the program is on a noncommercial station. Remember, too, that you don't have to pay it out all at once. Try a show for two or three months and then evaluate whether to sign up again.

Although most stations try to appeal to a very general audience, radio can offer very precise targeting. Many broadcasters provide a great deal of special-interest programming, either integrated into the larger format (for instance, a five-minute gardening show), or in its own block of half an hour or longer. Some stations build most of their audience around large special-interest blocks of up to three hours.

In any talk show, and in some nontalk specialty shows, radio moves from a background to a foreground medium. A music show may be on while the listener is working, driving, cooking, cleaning the house, or whatever, and provides a background to make the task easier. But a special-interest talk show is geared at active listeners—those for whom the radio message is the most important thing on their minds at that moment. Therefore, ads and PSAs on targeted talk shows not only provide the benefits of targeting, but increase the chances that the people hearing your message are listening carefully.

This doesn't mean you should ignore the music-oriented specialty shows, but it might be a factor in choosing among various radio show formats. An ethnic show that caters to a specific community will have this carefully focused, attentive listenership. But a program that plays just blues, or classical, or 1960s rock is more likely to function in the background.

Special-interest programs are popular with both commercial and noncommercial radio stations, and even the latter allow business sponsorship. On some commercial stations, a show's producer might buy a block of airtime for ethnic, religious, or other specialty programs at some off-peak time such as early Sunday morning. The producer then resells space to advertisers. For other programs, the station may handle ad sales directly—and your contract must specify the program(s) you've chosen.

Advertising on special-interest programs costs relatively little, yet reaches exactly the people you want to reach, requires only an ad or two per program, may cost less per insertion because the listenership is lower, and gets your message across in a climate where people are listening carefully, not just having the radio on for mindless background sounds.

With noncommercial stations, the approach is called underwriting rather than advertising. In theory, all you get is a mention on the air in return for money, products, or services. But underwriter's messages sound more and more like ads. Here's a real-life example that airs regularly on one university station in my area:

_____ [name of show] is brought to you in part by an underwriting grant from Spirit Haus Liquor Store, located at 338 College Street, Route 9 East in Amherst. Spirit Haus specializes in wines from all around the world, imported beers, and a complete selection of spirits. WMUA thanks Spirit Haus for their kind support.

The advertising coordinator at this store has chosen a general underwriting program in keeping with the store's general-appeal merchandise. This announcement airs on a wide variety of shows, but the station itself concentrates its listenership among several thousand college-age listeners within three miles of the liquor store. This particular "noncommercial" station charges $7.50 per insertion for underwriting.

Go back to your press list and call all the radio stations. Ask them what specialty programs they offer and when they are aired, as well as whom to contact for information on ads or underwriting. While you're at it, ask for an advertiser's packet. It will include not only rate information, but a useful breakdown of the demographics of the station's listeners. Listen to several shows before making an ad buy (if you're out of range and the station doesn't broadcast on the Web, ask the ad department for tapes).

Here are some types of shows:

Ethnic and Subculture Shows. Areas with good-sized concentrations of particular ethnic groups usually present shows that feature news and music of that community. Similarly, there may be programs (especially on college-affiliated stations) catering to various subcultures: disabled people, women, followers of particular religious traditions or lifestyles, speakers of various languages . . . the list is almost endless.

If you sell food, clothing, crafts, holiday supplies, or travel packages relating to any of these or similar cultures, an ad campaign on the show would almost certainly draw very well. Listeners who want exactly what you sell will hear your messages every week—and once they buy from you, they'll likely tell their friends.

Special-Interest Shows and Service Programs. Much as newspaper columns offer service information on the home, energy, raising children, car repair, gardening, religion, and a host of other subjects, so some radio stations have programs with a similar focus. Although these tend to be shorter—broadcast as brief segments within regular programming—many stations also devote half an hour or more to a show aimed at a particular audience. Both short features and longer programs attract a loyal following.

If your business seems like a good match for a specialty feature, try it out. On just one station in my area, a goldsmith underwrites gold price listings, a sixties record shop promotes its wares on a one-hour sixties showcase, a New Age book and music store sponsors a program of soft acoustic music, and a restaurant advertises during a food feature.

Do you promote concerts? Sponsor or underwrite the live entertainment calendar. Sell blues CDs? Donate a few choice, rare discs to your local blues radio program. Perhaps your store carries a line of gourmet foods and there's a nutrition program in need of a sponsor. Maybe you sell running shoes and would like to underwrite sportscasts. If no station near you offers a suitable program, suggest one; you may even become a radio host. (See chapter 18 for more information on becoming a talk show host.)

If the station produces concerts or charity events, offer to sell tickets. That will get your name mentioned on the airwaves for free, bring people to your store, and possibly give you a small commission.

Obviously, these sorts of ads and promotions are geared more to the small-business person than the community group or nonprofit agency. Those in the latter categories will probably do better with simple PSAs. However, if you can tie in a special event, it might be worth trying as an experiment. Say you're bringing a Native American speaker and there's a program on indigenous cultures. Send a PSA, of course, but you may also want to both show your support for the show and increase your audience's familiarity with what you are doing by running a small commercial. Air it for three weeks before your event; you'll probably spend between thirty and one hundred dollars.

Donating or Bartering Premium Prizes

Both commercial and noncommercial broadcasters give away amazing numbers of records, concert tickets, retail gift certificates, and other prizes; these are almost invariably donated by publicity-seeking merchants. Prizes may be raffled off in charity auctions, given to random callers or those who can answer trivia questions, or used as incentives for people to subscribe to noncommercial stations. (Charity auction premiums may even have the added bonus of a line in newspapers or brochures listing your prize and the time it will be auctioned.)

If you listen, you'll hear a rap on the order of "I have a hot tub pass for two at Heavenly Heat on Bath Street in Anytown for the third caller who can tell me Ringo Starr's kid brother's name" or, at subscription time, "Jeff Jacobs, who owns the Witty Words bookstore, has just offered a twenty-dollar gift certificate to the next two people who pledge thirty dollars or more. So if your library's getting kind of run-down, now's the time to call in your subscription."

Not only do you get the airtime, but when the lucky winner comes to redeem the prize, he or she will have to make the acquaintance of your business or service—and, ideally, be added to your valued regular customers. Meanwhile, the station gets more money. Everyone wins.

V*irtually all prizes and premiums given away by commercial stations are bartered for publicity.*

Virtually all prizes and premiums given away by commercial stations are bartered for publicity. Often, it's possible to barter goods and services directly for advertising—see chapter 13.

Better yet, get someone else to spring for "your" cost—as Jordi Herold of the Iron Horse Music Hall proves: "Whenever possible, you get somebody else to pay for the premium you're using. If we use tapes, CDs, posters, a weekend at an inn, somebody else has paid for all those things." Herold even manages to get subsidized ticket giveaways. "Often, when we use tickets as premiums, we are able to get the record companies to pay for them. They buy a block of tickets." Herold has also promoted unknown bands by selling enough seats to a band's record company to pay the performers, and giving all the rest away for free.

Here's a variation from *Guerrilla Marketing* author Jay Conrad Levinson: If you advertise on a show that's built around an on-air personality, give the announcer a freebie: lessons, product samples, a dinner in your restaurant, whatever. Then just provide your radio celebrity with an outline of what you want covered in your ad. The radio star may provide you with an eloquent, unsolicited on-air testimonial that may run far longer than the number of seconds you're actually paying for.

Writing Radio Spots

Be as simple or extravagant as you want, but keep your message focused and understandable. Your wording should be concise and to the point, just like a good PSA—but you can and should be more blatantly commercial. You are competing in the background with whatever the listener is doing, and people will not retain everything they hear. So stay away from hundred-dollar words, and repeat the most important information. Repetition allows the listener the chance to grab a pencil and jot down the details.

Jonathan Price, a former radio employee, urges you to mention your business name at least twice per ad: once toward the beginning, and again at the very end, with contact information. Repeating this information at the end cements the listener's identification of the product with *your* business, rather than with the generic idea of using the kinds of products or services you sell: if you run Heavenly Heat Hot Tubs, you want to tempt the listener into trying not just any hot tub, but *your* hot tub.

Commercials are usually fifteen, thirty, or sixty seconds. Thirty seconds probably affords the best value—short enough to save money, but long enough to get the message across comfortably. And get right to the point! There's no time for small talk in half a minute.

Match your ad's tone to the show. A loud, brassy, hard-sell commercial would be jarringly out of place—and ineffective—on a classical music show, while a soft, elegant commercial would get lost amid the noise and aggressiveness of AM Top Forty. Reverse the placements and these two examples work a lot better.

When reaching a carefully targeted audience on a specialty show, start very simply: an ad with one voice reading text—yours, the host's, or a professional announcer's. It may be most effective to have the host read it, so it appears to the listener to be an integral part of the show. Nationally syndicated commentator Paul Harvey presents the ads as just another piece of information in his highly personalized news report. However, if different announcers air the spot over several weeks, tape it so it sounds the same each time.

There is no production cost to read words on paper—just airtime cost. If the people who are listening already use the kinds of products you sell—and if you don't have a lot of local competition—you can be very straightforward. You won't need gimmicks. Just tell people who you are, where you're located, and what you sell; they will reward your support for their program and culture and seek you out. For example, on an Armenian program:

The Armenian Grocery is here to serve you. Offering a full line of Armenian breads, pastries, dried fruits, music, and fashions, we are located at 1362 Broad Street, South Falls, where we've been serving the Armenian community for over twenty years. We are open every day from 9 A.M. to 6 P.M. The Armenian Grocery, 1362 Broad Street, South Falls. 555-9009. [approximately 25 seconds]

If your audience is not quite as selective, you can still use an all-talk, one-voice approach, but put a little more sales flair into it. Try this one on an international folk music show:

Have you ever had a homemade *bourika,* straight out of the oven and still warm? At the Armenian Grocery, 1362 Broad Street, South Falls, that's just one of the many wonderful pastries we serve. And they're all delicious. If you've never had Armenian cooking, you're in for a treat! Armenian music, clothing, and lots more, too. The Armenian Grocery, 1362 Broad Street, South Falls. 555-9009. [approximately 30 seconds]

As your audience gets more general, add a second voice and aim to be more engaging:

First Voice: "Oh, I'd like to eat out for lunch today.

But I'm bored with the same old restaurants."
Second Voice: "Have you ever tried Armenian cooking?"
First Voice: "No—what's it like?"
Second Voice: "Really great. The Armenian Grocery has a terrific lunch menu: pastries filled with cheese and meat, whole grain cracker breads, stuffed grape leaves . . ."
First Voice: "Wow, that sounds delicious. What was that restaurant?"
Second Voice: "The Armenian Grocery, 1362 Broad Street in South Falls. They have cookbooks and authentic ingredients, too—I know you love to cook."
First Voice: "1362 Broad Street, South Falls. Will you join me for lunch?"
Second Voice: "Sure." [approximately 30 seconds]

Advanced Scripting Techniques

Since in radio you don't have to supply any visuals, you can be very creative at minimal cost.

Note the subliminal message in the last ad we looked at: Your social life will improve if you patronize this business. Advertisers often use subliminal techniques to boost customer response. Other advanced techniques include recorded or created special effects (abbreviated as SFX), personification of objects, humor or satire, a snatch of music, and/or multiple voices. Singly or in combination, these approaches can all work to professionalize your production. They serve to:

- Attract attention and provide drama and human interest
- Increase listener interest
- Portray your business as clever
- Create a perception that the spot is longer than thirty seconds (so much is going on that you get more for your time)
- Make you stand out in a crowd

Two concerns: First, secure permission for music. You will have to pay a fee to the appropriate music-rights clearinghouse (ASCAP, BMI, or SESAC), unless the station you're airing on already has blanket permission to use music in commercials. Second, your cleverness must complement your message. Don't get so hung up on writing brilliant copy that you forget to sell the product, and don't get so obscure that the average listener can't follow you. Using our fictitious grocery again, here are some examples:

Music: Khachaturian: "Saber Dance" (a fast-paced, distinctive piece of music). Music begins loud, dims to be heard faintly over voice, loud again at end.
Narrator: "Find your favorite Armenian classical and popular music at the Armenian Grocery, 1362 Broad Street, South Falls. We carry a full line of Armenian records and tapes, food, clothing, and craft items." [time will vary depending on how the music is used; text is about 17 seconds]

Simple and to the point. A natural for a classical or ethnic music show.

SFX: key turning, door opening.
Child: "Mom! Dad! I made dinner tonight!"
Parent: "Great! I'm starved!"
SFX: sounds of eating.
Parent (dislikes it but trying to be nice): "This is very, um, interesting. What gives it the crunch?"
Child: "Eggshells. I read they have lots of calcium. I made up the recipe myself."
Parent: "I see. Jamie, do you remember that yummy lunch at the Armenian Grocery on Broad Street? Now that you're interested in cooking, maybe we should buy you one of their cookbooks."
Narrator: "The Armenian Grocery, 1362 Broad Street, South Falls. For the finest Armenian cooking, food, and cookbooks." [approximately 30 seconds]

This ad is subtle, but effective. It uses gentle humor and a familiar situation (inedible food) to appeal to almost any listener.

This one is too clever and less effective:

SFX: jet landing on a runway.
Importer: "Beautiful landing. I can't wait to get through customs and bring these fresh apricots to the Armenian Grocery."

Apricots (several voices): "Help! We've been kidnapped! We belong in Armenia."
Importer: "Hey, apricots! I brought you to America so everyone can find you at the Armenian Grocery. They're lonely for good Armenian food! We need you!"
Customs Inspector: "Okay, buddy, what have you got in that suitcase?"
SFX: suitcase opening.
Apricots (sing): "Mean Mistreater."
Customs Inspector: "Wise guy. You're under arrest."
SFX: handcuffs being fastened.
Narrator: "The Armenian Grocery, 1362 Broad Street, South Falls. Food so fresh it talks back." [approximately 30 seconds]

It's funny, but it doesn't sell. The only product mentioned is readily available at any grocery store. The claim of freshness is a minor selling point, buried in the clever pun. There is nothing about the diversity or uniqueness of the store's product line.

You can either write your own ads or have them done. The first place to look for copywriting help is in the broadcaster's office. Many radio ad sales departments employ copywriters who will create ads for you at no charge, or for a small fee. Quality will vary widely; if you don't like the station's copy, or if you think it makes you sound too much like all the other ads on the station, you can still buy the airtime—and use the station's production facilities—but get your copy written elsewhere.

Many small writing and editing businesses, such as my own company, will also be glad to write copy for you, and their charges will generally be quite reasonable. If radio is going to be a major part of your promotional tool kit, public relations and advertising agencies are the next step up: expensive, but very slick.

— Television —

Television is an extremely potent medium, reinforcing messages with both sounds and moving pictures, and commanding wide viewer involvement. During the time after work or school and before bed,

TV watching is the most common activity in the United States.

But often, TV advertising is a mistake. Each minute of airtime costs many times as much as the same slot in radio, and production costs are also much higher. Anyone can tape radio ads, but TV production requires competent acting, scripting, and camera work. These skills aren't cheap. You must pay thousands of dollars per year to get your spots done right or look like a bumbling fool with amateurish commercials on late-night television. We've all seen those goony ads, and more likely pitied than patronized the local businesses who ran them.

Al Eicoff, TV advertising specialist at Ogilvy & Mather, claims short-form commercials simply don't work. In his view, two minutes is the minimum selling time, with twenty seconds spent just on the ordering information. His research shows that the best times to air are early morning, late evening, and weekends. January, February, and March pull better than other times of year. (This probably correlates differently depending on the target market and the offer.)

Interestingly, poor programming yields higher response from the commercials; they're an annoyance when the show is good, but a welcome distraction when the show is lousy. Me? If a show is bad, I turn it off. David Ogilvy suspects a reverse correlation between production cost and sales; the more you spend shooting the commercial, the fewer people will buy. (Source for both Eicoff and Ogilvy: *Ogilvy on Advertising*.)

While other media are consolidating, TV has fragmented. In recent decades, many new options have opened up: small local stations in the UHF band, new networks such as Fox and CNN, and the entire new worlds of cable and home video. More recently, the Web has eroded TV's market share. So viewership is divided and no one can offer the level of penetration ABC, CBS, and NBC used to present.

Viewer fragmentation alone would not be reason enough to ignore TV; radio, Internet, and print media suffer the same problem. But when combined with the problems of quality production and the expense, it's a pretty discouraging picture.

However, in certain circumstances TV advertising might make sense. Both are analogous to successful targeted radio advertising: (1) premium giveaways for public-TV fundraising campaigns; (2) low-cost, simply produced ads on relevant public-access special-interest programs.

Premium giveaways work the same way on TV as in radio, except that you're limited to the public station's annual or semiannual subscription drives. Again, the announcer will mention your business and your offer, and state the terms: how large a pledge the viewer must make to claim your donated prize. (There is no reason why you couldn't donate prizes for random giveaways at other times, but no one seems to do it. Maybe you'll be the first.)

Cable stations must provide community-service and public-access channels as a condition of their license. Many of the programs aired on these channels are special-interest shows similar to those on radio, and therefore provide a sensible way to advertise on TV. With the right audience, an ad could be as simple as a typed message displayed on the air for fifteen seconds while the announcer reads it.

Spots on cable can be surprisingly inexpensive. According to marketing consultant Dr. Kevin Nunley, even high-visibility spots on CNN or ESPN in affluent New York City suburbs go for as little as twenty-five dollars each (plus the cost of production, of course). In towns of under forty thousand, the airtime may cost as little as two dollars!

To hold down production costs, study Hal Landen's book, *Marketing with Video* (Oak Tree Press, 800-266-5564), and the free booklet, "Effective Cable Television Advertising," by Dale Carson (Tele-Communications, Inc., 800-220-9861).

Another TV option bypasses broadcasters altogether. Prepare a short professional video and mail it to qualified prospects. Again, production won't be cheap—but if you're selling an expensive product whose features are not well known, a ten- or fifteen-minute video demonstration might make sense. During an election campaign, one candidate mailed a video to every voter in Massachusetts. It cost him much less than paid ads.

To save big bucks, take a leaf from Bonnie Marlewski-Probert <mailto:brmp@aol.com>.

We wanted to expand from books to include videos for our market. Because I am always looking for a great value, I joined a local cable access station and took their courses for camera, lighting, and producing. I worked on several shoots for other producers and directors, until I was comfortable.

After producing a few thirty-minute shows for others, she bartered public relations services with a video production company.

We had a 60-minute, broadcast-quality video that is currently being distributed all over the U.S. for us by our distributors and through magazine ads. The video company president asked if we would be interested in doing a second video and continuing swapping for PR work. I said sure! We did—and I just received an endorsement from the largest group in our niche market that specializes on the topic.

Our total investment in the first video was the cost of donuts and coffee for the crew on the day of the shoot. We shot on a 14,000-acre resort, free of charge in exchange for a mention on the video. . . . If you want to do a high-quality video, don't let the money thing stop you. If you are short on money, get long on creativity! The first video retails for $34.95 and the second for $29.95.

You can preview the results for yourself at http://www.horsecrazy.com.

Video news releases are becoming more common. In most situations, I have my doubts: the long production time, the high cost, and the danger of bad impressions make this a tool to be cautious about. But media consultant Brian Jud <mailto:bjud@marketingdirections.com> points out that well-produced video (or audio) releases are ideal for securing yourself a spot as a talk show guest.

TV continues to grow. The industry is still only a few decades old, and its technology will change dramatically in the next decade or so. High-definition TV is improving picture and sound quality, much as color replaced black-and-white. Communications networks will allow two-way video transmission over phone lines. Personal computers can already incorporate real-time video; that technology has already spawned targeted TV presentations over the Internet—and PCs and television will continue to integrate with each other and evolve new markets.

Because cable brings the physical network into the viewer's home, TV may become interactive. We may have completely new kinds of TV shows, such as a live video conference call with viewer comments Instant surveys will become common: Viewers will press a button to vote yes or no on a question. It's going to be a whole new world out there, so re-evaluate TV as an ad medium every few years.

— Shopping Channels —

To me, this is perverse. Why would people watch a parade of products go by to order one that looks interesting? (Multimedia and online catalogs make more sense; prospects can pick and choose without wading through tons of garbage.)

I admit to being a catalog junkie, yet I can't think of anything more boring than watching this sort of thing. A catalog is there only when you want to look at it, but every product listing is available at any time. You can mull over a prospective purchase, comparison shop, request additional information, and so forth. To the viewers, I say, get a life!

Yet TV shopping seems, against all logic, to work. I don't know why, but products move in this format. If it appeals to you, talk to your cable company and find out more—or pick up a copy of *Electronic Retailing* magazine and contact some of the infomercial producers who advertise there. Don't expect this to be cheap, either.

Interestingly, home-shopping vendors such as QVC are now porting their entire catalogs to Web sites—but the TV versions still create huge demand. Tens of thousands of units can be sold in just a few minutes of national airtime.

20

New Media

New media—and thus, new marketing possibilities—seem to be cropping up under every bush and tree these days. Things are primitive but rapidly growing, much like TV around 1950, or cars around 1915. Dozens of options either didn't exist or weren't very practical a decade ago. We'll look at some of the more interesting ones here—other than the Internet, which gets a whole lot more attention a bit later.

— Voice Mail—

More and more places around the country offer a large information/response voice mail system (often sponsored by the local newspaper). People no longer have to log on with a computer, wait for the newspaper to come, or just not know. Even my community of thirty thousand has had it for several years: You dial the main number and then press a four-digit number to get everything from election results to weather. There are also interactive selections, allowing you to record a voice message as a letter to the editor, comment on a question asked in the previous day's paper, or enter a contest.

Nearly all of these are sponsored by local businesses, whose commercials precede the information the caller wants (the charge may be fixed, or set per "hit"). Some of these are effective, some not; the same principles of targeting apply as in any other media buy.

The most targeted ad I've heard is from a kids' activity and fitness center advertising on the menu selections that provide information on school closings in the event of bad weather—telling parents that the facility is an option on a snow day.

New York's *Village Voice* offers one-minute samples of different bands playing at local clubs. Other possibilities might include: a purveyor of umbrellas on the weather line, a tickets-by-phone outlet sponsoring the cultural listings, a sports equipment store underwriting basketball scores, and a comedian supplying the joke of the day.

Linda Chestney <mailto:nfp@nh.ultranet.com>, publisher of regional bicycle trail books in New Hampshire, teams up with a local bicycle shop that sells her book. She provides a weekly tip on where to ride (much like David Majercik's maple and foliage reports in chapter 18). The store pays for the spot, which concludes with plugs for both her books and the store that sells them.

Many similar possibilities exist in other media. For instance, if you'd like to market via computer to the captive audience aboard aircraft, call a service such as FlightLink, 708-573-2660. Opportunities for various types of electronic sponsorship exist in bowling alleys, supermarkets, movie theaters, malls, tourist information booths . . . anywhere people line up for information or entertainment.

— Automated Fax-Backs —

While over 70 million people worldwide are connected to the Internet, a far larger number have access to faxes. Many companies are setting up systems to send information automatically to a fax that dials in. Users love the convenience and quick response, and it costs much less than direct mail.

No need for an expensive service: PC software programs such as WinFaxPro can do this easily (I use a Macintosh and haven't tested it myself).

It's a great idea, but keep a few things in mind:

- Keep it under five pages—nobody likes to read through twenty-five pages on curly, blurry fax paper.
- Make sure it's in crisp, readable type, with plenty of white space.
- Test different brands of fax machines and fax modems calling into your system.
- Include ordering information.
- If the recipient might want more information, set up a mechanism to provide it.
- Provide a voice ordering number in case of technical problems.

— Other Fax Innovations —

Though it's been kicking around for over one hundred years, fax technology continues to mature. And as fax and computer technologies blend, the user benefits. Some examples:

Faxes can be sent and/or received through e-mail. No more scrambling to turn on your fax machine on a shared line—or worse, greeting voice callers with those horrid beep tones. For $12.50 per month, I receive faxes through JFax <http://www.jfax.com>, which allows you to pick a fax number from several cities around the world. As an extra bonus, when I print them on my 600 dpi laser printer, the faxes are the clearest I've ever seen; even 9-point type is easy to read. (This service sends as well as receives, but for sending, I use my own modem.)

This is also a fabulous way to experiment with an international presence; you can have a fax number in London, Paris, or Amsterdam. And for Americans who do a lot of international faxing, you may be able to hold down costs as copycat services spring up in other countries. A newer competitor lets you receive faxes for free, if you don't mind seeing ads.

Going in the other direction, mixing the Internet, databases, and fax sending yields great results for outbound fax broadcasting, too. A wonderful service called I-Media Fax <http://www.imediafax.com> allows you to select media from a list of many thousands, target them with pinpoint accuracy for the exact press release you're creating, and send faxes from your computer. This service provider, Paul Krupin of Direct Contact Publishing, also sells a comprehensive database and directory of media e-mail addresses for a very reasonable fee at <http://www.owt.com/dircon>. Or you can use the online "jumpstation" to visit over three thousand media Web sites directly from http://www.owt.com/dircon/mediajum.htm#Mediajump.

I recommend Direct Contact's services as a satisfied user—so much that I signed up to be an associate. If you visit his site, I would appreciate it if you put "Frugal Horowitz" in the Associates box.

Using a computer fax modem, sending a fax to many recipients (called broadcast fax) requires only a few mouse clicks and can work unattended (though fax software tends to be not very smart, and will require some cross-checking to make sure everything goes through).

— Infomercials and Multimedia —

Everything I said about traditional TV commercials (sixty seconds and under) holds true for these longer and more elaborate presentations as well. If you're going to do them, be prepared to spend a lot of money and have them done well. Marketers should expect to amortize the high production and airing costs by creating ongoing relationships with their customers, starting with a polite cross-selling or up-selling bargain offer during the prospect's initial phone response. And make sure to include a direct-response component (i.e., a toll-free telephone number).

Anything that incorporates several of the senses is a good candidate for a professionally produced, benefit-focused film or video—or interactive multimedia presentation. But whether the final product is shown on TV, posted on the Web, mailed to prospective clients, or used as an on-site selling tool at conferences or trade shows should depend on a good market analysis. Maybe you'll want to do all of these things. However you do it, make it as easy as possible for your prospects to respond. As we all get busier (or lazier), the more work you make them do, the less likely it is that they'll follow through.

Some products lend themselves very well to the long form. Imagine, for instance, how a resort operator could use a fifteen- or thirty-minute video to sell a vacation destination in a way that simply isn't possible in print media or in a traditional thirty-second commercial. *Electronic Retailing* magazine (July/August 1995) reported that one travel service upped its monthly bookings from six hundred to six thousand after establishing an interactive presence on the Internet.

Luxury goods are also appropriate. Car manufacturers have leapt to embrace these technologies, because they can put together presentations that customize themselves toward the exact model, style, and color a prospect is considering—and even display different interior and exterior angles as the potential buyer shifts viewpoints.

Consider Toyota's experience. The company put together an elegant CD-ROM highlighting every car and truck it makes. This info-crammed disc, called "Toyota Interactive," would take sixteen hours to view in its entirety. Toyota advertised the disc in both car magazines and computer magazines. The company was expecting only a few thousand responses and did an initial pressing of five thousand. But within five months, the company had sent out fifty-six thousand discs!

A follow-up telephone survey of three hundred disc viewers showed a number of benefits. First of all, they reached real prospects: People expecting to buy a new car within a year or so vastly outnumbered those who just wanted to satisfy their curiosity about interactive presentations. Second, consumers felt better prepared before going to dealers. And third, their view of Toyota was enhanced; the company was perceived as forward-thinking and considerate.

In these media, it's easy to forget that the purpose of your presentation is a *marketing* message. Don't let a sizzling presentation get so carried away with its technological and artistic sophistication that you violate your marketing fundamentals. Evaluate any video production on its ability to convey the ten points of great copywriting, discussed back in chapter 3. And if you've chosen an interactive medium (interactive TV, a presence on the Internet, or a branching CD-ROM computer disc, for instance), maintain the "viewer-driven" feel of successful presentations. The viewer should feel like he or she is the one making the choice as to what happens next. So anticipate your customers' obvious and not-so-obvious questions, and build links to the answers.

And—as infomercials subdivide into sitcommercials (modeled after situation comedies), video catalogs, documercials, and so forth—treat your viewers fairly. Craig Evans points out (*Electronic Retailing*, September/October 1995) that if consumers think they're watching an information program and then find out it was designed to sell a product, they'll feel betrayed, cynical . . . and reluctant to buy.

Once you've taken the trouble to create a first-class presentation, get as much mileage as you can. Put it on your Web site, of course. And mail a video or audiocassette, CD-ROM, or floppy disk to your prospects. People are flattered to receive electronic media in the mail (particularly if you attach a personalized letter). Perhaps this will change as they become commonplace, but for now, your recipient will likely give you a look or listen that you might not have gotten without the electronic marketing. And don't forget to note your TV credit in print ads, direct mail, and so forth (e.g., "as seen on CBS").

A recent trend is the conversion of print catalogs to electronic, multimedia ones, complete with color graphics, animation, sound, and so forth. Depending on your product line, this may enhance your impact. Pricing and quality vary widely, so be a good shopper, make sure you understand the terms of your agreement thoroughly, and ask to see samples of previous work.

Many technologies are appearing for electronically published books. The most common formats are HTML (which makes the document readable in any Web browser) and Adobe Acrobat (which keeps font and design choices and can be read with Adobe's free Acrobat Reader software). Some of these are simply downloaded to the purchaser's computer and printed out, while others are designed for various (as yet incompatible) handheld "readers" that allow you to bring an e-book to the beach, or an entire research library on a business trip. They're a good deal more portable than laptops, but it's too soon to know how the market will treat them.

And just as I was finishing this manuscript, I got a press release about a multimedia presentation device the size of a credit card, playable in any CD-ROM drive.

Money Savers and Money Generators

Do it cooperatively—buy a 20-megabyte chunk of space on a themed disk going to your audience. This would be a good way for prospects to compare ski resorts, for example.

Or charge for the disks, if you've got something of value on its own. MusicNet provides musical samples of some two hundred releases in each quarterly issue; prospects can not only listen, but order entire albums twenty-four hours a day, with a choice of toll-free call, fax, or modem (the latter just by pressing a button on screen). A four-issue subscription is $29.95.

Finally, if you air a long-format commercial on TV, buy late night slots at very cheap rates, obtain an automatic four-number VCR programming code, and publicize the spot; encourage people to tape your show and watch it later.

Anything you put up on the Internet or distribute through CD-ROM, tapes, or diskettes opens the question of piracy. However, there are ways to protect your intellectual property. For instance, a company called SoftLock <http:www.softlock.com> offers a way to protect Adobe Acrobat and other files. As of June 1998, their fee structure was $99 a year for the first product, plus commissions of 15 percent ($1.00 minimum).

CD-ROMs, Adobe Acrobat files, e-books, and other electronic media also generate the potential for another revenue stream. Not only can you make money selling the product, you can also sell advertising. I just took out a $20 ad in a downloadable e-book about marketing. I bought a spot on the page about press releases, directing people to my site and to my writing services. We'll see if it pays off in increased site traffic, book sales, and client orders for writing jobs.

— Software Brochures and — Brand Awareness Products

On electronic BBSs (bulletin board systems), Web sites, and information utilities, public domain or shareware materials can be posted and copied. Nothing prevents you from preparing a software brochure about your product or service, particularly if you're skilled in animation or multimedia presentation. Buick, for instance, annually distributes a computer disk highlighting its products. Anyone who sees their ad in a computer magazine can request a free copy. If you distribute your software through an online software library, you don't have to pay for expensive advertising.

Better yet, public domain software companies might pick up your contribution and list it in their catalogs, allowing you to reach computer users who don't have a modem. Look at their software listings to get an idea of how other companies are doing this. Often, a fairly simple multimedia presentation can be attractive enough as a source of art that users will want it.

Software can also serve a pure branding purpose even without direct marketing content. It's common to develop screen savers, startup screens, games, and utilities and distribute them free with a company logo. To quote from a January 1999 press release one screen-saver company sent me, "Think of Customer Savers as the complimentary pens and calendars of the 90s. Customer Savers help to keep your business in the minds of your customers. Customer Savers entertain and inform your customers and make them feel they are a part of your business family."

A January 1999 study by Conducent—a company that makes branded software products (and therefore has a vested interest in high numbers)—reports an astonishing 30 percent response from its 555,000 software users. In a sponsorship ad on the Internet Advertising Discussion List (February 2, 1999), the same company makes a claim of 94 percent response. Even if these numbers turn out to be inflated, it's still a channel worth investigating.

21

Getting Started in Cyberspace

Inventions have always changed our lives. The printing press, the automobile, the telephone, and television have all made sweeping changes in our society and in the way people interact—and market. But never in the history of the world has the social mindset changed as rapidly and broadly as in the "cyberspace revolution."

Call it cyberspace, online computing, the Internet, or the Information Superhighway, it's all the same place: a vast network of interrelated communities that know no geographical limits. The Internet, or Net, symbolizes humanity's rush to pursue business, education, research, and recreation on the new digital frontier.

A computer network is a group of computers that can exchange information and share printers or other resources. The Internet is nothing more than a worldwide network of these networks, letting the whole become something much greater than its parts—a shared virtual reality where almost anything is possible.

Science fiction novelist William Gibson coined the term "cyberspace" to describe this nonphysical experience. Cyberspace is a digital gathering of ideas,

concepts, and aspirations. The Net allows people to instantly and continuously communicate and share information, regardless of their location or the time of day—and thus has spawned a thriving new digital society, complete with virtual communities, virtual corporations, and virtual shopping malls.

Virtual corporations are partners who come together—often across wide geographical distances—to complete one project. For instance, a writer, graphic designer, and printer may join forces and bid together on an annual report. They may come together again for another project or dissolve forever once the job is done.

Virtual reality refers to a world that doesn't exist physically, but only in the computers that comprise it. The Net culture of people with common interests coming together through their computers creates hundreds of thousands of separate virtual communities—one kind of virtual reality—with each being no less real than a live club meeting. A virtual shopping mall allows a browser to explore many stores from his or her own computer.

For a brief history of the Internet, visit <http://www.frugalfun.com/nethistory.html>.

— Internet Savings —

Whether or not you're selling online, the Net can slash dollar and time costs. Posting commonly asked customer service questions on your Web site or e-mailing back and forth is cheaper than receiving a toll-free number call, mailing out a catalog, faxing, or replacing rapidly outdated print information several times a month. If you send a lot of mail, the Net can be a real budget stretcher. There's no postage cost, no fax paper to waste, the labor savings over traditional methods are substantial, and in most parts of the United States, you can connect with a local telephone call. And of course, any question your Web site can answer frees up your customer service staff for other calls.

E-mail accounts typically range from free to about twenty-five dollars per month for unlimited use. It's not surprising that e-mail now carries a higher volume than the U.S. Postal Service. Even at the high end, if you replace just twenty domestic postal mails a week, the postage savings alone more than cover the cost of the account. Add the costs of addressing, handling, paper, and printing, and the payback is even faster.

And if you have contacts halfway around the world, there's no need to worry about time zones!

Other advantages: The recipient can save the text to disk, modify it, forward it to others, respond quickly, and so forth. This is very powerful; it enables your message to build like a pyramid as many recipients forward in turn to their own large networks (you may see this referred to as viral, propagation, exponential, or ripple marketing, among other names).

And when a message doesn't go through, you're usually informed. Often the problem is a simple typographical or copying error. Unlike postal addresses, e-mail addresses require 100 percent accuracy. Your mail will be undeliverable if even one character is wrong, missing, or out of place.

Of course, successful delivery doesn't guarantee that the recipient opens or reads your message, so make sure your subject line is interesting and related to your message, your post is brief and to the point, and you've provided contact information.

Many companies stand to save huge customer service costs. Sun Microsystems's Neil Knox estimates his company saves about $8 million annually by using the Web—not even counting a substantial direct-sales benefit (*WebMaster,* November/December 1995).

Worried about the loss of personal contact? There are technologies that combine the best of both. For instance, a service called WebCallback allows a Web site visitor to enter a phone number and be called back instantly by a human customer-service representative. (Of course, this only works if the visitor has an extra phone line.)

Make sure your subject line is interesting and related to your message, your post is brief and to the point, and you've provided contact information.

In some ways, the Net makes personal contact easier and/or cheaper. It's already possible to have real-time phone conversations over the Net—goodbye to overseas long-distance charges! Within three to five years, as early adopters bring down the cost and increase the installed user base, this technology will be practical for many conversations. Also, as technologies converge, e-mail and Web pages can work with fax, voice calls, even television. The day will come when your Web connection supports live videoconferencing around the world.

Spend your online time efficiently. Do as much off-line as possible, even if you have unlimited service—but especially if you don't. Connect to the network, send and collect your mail, and exit. Then read the mail and answer it. Once past the initial exploration phase, go to Web sites to track down specific information, rather than idly "surfing" the day away. And if you pay by the minute, stay out of chat rooms unless you've got a good reason; they'll eat up an awful lot of time in a hurry. In many forums, you can download a chat transcript and read it later, running up a bill of three minutes instead of an hour.

— Making Money Online —

The Internet can be the most effective marketing medium for many businesses. However; there's an awful lot of hype and misinformation out there—all sorts of outrageous claims to sucker in naive business owners and part them from their money. There are definitely right and wrong ways to go about marketing online.

Is it worth the trouble to get e-mail and a World Wide Web presence? Definitely—if you know your marketing agenda and how cyberspace fits in—even for noncomputer-oriented products. Consider these real-life examples from Leah Woolford <mailto: woolford@trip.net>:

I have a real estate client that sells income properties by using the Web. He now has a list of investors across the world. He originally started selling residential, and then found a market for investment properties. He had his site up only one month before getting his first contract. As well, I have an international law firm that receives retainers from their Web marketing and public relations. Companies that need U.S. firms to handle contracts and negotiations have found this U.S. firm from as far away as Russia and Peru. I have other clients who are successfully selling services and products on the net. I myself have been awarded marketing contracts, as well as graphic design assignments, through my online marketing.

It's not just products that will sell, but the most important aspect is developing the marketing strategy behind the site, whether it is product or service that you are selling. There are success stories out there, but it's still a marketing strategy that makes the difference.

******
Leah Woolford
Alliance of Global Business Exchange
Where business meets on the web!
http://www.globalbiz.com
FREE Listings for companies and consultants
US Telephone 512.883.8833
US FAX 512.883A329
******

For me, the Internet has meant tens of thousands of dollars in my pocket and has broadened my geographic reach to handle clients as far away as Cyprus and London.

My experience is far from unique. Web designer Kathy Barthen <webmaster@irelandnow.com> sets up e-commerce (commercial transaction) sites from her office in Cork, Ireland. Although most Europeans pay per-minute charges for both the Net connection and the actual phone call, "every e-commerce shop we have set up so far has made their Web site investment back within 3 to 6 months" (Internet Advertising Discussion List, January 15, 1999).

The Web is only one part of cyberspace. Marketing possibilities abound throughout the Internet. If done properly, even the smallest of businesses can achieve amazing success online. However, marketing online is very different from marketing anywhere else. While Web sites can be very commercial, the Net, outside the Web, is definitely *not* a hard-sell medium. Many entrepreneurs have been badly burned by trying to adapt hard-sell direct-mail or advertising methods to a market driven by vast quantities of free information and mutual desire to help. Ignore the customs of the culture at your own peril; on the Internet, nothing spreads faster than a bad reputation.

What makes the Internet different?

Just for starters . . .

■ Potentially unlimited information: There's essentially no cost to publishing new information, and thus you can go as deep as you want. The more information you provide, the more your prospects will feel encouraged to do business with you. You can provide hundreds of pages of material at no more cost than one or two pages—and you can present it in small, manageable chunks.

- Hyperlinks: By clicking on a link, visitors can find the exact information they need—and even a huge site doesn't overwhelm.
- Interactivity and feedback: Your customers can now talk to you instantly, at any time, and also talk to their friends and colleagues. This has tremendous potential for market research, among other benefits. It also allows word to spread, positively or negatively, with amazing speed.
- Customization: With the right tools, you can use interactivity to develop individualized presentations and choices for your customers. They can pick and choose from various options, and you can tailor your responses depending on the answers.
- Rich media: Sound, pictures, interactive forms, even video and animation can now be incorporated into your presentation.
- The giving, anticommercial culture of the Internet: Within this culture, information is valued, and there is a desire to do business with those who provide it.

In the next several chapters, we'll look at some of these differences in depth. But first, let's answer the question I hear over and over again: "Is anyone actually making money on the Internet?" Even discounting the many secondary revenue streams online (i.e., advertising revenue and affiliate commissions, both of which we'll discuss later in some detail), the answer is a strong, loud, vociferous, *yes!* Thousands of Netrepreneurs actually sell lots and lots of product online. Here's another very concrete success story from the Internet Sales Discussion List:

We have a family-owned fruit farm that has been here in Florida for generations. We have retail stores and the associated costs that go with them. Mortgages, taxes, water, electricity, phone, workmen's comp, insurance, payroll easy 6,000 dollars a month for our smallest Indian River Fruit store. On the web, however, my Internet access for taking care of my store is $21.95 a month. My phone line is $42.95. My computer with all the bells and whistles, $1,500.00 (one-time cost only). Labor at 40 hours per week answering questions, submitting store to search engines and cross-linking, etc. $300.00. Retail sales last year at my two online sites http://www.giftfruit.com and http://www.indianriver.com: $1.5 million dollars. Retail sales at my smallest Indian River Fruit Store: $365,000.

Add it up. How can you not justify it? I think the big problem with online marketing is people trying to sell junk and scams. People with established products are not having the same problem.

It quite simply is very cost-effective for a small business to market this way.

******

Barry Gainer - President
The Indian River Gift Fruit Company
"We Ship the World's Best Gift Fruit"
http:// www.giftfruit.com
http://www.indianriver.com

******

The comparatively low costs and instantaneous delivery time online can create opportunities very quickly for those who can move as fast as the evening news. When President Clinton's televised grand jury testimony was released in the fall of 1998, video merchant Jaffer Ali of PulseTV.com <mailto:jali@pennmedia.com> rushed to e-mail his affiliates that he could supply the tape. In three days, he signed up over one hundred new affiliates and processed hundreds of orders, increasing his site traffic by a factor of 10.

A year earlier, after Princess Diana's death, it took him six weeks to produce and distribute a TV commercial. But by harnessing the power of the Internet, the Clinton campaign "took 1 hour to get it up on our site, e-mail the new release to our network of affiliates, and start taking orders immediately . . . I only wish we had 10,000 affiliates right now!"

(Internet Sales Discussion List, September 24,1998).

Another advantage: Media can find you! Howard Meibach <mailto:webmaster@hollywoodlitsales.com> sends out press releases one to two times a month, highlighting the new content at his movie screenplay Web site. He's been featured in both *The New York Times* and CNN by reporters who found his site.

Viatical expert Gloria Wolk <mailto:ggwolk@viatical-expert.net> says, "The worst marketing blunder was not setting up a Web site early on. This has turned out to be not only the best marketing tool but also the most cost-effective." She received coverage through a nationally syndicated financial columnist, was a guest on a syndicated radio show, and was featured by Kiplinger's, all because media people found her site.

My own experience bears this out. I received a phone call from a BBC TV producer in London who had found my Web site in one of the search engines. She is interested in filming me for a documentary on saving money (the theme of my other book, *The Penny-Pinching Hedonist: How to Live Like Royalty with a Peasant's Pocketbook*). I was able to instantly e-mail my press kit, along with a notation that I could help her find a camera crew if she didn't have the budget to make the trip. This was only one media contact among many. Another led to a large story in the *Cleveland Plain Dealer* that sold quite a few books.

— Online Glossary —

Cyberspace has its own lingo. Here are some of the more common terms you might encounter:

Affiliate (Affinity, Associate) Program: A marketing tool that pays commissions to referring Web sites.

Applet: A bit of computer code, usually written in a programming language called Java, that allows a Web page to do something out of the ordinary (with a long list of possibilities).

Autoresponder, Mailbot: An e-mail message that is automatically sent when someone requests it.

Bandwidth: Capacity of the data "pipe." The faster a connection to the Internet, the greater bandwidth it supports. And the more "bandwidth hogs" (animation, video, audio, huge graphics) on your Web pages, the more slowly your site will load and the more frustrated your visitors will be— especially if their connection is low bandwidth.

Banner: A graphic advertisement displayed on a Web page.

BBS: Bulletin board system. A small and generally local version of an online utility, offering rudimentary communication features. These have largely been supplanted by the major *information utilities* and thousands of *ISPs*.

BG, VBG: Big grin, very big grin.

Browser: The software that enables a computer to display World Wide Web pages. Modern browsers often offer other functions, too, such as e-mail, newsgroups, and file transfer.

Bulletin Board, Message Board: An area of a Web site or information service set aside for posts from readers.

CGI: A scripting protocol allowing Web sites to receive and process information from forms, often involving integration with a database.

Chat Room: A discussion group technology that allows many people to "talk" to each other in real time, by typing on their keyboards. Chats may or may not have a featured guest, a topic, or a focus. They've gotten a bad name in some circles because of their use as a sexual outlet, but they also have a great deal of use for business. For instance, it's much cheaper to set up a chat among several people in offices in different countries than to have an international telephone conference call.

Click-through, Click-through Rate (CTR): The ratio of people who click on a banner to visit another site.

Cookie: A bit of code that a Web site deposits on a visitor's computer, to track certain actions, information, or preferences. Cookies allow marketers to customize their presentation to each visitor. Some people turn cookies off because they fear privacy repercussions, but usually, cookies are limited in scope, and generally used only to let a site know that a previous visitor has returned.

CPA: Cost per action. A revenue model for advertising that charges by the number of people who take a certain action (fill out a form, call a phone number, etc.).

CPC: Cost per click. The most common form of CPA, charging by the number of clicks.

CPM: Cost per thousand. A revenue model for advertising that charges by the number of *impressions*—similar to the charges for print publications.

Digest: An e-mail discussion list delivered as one large message containing several posts, as opposed to getting each post separately.

Discussion Group: A group that comes together to discuss topics on a particular theme. There are many different types of discussion groups, including *mailing lists, forums, newsgroups, bulletin boards,* and *chats,* among others. Any of these can be *moderated* or *unmoderated.*

Domain Name: The part of an e-mail or Web address that identifies its owner. In an e-mail address, the portion that follows the @ sign. In a Web site address, the portion immediately following "www" (or following "http://" if there is no "www").

eCommerce, E-Commerce: Commerce over the Internet, and the software tools that enable it.

Emoticon: punctuation and/or letter characters put together to form a picture that conveys emotion, such as smiling, frowning, winking.

Eyeballs: A measurement of the number of people exposed to an advertising message.

E-zine: A magazine or newsletter whose primary delivery is by e-mail.

FAQ: Frequently Asked Questions document (pronounced "fack").

Filter, Filtering: Software that automatically performs an action on an e-mail message, such as moving it to a particular mailbox.

Flame: A nasty message.

Forum: A discussion group whose postings are placed on a Web site or BBS.

Frame: A Web site programming technique that provides more than one window at the same time.

FTP: File transfer protocol (a way of exchanging files between computers, including loading new content onto your Web site).

GIF: A graphics format on the Web that allows animation and other special effects.

Host: See *Web Host.*

HTML: HyperText Markup Language. The most universal and most important programming language used to display Web pages.

HTML Mail: E-mail that uses HTML commands to produce fancy formatting.

http: HyperText Transfer Protocol. All Web addresses start with this prefix.

Impressions: The number of people seeing any given message.

Information Service, Information Utility: A company that provides such features as e-mail, bulletin boards, thematic content, and shopping. Once the most common doorway to cyberspace, with many competitors in the field, this sector has shaken out in the past few years—feeling competition from the World Wide Web and a whole host of local and national ISPs. One company, America Online, has expanded tremendously, while most of its competitors have either shriveled up or folded entirely.

Internet: The famous "Information Superhighway"—a vast global network of interconnected computers, able to exchange information almost instantaneously.

ISP: Internet service provider. A company that provides access to e-mail and/or the Web.

JPEG: Another graphics format on the Web, used mostly for photos.

Listserv: A commercial software package that administers a *mailing list.* Also often used (incorrectly) as a synonym for *mailing list.*

LOL: Laugh out loud.

Mailbot: *See* autoresponder.

Mailing List: A discussion group whose postings arrive by e-mail. Postings may or may not be archived on a Web site.

Majordomo: Another mailing-list distribution software package.

Moderated: A discussion group whose posts are cleared by a human being before they are made public.

Newbie: An Internet beginner (this term is often used derisively to attack people who don't take the time and trouble to understand the culture of that particular community).

Newsgroup: A discussion group whose postings stay on a central computer and are accessed through news reader software.

Opt-In: A mailing list whose subscribers have asked to receive certain types of mail—often, commercial messages—from a particular sender.

Portal: A popular doorway Web site, such as a *search engine* or information service home page, which typically provides both jumping-off places and original content for visitors.

Real Time: A change that takes place as you watch. For example, on banner creation sites, you choose a graphic and a text message and then the software creates the banner in real time—very useful for comparing several options.

ROFL: Roll on the floor laughing.

RTFM: Read the fucking manual (hey, I don't write 'em!).

Search Engine: A navigation tool that suggests Web sites matching certain search terms.

Shopping Cart: Software that enables visitors to select items at any time during a visit, and have the site figure out the order and shipping totals at the end.

Sig, Signature: Online "business card" at the end of an e-mail, newsgroup, or forum message.

SIG: Special-interest group. A discussion group, especially on pre-Web BBSs.

Spam, Spammer: Unsolicited, untargeted bulk e-mail, and the people who use this tactic.

Spider: A search robot that crawls through a Web site to index its contents. Most search engines use spiders to bring back the search results.

Thread: One topic in a discussion group.

TYVM: Thank you very much.

Unmoderated: A discussion group where every post is automatically passed on to the entire group.

URL: Uniform resource locator—an address in cyberspace. Most of those you'll encounter begin with "http" (Web sites) or "mailto" (e-mail addresses).

Web Host: A company that provides space for a Web site. This may or may not be the same company as your ISP.

Webzine: A magazine or newsletter posted on a Web site. Note: E-zines can also be archived on a Web site.

World Wide Web (Web, WWW, W3): A portion of the Internet that allows access to graphics, database forms, sound and video files, as well as text. This is one neighborhood in cyberspace where commercialization is absolutely okay.

— Learning Your Way Around —

The prefix *http://www.*—or, more and more often, just *http://*—represents the World Wide Web, as you may have figured out. The rest of a Web name follows much the same logic as a regular e-mail address, with the domain name followed by more specific guideposts.

While a full tutorial on the Web is outside the scope of this book, here's a brief introduction. The Web is an incredible storehouse of information—and action. It is becoming both the library and the shopping mall of the world. Want to find out about Zulu culture? Select a travel destination and learn about it through articles and pictures? Get instructions for growing an organic garden? It's all on the Web.

What if you want to find the lowest possible airfare to Detroit or Hong Kong? Read excerpts and reviews of a book or CD before purchasing? Get the weather report for a city anywhere in the world? Try your hand at writing specialized poetry? Look up a phone number or area code for any individual, business, or category of business? Figure out the price of something in any currency in the world? Create a banner ad for your business and experiment until you get the look you want? This is just the tip of the iceberg of what's possible on the Web.

You'll find all this treasure primarily with two tools: search engines or directories, and individual links from e-mail messages, discussion group postings, or other Web pages. We cover these as marketing weapons in some detail in chapters 23, 25, and 26; that discussion will give you enough information to learn how to use them (it's pretty easy, actually). Start practicing, and in under an hour, you'll get a pretty good feel for how the Web works.

Save a lot of frustration by searching for key phrases or groups of words, rather than just individual words. (There's a good explanation of how to search efficiently at <http://www.frugalfun.com/search.html>.) And as you explore the Web, keep a list of sites you'd like to return to so that you don't have to keep typing out those lengthy addresses. Depending on your software, the list may be called "bookmarks," "favorite places," or something similar. Look for a menu option to add the current Web site to the list (back up this list and your e-mail address list regularly). Create macros—sequences that repeat a series of keystrokes—for your own (carefully proofread) URL and e-address so you can type them accurately in one keystroke.

— Modems and Marketing —

Online technology is growing even more rapidly than stand-alone personal computers did in the early 1980s. Make sure your modem is at least 28,800 or 33,000 bps—these can sometimes be found for as little as fifty dollars or so—and investigate faster options. You'll feel the difference in lower online bills, reduced eye fatigue, and more time to use your computer for other things. Plus, you need a fast modem to take full advantage of online graphics and the World Wide Web. Obviously, if you have access to faster equipment (e.g., 56K, T-1, T-3, cable modem, frame relay, or ISDN), go for it—especially if someone else is paying the bill!

A $300–$500 "set-top box" brings the Web into a television over cable lines. These machines are very limited, but selling well. Watch for a major influx of new users, and a lot of people buying computers for the first time when they discover how much more they can do online. Even many experienced users are spending a growing share of time using Web TV or a similar unit. (See Mary Lu Wason's post to the Internet Sales Discussion List, September 14, 1997, archived at <http://www.mmgco.com>, for an example of an Internet storefront owner who prefers to surf with Web TV.) Be sure your Web presence reflects set-top users' needs as well as those using a computer.

✠

Cable modems are becoming common, and will rapidly become popular. This in turn will make possible much more extensive use of video, sound, and complex graphics—but your Web site should always offer a quick-loading, no-bells-and-whistles option for those with older, slower configurations.

22

Domain Do's and Don'ts

As you establish a presence in cyberspace, you'll need to figure out where you'll get your connection. Choices include information utilities such as America Online (AOL), national or international ISPs such as Mindspring, Earthlink (which has recently merged with Mindspring), IBM, and AT&T, or one of the thousands of smaller ISPs. You may also need a Web-hosting company. In most cases, you'll need to pick and register your domain name(s).

The larger companies let you check your e-mail from practically anywhere, for a local call. However, small local companies may offer more personal service. In any event, there are ways of retrieving your e-mail from the road, either by logging on with a toll call, using a forwarding service, or even a service that reads or faxes your e-mail to you on request.

Yes, it is possible to bypass the ISPs and set up your own server—but why anyone would want the high costs, endless headaches, and need for twenty-four-hour technical support coverage is beyond me. Pick a reliable company with a reasonable price and let them do their job for you.

Meanwhile, let's look at some of the choices.

— AOL—The One Remaining— Major Information Service

Until commercial restrictions on the Internet were lifted in 1995, the vast majority of people in cyberspace (other than academics and government employees, who had access to the "real" Internet) got there through an online information service or BBS: America Online, Compuserve, Delphi, Prodigy, GEnie, or smaller ones such as San Francisco's The Well. Often, people had several different addresses, because the different services couldn't send e-mail to each other's networks.

By the end of 1997, about 12 million Americans had Internet access outside the workplace. Just a year later, America Online alone boasted 14 million subscribers, and some 50 million Americans were connected. America Online bought up Compuserve (its nearest competitor) and then Netscape—creator of one of the two dominant Web browsers—and Time-Warner. Its own and Netscape's home pages give it two of the most popular portals in the world. No other information utility comes close.

Three factors propelled AOL way past its competition: (1) Once users could send e-mail across the different services, AOL's easier interface, descriptive user names, and accessible content made it an easy choice; (2) AOL was the first utility to not only provide full Internet access, but to do it with a point-and-click interface; (3) by introducing a $19.95 flat-rate unlimited-use plan at the end of 1996, AOL encouraged its members to explore cyberspace in depth—so much so that at first, its computers overloaded and there were many jokes about "America On Hold."

AOL isn't a bad way to get your feet wet in cyberspace. Consider what you get:

- Monthly plans ranging from $4.95 for three hours to $21.95 for unlimited access
- Free classified ads in numerous interest areas
- Free worldwide e-mail—including attached formatted documents—with the option to read and respond off-line; e-mail to other AOL members can include formatted text (bold, italic, etc.)
- Internet services including Word Wide Web, Gopher, and WAIS databases (repositories of much critical information gathered and posted in the pre-Web days) and certain newsgroups
- Small (2-megabyte) personal Web sites, and software to create them
- Research resources ranging from today's *New York Times* to encyclopedias and databases (though Compuserve and the Web are much stronger in this regard)
- Numerous special-interest bulletin boards, teleconferencing chat rooms, and so forth
- Access to all sorts of business opportunities, contacts, and services—including the chance to "meet" and ask questions of nationally known experts
- Substantial quantities of downloadable software—and software and hardware technical support—for both Mac and PC
- Free connecting calls in most parts of the continental United States; 8 cents per minute

elsewhere in the country; international access from many other countries

I used America Online from July 1994 to July 1997—and it was my primary service until November 1996.

However, AOL falls down in other areas:

- Sooner or later, if you are serious about marketing online, you'll need your own domain name. By setting it up immediately, you'll first of all have a better shot at your perfect domain name, and second, you won't have the major headache of changing your address later on. While I have been told that AOL finally offers "yourname.com" Web hosting, I don't know anyone who has tried this service through them.
- The e-mail software, while easy to use, is very slow and lacks crucial features—including filters. And competing packages, such as Eudora, are powerful and easy to learn.
- Your Web site will not be spidered by many of the popular search engines, and you'll have a long and cumbersome URL. Both of these factors will make it quite difficult to bring people to your site.
- Based on my experience using AOL exclusively for over two years, I discovered that AOL is not considered a good neighborhood in cyberspace. If your Web site deals at all with eCommerce, online marketing, or other aspects of doing business on the Internet, or brings you in contact with the old-line Internet communities who were there before commercialization, you will encounter outright prejudice against doing business with people who have AOL domain addresses.

What about other options? For most marketers, the best choice will be setting up a domain name and an account with an ISP—either a national or a local company. Most of these offer an unlimited access plan for $9–$25 per month; some also offer a more limited plan for less. There are even a number of companies providing free e-mail, but the cost of a full-service account is so reasonable that I recommend getting one. As with AOL, a free account impairs your credibility online.

In fact, according to Jim Daniels <mailto: webmaster @jdd-publishing.com>, editor of *BizWeb Gazette,* some ISPs are blocking mail from these domains, because too high a percentage is spam. And credit-card-fraud experts recommend refusing to process orders originating in a free Web-based e-mail service.

— Internet Service Providers —

Beyond the information utilities, hundreds of options exist for Internet access. Every area has many providers. Typically, the software will require more setup and getting used to than the online services, but you'll be rewarded with more flexibility. ISPs offer several advantages over online services: better software, including a full-fledged Web browser such as Netscape Navigator or Microsoft Explorer as well as a decent e-mail program such as Eudora, Pegasus, or Outlook; mailbots; much larger blocks of space on the Web; faster connections; access to virtually all parts of the Net; attractive pricing; domain name registration; better credibility among old-school Netheads; and less junk e-mail flowing in. Some also offer nationwide access numbers.

If you'll be online a lot, look for unlimited use (or several hundred hours a month) for $9–$25 per month. Light users should get ten or twenty hours per month and pay less than $15. AT&T customers with PCs are now entitled to five hours free every month. Also, if you know a Web presence is going to be part of your strategy—and in almost every case, it should!—ask about hosting services. If choosing between two different e-mail providers, go with the one that offers a better deal on Web hosting. Some people find they benefit by having their Web-hosting and e-mail service with the same provider, which centralizes your customer service and means the various parts of your domain will work smoothly together—and some use separate providers to take advantage of their respective strengths. In any case, check references and test the

tech support before selecting either an e-mail provider or a Web host.

— Your Own Domain Name —

Internet "domain" names (the part to the right of the @ sign) are rapidly being snapped up. Protect your company by registering your domain, even if you don't have a host computer. You can get your mail forwarded to your regular provider. Currently, it costs $35 a year to register a commercial domain name in the United States; the first two years are payable up front.

Why bother with your own domain name? Here are several important reasons:

- When you do a Web site, your address will be significantly shorter, and thus easier for people to remember and type in. Make your domain name as intuitive as possible, especially if you have a well-known brand name.
- A short, memorable address can be used as a marketing tool on everything from radio appearances to billboards.
- If you change from one provider to another, you won't have to change your address with every contact you've had over perhaps years. And you might change providers frequently as your needs change, or if your original choice proves unreliable. (For these reasons, your own domain is also better than using a redirect service that points your old address to your current one.)
- How much pain are you avoiding? Longtime Net marketer Cliff Kurtzman says you'll not only have to reprint business cards, but also "hunt out and find all the hyperlinks on the Web that link to your old site address and ask the various Webmasters to revise their links (good luck!)."
- It's easier to register with certain search engines (the Web equivalent of telephone directories) with your own domain. Alta Vista, for instance, one of the most frequently used search engines,

will index only a few hundred Web addresses (called URLs) from any one domain—so if you're using an AOL free Web site, you can't get listed there.

The letters after the last dot are called "top-level domains." In theory, they give a clue about the type of organization: *com* for commercial, *net* for system administrators, *edu* for colleges, *gov* for government, *org* for other nonprofits (though in recent years, many commercial enterprises have gotten .net or .org addresses, and many nonprofits have sprung for .com domains), *mil* for military. If there are only two letters at the end, it's a country code (*ca* for Canada, *il* for Israel, etc.). Either way, there's no period at the end of an address.

*T*hough many of the good [domains] are taken, a little creativity can go a long way.

For years, there's been talk about introducing new domains, such as .firm and .store—but as of this writing, they haven't appeared. Until that changes, virtually all of the domains you'll encounter will be .com, .net, .edu, .gov, and .mil, or country-specific domains.

In most cases, you will want a "com" suffix for your domain. That's the domain for commercial businesses—and many browsers go there by default (type in "books" and you'll go to "books.com," for instance). Though many of the good ones are taken, a little creativity can go a long way; I recently helped a board of realtors choose the domain name "realestateorg.com." If a group of Texas realtors came along, I might suggest "texrealestate.com."

If you can get it, consider the commodity that you sell. Many of these will have been snapped up, but you may be able to come up with an alternate word. For instance, I'd bet that "papyrus.com" was available long after "books.com" was assigned. Likewise, a farmer may find that "purpleonions.com" is ready to use, while "onion.com" and "onions.com" were probably claimed ages ago. If you sell roofing shingles and you can obtain "shingles.com" or "roofingshingles.com," your site will come up if people search by entering a domain name.

There's also an outfit that offers a "to" suffix, representing the Republic of Tonga—a possible alternative if the name you want is already taken in its .com, .net, and .org variants. It charges $95 per year to redirect traffic to your existing Web provider. However, in the two years since I've learned about this, I've only seen about five .to addresses. If you want to try it anyway, visit <http://www.tonga.to/tonga/>, and let me know about your experience. This does *not* constitute an endorsement!

Your firm name (or a domain based on your own personal name) may or may not be your best choice for your primary domain—but at $35 per year, consider purchasing it anyway; multiple domains can point to the same site. Read the section on naming a business in chapter 2; many of the principles hold when naming your cyberbusiness.

Harvey Segal <mailto:hsegal@supertips.com>, writing in Michel Fortin's *Profit Pill* e-zine (January 20, 1999), points out a few more factors in naming a domain:

> It should convey effectively the nature of your business. A name such as golfnews.com will immediately give the reader an idea of what the site contains, with no further description. It will also be easy to recall from memory at a later time.
>
> But you must also plan ahead for any future diversity. Suppose you then decide to provide news about other sporting activities. It would make no sense to set up new names such as: golfnews.com/boxing or golfnews.com/tennis.
>
> The name of your site should be generic in order to allow for future variation. If you had chosen the more general "sportsnews.com" this gives you the flexibility to add sportsnews.com/golf, sportsnews.com/boxing, and sportsnews.com/tennis.

It should be easy to remember and to spell.

Think of the situations when you need to convey the spelling of your URL. It could be in spoken format (during a conversation, a phone call, in your voicemail) or printed format (on all your stationery). You want to make it as easy as possible for your customer to record it and to recall it later and, hopefully, to communicate it to others.

Avoid a name that is too long or one with confusing characters such as ~ or - or mixing 'I' with 'l' (and just how do you explain the tilde sign '~' over the phone?)

Until December 1999, Network Solutions (http://internic.org) had a monopoly on registering .com., .net, and .org domains. Now, with competition, prices range from $19 to $70 for the first two years. The good news: Some of these new competitors offer domains up to sixty-seven characters instead of the old twenty-eight-character limit.

The bad news: It's harder to check on domain availability, because you have to check all registration services—and as of this writing, the jury is still out as to whether these newer registration services are as reliable.

Important Note: When you register a domain name, make sure that *you*, and not your Web host or ISP, are the domain owner. The administrative contact should be an e-mail address that goes to your company. Otherwise, you may run into an unscrupulous ISP that will give you much grief and technical difficulty if you want to change providers; you don't want your domain held hostage over a dispute! And if you do change ISPs, be sure to update your administrative contact with Internic.net (the body that administers commercial domain names in the United States). I learned this the hard way when I tried to switch to a new Web host and my site got lost in cyberspace for almost a month—because InterNIC was sending "You need to confirm this" messages to my old ISP that I'd dropped a year earlier.

If you want to reserve a name but aren't ready to use it yet, pick a temporary host with the lowest monthly fee possible—making sure that it will be easy to extricate later—and fill out the forms, designating yourself as the administrative contact. You will need a working e-mail address. (If you haven't chosen an ISP yet, you might investigate <http://www.register.com>, which, according to my sources, will register your site at no surcharge and make life easy for you until you've chosen a host. I have not had any dealings with this company.)

Then, instead of the usual "under construction" sign, put up a more active message to the occasional visitor who wanders by. Something on the order of "Thank you for visiting. We expect to have our Web site up and running by [date]. In the meantime, please contact us at [e-mail, autoresponder, and phone contacts], and we'll be glad to send you information on [product or service]."

23

E-Mail Marketing Miracles

E-mail is a fantastic resource for marketers. Ask every contact for an e-mail address, and use it whenever it's appropriate.

E-mail is mostly used for unadorned text, but it's possible to send formatted messages—and almost any system can attach fully formatted files. Using attachments, as long as you're sure the recipient can open your file, you'll be able to send graphics, even multimedia presentations, virtually anywhere along the Internet. However, only send an attachment or formatted e-mail message if you've verified that the recipient wants to receive it and can indeed open your file format.

In May 1999, e-mail software maker Eudora announced that users of Windows computers could actually send videos by e-mail—one click and up comes the sound and moving picture.

How to Read an E-Mail Address

E-mail addresses go left to right from the specific to the general, just as U.S. postal addresses go top to bottom. To the left of the @ sign is a personal mailbox. Here's an imaginary example:

nthompson@k12oit.umass.edu

This is an elementary school teacher (k12) named N. Thompson with an account through the University of Massachusetts Office of Information Technology (oit).

I preface real e-addresses with <mailto:> and web addresses with <http://> so that readers using some electronic formats can send an e-mail or visit the site just by clicking.

Here's the most famous e-mail address in the U.S.A.:

<mailto:president@whitehouse.gov>

— Targeted Personal E-Mail —

One of the basic rules of cyberbusiness is to check your e-mail frequently; you never know what will be waiting for you! Monday through Friday, I typically bring in the mail between three and five times. On the weekends, I take one day off from the computer, and the other day I generally bring in the mail in the morning and evening.

And oh, the things I've found in my mailbox! Here's just the very tip of the iceberg:

- An offer from an Internet start-up company to be interim part-time Marketing Director—a few thousand dollars worth of work
- A new client in London who found my Web site and spent hundreds of dollars' on my marketing services
- Constant streams of messages from prospects—many of whom become clients, in part because they get a quick and appropriate answer
- Opportunities to generate free publicity through print and electronic media.

All of these were initiated by clients. Then there's the individual e-mail I initiate. That has brought me . . .

- Several thousand dollars for work I did on a book collaboration
- Many new places to publish my articles
- Tons of free content for my Web site, from some of the top names in marketing and small business
- Review copies of books I used while researching this book and other writing projects
- My first of several appearances as a chat guest in a business forum
- Partner relationships with all manner of business owners, some of which have led to paid consulting, new markets for my book, and many other opportunities

The list goes on and on and on.

When I see a posting of interest on one of the many e-publications I read, I often dash off a quick little note, spell-check it, and send it on its way. Sometimes these notes have led to amazing opportunities.

You don't always know where things will lead. Here's a correspondence I had in January 1999, starting with a simple request to reuse two different posts on my Web magazine, *Down to Business*. (Notice the online business card, or "sig," at the end of my message. Sigs are a vital marketing tool, and they get their own chapter).

Subject: Dear Dan and Anne—RE Your I-Adv posts

I'd like to combine these two into an article for my Down to Business magazine (http://www.frugalfun.com/dtb.html). May I have your permission?

We're a nonpaying market but we give a blurb and hotlink, don't demand exclusivity, and put you in the company of some very well-known names.
Best,

***
Shel Horowitz, mailto:shel@frugalfun.com, 413-586-2388 (v) 617-249-0153 (f) Editor/Publisher Global ARTS Review <http://www.frugalfun.com/review.html> Global TRAVEL Review http://www.frugalfun.com/travel.html> Down to Business <http://www.frugalfun.com/dtb.html>
For information about our books on low-cost FUN and low cost marketing, send any message to <mailto:pph@frugalfun.com> (fun).
<mailto:mwm@frugalfun.com> (marketing), or visit our Web site. <http://www.frugalfun.com>
***

This is the response I got from one of the writers:

From: DanOgma@aol.com
Date: Thu, 14 Jan 1999 11:24:57 EST
To: shel@frugalfun.com
Mime-Version: 1.0
Subject: follow-up

Shel;
I just spent some time reviewing your site and was quite impressed! (I also signed up for your newsletter).

There are two reasons I wanted to send another e-mail (in addition to my reply to your request to use my IADL post).

1) I've attached an MS Word 7.0 file that outlines a new service I've launched along with a personal bio and the company's bio;
2) I am seriously considering writing a book that to my mind has NOT been written and with my background would be a "snap" :-)

The working title is: The History of Commercial Media (From the Stone Age to the New Millennium) and I've already done the overall outline and an outline for the first section—Out of Home. Obviously, I'll need a publisher, but before that I'll need someone to "vet" the idea.

Perhaps we could work out a deal since you need ads, I need more unique sites to work with, and I want to publish something with merit!

Let me know what you think.

BTW [By The Way], I just returned from New York where I took one of my clients (from D.C.) into four major agencies to find a sponsor for his very targeted site. He was ecstatic since although he only wanted one participant, he now has to choose from all four!

Regards.
Dan

P.S. if you want other samples of my writing, I'd be pleased to e-mail you a copy of "Hope, Hype, or Happening," a pre-release copy of my current paper ("Digital Alchemy—Turning Your Website Into Gold") which is about to be published in the 1999 NAB MultiMedia World Journal, and past speeches such as the one I delivered to the ASIDIC 1998 Fall Meeting. (I'm also on the list for an upcoming Insight Information, Inc. event in March.)

Notice a few things about Dan's letter. First, he starts it by letting me know he visited and enjoyed my Web site and subscribed to my tipsheet—which puts him on a very good footing and makes me very receptive to what comes next. He lets me know his speaking and writing credentials—as well as his ability to perform well for a client—asks for my help for mutual benefit, and offers me some useful freebies.

The attachment was for a new product called Internet Media Maximizer, offering integration of traditional ad agency services with cutting-edge Web technology; prices started at $5,000.

If Dan is able to target ten individuals a week, that gives him a pool of five hundred potential in-

vestors per year. And if just two per month become clients, that's a $120,000 annual revenue stream from perhaps ten hours of prospecting. Not a bad rate of return!

Meanwhile, of course, I am looking for my own ways to maximize the return on this exchange. My reply to him keeps many doors open, and pushes some new territory, such as my ability to consult on the publishing process:

Hmmmm. I'm sure we can work something out. I'll try to look at your file over the weekend. I also have a lot of expertise in book publishing and marketing.

BTW, may I use our correspondence as an example of one-to-one marketing for my own new book, tentatively called Grassroots Marketing (Chelsea Green, spring 2000)? Do me a favor and keep this intact in your reply.

As I write this, no business relationship has materialized. But there's a good chance that by the time you read this, one or both of us will have benefited from a useful partnership.

— E-Mail Etiquette —

Keep in mind a few rules:

- Respond promptly. If you're away from your office for several days, ask your ISP to set up an "on vacation" message that lets people know when you'll return (be sure to test it before leaving).
- If contacting someone because of a post to a discussion list or newsgroup, or in reference to some content on his or her Web site, refer specifically to that issue—and it often helps to quote a few lines, enough to establish context.
- Use very focused subject heads. Keep in mind that some people might get five hundred or even one thousand e-messages every day. If you want yours to be opened, don't use a heading such as "hi there." Instead try "Dear Mary—RE

the History page of your Web site." And obviously, avoid headlines that sound like "spam" (I'll define spam shortly).

- Be brief. After an initial contact, there's plenty of time to go into more detail if someone is interested.
- Provide several ways for the person to respond, including a valid and current e-mail address.
- Make sure that the "reply to" address is valid, if it's not the same as your e-address.
- Even if you use autoresponders, check over the inquiries and personally respond to any that ask questions your autoresponder doesn't address. Similarly, if you've set up templates to respond to the same queries over and over, add a couple of personalized lines at the beginning.
- Send attached formatted files only if you've checked that the recipient can read them—and made sure they are 100 percent virus-free (some programs, including recent versions of Microsoft Word, can trigger nasty viruses by opening attachments).
- If you e-mail marketing materials to more than one person at a time, be sure to send the names blind, so every recipient doesn't get the names of all the other recipients. Two reasons: First, people don't like to pay to receive a long list of names (or even just to scroll down past them), and second, others will bombard your folks with their own messages—and you'll be blamed (and flamed).

Irish Web designer Kathy Barthen, whom we met a few chapters back, showed how this kind of courtesy can pay off (Internet Advertising Discussion List, January 15, 1999):

I get anywhere from 10 to 110 e-mails a day from visitors to our site (that is not counting IADL and other forms of e-mail). I answer EVERYONE even if I cannot help with their inquiry. I also go through our guest book and randomly reply by e-mail to comments left by our visitors. The biggest response I get back from this is, "Wow . . . you actually answered . . . no one ever has before."

I recently came across an entry in our guest book from a young man asking for information for a school project involving a pretend trip to Ireland. I sent him a few bits and pieces and we corresponded for over a week as he put his project together. I recently received mail from his mother thanking me. It seems he sent out over 50 e-mails and left comments in every guest book he could find and NO ONE else responded. . . .

What did this cost me? Total, over a 9-day period, it "cost" me MAYBE 10 minutes of my time. The first thing that comes to mind is that responding to direct e-mail from a visitor to my site is common courtesy. The second thing is it is a great marketing tool. My visitors know there are real people on the other side of the web site. Doing this from the conception of our site a year ago has done an unbelievable job of building trust. Because of this trust in Ireland Now, when we guarantee and back our e-commerce clients to our visitors, they buy from them based on that trust in us. It has also resulted in one of the oldest and best (not to mention cheapest) forms of advertising in the world: word of mouth. Did I set out with that in mind? To be honest, no. I was trying to make visitors happy in the hopes they might return to the site, a way to help build traffic. But this common courtesy is paying off in numerous ways.

Anyone that does not bother to answer e-mail from visitors (and in a timely manner) is missing the boat. Another point: if you can't be bothered replying to an e-mail, what is the point of even having a faster form of communication?

***

Kathy Barthen, Head Designer,
Digital Presence, Ltd. Cork Ireland
Specialist in E-Commerce and Web Site
    Promotions
Creator and Web Master of Ireland Now
http://irelandnow.com

***

Yet, many big companies either ignore e-mail queries or answer them very late, or only send form letters. Differentiate yourself from them, and do it right, as Kathy does.

— Spam —

As soon as you explore anything commercial on-line, you'll notice people sending out junk mail messages to a bulk list of names (derided on the Net as "spamming").

These, and the numerous classified-ad sheets you'll also encounter, may seem at first glance like cost-effective mechanisms to reach a technologically sophisticated audience—but beware!

The Internet is *not* like other marketing media! If you mail unasked-for and unwanted messages to untargeted lists, many Netters will be deeply resentful—and thousands of spammers have actually lost their Internet accounts because of complaints. Or, if they're smart, they'll never even see your message, because filtering will deliver it right into the electronic trash can.

If you do try them, expect microscopic response rates—and most will be flames or "remove" requests, not orders. In my early days on the Net, I experimented with one rapidly growing service. I got about 50 responses on a hard-sell mailing to 70,000, about 20 on a soft-sell ad to 200,000, and about 50 on a hard-sell mailing to 300,000—and exactly one response in a year with a classified on their Web mall. These translate to between .01 percent and .07 percent—about one hundred times *less* than the expected responses on a traditional direct-mail pitch. Worse, the conversion rate was abysmal. Out of my total of about 120 inquiries, only 5 or 6 actually bought a book. So my sales from the ads were actually measured in thousandths of a percent compared to the original circulation (and this was when I was a newbie in 1994, before most people had filtering software; I'd expect to do even worse if I tried again).

These lists tend to go to Internet "newbies" (beginners). Experienced Netters dislike them because they may already deal with hundreds of messages a day that are directly related to their interests, through mailing lists (also called listservs) and newsgroups. Also, there's a deep prejudice against any mass mail—even including blacklists of spammers. This may sound harsh—but remember it costs a great deal of time, and sometimes money, to sort through a large volume of e-mail. It is not fair to cost your prospects money to spam to them, and if you do it, your reputation will never recover.

Worse, because some recipients will even set up mail bombs that could bring your entire ISP to its knees, many ISPs will terminate your account if anyone complains that you've spammed them—before even hearing your side of the story, and sometimes without even bothering to tell you! This "shoot first, ask questions later" approach can play havoc with your careful marketing plans—so don't *ever* spam!

— Multiple Readers —

There are far more effective ways of reaching the right audience than spamming, and you certainly don't want to be the target of a hacker attack!

Here are some much better e-mail marketing strategies, each of which will be discussed in detail below:

- Circulate articles
- Participate in newsgroups, online forums, and mailing lists
- Use targeted internal-list e-mail
- Sponsor other publications
- Become an online newsletter publisher

Circulate Articles

Work up two or three (or ten or twenty) articles and circulate them to various newsletters, e-zines, and topic-focused Web sites (if what you have to say is relevant). I notice a spike in my Web visits and tipsheet sign-ups whenever one of my articles appears. Though paying markets do exist on the Net, don't expect money—your payment is a blurb with contact info, and sometimes a free ad (negotiate to run the ad in a different issue, thus doubling your exposure). Be sure to keep your copyright and re-use rights!

In fact, you can help the Net spread your articles around, if your contact box grants the right to distribute your article electronically as long as your contact information and credit line are included—and they send you a copy! That way, you may get far more penetration than just the original newsletter.

Participate

Everything I say about free publicity in print applies at least as much in this new medium—with a twist. In the Internet culture, giving away information and advice is standard operating procedure, whether you do it in newsgroups, e-mail mailing lists, and/or a Web site. Of course, if you give valuable information away on the Web, you can publicize it. But in a mailing list or newsgroup, you will become known by your helpful replies to questions posted there, your "sig" (online business card at the end of your e-mail messages) will point people to various ways to get in touch, and business will begin to flow to you.

In fact, many of the ideas and quotes in this book were originally aired in such discussion groups as the Internet Sales, Internet Advertising, Publishers Marketing Association (and its replacement, Pub-Forum), or the now-defunct Internet Marketing discussion list. To find these and thousands of other highly targeted lists visit topica, onelist, liszt, and egroups.com. Remember: for any mailing list, the subscribe/unsub-scribe address is different from the address to make comments on the list.

What's the difference between advertising and posting messages on a thread? Jim Sterne <mailto: jsterne@targeting.com>, author of *World Wide Web Marketing,* explains:

. . . a source of information, a voice of reason and a company worth talking to when it comes time to buy . . . Consider the difference between:

An e-mail in your mailbox that says:

We have the best bicycle tires in the Galaxy!!! !!!!!!!!!!!! Buy them today

vs. a post to alt.rec.bicycle.racing that says:

In answer to the post from Bob, we have found a

more rubberized tire will give a smoother ride and last longer but doesn't have the features necessary to win a race—you can find out more about this by reading our "All About Tires" page at <http://www.company.com>.

This is . . . participating in the gift-economy of the net and it doesn't offend.

Participation in discussion groups has been my single most effective marketing strategy—and it works because I understand the medium.

Spend the time to learn Internet culture. Many newsgroups and mailing lists are extremely hostile to commercialization—and will flame you or get your service cut off. And each subcommunity on the Net interprets the culture a little differently. Just as doors open up if you say "Thank you" in the local language when you're traveling, so, too, your travels in cyberspace will be far more productive if you understand and respect the local, individual customs.

Yet, these communities are extremely fertile grounds for marketers. In fact, at this writing, about a third of my income comes from clients or book customers who find me online—occasionally on the Web, but more often via e-mail.

You only have one chance to make a first impression. I've seen newbies shoot themselves in the foot over and over again and take years to build up a level of trust afterward. In fact, my own first attempts to use these tools—on a career services discussion list—were an unqualified disaster. I had to leave that list and identify completely different communities before I began to be successful. Even then, I was an active participant for six months before I got my first clients—this on a list that has brought me forty new clients in my first three years, including several who've put me on retainer. When you feel ready to stick a toe in the water, join a newsgroup or mailing list and read a few days' postings before you try to post a message. Get a flavor of what's being discussed, and look for ways to tie your expertise to the discussion. Always, the focus should be not on selling, but on providing information to answer the seeker's question—but include a great sig if the list uses them. It may take some months for your participation to bear fruit. Have patience and keep on developing a reputation as someone whose advice is worth listening to.

The ideal discussion group is one where you can both learn and teach. That way, even if you don't see direct sales, you're building your knowledge base.

Many lists encourage new participants to introduce themselves. Craft this message very carefully! Not only is it your best chance to tell people exactly what you do and how you can help solve their problems, but it's also the list members' first impression of you. Keep it conversational, and stay far away from anything that smacks of hard-sell.

Net culture is loose, supportive, informal. Tom Vassos of IBM calls the marketing implications "The Internet Underwear Theory." In his view, because many users are reading your message while relaxing at home, maybe even in their underwear, traditional "business suit" marketing doesn't work. They don't want to be shouted at or pressured, but they want to assist and be assisted with issues, information, and problems.

Never send an attachment or HTML-formatted e-mail to any mailing list. If you need to provide color, pictures, video, and the like, include a URL where you've posted it—or load the document to a "shared files area," if one exists. Few things are more annoying than printing out a digest and seeing twenty-five pages of computer code, which is what usually happens to attached files when they go through a list processor.

Though technically not e-mail-based, Usenet newsgroups (and, for that matter, AOL and BBS message boards and Web-based forums) are similar to e-mail mailing lists. The only significant difference is that you access them with a newsreader that visits the newsgroup on a central server, rather than waiting for messages to automatically arrive in your mailbox. And of course, if you want to respond privately to a newsgroup posting, e-mail will be your tool of choice.

Use Targeted Internal-List E-Mail

Engage in carefully targeted e-mail to your own internal list of prospect inquiries. When you respond, remind the recipient this was requested information (preferably by quoting back the original posting). Then either give a soft-sell version of your full spiel or a more toned-down version with the ability to request a second level. Another use for your "house list": send copies of your press releases so that your customers and prospects see your news before they read it (or don't read it) in the papers.

Here's how Jared Spool <mailto:jspool@uie.com> of User Interface Engineering <http://www.uie.com>, a consulting firm in Andover, Massachusetts, generated $80,000 in sales from just one message to his prospect list:

We've had tremendous results with targeted e-mail. . . .

The lists we use have been generated primarily from people who have responded to our autoresponder or contacted us in some way. Our list has about 6,000 people. We carefully remove duplicates so that each recipient only gets 1 copy of the message. (No better way to annoy people than to send them more than 1 copy.)

We keep the offer short with an address of an autoresponder to get more information, often something with value in its own right, such as some of our recent research results. This has multiple benefits: recipients get only a short message, they can easily contact us for more detailed information if they are interested, and we can track the response of the mailing.

Every message contains a complete signature from the sender, usually me or one of the other principals of our firm. It includes our 800 number and other contact information. I feel this adds a lot of legitimacy to the message. And our e-mail messages come from our domain, not [a generic] ISP.

Each mailing generates between 5 and 10 people who ask to be removed from the list. 99% ask politely. In all cases, we immediately remove them from the list AND respond to their message. We do not try to explain the benefits of receiving our mail—they've chosen not to receive it and we do not try to "sell" them again. We keep a list of all addresses in a special "nosend" list which we use to make sure that anyone who has asked to be removed never ends up on any list in the future.

In September, I sent out a message to our lists which generated over $80,000 in revenues. Most of our products and services have been sold through our targeted lists. I'd venture to say that it has been responsible for at least 1/3 of our annual revenues (which are over $1M).

The biggest surprise is the amount of times that we've gotten responses from a mailing from people *not* on the list. This is from people who forward our message to others in their organizations. We have a large "pass-around" rate, probably because the nature of the content.

My wariness about discussing this is the social stigma that follows this type of marketing. It's like companies that need to test with animals, not something you want to publicize to your customers. However, it has been very successful for us and [will be] a major part of all future marketing efforts.

Sponsor Other Publications

Sponsor a mailing list or newsletter that's closely targeted to your audience (or swap ads, if you manage a list of your own). Even some of the most prestigious lists on the Net accept sponsorships for as little as $25 per insertion. If you take a week on a daily digest, you'll get five to seven exposures to the people you want to reach, in a way that will be looked upon favorably: You're eliminating the need to charge for a subscription. Look for moderated lists that have a clear mission and a good psychographic fit.

If you're paying for a certain number of subscribers, it's nice to be able to verify that you're getting what you pay for. Some lists, such as my own, are hosted by third-party mail servers. Those lists have an essentially audited circulation. But others are managed by the publisher in-house.

Natalie Zubar <mailto:natalie@magics.net> suggested "two auditing models—similar to 'per click' and 'per view' for banner ads" in a post to the Internet Advertising Discussion List (January 12–14, 1999):

1. CPC model: The newsletter provides a link to a custom page on the publisher's site; this counts the click and redirects the visitor to the advertiser's page.

We use this for our weekly newsletter (40,000+ subscribers) and it works just great.

2. CPM model: You sell newsletter ads on a per-subscriber basis, place a direct link to the advertiser's site (or no link at all if it's an off-line ad). You send your advertiser newsletter distribution logs (with number of e-mails sent, number of bounced messages, timelines, etc.).

Our client with a dozen mail lists (daily and weekly, 70,000+ max) uses this model quite successfully. Sure, it requires long discussions with the advertiser (about log format, frequency, accuracy, etc.) and probably is no good without your own mail server and specialized software (this client uses our programs, but there are at least 3 other systems available, none are cheap).

As always, it's easier to sell basing on model 1, while model 2 is potentially more cost-effective. Our experience shows that CPC model is more profitable for the publisher when you have highly targeted newsletter ads, closely related to content (we have consistent 10+% CTR in our newsletter). I presume advertisers are happy too since they ask us to repeat placements.

Online gamer David Stansel <mailto:ceo@ RPEX. com> has had good results sponsoring entire Web sites in his specialized niche:

Since I wanted to gain recognition among the finicky market that runs from 13 to 40+, I set out to focus on one game at a time. What I did was to find several fairly popular fan sites that had a repeat customer base (from Chat, message boards, et cetera), then offer to pay to host their sites. No restrictions. Not long after doing that and helping notable players start their own sites under my domain name, I was one of the top visited web sites pertaining to BattleTech (the game I chose to start with). The sites still send enormous amounts of traffic my way. Even when I lost my computer and couldn't update the site for over two months, I still averaged over a thousand visits a day.

I believe one of the key forces behind sponsorship is the quality of the sponsored site. I picked a select few sites that I considered to be well designed and that have good content. Those sites that didn't want to move to my servers I sponsored contests on. I made sure that when hosting I made it obvious that they were hosted by RPEX but not overwhelmed by the fact. A combination of third-level domain names (e.g., http://Mordel.RPEX.com) and small micro-banners helped gently push the user to the fact that this was a sponsored site. On the contest page I made sure that people knew that this was a contest "Sponsored by Role-Playing EXtremes, www.RPEX.com" and that I had a contest on my site and was giving away an equivalent prize. (Internet Advertising Discussion List, January 12, 1999)

Become an Online Newsletter Publisher

There are tens of thousands of e-zines and Webzines out there, with more arriving every day. Yet the market is far from saturated. Find the right niche, publicize it appropriately, and people will sign up. There may be more than enough newsletters covering online marketing, but you may be the first on your block—and in cyberspace, your block is the entire world—to put together a monthly reader resource serving dolphin and porpoise trainers.

Publishing is incredibly easy on the Internet. All you need is a word processor and an e-mail account.

Dozens of different models exist: publication daily, weekly, monthly, or sporadically; with all-original content, a mix of your own and others' articles, press releases, reader contributions, historical material that's fallen into public domain as the copyright expires. Ad-free, one or two sponsorship ads per issue, a classified ad section, banner ads on the archives Web page . . . In short, there are endless permutations.

Sometimes the newsletter can actually become a full-time livelihood. Ray Owens <mailto:jokeaday@jokeaday.com> quit his day job as a corporate trainer and Web site developer when his humor list became commercially successful:

Is there a more common use of e-mail than forwarding something funny to a bazillion of your closest friends? Probably not—just like 95% of all microwaves in the world do nothing but make popcorn and heat coffee. Humor listings are a dime a dozen and there are no new jokes on the planet. So how is Joke A Day able to generate revenue close to $150,000 a year without telling a single original joke?

For those of you who may have started a mailing listing of your own, this is not an inconsequential question: "How do I make my mailing list unique? Different?"

Especially if you're using content that can be found in many other places. Because, let's boil it down to the basics: if you want to make any money, you've got to be sponsored by advertising, if you want advertisers, you have to have readers. To have readers, you have to have content that's different from any place else. . . .

Joke A Day is an extension of my personality. It grew from having 8 members to over 150,000 members in two years. The only difference between it and other, older humor lists is how I "talk" to the readers.

Owens's full article originally appeared in the Internet Sales Discussion List and can be found at <http://www.frugalfun.com/dtb.html>.

In a follow-up interview, he noted that he stumbled around before finding a winning formula. To get the first advertisers,

I cut the prices to the bone. I made them so inexpensive that anyone could say, "Ehh, it's $45, I'll take a chance." I finally got an Internet gambling company to . . . buy about $1,000 worth of ads. I thought I'd reached the big time. After that, it was like a snowball effect. Once others saw that someone else was doing some repeat advertising then that broke the ice. But it took the "hey SOMETHING is better than NOTHING" attitude to get the first sponsor in the door.

One of the joys of running a small business is the ability to react swiftly to decisions either good or bad. There was a time that I raised the prices significantly and sold absolutely nothing. After about two weeks of starving, I realized it was time to do a rollback of the prices. That worked. I've got ad spots sold for the next two to three months, so I've again raised the prices to the highest they've ever been. They're still a bargain (if you do a cost-per-thousand reader analysis). I've not had too many offers at the higher price yet but since I now have a cushion of sold spots, I'm not as nervous as I've been before.

Typically, ads on Owens's list draw a 1 to 2 percent response—more than enough to generate repeat business from his advertisers. With the general content of his list, it's not surprising that the better performers tout products for a general audience. Owens even suggests that niche marketers will do better elsewhere.

Grow your newsletter by exchanging ads with compatible ones (tips: *always* request a sample issue, ask for extra insertions if you've got a much larger circulation, ask for top placement if the publication lists a whole bunch of ads, and don't be afraid to decline if you don't like the sample issue).

Hint: Rather than trying to manage these lists by e-mail, take advantage of free list management services at places like onelist.com, egroups.com, makelist.com, and listbot.com. (They may add advertisements to your mailing; commercial list management services are also available, if you want to control the ads or need advanced reporting features. These same companies and many others, including oaknetpub.com, revnet.com, and databack.com, can manage a list for a monthly fee.) If you use a mailing-list server from the start, you won't have to convert your list later—and you won't spend frustrating hours manually updating your list every time an address bounces. Eventually, as the lists get large

enough, they may become a source of income in their own right, as you sell sponsorship ads. And almost from the start, you'll be able to use your list to trade sponsorship ads with other newsletter publishers, thus increasing both newsletters' circulation.

— Automated E-Mail —

Like a lot of other things on the Net, e-mail can be automated to some extent. Most hosts will allow you unlimited autoresponders. These tools are very flexible, and certainly have their uses—but also their drawbacks.

Some good situations for an autoresponder:

- Vacation notice if you're unable to answer your mail for a period of time
- Newsletter back issues—or articles each addressing a specific topic
- An initial sales or informational message containing your strongest selling points and most frequently asked questions
- Confirmation message and/or subscription verification when people sign up for anything at your site

A well-designed autoresponder should go out instantly—and give you a copy of the original request. You'll often find that people ask questions or make comments that require an individual response. This ought to be fairly simple to set up; however, I've had a great deal of trouble with this aspect. From two different ISPs, getting copies has been unworkable, and I get only the bounces every time someone spams my site.

Set your autoresponder up so that if someone hits "reply," it goes to a real person. And watch out for situations where you get spammed, your autoresponder triggers a return message on the other end, and endless loops of messages go back and forth.

Keep messages short, unless you're sending an article or newsletter. And don't expect amazing results, though be glad if you get them.

Autoresponders are evolving rapidly. Almost none of them still require a subject field; rather, the address is keyed to just one document, and a different address is available for the next document.

Recently, there's been a trend from several companies to set up follow-up systems. Typically, these will send up to seven form letters over a specified period. It sounds good in theory, but I have to tell you that when I receive one of these, I start getting annoyed on the third letter and generally unsubscribe (make sure if you use such a system that you let people out easily and graciously—and space them out infrequently enough that people don't feel bugged).

In fact, recent discussions on both the homebiz and epubs lists have shown me that I'm not alone. Many people loathe the follow-ups and resist even sending for an autoresponder with a recognizable multiple response-sequence address such as aweber or smartbot. E-zine editor Jerry Parkins <mailto: webmaster@paychecks-online.com> surveyed his readers and discovered that a full 25 percent hated the follow-ups—but 50 percent wanted to use them for their own follow-up! And Parkins, who is from the United Kingdom, has another peeve: "The thing that's really beginning to annoy me is I have started getting e-mails with a set of remove instructions which involve *phoning* a U.S.A. phone number to get my addresses off."

However, in October 1999, at least a few subscribers to the I-Sales Discussion List reported very good success with follow-up autoresponders—*if the* responses feel so personal that people can't tell it's an automatic response. For example, Willie Crawford <mailto:willie@williecrawford.com>:

I have met with considerable success selling software using autoresponders. I sell search engine positioning software on the try-before-you-buy model—as an affiliate. A customer downloads a free trial version of the software and this also triggers a series of follow-up autoresponder messages. While the customer is getting to know the software and determine if it really meets his [or her] needs, he [or she] gets a series of short messages pointing out

features, asking if he [or she] has any questions, and even making a special offer. I find that using this model, about one out of every six who download the free trial version of the software end up purchasing a copy.

The autoresponder messages are professionally written, personalized, and offer useful information. I often get e-mails responding to the autoresponder messages, which shows me how good they really can be. Prospects often don't realize that they are getting autoresponder messages.

Another software developer, John Vorwerk <mailto: jvorwerk@iname.com>, noted that since software is a complex product, often with unknown bugs, the autoresponders not only increase sales, but also enable him to do quite a bit of product research. When a customer places an order, he sends out an automatic e-mail introducing himself and his product, and then follows up later with another one that asks how the prospect likes the software, and if there are any problems, questions, or suggestions. And the follow-up message gets twice as many responses as the original. "The second message is the ultimate source of customer information for me, and it is free!"

However, I remain somewhat skeptical. After all, I've seen dozens of direct-mail letters that attempted to pass themselves off as individually written, and not one of them succeeded. (Of course, since I write the stuff, I may be harder to fool). If you use this technique, make sure the "reply to" field goes to a live human being, and doesn't call the autoresponder again.

I might mention—and this makes me a bit of an outcast among marketing gurus—that the same principle holds true in direct mail. Endless repetition of the same message, in any medium, is annoying. Far better to get those necessary exposures through a variety of different tools.

Is there a better way? Lynda Kan <mailto: lkan@ angelfire.com> thinks so:

It strikes me that follow-up should be requested. That is, there should be one automatic follow-up that asks "Did you receive the info you requested?" and then offers options such as "Received, would like follow-up information," "Received, not interested in follow-up information," "Did not receive, please resend."

This gives me the option to continue a relationship that I formerly believed would be good for me, or to back out of it because I no longer believe it will be beneficial to me. It also, basically, re-sights your scope so that you are still marketing to a targeted audience instead of a no-longer-interested audience. It's a win-win situation because I don't get deluged with information I don't want, and you don't get a reputation for deluging people with information they don't want.

This brings up a related issue: personalization—both on and off the Internet. Once again, I've noticed a lot of people whom I respect say that the traditional approach to personalization—using the prospect's name six times—is a hollow turnoff, whether in an e-mail message, a direct-mail piece, or a telephone sales call.

Yet true, meaningful personalization is a different story. If you send an e-mail responding to a question or interest that the reader has expressed, the response is likely to be positive. Later on, we'll touch on applying this to Web sites, but it's true in any communication medium.

A good rule to follow: If you wouldn't want a technique rubbed in your face by others, don't rub it in anyone else's face.

— E-Mail and Data Security —

For all its amazing capabilities, e-mail has its limits. It's difficult to prove an ordinary e-mail was delivered, or read even if delivery was successful. Messages can be delayed even several days. And the transmissions are not secure; a hacker could break in. Also, once a document is sent, the recipient can quietly modify it—which could wreak havoc in a contract or similar document.

Of course, entrepreneurs are stepping into the breach with secure data transmission, delivery guarantees, and so forth. Om Malik reported in *Forbes* *Online* (May 28, 1999, <http://www.forbes.com/tool/html/99/may/0528/feat.htm>) on several companies offering solutions: Click2Send.com, ZipLip.com, and InfoEx.com. The British banner network Safe-Audit.com also offers a product, but only for Windows computers.

— Rich-Format and HTML E-mail —

Like almost everything else on the Net, the style of e-mail is constantly debated online. A recent marketing trend is rich-format e-mail, which can be as simple as a line of bold or oversize or color type, or as complex as sound and animation.

E-publishing consultant Shannon Kinnard <mailto:shannon@ideastation.com> describes some of the advantages:

The level of interactivity with the recipient is increased with HTML mail. Writing advertorials is a totally different kind of writing from both journalism and marketing copy writing. It's a blending of the two (hence the term "advertorial"). Pair this type of writing with a "buy now" button, or better yet, a form at the end, and it's an unparalleled sales opportunity.

For example, if you're selling digital cameras, publish an article to your subscriber base that describes a step-by-step guide to using the newest camera on the market as a way to show the product's enhanced capabilities and then ends with a form that says: "Would you like to: 1. order the camera now, 2. request a printable version of this page, or 3. receive a call from a sales rep?"

You'll immediately know how many of your readers: 1. buy immediately, 2. already own the product, or 3. need more details to make a decision. So you can respond by: 1. following up on the purchase, 2. selling additional products, or 3. sending more information.

I've seen a few of the simpler ones—haven't yet seen one with sound or video—and they do have impact. However, like every other advanced Net technology, it causes problems for those with older computer systems or mail software—not to mention unpleasantness for those who pay for e-mail per use. Offer people a choice, and verify that your recipient has the right format, whether for a rich-format e-message or an attached file. And please don't assume everyone can read your file type, or even that everyone has a PC. As a Mac user, I'm constantly annoyed by file formats I can't use.

You can be reasonably safe using bold or italic in a message from one AOL address to another, but once you go outside a closed system, the variety of mail readers and computers is huge, and there's no sure way to know if your message will even be readable, let alone welcomed.

As you have seen, e-mail may just be the most crucial piece of the immense marketing juggernaut made possible on the Internet. And the key to e-mail success is the humble sig, the subject of the next chapter.

24

The "Sig"—Your
Cyberspace Business Card

Look back at Leah Woolford's signature, or "sig," on page 173: It's got her name and business name; Web, phone, and fax contacts; a general (and somewhat ineffectual) tag line; and an attention-getter—an offer of a free listing. But it should include her e-mail address! Some primitive e-mail software excludes the address. Also, people could contact her if other people forward the post—something that happens a lot, and not always with permission.

— When and How to Use a Sig —

Certain things should always be in your sig: your URL if you have one, your e-mail address, your phone number, and at least one offer, benefit, or service description.

Sigs are your cyberspace business card, and they can be as commercial as can be (within the culture of the particular discussion group). They are your key entry point to the noncommercial—and incredibly lucrative—sectors of the Internet where a blatant sales pitch could get you run out of the virtual town on a virtual rail. Don't waste your sig on a cutesy all-text graphic or a quote that says nothing about your business!

Almost every time you post to a discussion group, there should be a sig on the end of your post. Several crucial tools—newsgroups, mailing lists, and forums, for instance—are vastly strengthened in their marketing impact with a good sig. And don't forget one-to-one e-mail! Most e-mail programs allow you to automatically include a sig at the end of each message. Proofread it carefully and set it up. If your software doesn't support a sig, paste one in from a word-processing document—but turn *off* your curly ("smart") quotes and other special characters!

Sig Etiquette

Like everything else in cyberspace, sigs have their own "rules of the road." Your marketing message will be more effective if you pay attention.

- Keep it short: four to six lines is ideal. There will be exceptions (you'll see the longish sig I use with radio producers in a moment), but in general, be extremely brief. Few things are more of a turnoff than a thirty-line sig. If your sig is longer than your message, either trim it down or leave it out of that particular post.

- Don't scream or hype. Avoid whole sentences all in capitals. Stay away from series of exclamation points. Don't come across like a spammer or hard-sell huckster, but as someone people will *want* to do business with.
- Follow the rules of the group. The Internet Sales Discussion List limits sigs to a paltry three lines apiece—a marketing copywriting challenge if there ever was one, but definitely worth the effort. Since it's a moderated list, if you don't follow the rules, your sig doesn't run with your post. Also follow group etiquette on such matters as how much of the original post you quote back in your follow-up (be brief).

When *not* to Use a Sig

If you're posting several things to the same group at the same time, have mercy on them and either vary your sig or include it in just the first post. On the rest, close just with your name, e-address, and URL. Otherwise, you may wear out your welcome in a hurry—but every group is different, so watch the culture of each group.

Also, make sure to turn off your sig when you're communicating with a computer instead of a human being. Mailing list software will often reject a command that has a sig, because it will try to interpret the sig as an action to take. So when subscrib-

---

(1)
%%%%%%%%%%%%%%%%%%%%%%%%%%%%%%%%%%
Walter Daniels Carry Bags, Mugs, Mousepads, Sweat Shirts and
T-Shirts in Small Quantities at GREAT Prices! On the road or at home
Great products with no pressure. E-mail: fbngraph@indy.net
http://www.digiserve.com/fbngraphics/
Enter the bi-monthly design survey, and win a free mug.
%%%%%%%%%%%%%%%%%%%%%%%%%%%%%%%%%%

(2)
Evelyn Lee Barney, Producer NetProfits Radio & E-Zine mailto:
elb@netprofitsradio.com 413.256.3049 http://www.netprofitsradio.com http://www.home-work.net
Making the web more profitable with timely information for the Internet Marketer!

(3)
Nancy Roebke
Execdirector@Profnet.Org http://www.profnet.org
Learn to Network! Increase income, cut costs, and put an end to cold calling.
Subscribe to our FREE newsletter that teaches you the secrets of successful networking.
mailto:subscribe@just-business.com!
ProfNet- Helping Business Professionals Find More Business

(4)
IMAGES FROM THE PAST
History in ways that help people see it for themselves
Regional History-Cultural History-Historical Images
Fine interpretive exhibits presented as books
(Tel/Fax) 802-442-3204 P.O. Box 137 Bennington, VT 05201 info@ImagesfromthePast.com http://
www.ImagesfromthePast.com

ing, unsubscribing, or changing your subscription options, don't use it.

Let's look at a few more real-life sigs in the box on page 198 and below.

Daniels (1) worked hard to get a good sig: "I tried to use the old guideline of telling what you do in twenty-five words or less. Of course, distilling a core business statement to that small a space isn't easy. I had to start by focusing on what I really did. Fortunately, some friends acted as a focus group and helped me do it." Look at what Daniels crams into five lines: a USP (small quantities, good prices on custom-printed premiums), e-mail and Web addresses, and a contest offer. He also uses a graphic element—percent signs—to separate his sig from the text above it. Missing? A phone number. Plenty of room for it at the end of the last line.

Evelyn Barney used this sig (2) when she worked as a radio producer (her current e-address is <n2u@home-work.net>). This is a good basic sig, with a job title (one that will attract attention, since she's in the media), e-mail and phone contacts, two URLs, and a reason to go and visit.

The next sig (3) is from self-described "networking goddess" Nancy Roebke.

At six lines, the next sig (4), from a publisher of illustrated regional historical books, is about the maximum comfortable length. She uses spacing to

---

(5)
http://www.videoltd.com - The Fast Way To Rent Or Own DVD!
1,200 titles to choose and a free, twice-monthly newsletter

(6)
I-Sales Version
Jay Steinfeld
//////// No Brainer Blinds and Shades \\\\\\\\
World's most popular & trusted on-line source for blinds!
\\\\\\\\ http://www.nobrainerblinds.com ////////

(7)
General Version
//////// No Brainer Blinds and Shades \\\\\\\\
Incredibly Useful Site of the Month - Yahoo Magazine
World's most popular & trusted on-line source for blinds!
Jay Steinfeld, President jay@nobrainerblinds.com
\\\\\\\\ http://www.nobrainerblinds.com ///////monthly newsletter.

(8)
///No Brainer Blinds and Shades—Yahoo Site of the Month\\\
World's most popular & trusted on-line source for blinds!
\\\ http://www.nobrainerblinds.com - jay@nobrainerblinds.com////

(9)
Moderator. HelpDesk, http://www.audettemedia.com/i-help
Tax Professional ExtraordinAire - http///www.taxmama.com (soon)
Tax Newsletter Ask TaxMama mailto:taxwriter@taxmama.com
The Original GiftSurfer http://www.mywishlist.com
———SHOPTHEWEBIN99-PASS IT ON————

center the text for visual impact—something that may or may not work well, depending on each recipient's e-mail formatting settings. I might cut the three lines of description down to two and include her name as president. I'd also do another version listing specific book titles. Note that she uses capitals in her domain name to highlight the important words. Domains are not case-sensitive, and this is a nice little trick if your domain is a compound word.

Bob Pardue (5) <mailto:bob@videoltd.com> chose to stay within the strict three-line limit on the I-Sales list by leaving out essential contact information (though his address does appear at the beginning of the post, and his name appeared just above his sig). Personally, I think this is a bit too stark—though for those interested in digital video, it's compelling enough.

Note the difference between Jay Steinfeld's I-Sales sig (6) and his regular one (7). Like Pardue, for the I-Sales version, he put his name above the sig (a clever trick where space is tight) and left out everything but the company name, USP, and URL. I found it interesting, too, that the slashes he used to distinguish his signature remind me of window treatments.

The longer version is much more compelling, listing his award from Yahoo (and his name and e-mail address). I rewrote his I-Sales version (8).

What do you do if you have your finger in many pies? Eva Rosenberg's sig <mailto:evarose@ mmgco. com> uses an effective approach (9).

— Multiple Sigs —

Since my needs are even more diverse than Eva's, I've chosen a different strategy. I currently use twenty-five different sigs for different audiences. Each is custom-crafted to put forth the exact message I'm trying to get across. Below and right are a few examples (please note that the book you're reading replaces *Marketing Without Megabucks*).

I set this up easily, by keeping a document full of sigs open in my e-mail program. Every time I need one, I just turn off the automatic sig, copy the one I want, and paste it into the my outgoing message.

Mary Westheimer, president of BookZone, a large book mall, uses her sig to highlight a different client every day. Worth the effort? Since she posts regularly to several publisher lists, her potential customers see that she's giving her clients extra exposure while showing the world the breadth and depth of resources at BookZone. Something must be working, as BookZone continues to grow rapidly.

Once you have a Web site, a sig should point people there, and when possible, provide specific incentives to visit. As for setting up that Web site . . .

Radio Contact

Shel Horowitz, "The King of Frugal Fun" Author, 5 books.
mailto:shel@frugalfun.com
413-586-2388 (Northampton, MA) http://www.frugalfun.com
Featured on over 150 radio shows from New England to California to Taiwan.

Talking Points (Low-Cost Fun) Anyone can afford vacations, entertainment, food. shopping, romance, etc.—specific ways to slash costs.

Talking Points (Low-Cost Marketing): Flame-proof Internet marketing, Zero-Cost Websites, free media exposure, slash your ad costs while building results . . .
Celebrate International Frugal Fun Day, First Saturday of Oct.—over 100 ideas listed at http://www.frugalfun.com/frugalfundayideas.html

---

General Marketing Sig
(this is my current "automatic" sig)

Shel Horowitz, mailto:shel@frugalfun.com, 800-683-WORD/413-586-2388
News releases, brochures, newsletters, ad copy, resumes, etc.
Books to save you money on business (Marketing Without Megabucks)
and pleasure (The Penny-Pinching Hedonist) - preview them, get free marketing
advice, arts/travel zines & more: http://www.accurate writingandmore.com

---

Editing/Book Doctoring

Shel Horowitz, mailto:shel@frugalfun.com, 800-683-WORD/413-586-2388
Director, Accurate Writing & More * http://www.frugalfun.com
Editing * Book Proposals * Ghostwriting * Publishing Consulting * Marketing
Serving writers and publishers since 1981 Fax: 617-249-0153

Public Speaking—Short (I also have a longer one)

Shel Horowitz - Featured Speaker, American Marketing Association—Chapter
Conference; National Writers Union regional conferences; others. Instructor.
University of Massachusetts. Heard live on radio stations from Taiwan to Tennessee.
mailto:shel@frugalfun.com - 800-683-WORD/413-586-2388
http://www.frugalfun.com - Fax: 617-249-0153

Résumés/Careers

Shel Horowitz, mailto:shel@frugalfun.com, http://www.accuratewritingandmore.com
Director, Accurate Writing & More ph. 800.683.WORD/413.586.2388 (since 1981)
Affordable Professional Resumes - in person (MA) or by fax/e-mail/phone
Résumés published in five national résumé books
Assistance in starting, operating, and marketing a business
Author, Marketing Without Megabucks: How to Sell Anything on a Shoestring

---

Web Site

Shel Horowitz, mailto:shel@frugalfun.com, 877-FRUGALFUN
Webmaster, FrugalFun.com http://www.frugalfun.com
Over 350 articles to save you money and improve your life
Home of: Global Arts Review, Global Travel Review, Down to Business mags
Monthly Frugal Fun and Frugal Marketing tipsheets
Excerpts from Marketing Without Megabucks, The Penny-Pinching Hedonist

---

25

Wonderful World Wide Web

For the greatest return on your Internet investment, you need your own site on the World Wide Web. You'll be joining some pretty illustrious company: U.S. senators, rock superstars, major corporations . . . And unlike other neighborhoods in cyberspace, commercialism is actively encouraged— if it is accompanied by good content.

Price is a concern, but not the only one. For instance, when I set up my Web site, I looked for:

- An access number within my local calling area, or a toll-free number with no surcharge
- Multiple autoresponders that send a response (and notify me) automatically when someone writes to a particular e-mail address
- Support for forms processing
- Transaction security for credit card orders
- My own domain name
- A fast, stable server and connection that's going to be easy to get into when I need access, and isn't known to crash very often
- Activity-tracking logs (so I can see what pages are the most popular, whether there are spikes in traffic after a radio show, etc.)
- Low monthly cost

Other people might look for far more detailed tracking, message boards, and/or chat rooms, support for Microsoft Front Page, additional security features, real-time credit card processing, shopping-cart software or other eCommerce features, and so forth. Know what features you need before you select a host.

At <http://www.tophosts.com>, you can narrow down your choices and compare server performance in real time. Then compile your top picks using shopping-cart software, and the site will generate a comparison table on a single page. Eva Rosenberg, moderator of I-Sales Help Desk, suggests <http://www.webhostdir.com>.

Peter Kent, author of the excellent book, *Poor Richard's Website,* suggests starting with the directories of Web hosts at <http://www.budgetweb.com> or <http://www.hostfind.com>. Look on Peter's Web site at <http://www.topfloor.com> for his list of twenty questions to ask a Web host.

Shop around! I've seen basic (noncommercial) Web pages included free with a $10 or $20 monthly account, but some vendors charge businesses as much as $575 per month. You ought to be able to find whatever you need for somewhere between $15 and $60 per month. (I'm currently paying $18 a month for 10 megabytes of storage with my own domain name, plus unlimited e-mail, site updates, and Web access, through valinet.com. I find that valinet's technical support and server capability could be stronger, but I'm basically satisfied. I also have a two-way link with BookZone.com, a large publishing mall—my cheap and easy way to offer secure transaction processing. Please feel free to mention my name if you contact either host.)

There are some incredible deals out there. I've seen companies offer 200 megabytes of storage, CGI scripting (for forms), a secure server to encourage credit card orders, software to run your own mailing list, and unlimited autoresponders, among many features—for astounding prices in the $10–$20-per-month range. Suggestion: If it sounds too good to be true, don't just check references, but also try to call tech support a few times. Some of these companies only offer tech support by e-mail; you want one you can reach on the phone. E-mail-only support is pretty useless if a problem with your settings prevents you from logging on! Switching hosts can be difficult and time-consuming (I've done it a couple of times), so it's better to get it right the first time.

If you're new to cyberspace, you'll probably be tempted to get a "storefront" on one of the numerous Web shopping malls cropping up. The best ones offer nifty software tools such as shopping carts and a secure server, and engage in promotion to draw traffic to their sites.

But don't expect enormous results. Unlike a bricks-and-mortar mall, people don't enter by a main entrance and look around to see what's interesting. Rather, they follow a link from a posting, topic page, or search engine query. In other words, they don't have to come in by the front door, but can arrive on any individual page that has a link from another site. As a result, the mall model doesn't translate as well; it's more like an old-fashioned collection of town squares, with alleys connecting them. So you don't get much benefit from "walk-in" traffic spotting your site. Link your site to any malls that won't charge you, but remember that location is different in cyberspace. Rather than a Web mall, the most desirable location is a short, snappy, relevant domain name of your own.

After two years, I can track only a handful of book orders to my mall listings at BookZone. I've received many other orders through them, but most of them, I believe, came to BookZone through my site. These sales tend to correlate strongly with other promotions I do. Likewise, Amazon.com sells a few books for me every year. But my own promotion does most of the work.

— Creating Your First Web Site —

Creating your own basic Web site is not that hard. If you're going to create Web pages with any regularity, investigate some of the wonderful software that converts a word-processing document into HTML (the language of the Web). This makes creating a Web site almost as easy as doing a heavily formatted letter, and insulates you from the code-based programming you'd have to do otherwise. Recent versions of Microsoft Word and WordPerfect include this feature, and there are also many HTML editors that do the job. Me? I do it the old-fashioned way, plugging my documents into a template and adding code with search-and-replace routines between paragraphs.

Another big difference from other media: The way your page looks to your visitor will depend on how his or her machine is configured. It will change from computer to computer, and even from Web browser to Web browser running on the same computer. As of this writing, the most common tools for exploring the Web are Netscape Navigator and Microsoft Internet Explorer—and both of these are available in several versions. So before you put up a page, visit <http://www.bobby.com>, which allows you to see a page as different browsers view it; try it with a few different browsers (including Netscape and IE versions 2, 3, and 4, as well as Mosaic, Lynx [a nongraphical browser], and an older AOL browser to make sure it looks good. You may even want to customize your Web pages with versions available for different software. Avoid the trap of designing only for one browser, which cuts down your audience and alienates prospects.

If you really need a page to look a certain way, Adobe Acrobat and Sun Microsystems's Java both allow you to create images that will look the same no matter what kind of machine they're displayed on. However, Java tends to crash many less-robust computer systems—and hold others hostage while the Java applet loads at a crawl (at least on my 28.8 kbps modem). (GIF and JPEG images are also pretty consistent from one browser to another. Font tags specify the appearance of text, but if the user doesn't have the right font, this creates really ugly pages.)

Web pages continue to get glitzier: Many have sound, video, and 3-D graphics—but with current technology, display and downloading speed is often too slow. These technologies are really designed for a lightning-fast connection and can be painful to display at anything less than 56,000 bps. There are still users out there cruising the Web at 14,400 bps or slower connections. Content is far more important than bells and whistles. If your site takes over thirty seconds to load, many viewers will not stick around to see your fancy graphics and animations.

While average speeds will continue to rise, for at least the next few years, it makes sense to design for the lowest common denominator. That means avoiding (or providing alternatives to) frames, large and frequent graphics, animation, plug-ins, sound, and video. Any tool that adds to bandwidth should be used sparingly, and only where no better alternative exists. Never hijack your viewer by disabling the "back" command. And always provide an alternative that doesn't hog the user's resources.

Consider the experience of the Internet Marketing Chronicles Support Team <http://www. marketingchallenge.com>:

A while ago we launched a web site, and initially used a frames-based layout. We were aware of the potential problems, and spent lots of time tweaking it to be as browser-friendly as possible. But after asking for feedback we discovered that many visitors hated it.

And the scary thing is that unless we asked for feedback we probably never would have realized this. Everything looked and worked well for us, but a significant number of our visitors had problems with it. We redesigned the entire site and immediately our sales increased. (The Informer, December 15,1998)

Still, as long as your site is set up to give the viewer a choice, there are some arguments in favor of these bandwidth hogs. If a viewer gets the rich media component voluntarily and can stay with plain text if that's the preference, it does open up many possibilities. Product demonstrations, instruction sets, advertorials, and reader commentary are just some of the ways to use rich media.

In her manual *How to Make $50,000 a Year (or More) Creating and Selling Information Products Online,* Monique Harris <mailto:monique@onlinesalespower. com> lists some advantages of including audio in content or advertising (and clearly, similar arguments can be made for video, animation, etc.):

- Every day, 100,000 more people download the Real Audio player, which now has over 28 million users.
- Audio banners perform five times as well as static banners.
- Advanced media can create "28% more traffic, 33% longer visits, and 38% more click-throughs."
- Sound increases your site's appeal to auditory learners.
- If your target audience is high-tech, chances are good that your visitors are already set up for audio.

Offer every possible option to order or contact you—different people prefer different methods. Every page of your Web site should include phone (internationally accessible), fax, URL (Web address), e-mail, and "snail mail" (the postal address). Every outgoing e-mail message needs an e-address, URL, and preferably a phone number.

Since neither e-mail nor Web servers are truly private, take precautions with credit card numbers: Use a secure server or a transaction vendor. Major online services such as America Online are also secure, as are many ISPs and Web malls. A cheap alternative: Have clients send their credit card number in two halves, in two separate e-mail messages. The messages will probably follow different routes, so the chance of someone intercepting the number are greatly reduced.

More Web Site Design Considerations

Mary Morris <mailto:marym@finesse.com>, a well-known Webmaster and author, suggests these guidelines for successful Web weaving:

- Design every page so that it displays to the user within thirty seconds—keep it to 50K (kilobytes) or so.
- If you use backgrounds, keep them to about 5K—some software, including Netscape, forces you to wait until the background is displayed before anything else can happen.
- Keep the jargon out—or at least explain it—and keep the reading level simple.
- Don't use a feature just because it's there (for instance, don't let your text blink on and off). In other words, remember that the goal is readability. [Shel's note: In rare cases, it may be appropriate to blink one line—a line that contains a crucial instruction on an order form, for instance.]
- Make sure a novice user can easily find any links you've put in to other pages.
- Sign all your pages, and provide the full Web address [and, adds Shel, an e-mail contact] on each one.
- Remember that many surfers won't scroll—so don't fill up half a page with your logo, because it may be all the surfer sees.
- Warn users before they commit to downloading large files.
- If you're using a video player, start it only when the user puts the cursor over it—don't do a continuous loop.
- If you're showing off technologically, it should be content related, not just to prove how cool you are.
- Notify the owner before you establish a link to another site.

Loading speed is perhaps the most important variable. Web surfers are a notoriously impatient lot, and if they don't see something worth staying for, they may leave in as little as ten seconds. Thus, a page that takes a full minute to load is the kiss of death. Only those who desperately need the information will wait around. Casual surfers and shoppers will be long gone. Remember, too, that access speeds vary widely. A site that loads acceptably at 56K or faster may be intensely frustrating to a user in a developing country, struggling with a modem that's only 9600 bps.

Some more design pointers:

- Label your graphics using descriptive "alt" (alternate) tags, so those who surf with graphics disabled know what's supposed to be there. For example, on my site, I have graphic images of my book covers. My alt tags don't just say "book cover"; they state the names of my books.
- Provide *great* content, not just a sales pitch for your product or service.
- Make sure your site is both attractive and functional. Aim for a simple, clean interface that is easy to navigate and easy to read.
- If you're using any bandwidth hogs, such as animation, sound, or video, be sure they serve a true marketing purpose. For example, a video clip that demonstrates a complex procedure or a sound file from a CD that you sell is appropriate. A video of your logo as an animated rotating sculpture is not.
- Anything you can do without Java or frames should be done without Java or frames—both of which are not only unsupported by some older browsers, but also vastly increase the likelihood that your visitor's computer will crash. If you

must use these tools, provide an alternative page without them (and a description of what your visitors have missed).

- Keep all the text legible! Avoid heavy use of italics, bold, weird colors on noncontrasting backgrounds, reverse type, etc., and test the legibility and friendliness with both monochrome and color monitors—you'd be amazed at how many Web sites are completely unusable in black-and-white.
- Every piece of your site should move visitors to take the action you want them to take.
- Test and refine over time. One of the best reasons to use the Web is the ease of updating.

Organize your site in a way that makes sense to your customers and makes it easy for them to buy from you. Publishing guru and parachute author Dan Poynter reorganized his parapublishing.com Web site, which had been set up by product category: books, special reports, audiotapes, and so on. When he began categorizing by interest (i.e., self-publishing, printing resources, parachuting), he immediately experienced fourteen times previous sales once the redesign went live.

Instructional designer and Web developer Lorilyn Bailey <mailto:lorilyn@guestflnder.com> says that she creates effective Web sites by following a well-known five-step design model—and adding her own sixth step:

> When I develop any web page, I use the same approach as I do in developing any training materials, regardless of medium (computer, self-study, classroom, Internet, video).
>
> There are five steps:
>
> *1. Analysis:*
> Audience: Who is the audience? What do they want? What will they do? What hardware do they have? What software? Which plug-ins (if any)? I obtain all the possible information I can about them.
> Task: What do I want the audience to DO or KNOW? After they visit my Web site, will they have

been able to do or know what I want them to? I come up with a list of very specific, measurable objectives . . . e.g., "The user will be able to find an application form and a link to a fact sheet with no more than two clicks. . . ."

> *2. Design:*
> I design the page according to the audience needs and my list of objectives. Does the audience want fast downloading? Of course! Who wants to wait? Should it be a clean, simple design that encourages users to stay and look around? Yes! And so on.
>
> *3. Develop:*
> Only now do I put it all together, keeping in mind the results of my analyses.
>
> *4. Implement:*
> I put it out there on the Web.
>
> *5. Evaluate:*
> After visitors have "tested" it, I ask: Are my objectives being met? Are there changes? Problems? Of course! There will always be changes. This is an anticipated step, where the page is evaluated and changes are made.
> I suggest a sixth step—Maintenance. You must keep your page fresh and up to date. People will not re-visit a static page. The Maintenance step should be considered throughout the development process.
> These are simple steps, but they're worth a million. They seem so logical, but many people don't think about these issues. They end up with Web sites that visitors won't use because they don't have the right plug-ins, take forever to download, or are illegible, unappealing, or extremely confusing. (Publishers Marketing Association Discussion List, September 14, 1997)

Seasoned users scoff at "brochureware"—simple Web sites that essentially digitize a brochure and do nothing to take advantage of the Web's strengths. Content that is all sales or puffery gets ignored quickly.

And one of the Web's strengths is the ability to anticipate people's questions. If you expect to attract journalists, set up a page with press information. If you want to sell advertising, put your rate card, demographics, and insertion order form on a page. And provide clear navigation to these pages from any part of your site.

Paul "the soarING" Siegel <mailto:soarsegl@ix. netcom.com> believes the way to an effective site is to create what he calls a "learning fountain": a site that "does not teach or preach, but arranges conditions to make it easy for the visitor to learn."

Siegel, writing in *VirtualPROMOTE Gazette,* January 10, 1999, lists five types of learning fountains:

- Referrers (directories and search engines)
- Informers (offering useful information)
- Advisors (solving problems)
- Context providers (providing visitors with the tools to solve their own problems)
- Learning community stimulators (getting visitors involved in helping each other)

Cliff Allen <mailto:cwa@allen.com> has had good success with "anonymous personalization." He uses six checkboxes to provide 720 different content options. Without requiring the user to enter any personal information, he can customize the content based on their responses. Because it's not a lot of extra work—just one click per checkbox—over 50 percent of his visitors click, and receive the customized content.

Another way to personalize is to have an automated response that dovetails on the customer's action. Software merchant Brent Cook <mailto: brent@ transactiv.com> raised his cross-sell rate from 1 percent to 5–7 percent by offering another product in the same category. Amazon.com does this all the time; when you examine a book, the site will suggest other books.

Clear navigation is vital. Your visitors need easy, obvious ways to get farther into your site and to travel across to the key pages. My site uses a row of buttons down the left column of every page, with links to the most important parts of my site, including the pages of Frugal Marketing and Frugal Fun

resources, the site overview, information pages for each of my books, a site-specific search engine, the home pages for my magazines, favorite links, and, of course, my order page. Since some browsers don't support frames, I do this with a table. I also have my e-mail address and telephone number all over the site, and all the articles even vaguely related to one of my books provide a direct link to more info on that book.

A search engine that only searches your site is a nice touch once you get more than about thirty pages of content. You'll save your visitors an awful lot of unnecessary and frustrating work, and that means they'll stick around longer on your site. If you'd like to make things clearer for your visitors, "borrow" my search instructions at <http://www.frugalfun. com/search.html>. They're free, with attribution.

— It Really *Is* a Worldwide Web —

The Web—in fact, the entire Internet—is truly a global marketplace. The World Wide part of the name is not an exaggeration, and that, too, changes marketing.

Sheila Webber <mailto:sheila@dis.strath.ac.uk>, a professor from Glasgow, Scotland, warns Web designers to welcome international visitors. She points out several things to avoid:

- *The payment mechanisms effectively exclude those outside Country X (costly, difficult, or impossible for others); or*
- *You only give free phone numbers (which only work in Country X); or*
- *You haven't bothered to seek out a cost-effective shipping option for the goods, so I spend $3 on the product and $9 on postage (I know shipping costs money, but some routes are cheaper than others); or*
- *The site appears to want to attract all comers, but is made "homey" by including lots of in-references which only those in Country X would understand; or*
- *You forget that people outside Country X are having to pay for local phone calls on top of any*

Internet charges, so are even less likely to be happy about slow-loading sites.

It's a basic marketing question: if you really want to aim at international markets you have to think about that right from the word go and it will affect your whole marketing strategy.

There's nothing more frustrating than working through a site, thinking 'yes, I want to purchase this product'—then finding out it's incredibly expensive or an incredible amount of hassle, because I'm based outside the country in question. Presumably the people operating these sites would say that I COULD purchase—but they are deluding themselves (unless they've got a truly unique product)....

If you are going on to an international platform like the Internet, then you've GOT to think international, because you've got an international audience whether you want it or not.

One great (and easy) way to make your site global-friendly: link your order page to the currency conversion site at http://www.xe.net/currency. Then your customers can find out exactly how much of their own money they'll be spending. (If you accept credit cards, the currency conversion is automatic and inexpensive.)

I not only link my order page to the currency converter, but I also start my home page with links to brief welcome messages in a bunch of different languages (as many as I've been able to get people to donate). I think this feature provides a nice homey touch to surfers from elsewhere, and even if their language is not represented, they know we're global-friendly.

And I've had site visitors, tipsheet subscribers, media inquiries, and book and service orders from the far corners of the globe.

26

Build Brand Identity and Traffic

It's not enough to set up a Web site and wait for the world to stumble on it. You have to market it.

— Search Engine Tricks —

Search engines are like the Yellow Pages of the Internet; they're the places people go when they don't know exactly whom to visit. The results are all computer-generated on the fly, with new pages created each time a visitor performs a search. And different search engines will index sites differently, so the results of different engines may vary wildly.

The Internet includes five main types of search tools (the URLs are enginename.com, unless otherwise stated—e.g., <http://www.altavista.com>):

Spiders: These robots crawl through a Web site, indexing every word and phrase as they go. Popular spiders include Alta Vista, HotBot, Excite, Web-Crawler, Infoseek, Northern Light, and Lycos.

Metasearch Tools: These query the most popular search engines and sift all the results at once, saving the visitor a lot of effort. Dogpile, Inference Find <http://www.infind.com>, Metafind, and my personal favorite, Metacrawler, are a few important ones.

Directories: Sites here are manually listed by human beings. Yahoo is the most well known, but there are others, including About.com (formerly called The Mining Company) and the natural-language-oriented Ask Jeeves (actually both a directory and a metasearch engine—and very cool).

Discussion Group Search Tools: Liszt.com, Deja-News.com, ForumOne.com, and Tile.com search by topic for posts to discussion groups, and/or for discussion groups that you can join. Major host sites, such as Onelist.com and Egroups. com, also allow you to search and sign up for their thousands of discussion lists.

Databases: For serious research, much of the Internet's repository of knowledge (often considerably more well-documented than what you might find on the Web) rests in obscure Gopher and WAIS databases that predate the Web, or in the search libraries of commercial database services such as Nexis/Lexis and Dialog. You're not likely to get much direct marketing benefit here, but if you need to find facts . . .

For traffic-building purposes, only the first three types concern us.

Getting Found

First off, register all your crucial pages, and not just the home page (though do that first, to be sure!) Put "meta-tags" on every individual page. These help some of the spiders index your site. My main pages (and most of my minor ones as well) include keyword, description, and "robots all" tags; the last of which tells the spiders to go through your entire site. If you want to copy the syntax and replace my information with yours, drop by <http://www. frugalfun.com> and display the source code.

Better yet, visit <http://www.metamedic.com> to see what your page actually looks like to a search engine spider. I discovered through metamedic that my title page, meta-tags, and navigation bars were all that showed up. I quickly revised all my doorway pages (the ones that organize information for visitors and lead them to the content areas) to put some text between the heading and the navigation bars and thus get better rankings. I do the same for all new or revised pages I put up.

Your page title is another crucial element in the way the search engines list your site. Think of it as a headline, which is how browsers will display it. Never squander a title tag on meaningless drivel! Which page title do you think will return better search results: "My Home Page" or "The Money-Saving Frugal Fun/Accurate Writing & More/AWM Books Site"?

There are literally thousands of places you can list your new site. The seven spiders and three directories named above are the most important search engines and should be registered manually (or with mild aid from WebStep 100—see below); they are far too important to trust to an automated service.

Be especially careful with your listing submissions to Yahoo, where errors can be notoriously difficult to fix. Yahoo accounts for a huge percentage of searches, so a good impression is worth the effort.

Beyond these seven, start with WebStep 100 <http://www.mmgco.com>, a free service of John

Audette's Multimedia Group. This ever changing hotlinked list of some of the best places to submit is currently (October 1999) organized by order of importance. Do all the relevant four-star listings, then come back when you have time for the three-star listings. This site also offers a convenient single page to register with half a dozen of the most vital search engines, speeding the process immensely.

After WebStep, locate the best directory sites and the key "hot lists" (individually compiled lists of favorite links) in your product or geographic niches.

What about those places that promise to submit your list to hundreds of search engines for some smallish fee? There are some that have legitimacy, such as Submit-It. But most will probably be a waste of money. A lot of their listings will be for low-rent free classified sites that few people visit and even fewer actually read. There have also been troubling reports that some of these companies just take your money and do only a dozen sites or so. Check any service out and get references before you spend money.

Also beware of companies that guarantee you a Top Ten or Top Twenty listing in a search engine result. It's easy to do—if the company lists you under some obscure phrase no one is actually searching for; you want a guarantee that you'll be well listed on the most popular searches for your category. And with thousands of results, that's pretty hard to ensure. Some of these companies are reputable, but if you want to get found in a dozen different searches, expect to pay significant bucks.

Even if you do achieve a great ranking, you probably won't keep it for long. Between the constantly changing search engine algorithms and your competitors studying your source code, placement can be pretty transitory.

One thing that sometimes helps is to resubmit to the major "spider-powered" search engines (i.e., only the automated ones, *not* to directory sites such as Yahoo, where a human being manually sifts through the submissions) every few weeks.

In any case, don't rely on search engines to bring most of your traffic. Promote actively every way you can, and you'll find, like Jim Daniels <mailto: webmaster@jdd-publishing.com>, that it pays off:

> There was a time when I felt that ranking high in search engines was very important. I even spent hours every week trying to get those top spots. . . . Then a funny thing happened. I wised up. . . . There were literally thousands of other folks promoting related products and services. I knew that keeping those high search-engine positions would become quite a chore eventually. Hey, I'm just one guy, sitting at my computer. If the few hours a week I was spending on search-engine ranking grew into ten, twelve, or fifteen hours, something else would have to suffer. . . . I dropped out of the game altogether. That's right, I gave up the battle. And it was the best decision I ever made.
>
> You need more than search-engine traffic to make it online. You need relationships. You form these valuable business relationships by promoting your business in other ways. Regular e-mail contact, newsletter publishing, discussion group participation, offering an associate program—these are the methods that have brought me full-time income on the Internet. They are also the methods that will take me further.

Amazingly, Daniels now enjoys better search-engine rankings than ever—because giving up the struggle for placement doesn't mean abandoning his carefully optimized pages:

> All you have to do is create one good meta-tagged page, then use it as a template. Every time you create a new page, paste in your template and adjust the keywords for the content on that page. A quick tutorial on meta tags can be found at my free help area: <http://www.bizweb2000.com/freehelp.htm>.

Tips on Search Engine and Free Listing Submissions

Prepare a word-processing document with your name, e-address, URL, and 10-, 25-, 50-, and 100-word site descriptions. Spell-check it and proof-read it thoroughly, then keep it open as you wend your way through the listings. Then just copy and paste into the form. (If your site focuses on several topics, do this for each topic—and submit each category home page separately.)

Keep another document to record passwords and usernames as you enter them (not just in search engines, but throughout your Internet travels). Also, keep records of where, when, and which pages you've submitted: BookZone offers a nice tool kit for tracking submissions, accessible directly at <http://www.bookzonepro.com/mkttoolbox.html>.

Tips on meta-tags: make sure your meta-tags include close misspellings; if people make typos as they enter the search criteria, they should still be able to find you. Separate keywords or compound phrases with commas, and don't put the same word more than three times in a meta-tag or the engine will think you're spamming and drop you right out.

If you use gateway pages designed just for search engines, expect to put in a substantial amount of time, even if you use software like WebPosition Gold to make it easier. You'll need different pages for each keyword set *and* each search engine. So if you have three major themes on your site and you target ten search engines, you need thirty custom pages. And you'll need to update these pages constantly. Each page should also be attractive and useful to visitors, so they want to click into the belly of your site.

Personally, I've chosen not to bother. I do get traffic from search engines, but I have better things to do than make a fetish about it. My goal is not vast traffic; rather, I want to bring the right people to my site: people who will buy my books and services and/or give me referrals and testimonials, media exposure, co-op marketing opportunities, or other goodies. And I use many other promotional strategies to attract traffic, so I'm not dependent on search engine whims.

Great search engine listings are easy enough to get if you have a truly specialized niche. But for the more general categories, the numbers are daunting. Alta Vista returns over 10 million hits for "marketing," and over 20 million for "book." Changing "marketing" to "Web marketing" narrows it down to a mere 45,783 (*Web Marketing Today*, March 2, 1999). If you want to be on the first page of results in a search like that, it's going to be a full-time job.

How much can you actually expect from great positioning in the search engines? Again, I'll use Ralph Wilson's analysis in *Web Marketing Today*. If you draw an extra 50,000 visitors per week, 1 percent buy an item averaging $40, and your gross profit is 15 percent, you'll net $3,000 extra profit per week on revenues of $20,000. That's over $150,000 a year in your pocket (plus whatever you make in advertising revenue, which could be significant if your traffic is that high). Thus, it's nothing to sneeze at—but you have to ask yourself if it's worth the cost of a full-time employee or an expensive outside service to keep your high rankings.

Of course, you could make the same $150,000 profit with half the visitors, if you can raise your conversion rate from 1 percent to 2 percent!

Search engines constantly shift their algorithms, as they try to outwit people who subvert the directories by various techniques akin to ballot-box stuffing. Typically, someone will come up with a new way to fool a search engine, within a month hundreds of people will be doing it, and a week or two later, the engine will block that trick. The best way to keep on top of what works on this particular day is to read the resources and newsletters that make it a full-time job to stay on top of search engines.

— Buying Search Engine Results —

It wasn't all that long ago that search engines brought up results based strictly on automatic searches for the keywords entered in a search string. Now, however, prime real estate in a search engine is sold at least as much as it's given away. A listing within the first ten or twenty search results will display on the first one or two pages, and thus is likely to be seen. Meanwhile, the hundreds or thousands of results on following pages will be ignored by all but the most dedicated researchers. So it's not surprising that prime placements are for sale.

Typically, a company can either buy the actual listing or, more commonly, buy the right to display a banner when certain keywords are entered. This, of course, makes the field far from level for small sites without advertising budgets. Fortunately, there are many strategies in addition to search engines that can bring visitors to your site.

Doing the math is not encouraging. Let's say you purchase 500,000 impressions on a search engine, for $20 CPM (cost per thousand). So that ad costs $10,000. If you get 2 percent click-through (a very good number), you've brought 10,000 new visitors, at a dollar apiece. But a visit is not a buy. If 2 percent—again, higher than normal—of these new visitors make an average purchase of $20 on your site, your gross is $4,000, and it cost you $50 to attract each new customer. So you're $6,000 in the hole before you even count your other costs of doing business—and 10,000 isn't enough new traffic to interest most ad buyers, so you can't even offset the loss through ad sales! And at the more typical rates of 1 percent for click-through and purchase, it's even more dismal.

GoTo—a Keyword Bargain

Here's a better way to buy keywords: GoTo.com. This unusual search engine has far less traffic than the most popular players. But it holds out amazing possibilities for those who want to experiment with buying placement on a search engine.

GoTo auctions off results to the highest bidder, and sometimes the fees can be surprisingly small. Let's say you put in a bid for one cent per click. If you get the same 2 percent click-through and you want the same 10,000 visitors, your cost is $100 and your CPM is only 20 cents. If the same percentage convert to sales, the $100 marketing cost of that $4,000 represents a very affordable customer acquisition of 50 cents, compared to $50 in the previous example.

GoTo displays the current high bid when it brings up a banner. It also provides a list of alternative search terms, so if the current bid is too high, you can select another choice that perhaps no one has bought yet.

And you don't always have to be first! If the high bidder is at 8 cents and the second bidder is at 2 cents, a 3-cent bid gives you second place, and a penny per click gets you fourth place. Another strategy is to use a compound keyword. I looked at "bargain" and decided it was too expensive, but when I searched for "bargain travel," I could be first with a 2-cent bid, or second with a penny. I bought $50 worth of keywords, and so far, it's bringing a small trickle of visitors per month. That $50 will spread out over about a year at the rate things are going. In other words, it was a good investment since I only pay for click-throughs, but this engine doesn't get nearly the traffic of the major engines.

Robert J. Woodhead <mailto:trebor@animeigo.com> had some interesting thoughts about GoTo.com:

> *The algorithm to use in optimizing your GoTo.com bids seems to be (at least for me) "bid the minimum needed to get into position 5 or higher, but not more than some maximum bid." In my case, that maximum is about 15 cents. You usually don't want to be in the #1 position, because that will get you some mindless "top of the list" clicks. A little lower down, but "above the fold" on a 640 x 480 monitor page, gets you click-throughs of higher quality—though I don't have the numbers to back up this gut feeling.*
>
> *Even with the bid competition that has been going on recently (a good thing in the long run), I'm still earning $5 for every $1 spent with GoTo.com. Not as good as the $10:1 rate of last summer, but their traffic has increased, so my total earnings from GoTo.com are up.*
>
> *One way to really up your traffic from GoTo is look at their top search terms, and see if you have a page on your site appropriate for that term. Then you apply for the search term, using a very specific description that you hope will only generate click-throughs from potential customers, and redirecting to the specific page on your site.*
>
> *GoTo is very careful about letting people bid on the top search terms, so you have to have relevant content, but the side-effect of this is that many of the top terms can be had for surprisingly little. I man-*
> *aged (after a round of explanations about why it was appropriate!) to get onto one of the top search terms on GoTo, and the price was about half of my average cost per [search] term.*

Incidentally, Woodhead's site at <http://www.selfpromotion.com> offers excellent advice about getting listed in Yahoo, among many other goodies. Other enormous riches in Web publicity/promotion information and tools can be found all over the Net. Some of my favorite sites: <http://www.virtualpromote.com> (Jim Wilson includes forums on each major search engine, along with hundreds of other hands-on, practical resources that he's published in *Virtual-PROMOTE Gazette*—you may not enjoy his politics, but his information can't be beat), <http://wilsonweb.com> (Ralph Wilson—no relation—gets my vote for the smartest advice in Web marketing; back issues of his newsletter are another absolute must), <http://www.bizweb2000.com> (Jim Daniels's continuing story about how he has succeeded, with lot of practical applicability for others), <http://www.searchenginewatch.com> (Danny Goodman's moment-to-moment search engine update), and my own *Down to Business* magazine at <http://www.frugalfun.com/dtb.html> (over eighty articles on many aspects of business, including a great deal of information on many facets of Internet, marketing: avoiding credit card fraud, managing online resources, eCommerce, etc.).

— Keep Your Visitors in Front —

Amazingly, many businesses with Web sites fail to generate contacts from their Web site—or capitalize on the contacts they generate. I strongly suggest some way to do this—but remember that if you ask people to register on your site, you've got to give them a reason. Assume that in most cases, visitors will *not* return to your site once they've concluded the initial session. Any that do are an extra bonus; plan for the one-time visitor.

On my own site, I've set up two monthly tipsheets that visitors can subscribe to from almost any page.

Each of them lets me promote my books to prospects every single month, while I provide those same prospects with useful information.

As we discussed earlier, a newsletter can be enormously successful, both in direct revenues and in branding yourself in front of your best prospects.

In addition to mailing lists, sites can build return traffic in many other ways:

- Contests with worthy and relevant prizes
- Discussion boards or chat rooms (this works especially well for discussion of software usability or cutting-edge topics in a specific field—or if you feature prominent experts or celebrities in a live chat)
- A notification form if the content changes (generic messages are very tiresome to the recipient if your site changes frequently—so if you use this, your message should state specifically what you've added)
- Surveys
- Fresh content daily

Contests can definitely build traffic. Stephen Jackson <mailto:sjack@earthlink.net> reported 1,365,000 contest entrants in a thirty-day period, a 47 percent traffic increase. Web sites that sponsored the contest reported a 33 percent increase in visitors two weeks after the contest ended.

Of course, there were two strong reasons why Jackson's contest did so well: the nature of the prize (a vacation in Jamaica), and a massive publicity campaign.

We promoted the contest by placing announcements in newsgroups and Web sites that listed contests. We purchased and exchanged ad banners on Web sites that attracted our target markets. We promoted the Web site offline through press releases, flyers at large gathers like expos, concerts, etc. We had interns announcing the contest in chat rooms and placing announcements in AOL general message boards—and we still fell short of the 1.5 million we were seeking.

I still think it's easier to institute a "push" mechanism that goes to the prospect, rather than relying on repeat traffic. You can even process the registration information directly into a database or e-mail mailing list.

— Links! —

Web pages support something wonderful you won't find in traditional media: hypertext links. These allow Net "surfers" to either go a level deeper and find out more information, or be transported in seconds to another related site. (Many marketing possibilities here! If you stumble on a Web site that's talking to your audience, ask to set up reciprocal links—or work out a small "per-click" fee to have a one-way link from that page to yours.)

These text links are a key strategy, but are often overlooked by beginning Web marketers. They are important for a number of reasons.

- Some search engines factor in the number of links from other sites to you (and, to a lesser degree, from you to others). You will get a better ranking with lots of links, all other things being equal.
- Links bring in visitors directly. Many sites get more of their traffic from well-placed links than from search engine hits.
- Links provide a degree of third-party validation, much like the implied endorsement of editorial coverage. Of course, one individual Webmaster's recommendation may not mean as much as coverage in your local newspaper—but it shouldn't be ignored. Some Web sites have fiercely loyal followings, who will click on links they find within those sites. My own page of links always surprises me with its high ranking relative to some of my more content-focused pages.
- Links allow you to create income streams, through affiliate programs, classified ads, and other devices.

- Many writers will provide free content in exchange for a link. I have gotten over two hundred articles for my three magazines this way. The links are directly accessible through their articles, and not exiled to my links page.
- Without the need to spend time copying and reformatting a page, links allow you to offer additional content by linking to it. For instance, on my *Down to Business* Webzine, I have four of the eighty or so articles I've written for the UMass Family Business Center—and a link to the FBC's own Web site, where anyone interested in those topics can read for hours. The director also has a link back to my site from my biography blurb.

A Georgia Tech survey <http://www.gvu.gatech.edu/usersurveys/survey-1998-04/graphs/use/q36.htm> conducted in April 1998 noted that links outpulled search engines for the second year in a row. On a survey that allowed respondents to check multiple options, 86.6 percent cited another web page, while only 83.5 percent cited search engines. Incidentally, the only other options to score over 60 percent were directories (64.4 percent), friends (62.7 percent), and printed media (60.5 percent). The next best method was sigs, all the way down at 33.8 percent.

John Lustina <mailto:lustina@vow.com> reports (Internet Sales Discussion List, October 9, 1998) that his company, Voices of Wellness, supplies a link to a changing-daily "Daily Quote About Living," featuring the world's great writers and thinkers. A host site only needs to put in one link, once, and Lustina's company rotates and hosts the content. Twenty sites signed up within the first two days, and after six months, "our applet is now on over 8,500 sites around the globe," displaying to over 100,000 people per month—and building traffic from 7,000 to 60,000 visitors per month.

He suggests that other businesses can follow this model, too. "Find an interactive activity related to the theme of your site or business and offer it as a free download with an easy setup. . . . Your visitors will remember your name as they utilize the free application. . . . You've suddenly placed a link to your site on their desktops."

Not everyone sees two-way hyperlinks as a great marketing tool. Software supplier Cyberian Outpost's links bring visitors to customized pages, where the only way out is back through its on-line store. Thus, there's less danger of a customer browsing and leaving, and failing to come back and complete a purchase because another site was more enticing. (However, there's a flaw in this strategy: Most Web browsers allow visitors to retrace their steps either through the "back" command or by visiting a pull-down menu that includes every site visited in that surfing session.)

Web Rings

A special kind of link, called a Web ring, allows several Web sites with a common theme to join forces and all link to each other's sites. The programming is a bit more complex than a straight link to one site, but the idea is that a visitor can visit all the links or some subset. If you'd like to investigate, do a search that includes either "webring" or "web ring" *and* a keyword about your topic area.

— Affiliate Programs —

Affiliate programs are links that have cash value; the merchant pays a commission on either sales or visits. This can be a great way to add content: the tool to buy products or services you recommend. But like everything else, there are good and bad ways to do this.

At its best, this automated high-tech variant on multilevel marketing creates a win-win for both partners: The referring site receives not only an income stream, but a way of making its own site more valuable to visitors, who can enjoy the convenience of shopping right from the relevant content. And for authors and musicians who publish traditionally, the commissions from people buying your book or CD by clicking on a merchant link from your own Web site may actually be greater than the royalties you get from your own publisher.

The commerce site gets obvious advantages as well: With hundreds or even thousands of people to do its marketing, it cements a brand, is seen as big and important—and a company to do business with—and of course, it brings a flow of new traffic, many of whom become long-term customers at a very minimal cost to the selling site.

There are disadvantages, too. With any third-party income stream, including banners and affiliate commissions, you risk compromising your editorial integrity as a Web publisher. If you collect money by recommending certain products, people may be skeptical about your intentions. Of course, this is a problem in traditional media as well, and is one reason why some of the larger media outlets carry more weight. They are seen, rightly or wrongly, as having an insurmountable wall between advertising and content.

Another downside: If affiliates feel they're not getting enough reward, bad vibes can spread rapidly. Around 1997, Amazon.com—the first really successful affiliate program—was roundly criticized for paying only on those orders generated *before* a customer went anywhere else in the site. Amazon changed its structure to pay commissions on any purchases made during an entire visit that originated at an affiliate site. Now, with recent buzz about paying commissions over the life of the customer and not just the initial visit—and the presence of affiliate networks such as PulseTV.com that do pay every time a customer visits—I expect that Amazon and other affiliate networks will eventually move in that direction. This is crucial to attract affiliates for, say, a fine-art site, where it may take many visits before a sale is made. Another likely trend: keeping the visitor on the referring site while making the affiliate purchase, as pioneered by Nexchange (Internet Advertising Discussion List, June 8, 1999).

In my own experience as an Amazon affiliate, I certainly am not motivated to push a lot of traffic their way. After six months sending a small but steady stream of visitors there, I've earned 56 cents commission! I keep the program only as a convenience to my readers, who can buy books they've read about on my site.

Incidentally, Amazon is an example of cost-no-object marketing and branding. Despite its 200,000-plus affiliates, 1998 revenues approaching $1 billion, a high stock price and even higher visibility, Amazon continues to gush red ink. The site has never yet been profitable! In 1998, it had a net loss of $124.5 million, up from $31 million in 1997, on total revenues of approximately $6.4 billion (that's $6,400,000,000).

Interestingly enough, Amazon spent $133 million on marketing and sales; maybe if they'd read this book, they'd have made a profit! Perhaps I should do a media event and give a copy of my existing marketing book to Amazon CEO Jeff Bezos. (These figures were stated in or extrapolated from a report in *Publishers Weekly Electronic Edition,* January 27, 1999, quoted by Publishers Marketing Association Executive Director Jan Nathan on the PMA-L discussion list.)

Leo Sheiner, who heads the banner network SafeAudit <http://www.safe.com>, says anyone considering an affiliate program should ask: How can I know how often the payment-triggering action occurs? Can I trust the vendor to report accurately and pay consistently?

And, let me add, does the affiliation contribute to the mission of my site, and my personal belief system?

Of course, another alternative to affiliate status is the traditional drop-ship model: You provide sales information on the products, capture the orders, and forward them to the supplier, less your commission. Terry Kluytmans <mailto:webmaster@stairway.org> pointed out the advantages over the affiliate model in the Internet Sales Discussion List, October 14, 1998:

I run a site devoted to online children's music. As part of that site, I sell a selection of related albums and books which I purchase directly from wholesalers and/or the artists themselves. Average cost is 50–55% of product, which leaves me 45–50% gross profit per item.

Music Boulevard recently invited me to join their affiliate program. . . .

On monthly sales up to $499, I'd receive a 7% commission. It increases in 1% increments to 10% at the $3,000–$4,999 level, and *15%* at $17,000 a month. Gee, isn't THAT enticing?

In the meantime, I send people off of my site to Music Boulevard's to purchase their products instead of mine. Hmm. Not sure I like that idea. And thereafter, what are the chances that the customer would enter Music Boulevard through MY site to place their MB order? Not too likely.

An affiliate program might be okay for someone who just wants to earn a few bucks from, for example, their personal Web site, but in my case, with direct product competition, I think it would be a losing proposition, and opted to "just say no." :-)

Terry Kluytmans <webmaster@stairway.org>
Web Site Design/Hosting:
<http://www.stairway-to-webbin.com/>
KIDiddles: <http://www.kididdles.com/>

Those three funny characters at the end of Terry's post are an emoticon, in this case a smiley face. Look at it sideways.

Affiliate programs may have added benefits other than a financial return. Voice of Wellness <http//www.vow.com> signed up for affiliate programs in order to do market research. The company wanted to sell products and didn't know what would work well for their niche. By signing up as affiliates, they were able to track products of interest to their visitors through real-world data. After five months, they knew enough to set up their own catalog and discontinue some of the affiliate programs. And, of course, many sites have become affiliates as a way of enhancing their content and offering convenience to their visitors. Any dollars generated are gravy.

Administering an affiliate program of your own is complex, and probably best outsourced, says Herbie Olschewski, CEO of ICC Worldwide. He recommends working with either Commission Junction, ClickTrade, Linkshare, or BeFree (I-Sales Discussion List, June 3, 1999).

As with banners, affiliate programs change too fast to enshrine any information in a book. Do extensive research before joining an existing program as a referring merchant or setting up your own affiliate program. Good resources to learn more include: <http://www.associateprograms.com>, <http://www.associate-it.com>, <http://www.adbility.com>, <http://www.refer-it.com>, and Olschewski's affiliate information page at <http://www.iccworldwide.com/affiliatewatch/directory/>.

— Off-Line Promotion —

A number of marketers have reported good results from advertising a Web presence on traditional TV. Cyberian Outpost reported a ninefold sales increase after running an oddball (and controversial) image ad on national TV. Jaffer Ali, of Pulse TV (a video retailer with a large Web presence), reports (Internet Advertising Discussion List, December 11, 1998) that TV seems to bring buyers to his site, while the Web brings tire-kickers. He claims that a much higher percentage of people visiting as a result of a TV ad buy the product.

While I'm not a big fan of TV advertising for the cost-conscious marketer, other off-line media can deliver the same positive exposure. Radio, speeches, articles, in-store signs or leaflets, and print ads can all drive traffic. Cross-promote every chance you get in traditional media: List your URL in your e-mail signature; stick it on your printed business card and letterhead; send out press releases about it (and mention it in the body of any other press releases); list it in all your print ads, newsletters, and so forth. Put up signs in your storefront with a special offer for existing customers who visit you online. You can even put your URL right on your product: The elastic strap on every pair of Joe Boxer's underwear prominently displays the company's Web address.

With every mention, give a reason to visit. When I do radio appearances as "the King of Frugal Fun," I provide at least one specific benefit of visiting my Web site. Example: "In the January 1998 Frugal Fun tipsheet, archived on the Frugal Resources page at <http://www.frugalfun.com>, I have hotlinks to some of the best cheap airfare sites on the World Wide Web." Other examples include sections on how to have a three-hundred-dollar wedding or how to spend almost nothing on holiday gifts.

Of course, if I'm doing a pitch on marketing, I'll highlight parts of my site of interest to entrepreneurs, for example, "If you'd like to set up a Frequent Buyer program to bring repeat customers, look at the February 1998 issue of Monthly Frugal Marketing Tips, archived on the Marketing Resources page at <http://www.frugalfun.com>."

— Tracking Your Traffic —

Traffic is a marketable commodity on the Web: a way of getting advertising revenue. And the Internet allows much more accurate quantification of an ad's effectiveness than traditional media. With the proper software tools installed, you will know how many visitors came to each page, how long they stayed, where they came from, and where they went. If you have banners or links on your site, you'll be able to track both click-throughs and impressions. While this count won't be 100 percent accurate for various technical reasons—for instance, all 16 million AOL users worldwide look like the same visitor from Vienna, Virginia, to some software—it's much more quantifiable than print or broadcast advertising, for example.

Web software allows you to count the number of "hits" (page accesses) and thus more or less quantify the return on your investment. But here's a key distinction: *Hits are* not *the same as visitors.*

Each time someone views a graphic or text block, it's another hit. So if you have eight graphic images

and some text on a page, every time someone visits that page counts as nine hits.

You want to count how many individuals come to your site in separate sessions (ideally, separate counts for new and repeat visitors)—not how many times buttons are clicked or how many times in one Web surfing session the same person passes through your site.

If you're doing a lot of different promotions to bring traffic in—and I hope you are!—how do you know what's working? One trick that will help you with tracking all your online promotion is to use the humble question mark. When embedded in a clickable URL or mailto address, the question mark allows you to track the referring source, specify a subject line, and so on. Here are a couple of examples (you don't need to use the brackets at the ends; I'm just using them to be consistent):

<mailto:info@frugalfun.com?subject=tradeterms> (This will create an e-mail addressed to info@ frugalfun.com, with tradeterms as the subject. If I get an e-mail like that, I know someone wants to get the information on reselling my books to their own customers.)

<http://www.frugalfun.com?businessdigest> (This would be a link I might use if advertising in an e-zine called *Business Digest*. When visitors clicked in from their e-mail, it would register a click to that special URL.)

Since I do a lot off-line promotion, where it's to my advantage to keep my URL as short as possible, one of the ways I track is through the sign-up form on my free Monthly Frugal Fun Tipsheet. The list management software allows me to ask people questions as they sign up, and I ask what led them to my site. I don't get a lot of people answering, but enough do that I can extrapolate. So if one-third of the people who do respond cite radio, I know the promotion I'm doing on the air is working, even if it's not immediately reflected in book sales.

Of course, you can also use traditional measurement/attraction tools such as coupons or other special offers. For instance, if you leave a mailing address with Ragu on the Web, you'll get sauce coupons in the mail. And many other Web sites will actually let you print out store coupons from the site, right on your own computer.

Still, many people are reluctant to register unless there's a clear benefit. People are strongly protective of their privacy. For this reason, I don't even ask my visitors their postal address or telephone number unless they're buying a book.

However you measure, you probably won't know the full extent of the results. People may research a purchase through the Web and buy through traditional means—especially if they're nervous about sending credit card numbers over the Net (a pervasive but essentially unfounded fear—actually, merchants take on far more risk than customers). Often, the same people who'll ask you to justify the investment in your Web site are the ones who blow millions on traditional image advertising. Take them with a shaker of salt. If the Web stimulates the traditional AIDA formula (Attention, Interest, Desire, Action), it's doing its job, even if the final step isn't taken online. Jeanne Dietsch <mailto:jadeitsch @activmedia.com>, an Internet consultant, cites a woman who chose her ski vacation (and booked through an off-line travel agent) after searching the Net to find out who had snow during her December vacation week.

27

Banner Advertising on the Web

Banner ads—analogous to print display ads—are all over the Web these days. Irresistible text and graphics in a banner posted to the right Web page can bring in large numbers of "click-throughs"— people intrigued enough to follow the link to your site—*if* your visitors have graphics turned on, the banner loads smoothly, and it's fast enough to display before they go elsewhere. Of course, once they've clicked through, you still have to convince your readers to buy.

While this chapter will focus on using banners to pull visitors from other sites to yours, there is some discussion of banners on your own site, to generate revenue. For a more thorough discussion of supporting your Web site through advertising, read *StrikingItRich.com* by Jaclyn Easton. This chapter also uses a lot of technical language; feel free to refer back to the glossary in chapter 21.

Banners have several important differences from traditional media buys. A magazine ad is static. Once it's printed, it cannot be changed. But a Web site is dynamic, displaying the page anew each time the URL is loaded into a Web browser, or even rotating banners right in front of you—so site owners can sell essentially the same inventory over and over again.

Unlike most other media, a banner has the advantage of near-total trackability. You will know exactly how many computer monitors displayed the banner, how many viewers were enticed to click through and visit your site, and how many of those visitors actually followed through on your offer.

Another crucial difference: If a banner achieves its desired result—getting the visitor to click—it hurts the hosting site (also referred to as the "publisher") by removing the visitor. In a print publication, an ad is side-by-side with content. On a radio or TV broadcast, the ads interrupt the content for a specified time, and then the content returns. But on the Web, once a visitor clicks off to another site, a return visit isn't automatic, and may not happen at all.

On the whole, once the novelty wore off around the middle of 1997, banner click-through rates started plummeting, even as the number of banners shot through the roof. After all, many people go on the Web to work, not to play. If you're in search of a particular piece of information, you don't want to be thrown down a side road by clicking on a banner and moving away from your quarry. In fact, many people use the Web with graphics (including ads) turned off, or ad-blocking software turned on; they won't see your ad.

In February 1998, Natalie Zubar <mailto: natalie@ exoridor.com> surveyed 7,483 visitors to mypostcards. com—a site that accepts only those banners that seem relevant to its audience. Asked "Had you ever found a useful service product or information via the Web site ad banners," 29.81 percent said never, and 47.83 percent said rarely. Thus, banners were effective in marketing to only about a quarter of those surveyed. A competing site that did not target its ads reported even worse results: 65 percent of respondents said banners had never been useful (I-Advertising Discussion List, July 31, 1998).

Still, banner advertising is far from a dead horse. For example, Diane W. Collins <mailto: dcollins@ marketingweb.com>, president of MarketingWeb. com, has reinvented banner size and placement. Instead of relying on 468 x 60 pixel banners at the top of the page:

we are implementing different IAB [Internet advertising banner] standard sizes with locations beginning approximately one-third down the page on the right-hand side next to the scroll bar. (The banner ad study at webreference.com has merit.) In addition, we have placed a half banner at the bottom of the page which we believe will have a better response rate. Slow loading, top-of-the-page banner ads are scrolled past. (Side note: Those inhibiting text down-load to assure that topheavy banners load first must have forgotten that users don't wait.) We are also trying a Sponsorship advertising plan which offers banner ads and opt-in e-mail advertising for one price . . . [in] Marketingweb News, our monthly news-letter, and Editor's Notes, our weekly Internet news commentary. Both of these services have a Web and e-mail presence. If you wish to review our philosophy our advertising policy is located at http:// www.marketingweb.com/Advertisers/advertisers.htm (Internet Advertising Discussion List, January 8, 1999).

Banner placement is evolving. Monique Harris's manual (see page 203) reports on a study that found an ad in the lower right-hand corner of the first screen got 228 percent more clicks than an ad at the top of the page (though with so many different screen sizes out there, I question their ability to identify this so accurately)—and ads one-third of the way down the page got 77 percent better click-through. (She also cites three successful banner offers: a prize, information, and a freebie.)

— Creating a Great Banner—

Great copywriting is vital in any medium, but perhaps nowhere as crucial anywhere else as in a Web site banner ad. And successful ads must understand the very different culture of the Internet compared to more traditional media.

Online marketing guru John Audette <mailto: johna@audettemedia.com>, CEO of mmgco.com, moderator of the Internet Sales Discussion List and editor of *Adventive*, posted on November 16, 1998:

On the Internet we are increasingly casting our votes against obtrusive advertising by refusing to click on banners. In response to this, advertisers have been developing ways to make banners more obtrusive, using devices such as blinking text, animation, even streaming video. Meanwhile Web users in focus groups have been observed literally holding up a hand to cover particularly obnoxious banners. This is similar to the way we protect ourselves from obtrusive commercials on television by hitting the mute button or clicking to another channel.

When I watch myself using the Net, I find that I'm almost always in the mode of looking for information: current news, sports news, financial information, latest happenings at Guinness—whatever. And when I'm looking for information I'm not going to be distracted by a banner ad that is trying to sell me something. It's hard to distract someone when they're deep into a task, in this case a search for information. I mean, really, have you ever seen an ad in a dictionary? So instead of distracting them. why not help them? Advertise information. Here's a fictitious real-life example:

You're in business to sell music online. So you purchase the keyword "Mozart" at Yahoo. Good move. Now when someone searches on the word Mozart, your banner appears at the top of the search results. What is the message they see on your banner? Could it be something like:

"Movie Soundtrack Sale? Save on music from the best musicals of the 90s Click Here"

Yech! You are advertising a sales message (albeit not a very targeted one) and your potential customer (who is in charge) is most likely looking for information. Do they click on this banner? Not very often.

Wouldn't it be more effective to advertise information? After all, the viewer is looking for information about Mozart—why not offer it to him? Maybe a banner along the lines of:

"Did You Know That Mozart Never Attended School? Click Here for the Web's Definitive Site on Mozart, Including a Collection of His Works"

Or use rich media to build a live banner something like this:

"Do You Know What Level of Schooling Mozart Completed? Check One:
__none __ grade school __high school __ college
For the Surprising Answer, Click Here"

Then, after the viewer has arrived at your site, you can present him with a wealth of information about Mozart and subtly present your sales message. You will more than likely develop a customer, create sales—and give yourself a chance to grab some beach time.

The current advertising model was developed in response to a media environment that was severely limited in terms of space and time. Advertisers have adapted cleverly to these limitations by concentrating their efforts on eliciting an emotional response from the viewer. It has worked so well that many believe that tweaking emotions is the only way to advertise, forgetting that it's simply an environmental adaptation. The Internet offers almost unlimited time and space. We now have the ability, indeed the need, to appeal to viewers' intelligence, as well as to their emotions.

There are countless other ways to market effectively on the Internet, many of them having nothing to do with banners. The point is that the essence of the Internet today is information. Market information, advertise information, provide information—and the customers and sales will follow.

Or, another way of looking at it, now that things are upside down and the customer is in control, is that marketers need to meet customer needs—as opposed to manufacturing them as in the past.

Writing in *WebPromote Weekly* (September 5, 1998), Brian Chmielewski <mailto:newsletter@webpromote.com> noted that the Web advertising industry can now expect revenues of about $1.4 *billion* a year. Yet much of this money is thrown away on ineffective ads and click-throughs of 0.5 to 2 percent.

Chmielewski provides a three-part recipe for effective banners: Target your audience, incorporate interactivity in the banner design, and place them on high-traffic sites. He cites an ASI Interactive study that claims interactive banners perform 71 percent better than static banners—and that larger ads increased click-through by 44 percent and the ability to recall the ad by 45 percent.

What exactly is an interactive banner? It's one that the visitor controls, that displays differently depending on the visitor's action. For example, a press release for WebSpot describes a banner for Shop Vac that allows the visitor to vacuum any part of a virtual handyman's workshop on screen. An animated banner with no user input is *not* interactive—just annoying!

Make sure your URL is visible in your banner (and in your alt tag), even without clicking. A memorable domain name gets you branding benefits.

Test!

If you use banners or any similar advertising vehicle, test, test, and test some more. Researcher Josh Reynolds <mailto:josh@brain.com> reported a jump in response rates from the 2 to 5 percent range all the way up to 20 percent and 30 percent after minor tweaking. In his words:

We've tested copy (without graphics) where changing a few words, such as *quick* vs. *3 minute,* represented up to an order of magnitude difference in response!

Again, the key to this is testing, re-testing & being patient. In the final analysis, content, design & positioning are the ONLY elements from which your click stream is created. The stronger they are the less your ad is subject to chance.

Bottom line:

- Find something unusually alluring, informing, or entertaining to offer at your site (it could be your product but doesn't have to be)
- Test the copy (positioning) until you see a big jump in response (often 5–10 times normal)
- Wrap graphics around it, creating the banner— but make sure you test it too (strange things happen in this game—take nothing for granted). Obviously testing means at AND AWAY from your site [in other words, from your own computer and from other computers not on the same server].

Go to the thousands of medium-sized sites hungry for ad rev $ & work out a click-through rate that you know leaves you a margin for error plus a profit. You must know your Revenue Per Visitor (as well as know how to tweak it). This forms a ratio of Revenue vs. Cost Per Visitor = RPV/CPV. It's taken us 6 months to get our ratio up from <1 to >5.

Reynolds noted a significant change in his banner's "pull" just from *reversing two words!*

Eventually, as you build traffic, banner ads for other sites may even produce revenue for your site (if you don't mind your visitors going elsewhere). Plan ahead, and capture your visitor statistics right from the beginning.

However, be careful if you're paying market rates for banners to pull people from other sites to yours. Like any form of display advertising, they can gobble up a lot of money in a short time, and the results

may or may not be what you bargained for. In one study reported to the I-Advertising Discussion List, B. Taylor <mailto:btaylor@inreach.com> reported that half an hour after viewing a page with a straightforward banner ad, 32 percent of respondents could not even identify the product category (a car), much less the brand—and 47 percent failed when the banner alternated the question, "Think you gotta give up ZZZOOOM for ROOM?" with the response, "The New Saturn's got both." (Perhaps the low retention rate had something to do with this ad's poor grammar and uninteresting text.)

Click-throughs—the number of people who actually used the ad to visit Saturn's site—ranged from 18 percent when a giveaway was featured, down to 2.5 percent for the question banner. A product-oriented banner achieved 3 percent response. So in other words, if you use banners to give away something desirable, you'll get higher click-through— but as with trade shows, make sure the offer is germane to *your* prospects, or you'll waste a lot of money bringing tire-kickers to your site.

Run the numbers to see whether any ad buy will make sense. A marketing client was approached by a niche site that wanted her to advertise, and asked me to evaluate the Web site ad buy:

My first impression—this would be a great site for you, but their prices are OUTRAGEOUSLY high. $2.50 per click???? That's about l0x the norm for a highly targeted site. $36 CPM means the minimum cost to you for 10K impressions is $360. Yet their targeting is only by age, not necessarily your key audience.

Look at it this way. If you convert 10%, that means it's going to cost $25 per sale. And 10% would be extremely high! 1–2% would be more believable. The only point of entry I saw that might be a good value was the article-with-link for $99. However, in general, site owners should either pay for content or at least not charge.

I noticed they have an e-mail newsletter with 35K circulation. Their cost for sponsorship is again outrageously high—but if I were you, I'd subscribe and see if they use outside authors. Then you could reach this market FOR FREE with a good article and a blurb including website and ordering info.

It's not only the advertiser who has to be careful; host sites can also get burned. David Doggett <mailto: ddoggett@lovepoetry.com> reported (Internet Advertising Discussion List, December 23, 1998) that his site served 325,394 banners in one month for his ad network, but because of the way the program was structured, he received nothing. The broker's fee, ad-serving costs, and so forth ate up all the revenue.

On the same day, Brad Byrd<mailto:brad@ newgate.net>, Director of Business Development at the online marketing firm NewGate Internet, responded with an alternate model:

It doesn't have to be all or nothing. I proposed an industry compromise—a CPM+ model that guarantees a base CPM pay rate to Web sites for hosting the ads, and pays a *bonus* for above-average CTRs. The most likely way this model would work would be something like a sliding scale CPM, adjusted to the click-through percentage . . . $20 CPM for "average" click-throughs, $22 CPM for click-throughs 2.5% higher than average, $24 for 5% higher; etc. Under this approach, the advertiser will see that their CPC/CTR actually *decreases* as the percentage rises. Actual pricing would have to sit in the pocket between CPM and CTR deals, and the market would (theoretically) adjust to this new pricing strategy.

This model seems to reward Web sites for aggregating not just target audiences, but ACTIVE target audiences; it places a higher value on *quality* audience building, and provides a mechanism and incentive for sites to *prove* the value of their audience. Most importantly, IMHO [In My Humble Opinion], I believe it gives advertisers what they want. I have no doubt that they'd be happy to pay your site a bonus if you brought them better results than the industry average . . . they'd certainly rather adopt a CPM+ than pay $5 per click-through.

And branding expert Rob Frankel <mailto:rob@ robfrankel.com> proposed another alternative:

Find your psychographically compatible sites and contact them directly. Ask them about their activity and impressions. But junk the whole CPM thing in favor of a flat 30 day fee. Believe me, Web hosts would rather take a fat check now than the disappointing few cents they get from the ad brokers who burn them. Plus, when you negotiate directly with a site, you can firm up the deal with extra goodies (like extra graphics) and kill yucky stuff like banner rotation. Play your cards right, and you might even parlay the whole gambit into a month-long sponsorship. [This quote is copyright 1998 by Rob Frankel.]

As a side note, this conversation shows the power of threads as both informational and marketing tools. Both Byrd and Frankel grow their own exposure by responding to the thread Doggett started, and both include signatures that make it easy to follow up. Frankel, in particular, author of *Big Time Branding* and publisher of the mutual-aid newsletter *FrankelBiz* <http//www.robfrankel.com/frankelbiz/form.html> is a very active participant in several Internet discussion groups I monitor.

In the following days, this thread brought in many comments. Respondents argued that CPC (cost per click) makes sense to sell inventory you couldn't get rid of by selling impressions—but that a site should only accept a per-click deal if the host site can set the terms. Jim Reardon <mailto:jim@ freecenter.com> negotiates a floor of one click per hundred impressions; if the ad brings in fewer clicks, the advertiser still pays that rate (December 30, 1998).

Banner ad expert Mark Welch <mailto:markwelch@ markwelch.com> warns site owners never to guarantee a certain number of clicks, or else you'll be forced to keep displaying an unsuccessful ad. He also reserves the right to bounce an ad if a better deal comes along. He has sometimes replaced ads that pay 25 cents per click with those that pay 15 cents but draw more clicks—and he controls the actual banner installations, to protect against advertisers switching banners to those that are designed for high visibility but low click-through (December 30, 1998).

And moderator Adam Boettiger <mailto:ab@ internetadvertising.org>—noting that ultimately, good performance on a CPC campaign is also in the advertiser's interest, since a host would turn down a repeat campaign if it performed poorly the first time—suggested writing protective clauses into the advertising contract:

- The advertiser must supply a new banner if the response drops below a certain percentage.
- The host may terminate the banner flight (insertion run) if the banner doesn't meet specified performance standards.
- Test the creative with an initial run of 50,000 impressions before committing to a larger flight (December 29).

If you wish to accept banners or other ads, put up an online media kit on your site. Mine is a simple page outlining various sponsorship opportunities. *The New York Times Online* has an in-depth media kit online, covering ability to target, audience demographics, achievements, format and placement options, statistics and reporting, as well as, of course, rates and contact information.

— A Bargain Banner Strategy —

This idea involves a good deal more work on your part, but the rewards may be worth it.

David Beroff <mailto:david@note.com>, writing in the Internet Advertising Discussion List on May 4, 1998, suggests:

1. Find sites whose content is a very good fit for your offer but that currently have *no* ads, and not even a rate card—in other words, sites that haven't thought about taking ads so far.
2. Approach the site owner and see if they'd like a bit of free money for running your ad.

3. Offer a nominal amount of money (say, $20) to link to your banner.
4. Keep your banner on your site, and track the results.
5. If the results are good, repeat—and if the site owner wants more money, give it; it's still a bargain!

Using this approach, he paid about $300 to get 300,000 targeted impressions per month, versus about $10,000 through more conventional channels. A man after my own heart!

— Banners and Technology —

Like other Web-based promotion, banners offer a remarkable ability to track your results. With the right software, you will know all sorts of incredibly useful information: How many times your banner was displayed, how many people clicked on it and at what dates and times, what site they were at when they saw your banner . . . This sort of information is a direct marketer's dream. You can easily do split runs, where you can test different versions of a banner, either across a random sample or by geographic/ demographic/psychographic information.

You can even find out whether a competitor has bought a keyword at a search engine. A site called Bannerstake <http://www.namestake.com> will query the search engines for a particular keyword and deliver the banners coming through.

Another service, Tritium.net, allows users to control banners much like a CD player: visitors can pause, fast-forward, and return to a previous ad (it changes the display every thirty seconds), as well as click.

Right now, banners are in a state of rapid change. Techniques such as animation, audio and/or video, forms embedded in the banner, nonstandard sizes or placements, "interstitials" (ads that intercept an incoming Web page, display themselves, and then allow the page to come in, much like a TV commercial), and even the simple copywriting trick of saying, "Click Here to____" can increase a banner's "pull." In fact, according to a *Wired Digital* study in March 1999, "rich media" banners outpulled traditional banners by 13–18 percent.

Yet some of these techniques can backfire. I personally hate distracting animated banners and boycott any site that uses them. I don't much love Java either, which imprisons my computer while it goes through its slow and usually uninteresting routine. Java also crashes many older computers, and thus leaves a bad taste instead of a positive impression.

A number of ways have been invented to solve the problem of tearing a visitor away from your site. Some banners open new browser windows so that the referring site is still underneath and accessible. Others open in a frame, so that two sites at once are usable on screen. Ads can also open a "microsite," a small hint of what the whole site would be, so that the visitor knows whether it will be worth the trip.

All of these, however, have their own problems. Frames play havoc with navigation, since your "back" button may take you back in one or the other frame, or back an entire site. And frames confuse search engines. There are also still people out there using old browsers that don't support frames (Internet Explorer 2.0 and below, for example). New browser windows have no technical problems, but some users resent them very strongly. And microsites only delay the point at which the user must choose whether to stay or go.

A recent technology promises to keep the advantages of banners while minimizing the disadvantages: autoresponders initiated by a Web site click—and accompanied by the magic words, "Click Here to ____ and NEVER Leave This Site." This approach has been pioneered by e-ads.net.

Bob Cortez <mailto:bobcortez@tqm-online.com>, moderator of the homebiz discussion list, suggests thinking of the e-ads system as turning a banner into a direct-mail reply card. The user can select the information he or she would like to receive as e-mail, in a new browser window, without leaving the original site. And he sees an exciting future:

When your information arrives in the prospect's in box, in addition to the information they requested, you also provide them with an overview of your site, with direct links to specific sections of interest. Now they have a directory of your site that they can refer to and visit at their leisure. What if that reply card gave them the option of receiving your message in multiple languages? What if you could customize the card so you could ask for more information from your prospect? What if this reply card was part of a system that automatically followed up with additional information on a scheduled delivery? (I-Advertising Discussion List, December 16, 1998)

This is only one of many ways to integrate personal e-mail with a Web site. You can let visitors send an e-mail to friends recommending your site—or even e-mail actual Web site content—and, of course, collect e-addresses for a newsletter, to mention some possibilities.

If your site leads the viewer to an action, your "Thank you, your message has been sent" page could be a great place to put banners. You're done with these viewers, who have filled out your form or purchased your product. Why not get revenue for their next stop on the journey?

Before you buy or sell banner placements, try them out; exchange banners with a compatible Web site.

What about the free exchange services such as Link Exchange? Typically, for every two or three times you display someone else's banner, one of yours gets displayed. Tread cautiously; you give up control over the content, and banners from incompatible sites may not do you much good. Search the Web for "banner exchange" and you'll surely find a few up-to-date articles comparing different ones. Also, check the I-Advertising Discussion List archives <http://www.internetadvertising.org>.

⚞

The power of the Web has only begun to be tapped. Turn the page to learn about the most important new trend on the Internet.

28

Integrating Databases and the Internet

While the Web is a powerful tool even just by itself, when you add the ability to work with databases from the Web, you create a vastly more powerful synergy whose possibilities are just about unlimited.

There isn't space here to cover this in depth—someone could do a whole book on this—but let's quickly examine some possibilities:

- Shopping agents
- Print-on-demand and e-book technologies
- Integration of direct mail and the Web
- Web browsers as database front ends
- E-mail as a database front end
- Data warehousing and communication

— Shopping Agents —

Databases allow you to search the entire world in order to get a good value on shopping. Using "agent" software, many people are saving money by finding the best price before they purchase high-ticket consumer items. If you're a discounter, obviously this works to your advantage, but even if you're not, watch this trend. The same technology ought to

enable agents to automatically return results based on other criteria. And the best price, of course, isn't always the same as the best value.

— Print-on-Demand and — E-Book Technologies

The Web can combine with databases to replace some sectors of traditional book publishing. Customers can now use the Web to locate a book, give credit card and shipping information, and receive either a custom-crafted printed, bound book or a password-protected electronic book.

From a publisher's point of view, instant-book technology can offer several advantages over traditional large-run book publishing. Publishers now have a very low entry cost, making self-publishing an even more viable option. When orders of one, five, or fifty books are economical, or when the publisher develops an e-book and doesn't have to print at all, many things become possible. Publishers can:

- Test the market to see whether they can generate customers for a book without committing to a full press run

- Keep books in print essentially forever, where demand is not strong enough to go back to press but too strong to let the book die
- Run galleys (advance review copies) cheaply and use them to create additional markets such as foreign sales, new networks of drop-shippers, etc.
- Offer personalized content
- Update titles as often as the information changes
- Publish literary and narrow-niche specialty books that would be otherwise unviable economically

Even if you hadn't thought about publishing a book as a marketing tool, this technology may open up ideas and options for you. Certainly, if you make part of your living consulting or speaking, certify your expertise (and open up another sales channel) with a book!

— Direct-Mail/Phone Ordering —

Evan Jennings <root@interlog.com> notes that a Canadian lettershop, Westminster, offers IMail <http://yourmail.com/imailweb>, a technology that sets up individual custom Web pages for each mail recipient, and then mails out direct-marketing pieces that encourage visits. From there, it's an easy leap to creating custom-printed brochures based on information from a data form on the Web. This same company's home page <http://www.westminster.ca> allows you to clean up mailing lists. Enter a U.S. or Canadian address and it will fill in any missing fields. (Internet Advertising Discussion List, July 17, 1998). Other companies are also integrating custom-printed direct mail with Web-based databases.

Paul Purdue of ifulfill.com <ppurdue@ifulfill. com> has even integrated the Web with his toll-free telephone number for customers who don't recognize a credit card charge. The bill has both the ifulfill Web site and the toll-free number. He reports that this phone number doesn't even have an audible ring. Since these orders originated on the Web, the majority of his callers log on to find out exactly what

they bought. When human attention is needed, the phone will beep him (Internet Sales Discussion List, February 10, 1999).

— Web Browsers: — Database Front Ends

Suppose you're looking for a new house. You access your state's Multiple Listing Service on the Web, select the community, price range, and features you're interested in, and out pops a list with capsule photos. When you click on the photo or text link, you get the whole spec sheet.

A time-saver? You bet! Far-fetched? It's already up and running in my own state of Massachusetts.

Of course, this process can work with any product. Amazon.com is one of the best-known database-driven sites, and has used this technology to expand from books into electronics, online auctions, and a host of other product lines.

— E-Mail Database Integration —

As the volume of traffic increases, people need ways to manage their e-mail. Systems that were adequate in your first days in cyberspace, when you got ten messages a day and eight of them were from friends sending you jokes, aren't likely to be effective if you have two hundred new messages every day.

M*ost good e-mail programs have at least some built-in management tools.*

Most good e-mail programs have at least some built-in management tools. For instance, you can set up "filters" so that all the messages from a particular sender, or containing a specific subject line, go into a specific folder in your in-box. (This is also a great way to control junk mail. Filters send 85 percent of my inbound e-junk into a mail folder called "spam"; every couple of days, I quickly move the few important ones that got in by mistake into my in-box and trash the rest unopened. To learn about filters, check the homepage of your e-mail software provider.)

Still, you may find that this won't be enough, especially if several people at your organization are working with the same incoming mail.

Publicist Sherree Geyer <mailto:sherreeg@ ix. netcom.com> wrote to me about software that pours new e-mail into a database. While I have no direct experience with this technology, it sounds as if it could significantly improve workflow under the right circumstances:

ResponseNow allows the staff at the CambridgeSoft testing center to manage and distribute incoming e-mail more efficiently. Staff members used to spend between 16 and 20 hours per month cutting and pasting e-mail messages, and then filing them in folders. ResponseNow automatically files incoming e-mail into CambridgeSoft's database and tracks messages throughout the system, ensuring timely answers to questions and facilitating better report generation. As a result, staff members spend more time on important tasks and less on the tedious task of e-mail administration.

— "Data Warehousing" —

According to software consultant Eric Anderson <mailto:blaine@infinet.com>, the real reason to increase the Net's bandwidth is not to support video presentations and the like. It's to exchange massive quantities of data between manufacturers and their distributors.

We can pick up data from a particular field in a particular database, manipulate it, and then dump it into another field in another database someplace else. The best part is that the databases can be anywhere; all you need is an IP address. This process can be completely automated, and described programmatically. . . .

Barnes & Noble could sweep all of the sales at all of the stores each night, manipulate that data, and then deposit it appropriately in each publisher's database. In other words, if you're a publisher, each morning when you come in and turn on the computer, you could see how many copies of your book Barnes & Noble sold yesterday in each of their stores. The marketing implications are pretty obvious. Did you send a press release to the Bay Area? You'd know if it did any good. Appear on a radio program in Iowa? You could tell if anyone bought. In other words, you'd be able to tie marketing activities more closely with sales. . . .

Now, think what happens when Auto America does the same for their parts inventory, Sears does it for their tires, etc. That's where the real bandwidth problem comes into play.

The complete article is available at <http://www. frugalfun.com/dtb.html>.

≍

Again, this short chapter only scratches the surface of the possibilities. How could the Web automate time hogs or manage inventory in your business?

29

Other Online Advertising and Promotional Tools

Though banners are the most obvious online advertising and promotional tools, dozens of alternatives exist—some of which are really nothing more than banners in a nonstandard size. I-Advertising moderator Adam Boettiger mentioned thirty different possibilities for online promotion in his October 9, 1998 issue. Some ideas:

- Ad navigation bars
- Advertorials
- Affiliate programs and other strategic partnerships
- Audio or video ads
- Badges
- Buttons
- Classifieds
- Contests, giveaways, and other promotions
- Cookies and database integration
- Domain names
- Newsletters or tipsheets
- Content exchanges with other sites
- HTML banners
- Interstitials (ads that appear before the content you've requested loads, then disappear)

- Keyword purchases
- Discussion group moderation
- One-way links (free or paid)
- Opt-in e-mail services
- Postings to newsgroups, discussions, forums, BBSs, etc.
- Pop-up ads (opening a new browser window when the ad is clicked)
- Reciprocal links
- Response forms
- Search engine optimization
- Sponsorships of discussion lists and newsletters
- Syndicated content
- Text links
- Web- or e-mail coupons

We don't have space to go into detail on these, but in view of the growing popularity of Internet radio broadcasting (both stations that were first established in physical space and those that are Internet-only), let's spend a quick moment on audio ads. Wanda Atkinson <mailto:wanda@ 3wk.com>, general manager of 3WK Underground Radio, comments,

Yes, impressions can be measured. Yes, audio works. Our experiences are that audio ads are 3 times as effective as banners alone. And yes, the sound quality is much better than previously, drawing more and more people to listening on the Internet.

But the really wonderful part to us broadcasters is that audio ads are a fixed inventory. After all, there are only so many minutes in an hour, no matter how many people are listening, and there are very few sites that can deliver audio. So unlike banners that increase total inventory every time another Web site hits the Internet and as such have a steadily decreasing value, the very limited audio inventory has the possibility of selling out, which will cause prices on audio ads to actually go up. Can you imagine an ad vehicle on the Internet that not only works for advertisers, but actually makes money for a content provider? No wonder the big guys are so hot about audio right now.

Every person who elects to click on their audio channel is going to listen. Every single person. There is no 20–40% listening with the audio turned off. It's 100% audio involvement. There is no way to escape an ad by not clicking on it, and the ads are typically so short that it isn't worth the trouble to turn the audio off. And because 100% of the people who listen to Internet audio have also listened to commercial AM/FM stations, they are comfortable with listening to audio advertising. (Internet Advertising Discussion List, June 8 and 10, 1999)

Of course, anyone visiting an Internet radio broadcast will have the audio turned on. However, that's not true for Web pages in general. Joe Vargas <mailto:jvargas@elp.rr.com>, of El Paso Internet Courier, took a small, informal survey of fifty readers. Thirty-nine were using the Web with audio off, seven said the audio was annoying, and only four acknowledged hearing the ad (Internet Advertising Discussion List, June 10, 1999).

— Licensing Lists and Content —

So far, we've looked at a few different ways to make money online:

- Present yourself as an expert and have people seek you out and hire you.
- Sell your own products directly from your Web site.
- Sell others' products on your site.
- Sell advertising or sponsorships.
- Earn commissions through affiliate programs.
- Generate business from other sites through your own affiliate program.
- Follow up leads and contacts from discussion groups, individual correspondence, forms on a Web site, etc.

In business off-line, there are at least two other direct revenue streams: your customer list and your original content. Can these make money for you online?

Your Own Customer List

Renting your e-mail contact list is almost always a really terrible idea. My strong advice: *Don't* go near this one! The waters of this particular swamp are a lot murkier, and the alligators hiding below the surface have much sharper teeth, than it appears at first glance.

Because there's no face-to-face contact, it's hard enough to establish trust on the Internet. To throw that trust away by violating your customer's privacy and letting them be spammed is just plain stupid. Word will get around, and your online business will be utterly destroyed.

Of course, nothing prevents you from using your own in-house list to market your own business. However, remember that the annoyance factor for unrequested e-mail can be pretty high. Make sure you have a new and fresh offer, a soft-sell approach, and an infrequent appearance in prospects' mailboxes. Don't use this to announce weekly sales and so forth unless you've asked permission with a specific sign-up list just for this purpose. Much better to let people sign up for your own newsletter and plug yourself at the end.

Opt-In: The Only Exception

If you have a list that is clearly designated as available to other marketers, and it is 100 percent opt-in—you won't place people on the list, but people sign up themselves—then and only then, it might be worth exploring marketing this list through a reputable firm such as Postmaster Direct. *Do not* try to send out this kind of mail on your own. Some companies have fairly innovative approaches to opt-in lists—for example, actually paying recipients who sign up to get the junk mail.

Renting Lists from Others

And if you're in the business of sending out bulk marketing materials, do yourself a big favor and use an opt-in list rather than a spam list. Results are a lot better, too.

For example, Lawrence Goldman <mailto: lgoldman@ decisioneering.com> tested three different bulk e-mail mailings with three different opt-in list companies. He reported response rates of 1–7 percent, and 25–35 percent conversion rates, at a cost of between 5 and 25 cents per name. I dare any spammer to come anywhere near that!

Says Goldman, "E-mail is tangible: it can be stored, saved, or even forwarded. We ran one campaign almost a month ago . . . and sales leads continue to trickle in at about one or two a day. Ever see a banner campaign do that? In addition, roughly 90% of visitors from opt-in that convert to a sales lead also join our own newsletter mailing list" (Internet Sales Discussion List, November 25, 1998).

Goldman does warn marketers to go in with their eyes open: Check out any service and only use a reputable one; ask for referrals. Be sure you understand the difference between list owners and list brokers—and if you use the latter, protect yourself against mailing to a list you've already used. Be as specific as possible in targeting your lists. Track visitors with a custom URL for response, and watch what they do when they visit your site. And don't put all your eggs in the opt-in list basket.

E-mail marketing has become big business, and precious little of that goes to spammers! Forrester Research reports that the more than 3 billion nonspam commercial e-messages sent in 1997 are expected to grow to 250 billion by 2002, with a market value of over $950 million.

Licensing Content

Licensing content, on the other hand, is a very different matter. There are two avenues: selling the right to post your articles to other sites and magazines (on- or off-line), or charging a subscription or membership fee to access some portion of your material (which will then need to be password-protected and in a format where it can't easily be passed around).

The problem with both approaches is competition that costs nothing. On my own *Down to Business* Webzine, I currently have over one hundred articles, including some from many famous names in sales, marketing, and/or eCommerce. I haven't paid a dime for this content; these experts all recognize the value of free exposure in promoting their own business and have allowed me to use their material in return for a blurb and a hotlink. And with my writer hat on, I've sold exactly three pieces to paying online markets, with total fees of $175. Yet I've been published in dozens of Webzines and e-zines, because I, too, recognize the promotional benefits that accrue to me.

To make a go of either subscription-based content or licensing your material to others, it has to be very fresh and timely, not easily available elsewhere, and presented in a very user-friendly way to the correct audience. If you can meet these criteria, then these income streams may be open to you.

There are people succeeding with this. Often, they have a free publication that provides useful information and up-sells to the more in-depth material. Two examples: We've already cited Ralph Wilson's excellent *Web Marketing Today*. He also runs a paid newsletter, *Web Commerce Today*. Wally Bock publishes a weekly freebie, *Monday Memo*. Every issue has a section about the contents in his latest for-pay publication. Some well-known publications in the print world also have paid online products—including *The Wall Street Journal*.

Certainly the technology is there to support many different revenue models. Mark Ketzler <mailto: mdk@softgood.com>, whose company provides these kinds of mechanisms, lists some of the possibilities:

- Pay-per-access (charge each time an article is viewed)
- Pay-per-license (charge per article with rights to access over a period of time)
- Fixed subscriptions (e.g., an association's 1998 proceedings)
- Rolling subscriptions (twelve months of a magazine with any start date)
- Debit (e.g., discounted prepurchase of ten downloads from an archive)
- Metered (e.g., charge per megabyte downloaded from the database)
- Timed subscriptions (charge by the hour, day, week, etc.)

Lead Generation

By now it should be obvious that the entire Internet is well suited to follow-up. If you can't think of how, go back and reread the sections on personal e-mail, autoresponders, and e-zines/newsletters.

— Totally Local Business —

Before leaving cyberspace, does it makes sense for a business with a purely local clientele to be on the Web? The Internet Sales Discussion List discussed this issue in a thread entitled "Should Barbers Go Online?" Web developer Muhammad Lee <mailto: lee@adgconsulting.com> says it depends on your business model. If you can use the Internet effectively to generate local business, it's a good investment. "If he offers people a way to schedule appointments . . . an information resource to people moving into the area, if people can design their own hairstyles online. These are methods that will con-

vert visitors to customers" (December 28, 1998).

In the same issue, Jeffrey Baumgartner <mailto: jeffreyb@jpb.com>, a marketing specialist based in Bangkok, suggested a similar strategy: Post hours of operation and schedule appointments online; offer climate-specific hair-care tips and pictures of various hairstyles, and post a changing list of barber jokes.

A few days later, Bill Hunt <mailto:billh@ mmgco.com>, Senior VP for Account Strategies at John Audette's Multimedia Marketing Group, noted that local businesses can promote through other parts of the Internet as well as the Web. Personalized e-mail reminders, using a database merge, would allow a barber to mention the customer's family members by name, direct them toward products of interest, and allow orders to be placed online and picked up at the next haircut appointment (December 31, 1998).

In the same issue, Sonny Cohen <mailto:scohen@fers.com>, sales and marketing director for Prime - com Interactive, asks why barbers can't provide Internet access just as coffeehouses have. (And by coincidence, earlier that month, Hadley, Massachusetts, opened my area's first cyber-hair-salon.)

Cohen also states that even if a barbershop chooses not to market on the Net, the business can use the Net in other ways: as a customer of hair-care products and magazine subscriptions, a tenant, and so forth.

And Greg Hayward <mailto:greg@otn.com>, director of sales at otn.com, cited the opportunity cost a nonwired barber will pay if potential customers find someone else on the Web.

Rick Beneteau <mailto:rick@interniche.net>, former owner of a dry-cleaning business, demonstrated that the Web is applicable even to stores like his with a purely local clientele:

- Set up a Web site with such sections as the company history (including historical photos and memorabilia), the history of dry cleaning, environmentally conscious approaches, wedding-gown preservation, links to local and national business and trade organizations, Employee of the Month, an advice column with real customer questions—and online coupons.

- Fund the site and its promotion by cutting back on newspaper and direct-mail coupon advertising.
- Add the URL and the availability of coupons on-site to all new and existing promotional efforts, including captions on existing TV commercials, billboards in high-traffic areas, remaining newspaper and direct-mail promotion, letterhead and other collateral materials, etc.
- Make the URL easy to spot on all company vehicles as well as family and friends' cars.
- Put PCs on the counter of each store and let walk-in visitors surf the site.
- Collect visitor e-addresses by letting them subscribe to a useful free newsletter.
- Provide referral discounts.
- Use the site to provide convenience by offering a range of other products through affiliate programs.

Rick's full article is available at <http://www.frugalfun.com/dtb.html>.

Determining Visitors' Geographic Location

Some organizations have to focus locally; they aren't even allowed to solicit outside of their geographic territory. For example, William Greene <mailto:william.greene@grizzard.com> heads the Internet division of a direct-mail house specializing in non-profit fund appeal letters. If he's soliciting for a state chapter of a particular nonprofit, he will ruffle some major feathers in the next state over if he goes into that territory.

So how does he pinpoint his prospects in a medium where the whole world might pass through? He targets sites with a geographic constituency and uses forms that require a zip code. Once a prospect provides a zip code, the agency can coordinate responses with the appropriate local chapter.

An Australian writer identified only as <mailto:plake@zip.com.au> commented (Internet Advertising Discussion List, October 2, 1998) on various ways to identify visitors geographically, which I've summarized in the table below.

To summarize: Cyberspace is far and away the hottest marketing development of the 1990s—one that can help almost any business, if done right.

Feel free to contact me at <mailto:shel@frugalfun.com>. I'd love to hear about your cybermarketing adventures. And please visit my Web site <http://www.frugalfun.com> to read many other articles about various aspects of eCommerce and cyber-marketing (as well as off-line marketing)—not to mention lots of content about low-cost fun.

Method	Advantages	Drawbacks
Match host (IP) addresses against a "whois" database.	Transparent to the visitor. Useful for identifying country domains.	Highly inaccurate; assumes the host is in the same location as the visitor.
Map the physical Internet access point against a custom database.	Transparent. More accurate than the previous method.	Assumes the visitor is making a local call to get access. Won't identify visits originating from private networks or proxy servers.
Ask for a zip or postal code and add it to the user's browser cookie; reward accuracy by providing incentives (i.e., local weather).	Accurate if visitors answer accurately. Easy to implement and with a high potential ROI (return on investment), as the site can then solicit ads from local businesses.	Somewhat intrusive. Incentives have to be great enough to generate accurate answers.
Build a locally oriented site.	Targeting will reach both residents and visitors.	If you want to separate the residents from the tourists, you'll have to combine this with another method.

30

World-Class Customer Service

Your clients will remember outstandingly good or outstandingly bad customer service and product quality. Attention to customers' needs must come from the heart. Nobody likes a phony! If every time you process a refund, the customer can feel you mourning the lost dollars, no amount of smiling and attentive listening is going to sit well. If you can't be nice to people and put up with their demands, hire the sweetest manager you can, and step out of the way. But watch this person as he or she smoothes ruffled feathers; you might learn that genuine caring about your clients and their needs feels good to you, and not just to the person on the other end.

In his book *Cash Copy,* Jeffrey Lant suggests you "romance every prospect . . . make that single individual feel that . . . nothing else matters so much to you as that he succeeds in getting what he wants, thanks to your kindly and knowledgeable ministrations." Keep that attitude once prospects become customers!

Clients *deserve* to be treated well. They've paid for something to solve problems or improve their lives; they have the right to expect results. And often, all they need to realize that improvement is a gentle, clear explanation.

Your philosophy should echo trade association director Frank Fox's: "We're here to do everything we possibly can to help members survive, grow, and succeed. We work for the members." In return for dues, "a member has hired a five-person staff who works on their behalf, trying to find new profit centers, solve problems, come up with ideas and information that will help [them] run [their] business better."

Customer satisfaction can be thought of as an equation: High quality + excellent service = repeat and referral business.

You need both ingredients. You can have the best product in the world, but your clients will buy from someone else if you treat them like dirt. And the best customer service in the world is not going to make up for shoddy goods. Even if you replace defective products immediately and for free, clients will try a different brand the next time if they have to replace the same item two or three times in a year.

Here are a few pointers on great customer service:

- Don't keep the client waiting. If you can't provide immediate attention, interrupt what you're doing to greet the customer, explain how long the wait will be, and invite him or her to wait in a well-lit, comfortable area with plenty to read and perhaps light refreshments. Rather than keep someone on hold for ten minutes, take the caller's number and return the call as soon as possible.

- Listen to the client. Assess the customer's needs and really think about what the best solution would be. Sometimes it might be a gracious referral to one of your competitors. Don't push a product that only does half the job, just for the sake of a one-time sale.
- Know your product inside and out. Train your sales and customer service staff to understand what they're selling.
- Provide technical support if it's required—in plain language, without patronizing or trivializing the client's lack of knowledge.
- Go the extra mile. If you sell complex equipment, throw in some training and hand-holding—not grudgingly, but with a smile. I will often spend five or ten minutes giving free advice on the phone. It pays itself back many times over in goodwill, referrals, and repeat business. Similarly, if an acquaintance wants a quick critique of a résumé or brochure he or she has done up, I'll look at it quickly and suggest overall improvements. Nine times out of ten, the friend will schedule an appointment to have it done right.

Throw in Something Extra

Increase the value of your product or service with extra touches that don't cost you much, but make customers feel like they are getting more than their money's worth. In the résumé portion of our business, we provide multiple copies on a choice of elegant papers. This is a profit center for us, but our clients love it because it offers them one-stop convenience and high quality. We also have free sample formats for cover letters, thank-you notes, and resignation letters.

Value-enhancers differentiate your product from the competition. A word-processing program might include a utility program to type commonly used paragraphs with one keystroke. A night's stay at a bed-and-breakfast can include gourmet chocolates on the pillow, brochures on area attractions, and a memorable breakfast. A toy store might provide a free yo-yo with every ten-dollar purchase.

Increase the value of your product or service with extra touches that don't cost you much, but make customers feel like they are getting more than their money's worth.

But avoid something that seems odd or worthless. Our local Cadillac dealer once did a very strange promotion: a free Yugo with every Cadillac. Cadillac buyers want a quality, luxurious car. Would they want a stripped-down economy car with a poor reputation for quality? Furthermore, if the dealer can afford to give away a five-thousand-dollar premium—even if people think it's junk—wouldn't it encourage the buyer to negotiate a much lower sale price?

Keep in Contact

Check in with your clients by phone one month and six months after a major purchase. This is the essence of a long-term relationship; it gives you the opportunity to make sure the product is meeting their needs and fine-tune any difficulties. Again, make the client feel you really value your relationship, not just as a customer, but as a person. It should be easy to create this perception, because it will be true. Honest, ethical caring for other human beings is one of the strongest tools we have for creating the world we want to live in.

Guarantees and Warrantees

If you don't believe in your own product, why should anyone else? Therefore, show your faith in the product by providing some sort of guarantee of customer satisfaction.

At Bread & Circus, if a customer returns spoiled merchandise, the store both refunds the full price and gives the customer a free replacement—and if the customer just didn't like an item, the store will still refund the purchase price. The store's reputation for quality, selection, and service is far more effective in attracting new business than its extensive traditional print and radio advertising, according to manager Dave Lannon.

At the Iron Horse Music Hall, talent booker Jordi Herold offers to refund the ticket price to anyone in the audience who isn't satisfied after twenty minutes of the headline act. It provides excellent customer relations at very little risk: He refunded only two admissions in the first year of the policy.

— Troubleshoot —

When a customer has a problem, fix it courteously, promptly, and fully. Give it your best; if you don't come through, all the customer's friends will hear about it—and that might include thousands of people on the Internet.

This checklist of customer service do's and don'ts is modified from former Apple Computer executive Guy Kawasaki's *The Macintosh Way:*

Do

- Put the customer in control
- Take responsibility for the problem
- Track down and solve the problem, even if it occurred because of the way your product interacted with someone else's
- Promise less than you can do, but do more than you promise
- Hire empathic, knowledgeable customer service employees
- Treat support as an important, integral part of your operation

DON'T

- Blame the victim
- Hide behind bureaucratic inflexibility
- Hire uninformed tech support (even if they're polite)

— Two Tales of One City —

Here are two true stories of horrendous and delightful customer service that happened on the same night. I was in New York for the weekend. Saturday night I went to an ethnic restaurant in the East Village for dinner. The food was both interesting and excellent, but I'll never go back. It was a hot night and the restaurant had no air-conditioning; I drank my water down to the bottom before we even got our menus. There was only one waiter, who could neither speak nor understand English. My companion ordered a dinner-special package that came with wine and salad. I ordered a soup and two appetizers. No bread was served. There were no flowers, candles, or even condiments on the table. After a while, the soup and main dish appeared. The appetizers, wine, and salad did not appear, nor did more water (although the food was spicy).

While we were waiting for the rest of our food, the party in the window booth left the restaurant. Half an hour later, their plates had not been cleared. The waiter was sitting down. A group came in; they waited about twenty minutes for menus and finally walked out.

A man came in with a discount coupon that the restaurant refused to accept. He finally stormed out. The establishment had now lost business from two parties within a half an hour, one of them a group of four. At no time during our nearly two hours in the restaurant were more than four tables occupied.

Eventually, we reminded the waiter that the dinner special came with salad and wine. He looked confused. Then he came back with a plate of iceberg lettuce, supermarket tomatoes, and a couple of sprigs of coriander and watercress, no dressing—and two glasses of wine. We sent one back.

Some forty minutes after we'd gotten there, we asked how much longer it would be before the appetizers came, and also asked for more water. The waiter seemed incredulous that we'd never gotten them. Ten minutes later, he came around with the water pitcher, and shortly after that, he brought us one of our appetizers. The other one never came. Then he argued with us when we told him to take it off the bill.

After dinner, we walked to the Thirteenth Street Repertory Theater, where we had reservations for a 9:30 P.M. show. The attitude there sharply contrasted with our disaster at the restaurant. We noticed a sign that offered half-price tickets to the late show if you also went to the early show. (Both shows were the same price.) We asked the box office clerk if we could buy our full-price tickets for the late show and get half-price tickets for the earlier play the following night.

He sent us to talk with Edith O'Hara, the *grande dame* of the theater company, who was socializing with patrons in the lobby. We made our proposal, and she said, "Usually that's if you come the same day." We said, "But isn't the other show already over for tonight? We didn't know about this until we got here." She agreed—and so as not to confuse the ticket clerk, she went into the box office and processed the transaction herself.

Shortly before curtain time, Edith announced that one of the actors in this play was sick. His understudy hadn't arrived, but there was another actor available who knew the play and could fill the role. However, he might have to refer to the script book, since he wasn't used to playing this part. Did we want the show to go on? And if we did—here she was interrupted by choruses of "yes, let's do it"—she'd give each of us a free ticket good for any show, any night. Edith had turned a potentially destructive event into a customer service bonanza. Every person at that performance will remember that free ticket and spread goodwill all around.

Edith didn't have to do this, especially since the audience had already decided that the play should go on. She also didn't have to be flexible about our proposal for a discount. But she chose to do right by her customers.

— How to Resolve Complaints —

First and foremost, complainers want to feel listened to. They want to know that you've heard their concerns, that you're moved to help them. The best marketing you can do here is not to push any product or service, but work with the customer to make him or her feel happy.

A dissatisfied customer whose grievance is properly resolved may become one of your firm's strongest boosters. Also, each complaint you receive probably represents many others who are stewing in their dissatisfaction but never call—so your complainers are actually doing you a favor: They've given you a chance to make it right!

The best marketing you can do here is not to push any product or service, but work with the customer to make him or her feel happy.

Thank the customer for bringing the problem to you and giving you that chance. Listen a lot, ask some probing questions to make sure the problem being presented is, in fact, the real problem. Consider a small gift certificate toward a future purchase, in appreciation that the customer took the time to alert you (and, of course, in order to use it, the customer has to come back and buy from you again).

You might even put signs up at your place of business (or notices in your catalog and on your Web site), encouraging customers to bring their grievances to you. If you're not naturally a sympathetic listener, invest in a course in customer service listening skills. When people feel their concerns are heard, they feel valued and respected—they may not even need the actual problem solved. You want to make them feel that you and they are working together as a team, looking for the best way to resolve the problem—and this should be sincere.

"Don't sweat the small stuff." Your profit on a twenty dollar or even fifty-dollar item is made up many times over in the lifetime value of a happy customer—or eaten away like cancer many times over as that unhappy customer tells friends not to deal with you!

If the problem is a defective product, replace or repair it for free (including any shipping charges, etc.). Do this even if the warranty is over. If it's an expensive item, get on the phone with the manufacturer's vice president for customer service, and go to bat for the customer (yes, while he or she is sitting in your office!). If the product is low quality, issue an immediate refund and an incentive for coming back. And if the product is the wrong solution for the customer's problem, issue the refund and suggest appropriate alternatives.

This is key: Don't take the customer's anger personally, and *don't* respond with your own anger. Let it out later by smashing your fist into a pillow and screaming, when no customers are listening. No matter how rude and obnoxious the complaint, you want to defuse, not escalate.

Also, empower and educate your employees. If customers find defects before purchase, let the cashiers knock off 10 percent without having to talk to a manager. If customers bring in returns or call in with a problem, even the lowest clerks ought to be able to process the transaction without needing a supervisor—and those clerks should also be trained in effective listening and positive attitude. Few things are more frustrating to an unhappy consumer than the need to go through several levels of bureaucracy to get someone who can help.

31

Friendly and Welcome Telemarketing

Few things annoy me as much as listening to a bad sales pitch, whether it's over the phone or in person. Unfortunately, bad examples seem to outnumber good ones by a factor of about ten to one. Incompetent telemarketers are bad enough, but a worse nuisance than bad telemarketing is an inappropriate face-to-face sales call—which is going to waste a full half hour of my time while I try to extricate myself from bad sales techniques. When a phone caller is insensitive, at least I can hang up.

Don't think I'm alone, either. Do a little informal market research; you'll have a hard time finding anyone who bought anything because they liked being offended, insulted, and unlistened to by a sales representative. In fact, in November 1991, the U.S. Congress outlawed as a nuisance the ultimate bad listener—automatic-dialing telemarketing robots. Congress seriously considered banning person-to-person telemarketing as well, precisely because of the alienation millions of Americans feel at the receiving end of an uninvited, canned sales pitch.

If you do a bad job with media relations or space advertising, the worst that will happen is you'll be ignored. You waste only the money you spent on your campaign. But in telemarketing and face-to-face selling, if you do a bad job, you run the risk of permanently alienating your prospect from your company. You will be perceived as a low-quality boiler-room operation, a product pusher rather than a problem solver. Those few people who do buy from you will do so in spite of your marketing and not because of it. Yet, when used properly, these can be among your best tools. We'll look at the telephone first, then go face-to-face in chapter 32.

— What's Wrong with This Picture? —

Me: "Good morning, may I help you?"

Telemarketer: "Hi, my name is Bob Smith. How are you today?"

Me: "Busy. What can I do for you?"

Telemarketer: "Well, I would like to take a few moments of your time to tell you about our new special on industrial floor cleaner. If you buy our Lemon Pure today, we can save you two dollars on every case, if you order any number of full cases. Are you already using Lemon Pure in your factory?"

Me: "No."

Telemarketer: "Let me tell you why you should use Lemon Pure. It will—"

Me (interrupting): "Look, I'm with a client now and I said I was busy. I don't need to listen to this." (hang up)

Okay, what problems did you see?

First of all, this oaf didn't even bother to find out if he was talking to the right person. I don't have a factory; I manage a two-person office and a four-person household. I have no need for a whole case of floor cleaner. He didn't qualify prospects in advance. And even if he did reach a factory, he didn't ask to speak to the person who buys janitorial supplies.

Second, he wasted my time with small talk. He'd have been a lot closer to a sale if he'd asked, "Is this a good time for you?" instead of, "How are you today?"

Third, he didn't give me a chance to state my needs. He wasn't looking to solve my problem, only to force a case of cleaning fluid down my throat.

Fourth, the person being called was not familiar with the company or the product. In-person marketing works best when the prospect already has an idea of what the product can do.

Fifth, his offer wasn't significant enough. Why should anyone change from a known to an unknown supplier to save two dollars? He would have been much smarter to offer a free sample bottle and then follow up two weeks later with a sales pitch and a discount trial offer.

Sixth, he wasn't flexible enough to deviate from a prepared script. Scripts are death in a marketing situation, because real people rarely fit the script; you have to address your prospect's needs as they come up.

Let's role-play out how he might be successful:

"Hello, this is Richard Jensen calling from Lemon Pure. May I speak with Jane Levin in Purchasing, please?"

"Just a moment."

"Hello, this is Jane Levin."

"Ms. Levin, my name is Richard Jensen and I'm with Lemon Pure. I understand you're the person who buys janitorial supplies. Is that correct?"

"Yes."

"Is this a good time to talk?"

"Well, I have a lot to do, but I can spare a few minutes. Thanks for checking."

"I'll be quick, then. Two weeks ago, I sent you a sample bottle of our new-formula Lemon Pure floor cleaner. Did your people have a chance to try it?"

"Yes."

"Did the janitors tell you what they thought of it?"

"Yes. They were impressed with the built-in wax, although there was some concern that the degreaser wasn't strong enough."

"We have a separate product to cut grease that's designed to work with Lemon Pure. That way people only have to pay for the expense of grease removal where they really need it. I'll make sure you get a sample, Ms. Levin—and thanks so much for letting us know about the degreasing problem."

"Thanks. What was your name again?"

"Richard Jensen. And I'd like you to know that your feedback is always important to us. We'd really like to see you be a satisfied customer, and we have an introductory special on cases of Lemon Pure. Plus, if I can get you to try us today, I'll throw in a four-pack of the grease remover. We also have a thirty-day, no-questions-asked, money-back guarantee on all our products. How many cases would you like to order today?"

Unlike Smith, Jensen is a confident problem solver, willing to answer objections as the prospect presents them, polite, cooperative, and ready to close the sale without being pushy. This person will make lots of commissions long after Smith has given up and started collecting unemployment checks.

— How to Do It Right —

Good telephone and in-person marketing depend mostly on common sense:

- Do your homework so you're talking to the right people.
- Be polite.
- *Listen* to your prospect.
- Present yourself as a solver, not a seller.
- Maintain assertive friendliness.
- Make the prospect feel valued.
- Answer objections.
- Ask for the sale.
- Accept rejection graciously, with room for later follow-up.
- Combine telemarketing with other strategies, particularly direct-mail or face-to-face sales.

Do Your Homework

Make sure you're talking to someone who:

- Is legitimately interested in your offer
- Has the authority to make the purchase

If you waste someone's time with a long spiel about a product they don't want or can't buy, you lose the sale and waste your own time. Furthermore, you make it much harder to sell to that prospect again. He or she may one day need your product, or you may have something else of interest, but someone else will get the sale. The insulted buyer will remember your firm as boorish and insensitive.

Be Polite

Look for cues about (or just ask) what the prospect wants to be called. And if that's a whole name, don't turn it into a nickname. If it's a title and a last name, don't use a first name. If it's a shortened name, don't use the longer version.

And don't badger the customer by repeating his or her name a million times. Yes, I've seen the sales training materials that claim the sweetest sound is a prospect's own name. But I don't think I'm alone in being creeped out when someone shoves my name into every sentence. Two or three times in a conversation is usually ample.

People's names are one of the most important pieces of their identity, and if you want the prospect

to become a customer, follow the customer's cues:
You: "Hello, may I speak with Shel Horowitz?"
Me: "This is Shel."
Or "This is Mr. Horowitz."
Or "Speaking."

If your prospect doesn't cue you, use the most formal address (in our example, "Mr. Horowitz").

This is also an opportunity to correct misinformation. Because I have an unusual and androgynous name, I often get calls for "Sheila Horowitz," or "Saul Horowitz," or any of fifty other variations. If I correct my name and the salesperson ignores the correction, that's it—the sale is lost.

Once you get the right person, *find out if this is a good time.* If it's not, set up an appointment to call back—and follow through when you said you would. Never get hostile on the phone, even if the prospect is rude or curt.

Listen to Your Prospect

Listening actively is not just letting prospects talk and then responding from your script. It's also not speaking to your prospects in "psychobabble" such as "I appreciate your sharing that," before returning to a canned sales pitch. Let them get give you some details on what problems they want to solve. Listen hard and ask clarifying questions; don't try to make the sale yet! Only after you've identified the problems should you start a sales pitch.

Because he was following up on an earlier encounter, our hypothetical Richard Jensen didn't wait for this step. But he did make sure to gain the prospect's trust before starting his pitch. Active listening—carefully identifying the problem the customer presents, and then checking in with the client that you have indeed identified the problem—is the most effective prelude to a sale. Discuss solutions only after the prospect has confirmed your analysis.

With these techniques, you and the prospect become allies; you solve the presenting problem while increasing your own sales performance. Even better, you and your customer-focused approach will be set apart from the jerks and goons who arm-twist prospects into reluctant purchases. In short, everybody wins.

Present Yourself as a Solver, Not a Seller

Let's bring in Richard Jensen again for a different industry.

"Hello, this is Richard Jensen from Datasecure Insurance. Who am I speaking with? [Note that Richard's choice of phraseology is deliberately ungrammatical. Textbook English here would be "With whom am I speaking?" But that isn't how most people speak in everyday life, and Richard would be immediately pegged as a pretentious twit.]

"Jason Gross."

"Good morning, Mr. Gross. Are you the person in charge of the computer network, and do you have a few minutes?"

"Yes, and yes. Call me Jason."

"Thanks, Jason. Have you ever experienced a catastrophic hard-drive crash and then discovered your backup copy was corrupted?"

"Yes, that has happened."

"That must have been a real nuisance for you. It's certainly a pain to have to re-create lost data, and it makes a mess of the most careful budget. Tell me, does your computer insurance protect against data loss?"

"No."

"Can you put a dollar value on lost data, in terms of the money you have to spend to rekey or re-create it?"

"I haven't done that yet, but I could come up with a number."

"Jason, would you be interested in an insurance policy that not only covers your hardware against fire, theft, vandalism, and any other damage except mechanical failure, but also pays you back the cost of entering the data again, under any circumstances? Do you think that might solve your problem?"

"Yeah, that would be great. But what does it cost?"

"That depends on how much coverage you buy. To take an example, a $20,000 policy is only $185 per year. Would you like to schedule a time when I could explain the plan in person?"

"Sure."

At least to start with, your prospect has no interest in your career—or, for that matter, in your offer. He or she is interested in the *benefits* of your offer: how to work more productively, increase earnings, save money, achieve status, or whatever. It's up to you, after listening to the client, to match what you're selling with what the client wants to achieve.

Incidentally, if you realize you don't offer the right solution, recommend someone who *can*. Follow up with a note or call to check in on how that worked. This quietly reminds your prospect that you're there to help. You'll be remembered positively.

Maintain Assertive Friendliness

Assertive friendliness means showing the customer that you care about him or her. It involves both a willingness to keep cheerful—but not saccharine—even on a difficult sales call. It also entails the ability to steer the conversation back toward your goals (closing the sale). Assertive friendliness means *you* control the call—while at the same time being sure to let the client define and "own" the problem, and raise all his or her objections so that you may successfully answer them.

Assertive friendliness is *not* the typical aggressive sales demeanor. You're not trying to win a one-shot sale through high-pressure techniques; rather, you want to build a long-term relationship of trust, perceived value, and continuing sales. But assertive friendliness is also not the saccharine insincerity stereotyped in airline flight attendants. You want to be honest, not smarmy. If you're cloyingly sweet, the prospect will leave disgusted.

Make the Prospect Feel Valued

You want the sale. Letting the customer feel special is an excellent way to get it. Just as Richard Jensen threw in four bottles of the degreaser, you want to strengthen the client's feeling that his or her business really matters to you.

Answer Objections

Every objection the prospect raises is an opportunity for you—as is every complaint the client has with an existing supplier. Give each prospect ample time to state objections, then restate them and answer them. Any unanswered objection is a legitimate reason not to buy.

Going back to our Lemon Pure example, the prospect raised an objection about grease. Richard could have said, "I guess you're right. It doesn't cut grease well." Jane would have been right, then, not to buy. Instead, Richard pointed out that he had another product that was specially designed to solve her problem. He made her feel special by offering a sample, and then actually giving away a good-sized amount; her next order from him will probably include both the floor cleaner and the degreaser.

Ask for the Sale

You've established the prospect's need for a solution you offer—and you've answered all the objections he or she can present. Now it's time for the next step: closing. In a telephone call, this either means asking the prospect to buy ("How many cases would you like?") or making an appointment for an in-person sales call ("Would you like to schedule a time when I could explain the plan in person?"). When moving into the close, use language that assumes you have the sale, for example, "Will you be paying by check or credit card?" or "Is Wednesday convenient for me to do the installation?" This makes it harder for the client to say "I don't want to buy it."

Avoid questions such as, "Are you ready to buy?" This only presents the prospect with an opportunity to back out of the deal, just when you ought to be firming up the final details; it shows that you yourself are not sure. When you try to close before the prospect is ready, you'll hear about it immediately—and then you need to go back a step, seek out and answer the remaining objections. But if you try to close halfheartedly, the deal may just fall apart.

If your attempt to close fails, go back and look for more objections to answer. Something on the order of, "I can see you still want some time to think this over, and I understand. Is there anything you haven't told me that makes you uneasy?" If, after that round, the client still isn't sure, set up another

time to check back. Particularly on major purchases, clients want to make sure they and their bosses believe they're doing the right thing.

Accept Rejection Graciously

If, in spite of your best efforts, you still don't get the sale, exit gracefully. If the prospect even hears a hint of "Boy, that jerk wasted my time," all the hard work you've put in building to this point is lost. Instead, try "I'm sorry I have nothing that meets your needs right now. But needs change. Please feel free to call me again if I can be of help. May I check back with you in three months anyway, just to see how you're doing solving [restate the expressed problem]?" Then, of course, check in when you said you would.

Combining Approaches

Cold-calling a new prospect is a tough way to make a sale. If you're approaching someone you haven't sold to before, send a prospectus ahead of time, outlining your product, service, or idea—and why it is right for this buyer. When you call, ask if the person received it and had time to look at it. If the answer to either question is no, don't even bother trying to sell yet. Set a time after the prospect has had a chance to look the material over.

Similarly, many large purchases are more easily sold in person. Consultant Bob Wieler, of the National Association for the Self-Employed, says, "Follow the telephone call up with mail, and then with a personal visit. You don't waste your time making cold sales calls [in person] when you can prequalify two hundred leads in a day. But if you get one qualified customer out of every two hundred leads, it saves a lot of knocking on doors."

Notice that our Mr. Jensen asked Jason Gross for an appointment rather than an immediate sale. But he took the time to (1) prequalify Jason as a prospect, (2) establish rapport, and (3) presell the client on the idea of the product—and on himself as the vendor.

You can alternate between phone and mail: Qualify the prospect with an initial phone call (without trying to sell), follow up with direct mail—tell the prospect to look for it, especially if it includes a sample—then check in a week later to make the sale. This combines the immediacy of in-person or phone selling with the breadth of material of a direct-mail package. The prospect can't forget to mail in an order, nor do you have to do all your convincing on the phone.

— Good Telemarketing Situations —

Now you've got an idea of basic techniques. Let's look at when telemarketing really makes sense.

Telemarketing is an ideal way to renew contact with past customers. It shows that you care about them enough to make some enticing offer to come back into the fold.

Making a customer service call or following up on a sale to make sure everything is all right lends itself naturally to proposing additional solutions to specific problems—and builds on your reputation as someone who puts the client's interests first.

Of course, if regular customers have bought particular kinds of items, and you have something new or a better price, that's a great time to pick up the phone.

When reaching new clients, your best bet is to follow up on people you've previously identified as serious prospects. At the very least, present potential customers with a "get-acquainted" offer not available to your regular customers: a premium, discount, or whatever. Put a time limit on the offer: no more than two weeks from the date of your call. If you handle it right, as Richard Jensen did with the janitorial products, you can make an offer that's only good that day—but be very careful to avoid the appearance of high pressure.

— Telemarketing for Charity —

At least when a business makes a call, there's a product involved. When you ask for money for a cause, you have a tougher job; there's no direct benefit to the person you're calling.

These calls are so pervasive—and generally so badly done—that my wife and I have established a policy of not giving money over the phone. We ask to be sent information in writing, and about twice a year we go through the fund appeal letters that caught our interest and write a bunch of checks.

It's amazing how poorly our refusal to pledge by phone sits with some telemarketers. We've been met with attempts to hard-sell us on the phone, pleas to save the organization the expense of mailing to us (usually from groups we've never heard of, interestingly enough), actual rudeness, and other techniques that do not endear these organizations to us. And yet, when my college calls to request a contribution to a specific scholarship fund, I'm likely to make a donation—because I know the program and its record of innovation in education, and I know what it meant to me to have scholarship funds, without which I could not have even entered the school.

So here's lesson one: Take your cues from the person you're calling. We all have our own preferred methods of communication. I do not have to do you a favor and accept your pitch in the way that's most convenient for you. If you want my money, you have to make your pitch the way I want to receive it. If you ignore that, or if you're rude to me, you've lost the chance to mark me in the donor column.

Lesson two: Just as businesses will have far greater success telemarketing their existing customers with a targeted offer (based on past purchases), so you will have the best luck with people who've already supported your organization. Give them a new reason to pony up again—for instance, a new program you're starting that expands the constituency you serve, or a crisis response to a bill before Congress.

Lesson three: Don't wear out your welcome! Any more than two phone pitches a year and you had better have a very good reason for calling.

Lesson four: Use the same principles of respect that a business should follow. Make sure you've reached the donor at a good time, or else find a better time—and call back when you're requested to. Be brief and to the point, without wasting the donor's time with idle chit-chat.

— Telephone Surveys —

This is another kind of nonselling that can be either beautifully or badly done over the phone. My biggest gripe with telephone surveyors is the tendency to flat-out lie about the length of time required. If the caller says it will take five minutes and we're not done after fifteen, I'm going to be pretty angry. Worse, some survey companies will disregard any responses if the survey isn't filled out completely. So not only do they waste your time, but your answers don't even count if you bail out! Again, I don't think I'm the only one who gets hostile over this kind of manipulation. Of course I want my opinion to count—but time is a very precious commodity to me. I often time survey calls, and if they go over the allotted time, I disconnect.

The other caution with surveys is questions that are worded in such a way that the bias of the surveying company is clear. No one likes his or her statements taken out of context or words put in his or her mouth. If you play fast and loose with the ethics of your survey, expect the people receiving your calls to play fast and loose with your reputation. (I hope some of our major political parties are listening!)

—Inbound Telemarketing —

People will call you—to complain, to get information . . . and to order. We've already covered complaints in chapter 30.

Informational Calls

When handled properly, informational calls are a potential goldmine. They're getting ready to buy—from *someone*—why not you? You want to do everything you can to move them to the sale, but not be so aggressive that you push them away. Answer the prospect's questions, but also highlight your particular strengths and expertise. Ask questions of your own—find out how the prospect will use your product.

Don't be afraid to add information—even if unasked for—that highlights your particular strengths—your USP. When I get a price-shopping call from a résumé prospect, I know that our prices are very competitive but not rock-bottom. But I also know that buying a résumé should not be done solely on price. So I actually say, "If you're shopping around, another question you ought to be asking is, 'What are your credentials to do this?' And here are ours: We've been writing résumés since 1981, our work has been published in five national résumé collections, we've had articles published in the Professional Association of Résumé Writers newsletter, and we were named Best Résumé Writers in the *Advocate* [local newspaper] reader poll."

W*hen handled properly, informational calls are a potential goldmine.*

Interestingly enough, about half the people who hear this little rap book an appointment on the spot. About three-fourths of the rest of them call back when they're done shopping around. So by adding this unasked-for information, I convert about 90 percent of my prospects. Before I added this, I was closing more like 60 percent.

And When They Call to Buy

Everyone's favorite kind of call. Don't blow it with a bad attitude! Get all the necessary information as quickly and professionally as possible, but don't be afraid to chat a bit if the caller initiates it. Also, most people will answer a simple marketing question or two from your end, such as "How did you learn about us?"

When people order my book after hearing me on the radio, I sometimes ask, "What part of the interview made you decide to buy?" This has given me great feedback on how to use these interviews as productively as possible.

Yet it's amazing how many businesses actually turn off prospects at the exact moment they want to buy. My wife and I went to an electronics store recently, wallets open and ready; the clerks were so uninformed and uninterested that they lost the sale. They just couldn't be bothered to pretend they cared about our needs. If your staff doesn't know the answer to a question, they should know where to find out—and make the inquiries as if they care.

— On-Hold Information Systems —

You lose people when you keep them on hold for a long time. And the longer they stay on hold, the more irritated they are when you finally speak with them. Radio is better than dead silence, but suppose the caller doesn't share your musical taste? Hears a commercial from your competitor? Reports your unauthorized use to the music publishers associations?

If long on-hold time is a necessary evil in your business, install a system that provides useful information during the wait—and no, this isn't voice mail, but something different. Be sensitive, though—don't fill your customer service line with messages about what a great company you run. After all, the caller already needs to work out a problem! Appropriate messages include information on new or underpublicized products and services, special deals for callers, new and creative ways to use your product, news items of interest in the industry, and so on. Banks and hotels have been using these systems with a high level of customer response; many others can benefit, too.

— The Telebridge —

A telebridge is an improvement on conference calling (a technology that's been around for years). Costs are lower and the system is friendlier. All participants call a "bridge" number and are automatically patched in to the conversation (no operator needed).

Being a guest in a teleconference is much like being a guest in an online chat—except that you respond with voice instead of by typing. Of course, the same marketing possibilities exist here as in any seminar or public event. Typically, telebridges can accommodate 30, 100, or 150 people.

I recently attended a free trial telebridge class with a public-speaking coach and lecture agent, Vickie Sullivan. I found the class useful enough to sign up for the series of two more paid classes: a classic example of marketing by showing the value of the product in a demonstration.

These classes were organized by business coach Sherry Lowry <mailto:NexusCoach@aol.com>. Sherry learned about this medium when she was organizing entrepreneurial ventures for transferring NASA war and space technology into the business world. When she became a business coach, with clients in six countries, she decided to permanently lease a telebridge. She found it "a simple way to bring people together from anywhere in the world. It was also a very good way to leverage time and to charge more affordable fees."

Now she participates in "telegroup conference calls" five to seven times a week—often as host, facilitator, or presenter.

Sherry summarized the marketing advantages of telebridges:

- Cost-effectiveness
- Elimination of travel time and expense
- Linkage for nationally based and international participants is easy to understand and organize
- Everyone is comfortable with and familiar with phone usage (though it takes usually at least part of one group call to get comfortable with the idea of a medium without the visual cues accessible)
- Increased capacity to learn auditorally
- A whole new means to organize distance learning that is also interactive
- People can learn faster and retain better than in live seminars if the training is well designed and conducted
- Very fast way to build trust

Annual costs start around nine hundred dollars; Lowry prepays to get a discount. They're also available per use, starting around twenty dollars an hour for a bridge for up to 30 people—and drop on down to lower rates depending upon the volume of hours needed and the length of the commitment in terms of months. According to Lowry, this is a significant savings over traditional teleconferences.

If you go through the major phone service companies like AT&T, MCI, or Sprint, you'll probably pay by the person and the rates will be at least $100 to up to $400 an hour. Also—you'll pay for everyone if you organize the call. The last one I used would charge between $160 to $220 for a 20-minute call for 5 people. They charge the highest going rates for the long-distance, from what I can determine.

The way the bridges I use work—everyone initiates their own call and pays for their own call. And the host does all the enrolling and registering and manages all the logistics of their own roster also.

Lowry sees value in telebridges for consultants, trainers, speakers, distance learning programs, coaches, and corporations with far-flung offices, among other uses.

32

Successful Sales Presentations

A personal introduction is 79 percent more likely to result in a sale than a cold call.

We all know an introduction is better, but just how much better may come as a shock. According to sales trainer Susan Bellows <mailto:bellows@ultranet.com>, the chances of closing a sale are only 1 percent on a cold call, 50 percent on a call with a referral, and 80 percent or better on a personal introduction. And the very best time to get referrals from your customers is right after they've agreed to buy from you.

This also means that a sales call that leaves a positive impression and generates referrals, even if the prospect didn't buy, may be more valuable than a call that actually results in a sale—but leaves the buyer reluctant or feeling pressured.

Of course, not only are existing clients the best source of new clients, but they are also your best prospects in and of themselves; it's seven times easier to sell to someone who's already bought from you than to a new customer.

Treat any encounter with a client as a potential sales call—and apply all the principles of high-quality telemarketing. In person, you'll also have

additional tools at your disposal: your body language, and a "pitchbook," or portfolio.

Your body gives the prospect direct insight into your mood. Your body language and tone of voice should reinforce your message. When you want to emphasize something, speak slowly and look intently at your client. If you're showing excitement, lean in, speak a bit faster and louder. Whatever your message, reinforce it with your whole body.

Naturally, avoid body language that implies boredom or inattentiveness. And take your cues from the prospect in matters of decorum. If you haven't been invited to sit down, ask if you may. Never smoke, eat, drink, or chew gum without permission.

With smoking in particular, refrain from cigarettes for at least thirty minutes before you meet the prospect. Many people who are irritated by tobacco are automatically subliminally prejudiced against anyone who reeks of cigarettes; it becomes one more unnecessary barrier you have to overcome—and yes, people *will* notice an odor of recent cigarette on your breath and on your clothes.

According to Bellows, a former bank marketing VP and a trainer in David Sandler's sales methods, good sales technique is just force of habit. Her firm, Susan Bellows & Associates, trains managers and sales staff in a whole raft of effective communication techniques.

Changing a habit, she says, takes twenty-five to forty-five days of concerted effort. There's a tripod of attributes behind every habit: behavior, attitude, and technique. So every day, initiate one new behavior that will result in more sales and a better attitude. Consciously reinforce these new behaviors until they become the habits of success.

Bellows uses a series of techniques called neuro-linguistic programming (NLP) to replace failure-prone habits with success-prone ones. A lot of this involves paying close attention to your prospects. Listen twice as much as you talk, pick speech and breathing and body language rhythms that are in harmony with your prospect's; try to meet the prospect on his or her own emotional ground.

She separates prospects into four categories: Controllers, Analyzers, Promoters, and Supporters. So when selling to a Controller—fast-paced, no-nonsense, achievement-driven—successful salespeople will use a "give 'em the facts, no small talk" approach. But when selling to a Supporter, emphasize acceptance, patience, communication, sincerity—feelings—much more than facts.

Many salespeople fit the Promoter profile. They're aggressive, driven by ideas, constantly seeking stimulation. And CFOs are the Analyzers, focused on the process and valuing accuracy far above speed.

In fact, these categories are helpful in other situations. Recognizing these four personality patterns will help in communication with family members and employees, as well as customers.

When dealing directly with a client, face-to-face, salespeople who understand these principles are at a decided advantage. Bellows says words are only 7 percent of what's being communicated. Tonality (tone of voice) accounts for 38 percent of the message received, and physicality (body language, appearance, breathing, eye movements) makes up a whopping 55 percent of the input to the prospect.

Over the phone, you lose that 55 percent. The importance of the words goes up to 17 percent, but impressions are overwhelmingly based on voice: 83 percent of the total message is communicated by the tonality, not the words.

Of course, in postal or electronic mail, the words (and graphics or layout, if applicable) must carry the whole burden; this may be part of why spam is so ineffective.

While establishing genuine rapport is far more important than what words you say, carefully chosen words can oil the wheels of perception. Words such as "naturally," "obviously," and "typically" can provide a smooth, flowing method of moving the conversation toward a sale.

One of the most interesting parts of Bellows's Sandler approach is that the goal isn't always to get a yes. The goal is to establish whether there's a good fit, and if there isn't, to move on quickly to a more likely prospect—while leaving room to come back if needs change and the fit improves. You want to find prospects who:

- Have a problem you can solve
- Can afford and commit to the solution
- Have decision-making power
- Answer their own objections, point by point

Finally, Bellows reminds us that a sales call is *not* the place to get your own needs met. If you need recognition or material rewards, for instance, don't look to your client for it. Your focus should be on identifying and meeting the client's needs. Once you get the commission check, *then* go out and meet your own needs.

Another relevant NLP technique, documented in Barry Siskind's book, *The Successful Exhibitor's Handbook* (Self-Counsel Press), is to look for clues about the prospect's primary learning style (which is different from the personality type). Some people learn best visually, some by listening (auditory), and some by feeling (kinesthetic). If you use phrases that resonate with your prospect's strongest learning style, it eliminates another barrier. So you might ask a Visual, "Do you see what I mean?"; say, "How does that sound to you?" to an Auditory; and use, "What does that feel like?" for a Kinesthetic.

A pitchbook, or brag book, is a sales presentation in a notebook. It may be simple or elaborate: photos of successful users, testimonial letters, samples of your work (particularly for writers, designers, and craftspeople), highlights of product benefits.

Pitchbooks are all too often misused. Many salespeople use their book (or an audiovisual presentation, which is even more rigid) as a crutch, to help remember a canned speech.

So how should you use a pitchbook? Just like the whole sales encounter, let your use of the book be customer-driven. If you're discussing a point—warranty or delivery terms, for instance—and a page is relevant, quickly turn to that page to reinforce your message. If you're selling any kind of contract work, offer to show samples and/or testimonials from satisfied clients.

— Audiovisual Presentations —

Many salespeople want only to get their clients in front of a projection screen or video monitor—but that's often a recipe for disaster in a sales call. Videos, slide shows, and overheads certainly have their place—and that place is not in sales, but in imparting information. If you're hired to give a lecture, fine, use your AV presentation. If you're trying to identify a problem you can solve, your listening skills are going to get you the sale far more easily than your ability to ram a presentation down your prospect's throat—even if it's a world-class presentation.

Of course, if you identify a highly technical problem, or one that's best explained through visual media, you might invite your prospect to look at a video *outside* the sales meeting, as a gesture of helpfulness. The prospect can then have a look at his or her own convenience, and without feeling any pressure because you're in the room. A cheaper way to

accomplish the same thing and not spend money duplicating videotapes (you didn't really expect to get that tape back again, now, did you?) is to put the presentation up on a Web site. Do up a card or flier offering all your free, helpful information-sharing presentations and listing the URLs.

Look at your presentation as you would any piece of marketing. It should:

- Hold your prospect's interest—maybe even be entertaining
- Offer professional production quality (no one will watch a video that looks like a 1950s used-car commercial!)
- Focus on benefits, problem solving, information sharing, and other good copywriting hooks
- Concentrate on the aspects of your product that are hard to explain through other media
- Be scrupulously honest
- Be much more than just a drumbeat for your company and/or product—it should contain value in and of itself (kind of like the tipsheets we discussed earlier)
- Respect your viewer's time (keep it as short as you can and still get your point across)

— Managing a Sales Force —

Every employee is part of your sales force. The impression your workers make when they deal with clients on the phone, fulfill orders, or even sweep the floor at night will contribute to your clients' perception of your business, and their willingness to do business with you. Therefore, good management becomes one more marketing tool. If your workers feel exploited, unlistened to, or unrespected, their feelings will show up in slipshod work, poor interactions with customers, morale problems, and high turnover.

But happy, motivated employees who feel their bosses will go to bat for them, who know their suggestions are taken seriously, and who enjoy the personal freedom to go beyond their formal job description will not only make your business function better, but will impress your customers.

So treat your workers as well as you treat your clients. And regularly evaluate employee performance, including any interactions with customers. Monitor not only performance but attitude, and take the time to provide effective motivational training.

Dave Lannon of Bread & Circus provides a good example. "Our associates are not immediately thrown into working here without a lot of training, a lot of information from us about how to talk to customers. They go to orientation, product training, and when they're first brought into the store to work, they're buddied up with a really strong associate."

Lannon points out that training salespeople is an ongoing process, including attention to the everyday details of patron/worker interaction. "There are a lot of little things: Never point—always take the customer to the product. If you don't know the answer, always stay and listen when another associate answers."

Also, model appropriate behavior to your workers. Instead of shouting at employees, or staring them down silently when there's a problem, talk quietly and calmly—and in private!—about what is going on, how you feel things should be improved, and what steps need to be taken. Use nonthreatening "I-messages" rather than accusational "You-messages." For instance, instead of "You idiot, how could you be so stupid?" try "When you treated that customer so curtly, I worried that she wouldn't want to come back." Listen to the employee's side, too. Do what you can to make the employee feel just as valued as the customer. And actively solicit advice from workers about how you could improve your management, your product, your cost control, or your level of service.

As Dave Lannon walks around the store, he inspects every detail. But as he suggests improvements, there's no hint of a judgmental tone. Rather, it's "When you get a chance, please clean under that scale," or "Can you put a bit more ice over here, please?" In short, courtesy to both customers and workers, is good business.

Understand Your Clients' Personalities

Sales reps should be properly trained in client-focused tactics. They should not only continually stress product benefits, but also target their message differently depending on who is listening. Roger Dawson, a nationally recognized expert on sales and negotiation, identifies four different kinds of people, each of whom require different sales methods:

- Pragmatic: Quick to make decisions, assertive, organized, good time- and thing-manager, short attention span. To a Pragmatic, information content is the most important part of presentation.
- Extrovert: Another quick decision maker, but highly emotional, not detail-oriented, and with poor follow-up. Likes the excitement of a crowd—enjoys spectator sports and "motivational" speakers.
- Amiable: A slow decision maker, who wants to like and be liked. Usually fairly shy, and not very assertive. Most of all, an Amiable needs to feel safe—and won't buy from you unless he or she trusts you.
- Analytical: Wants *all* the facts. Extremely detail-oriented. Unlike the Pragmatic or Extrovert, an Analytical has a vast attention span, and wants huge amounts of information before deciding.

Among the four categories, only Extroverts respond well to traditional sales techniques such as full-blown presentations stressing the "feel-good" attributes, rather than concrete benefits. A Pragmatic or an Analytical will be deeply insulted by an Extrovert-oriented sales rep who refuses to answer questions until he or she is finished boring the prospect with a canned sales pitch. A Pragmatic will want to know "What's in it for me?" while an Analytical will ask "How does it work?" or "How do you know?"

An Amiable won't make the decision until he or she feels secure. He or she will have questions about customer support and continuity of the sales relationship—but may not verbalize these concerns without prompting.

This may sound familiar; it's another way of slicing the same information that Susan Bellows discussed earlier in this chapter. There are probably hundreds of ways to set up a personality matrix, all of which shed some light on your relationships with customers and employees. Even very similar systems of organizing people will show major differences. Also, many people will not fall clearly into one category. Someone may seem to be of one personality type but present strong elements of other types, or people may shift modes according to the situation.

In a wonderful book called *CareerMap*, Neil Yeager creates these categories: Interactive (oriented toward feelings rather than results), Creative (idea person, not that great on follow-through), Methodical (long-term planner, much less concerned about the interpersonal side), and Practical (task-focused, not a people person). Yeager's categories are roughly analogous to Dawson's Amiable, Extrovert, Analytical, and Practical, respectively. However, there are also major differences. An Extrovert may not be a Creative, for example.

Use appropriate psychographic categories for each situation. You would sell very differently to an anti-authoritarian former hippie exploring the limits of personal freedom than to a socially conservative fundamentalist. There are Pack Rats and Minimalists, Hedonists and Survivalists, Innovators and Traditionalists, Explorers and Homebodies, Do-It-Yourselfers and Have-It-Dones, Experts and Amateurs, Humorous and Serious . . . Don't forget the traditional demographic categories: ethnicity, race, religion, income/class status (past, present, and aspiring toward), language, education, number of children, and so on. Determine which categories are important in selling your product, and do the same kind of analysis to determine effective selling anywhere on any of these scales.

What all of these groupings have in common is this: (1) people can shift themselves anywhere along any continuum at any time, and (2) people's self-perception of their placement may be different from others' perceptions of them.

No matter how you categorize them, people are individuals and want to be treated as such. Psychographic scales and charts are only tools to open communication, find common ground, and treat each prospect as special, important, and valued; you're not rigidly grading eggs or lumber. With a true client-centered approach, prospects will sell themselves on working with you. Back up client-centered sales with great service, great products, and great marketing, and the world might just beat a path to your door.

You can extrapolate Dawson's approach to any other way you come across—or invent—to learn better whom you're dealing with. But always remember you're talking to a human being, not just a set of personality traits.

Let's look at Dawson's four personality categories on a grid:

	FAST DECISIONS	SLOW DECISIONS
FACTUALLY ORIENTED	Pragmatic	Analytical
EMOTIONALLY ORIENTED	Extrovert	Amiable

Salespeople are at their most effective when selling to someone in the same category, and their least effective when working diagonally. In other words, business relationships between Pragmatics and Amiables, or between Analyticals and Extroverts, will be rough going. There will be conflict both about the speed of the process and whether to focus on feelings or facts.

Slow decision makers will perceive fast decision makers as pestering them to jump in when they aren't ready—and will bore or frustrate fast ones into abandoning the deal. A highly emotive person's evasive answers will annoy a Pragmatic or Analytical, while a "just the facts, ma'am" person won't establish the intimacy an Extrovert or Amiable needs in order to feel ready to do business.

An effective sales representative will identify each prospect's dominant category and tailor an appeal appropriately. This isn't dishonesty, just good salesmanship. It serves the prospect, by trying to address his or her felt needs.

If several people from your prospect's organization are meeting with you, your sales pitch should be able to touch on points that will warm hearts across the grid: You will provide both feeling and factual reasons why they should buy from you, and let the group give you its own cues about decision speed.

True Rapport

Master salesman Alvin Donovan, author of *Make More Money Now,* reminds us that all the factors Susan Bellows identified are important to make your prospect feel at ease. It's not enough to pay attention to the way your prospect moves, talks, even breathes. Your prospect will feel much more in tune with you if you gradually change from your patterns to his or hers. If you're breathing in the same rhythm, speaking at a similar tone and speed, using the same types of body language, this "mirroring" can be incredibly effective. Combine this with leading adjectives as we discussed earlier, for an incredibly powerful subliminal sales message.

It won't feel natural to everybody, but these patterns can create habits that replace the "barrier habits" your salespeople may be unconsciously putting up between themselves and their prospects.

"No" Can Be a Good Thing

Jacques Werth and Nicholas E. Ruben's book, *High Probability Selling,* points out something that ought to be obvious: you have the best chance of selling when you approach those who need, want, and can afford your product—those to whom you can offer solutions to their problems or some other direct benefit.

Rather than banging your head against the wall, pressuring nonprospects to buy something they don't need, Werth <mailto:jacquesw@highprobsell.com> and Ruben turn the sales process on its head: the primary purpose of a sales call, in their opinion, is to establish whether there is a mutual basis for a business relationship. If the answer is yes, you look at how you can solve their problem. If the answer is no, thank them for their time and move on. Your resources of time and energy will be more effective in eliminating nonprospects and moving on as quickly as possible.

This may involve an extended series of questions to your prospects. Rather than presenting product, you continue getting information. Then you know if there is a high probability that these folks need what you offer—and because you've listened so hard and so well, your chances of getting the sale are very high indeed.

Commissions, Bonuses, Awards, and Incentives

The best sales force is highly motivated, because its members are rewarded for performance. Written and spoken appreciation are important, but concrete benefits will motivate your sales reps to go the extra mile. There are four major types of reward: commissions, bonuses, awards, and incentives.

Since sales agents are independent and get paid exclusively on commission, the best ones will be highly motivated.

Money is a powerful inducement to perform. Provide a commission structure, so that reps get a percentage of every sale they close. In different industries, commission rates range from 5 percent plus a base salary to 60 percent or more. Think about increasing the percentage above a certain sales figure: for instance, 33 percent on the first $10,000 in annual (or monthly) sales; 36 percent on sales between $10,000 and $50,000, 40 percent above $50,000.

Cash bonuses also reward performance. If a sales rep brings in three new accounts at $30,000 each, a $1,500–$2,000 bonus will make him or her try harder again. Bonuses must be administered fairly and without favoritism.

Awards such as "Sales Agent of the Month" keep morale high while publicly recognizing your best performers—and encourage your other reps to strive to win the next time.

Finally, consider incentives—noncash awards for achievement of concrete goals: trips to Hawaii, large-screen televisions, time off . . . (Often, you can barter for your incentive prizes.)

If your business relies on either telephone or walk-in inquiries, reward the person who first dealt with a customer, as well as the person who happened to close. If one of your salespeople puts a great deal of effort into convincing a prospect to buy, but the prospect goes away to think about it and then closes the sale with another rep, find an equitable way to split the commission or incentive points. Otherwise, your staff will be rapidly demoralized; you'll probably suffer high turnover and poor performance.

Professional Development

Send your sales force to at least one or two conferences or seminars every year. Go for a mix of those covering sales techniques—now you know how to evaluate them, right?—and those emphasizing product knowledge. Share the cost of your employees' outside professional development. You'll be rewarded not only in a more skilled sales force, but also with sales reps who know that you back them 100 percent, and who'd like to do the same for you.

— Multilevel Marketing —

In multilevel marketing (MLM), you sell a product as an independent business owner, but also recruit additional salespeople who are themselves independent. Your recruits, and their recruits, generate commissions for you—and you in turn provide a commission to the person who recruited you, and his or her recruiters.

MLM offers low overhead and minimal support or training costs, plus passive income. Furthermore, since sales agents are independent and get paid exclusively on commission, the best ones will be highly motivated.

And the Internet has opened up fabulous ways to build a downline (the organization under you that brings you commissions) and market well beyond your friends and neighbors, making MLM a good deal more attractive for many. Jeffrey Lant has used many of his existing marketing resources—the Web, e-mail, his catalogs and card decks—to build vast and lucrative MLM downlines.

But I wonder how many of the people in his downline are really making decent money. Many people discover they don't enjoy the constant pressure of straight-commission sales with low margins. And it still takes lots of work to build up a quality sales organization underneath you.

Far too many people join MLMs as a get-rich-quick scheme. Starting any business should not be driven by a passion to make money, but a passion for your core mission. You should really believe in your products or services and want to use them to make a difference in the world. Talk to any group of self-made millionaires: Virtually all of them will tell you they were motivated by a desire to help—and they will still have a fire in their eyes when they tell you this. If you are just jumping from one MLM to another without any commitment to what you do, you will not succeed, and you will lose a lot of friends.

Picking the Right MLM Company

Use this checklist to evaluate any potential MLM investment—if they're all "yes," you'll probably succeed:

THE PRODUCT

- Do you use this product in your own daily life?
- Is this brand significantly better and/or cheaper?
- Do others get enthusiastic about the product when you ask about their interest (without any sales pitch)?
- Is the product consumable, so that customers come back to you again and again for more?
- Can you promote it easily in conjunction with your existing marketing?

The Company

- Has it been in business at least a year?
- Does it pay accurately and promptly?
- Is the commission structure workable and profitable?
- How fast will you recoup the initial investment?
- Is that initial investment primarily for actual product, and not for large start-up fees?
- What brand-building marketing or advertising does the company do—*outside* its own network?
- Does the company support and train its reps?
- Do questions get answered quickly and accurately—and are there enough toll-free phone lines and operators to handle the volume?
- Do you feel good about the people above you in the organization—not just your immediate upline, but people at the top of the company?
- Is your upline successful at this business?
- Are you happy with the brochures, audiotapes, and other sales/recruitment materials?

As for my own experience . . . I tried one MLM that seemed to meet most of the criteria, except two very important ones. It was a really good long-distance phone plan. Everyone uses it, people come back for more, the sales materials were good, there was essentially no start-up cost (it was only ten dollars) . . . but the company support was poor and it didn't pay out! Questions were lost in voice mail, left unanswered, or couldn't be asked because the line was always busy. Commissions would trickle in six months late, months of commissions would just be missing, and trying to track them got me nowhere. Worse, the line for new customers to sign up was often dysfunctional.

After a year or so of this, I switched to another phone company, got out of the MLM end, took down my telephone Web page, and went back to my core business. If I ever try another MLM, it will be one where I'm darn sure the company is properly capitalized and able to support its representatives.

House Parties

Many of the most successful MLMs use a house-party model. Tupperware, Mary Kay, and Amway were early pioneers of this marketing method, which can be wildly successful. In a sense, the popular affiliate model on the Internet is nothing more than a cyber-version of the old-fashioned house party.

Invite a few friends over for a social event, and demonstrate cookware, children's books, vitamins, or a host of other products.

In my observation, house parties work best for a female audience. If I were selling a typically male product such as power tools, I might investigate a variation, such as a bowling-alley party—or better yet, a carpentry project round-robin, where a group gets together for an hour or two every weekend at different members' homes, to build something together for someone in the group.

33

Trade Show Triumphs

Trade shows: lots of glitz and hype, huge crowds, sound and light extravaganzas . . . and a fantastic opportunity to sell to people who have already defined themselves as interested.

Attend a few shows before you enter as a vendor. Keep an eye on what other people in your industry are doing, what's effective, what's just a waste of money. Go through every aisle, including the far corridors that have small booths but often the most interesting vendors.

Here's how to keep your costs down and increase your effectiveness.

— Know Your Objectives —

Know why you want to exhibit; you'll be much more likely to match your actions with your goals. Here are some good reasons:

- Establish new dealers and distributors
- Meet users of your product and get face-to-face feedback
- Sell merchandise or services directly at the show
- Develop sales leads
- Interest journalists in covering you
- Demonstrate new products
- Explore new products to sell or distribute—and develop personal relationships with their manufacturers and distributors
- Keep current on new trends
- Shop for great deals

Show Floor versus Booth Space

The last three items in the above list can be done just as well, perhaps even better, by attending rather than exhibiting. So save your money and just buy a ticket.

For example, I attended a huge book-industry trade show in Chicago—and came away with four potential foreign-rights republishers, three potential distributors, two possibilities for book authorship or coauthorship, several people interested in my marketing services, a few easy no-work comarketing deals, and a new agent to represent one of my books. And for my wife the fiction writer, I brought home three agent and six publisher contacts who would seriously consider her new novel.

If all these deals had materialized (admittedly unlikely), I would have gained tens of thousands of dollars. Even so, I had covered my costs several times over.

Booths cost $2,400, and on-site costs such as electrical hookup raised the typical point of entry to about $4,000—but my cost to reap all these contacts was only slightly more than plane fare.

That's because I didn't take a booth. I did participate in two cooperative exhibits, where for a small fee I could display my book titles along with other independent publishers—but the way I got most of these contacts was by walking the floor myself.

Some tips to make a trade show work for you, along the lines of the way this one worked for me:

- Offer the best products or services you can— things that have real value—and be confident in what you offer.
- Make yourself a walking advertisement for what you have to offer. I made three custom T-shirts with a color photocopy of one of my books, the name of the other book, my phone numbers and URL; two of the key contacts were initiated by other people who saw my shirt.
- Go where the action is. If I had known how easy it was going to be to generate foreign interest in my books, I'd have hit the foreign publishers' area much earlier in the show—and perhaps landed another four to six worthy contacts.
- Select a strategy that makes sense. I browsed the foreign publisher displays looking for compatible books (got a South American publisher interested that way), talked to the country coordinators for recommendations (came away with a contact in Germany), and—when I showed my titles to someone who didn't feel it was a good fit—asked for other companies that would be more in line with what I offered (landed my most serious bite here, from a publisher in England).
- Don't neglect competitors. If you have products that complement each other, you may be able to strike comarketing deals. For instance, I met a publisher with a book on attracting the opposite sex. She took fliers for my Hedonist book on cheap romance and distribute them at a singles convention, while I mailed her flier in my next mailing to a list of singles for a sideline business. The cost to each of us is only photocopying, and we paid each other a 40 percent dealer commission.
- Be creative. Consider your product as a premium (or look for premiums you can bundle with your product to make it more attractive). Think about bulk-quantity sales in the corporate market. Consider what markets you already reach, who would like to reach those markets, and how you can find some mutual benefit in working together—and likewise, what markets you'd like to reach through other people.
- Follow up your contacts promptly and appropriately when you get home.

The following year, I went back to the same trade show, wearing the same T-shirts. One of the results was the contract to do the book you're reading: I stopped to talk with Chelsea Green's publisher, Stephen Morris, because he was promoting a book on sustainable hedonism; the book on my shirt was *The Penny-Pinching Hedonist: How to Live Like Royalty with a Peasant's Pocketbook*. I pointed to the shirt and began a conversation. We worked out a win-win deal to do a marketing book, and perhaps if this book is successful we'll do a similar deal with another book on frugal fun.

— And When You *Do* Exhibit —

If you want to take the plunge and rent exhibit space, be sure to make the most of your investment.

Pick the Right Shows

Examine the quality of the show: Who's sponsoring it? How many years has the show run? If you've attended previously, did it excite you or put you to sleep? How many of the major players were represented? Could you find the little independents among the stars? Did the conference sessions mesh well with your philosophy? How will the show promote its vendors? Will they promote you heavily in advance? Do they give you adequate description space in the program guide, or will you have to buy display ads to get more than a listing? How have other vendors of your size been treated by the management? How much press attention does the show receive? How many people attend?

Finally, who will attend? Look for these categories:

- Your target market
- Your own profession
- People marketing noncompeting products to your customers
- People in your geographical area

Choose Staff Well and Treat Them Right

If your goal is pushing product, focus on salespeople. But if your primary goal is user feedback, let product developers predominate. For most shows, it's good to have a mix: sales, demonstrators, technical support, product development, regional marketing managers. Your staff must answer questions from existing and potential customers, retailers, engineers, and passersby.

You'll do much better if your booth staff is always fresh and comfortable. Provide high stools with backs so that your staff can sit down and still be at eye level with people in the aisle. Use creative, comfortable costumes (for example, matching, eye-catching, professionally designed T-shirts) that provide visual identification with your product. Rotate your staff every three hours—this will not only keep people from getting worn out, but will also give them a chance to enjoy the rest of the show. Make hot and cold drinks and light refreshments available to your staff at all times. Keep your booth as easy to set up and take down as possible. And perhaps hire a massage therapist to give everyone a five-minute pick-me-up at the middle and end of each day.

Downsize Your Booth

Trade show booth space is expensive. The larger your booth, the more you will pay—both to the show organizer and to build your display. So keep it small. You'll be able to set up and take down easily, and the cost of the show won't force you to raise all your prices for six months just to catch up.

Unless you can afford a fancy room-sized floor display with lots of chairs and a big screen for an eye-catching audiovisual or live demonstration, you may as well stick with the basics: a counter or table, samples, merchandise to sell, and a big display banner.

Keep a stack of product literature available, but only give it to those who ask for it—otherwise you'll waste a lot of printing on people who really aren't interested, and your flier will be buried in a shopping bag full of other offers. Better to follow up quickly with a mailing or telemarketing to serious prospects. Thank them for visiting you at the show and extend your show discount offer for another couple of weeks, just for them.

Consider a Co-op Booth

Joining together with one's "competitors" leads to better visibility, higher impact, and a spirit of cooperation—especially at trade shows. Whatever your industry, find people whose products and services complement but don't compete with your own, and make the show more profitable and less costly by joining forces. You save money on the space and possibly on the literature you distribute, and you share the labor of actually staffing the booth (pretty exhausting if you try to do it on your own).

Here's a real-life example: I wanted my books at the American Library Association national conference. Small-press tables were $650, and my two books would be a pretty stark table. So I found seventeen other publishers with compatible titles, willing to pay me a fee to exhibit. I gave a significant discount if they would help staff the table. We captured names through a daily drawing for free books.

Results:

- I got to be paid to attend the show (though with several dozen hours of organizing time, I didn't get paid well).
- Other publishers got exposure at a reasonable cost of $65 or $110 per title.

- There was enough of a critical mass to generate significant library interest—far more than any one of us could have done on our own.
- Because there were other staffers, I had plenty of time to walk the show floor and make contacts specific to my own agenda.

Of course, there are more conventional ways to exhibit cooperatively. In the publishing trade, many organizations will exhibit your book among dozens of others. However, I liked the do-it-yourself approach for several reasons: The titles made sense thematically; there were few enough titles to avoid any book getting lost in the display; and it gave us a reason to be at the show and develop useful contacts, rather than waiting for them to come to us.

Your Press Kit

As an exhibitor, you're entitled to put kits in the press room. While it's always in your interest to produce a simple, straightforward, *useful* kit, at a show, it's crucial. Consider *VirtualPROMOTE Gazette* editor Jim Wilson's report from the press room at Internet World:

Several reporters sitting on the couches, each with a massive pile of press kits on the floor in front of them adjacent to a large trash can. Each kit was carefully examined for any meaningful content, which was extracted and the remainder of the press kit went into the trash can. Many kits went into the trash in their entirety.

As reporters walked up and down the press kit tables, giggles and sounds of frustration accompanied the examination of each kit. "Hey, anybody know what this company does?" or "Wow, this kit includes eight-by-ten glossies of everyone that has ever worked at this company."

It seems that public relation firms and marketing departments are of the opinion that reporters can carry unlimited pounds of press kits while covering the show. The truth is that only a small portion of each press kit actually avoids being trashed immediately. Weight is the great press kit equalizer.

Here's how a press kit gets evaluated in real time.

1. *I walk up to the press kit's bin and look at the cover. If there is enough information for me to tell what the company offers, and it is an area I am interested in, I stop to look closer.*
2. *The press kits are standing up, so I peel back the presentation cover to reveal the materials in the inside right pocket. The left pocket is invisible and remains so until I am home and can open the press kit fully and examine the contents. I am looking for a bold statement of what the creator of the kit wanted me to know about. If I find it, and it is something I might want to write about, I put the kit in my pile of kits and move on.*
3. *When my turn to use the couch arrives at last, I pile the kits up in front of me and start processing them one at a time. Anything I might be able to use goes into my backpack. The folder, catalogs, glossy photos and press releases about hirings and firings go in the trash can. Now I have extracted the meaningful information from 100+ press kits and it all fits into my backpack which I now carry out to my car and get back to the show.*

So, who had this year's best press kit? A service called CollegeNet.com, which offers help for students applying for college admission.

The press kit's cover had pleasing graphics, but more importantly, it contained two pieces of valuable information. First a bold listing of the URL www.collegenet.com followed by the bold-type statement: "The Force Field for College Admissions" which gave me enough information to know what the kit was about.

Peeling back the cover, I discover on the right side a simple and well written CollegeNET Fact Sheet. This was followed by a comprehensive Company Profile. Finally, a simple sheet of testimonials.

I pick up the kit and it is very lightweight. It goes directly into the backpack.

Now comes the hard part. With so many badly done press kits, how do I select the worst? As luck would have it, the grumblings of another reporter led me to the winner.

This year's Annual Worst Press Kit Award goes to PlaceWare. Now you know as much as I did when I looked at the cover of the kit. "PlaceWare." Probably would help if there were any other words on the cover, but design consideration led to the complete absence of any other words that might take away from that powerful message: PlaceWare.

Peeling back the kit's cover I am greeted with a press release about the hiring of a new Vice President of Marketing, followed by a release letting me know who was named as Chairman of the Board. Next comes a release about the appointment of a new Board member, followed by a release revealing a clue: Placeware Conference Center Enables More Than 800 Participants In Live Web Conference. At last! A clue! Next comes a release about the same event as the previous release. That's good. You can never write too much about an event.

The right pocket yields up eight press releases and nothing more. No information about the company or its products or services. Just hirings and events.

Picking up the kit I notice that it weighs more than any other kit I've seen today. Way more. Must be that glossy brochure blocking my view of the company backgrounder I had been looking for. All in all, a great presentation of meaningless information in prime selling space. Especially notable was the absence of a business card in the little slot cut out for one.

I am sure PlaceWare did not appreciate seeing all of its expensive press kits being thrown in the trash in their entirety at the hands of frustrated reporters.

And finally a sad story about an Almost A Winner. One bin contained a nicely packaged CD-ROM press kit. What a great idea. Lightweight and any technology reporter would obviously have CD access. Unfortunately, the CD was only part of the kit. There was an accompanying press kit folder that had the dead tree presentation required to make any use of the CD information. Had they put the entire presentation on a CD they would have gone into every reporter's bag and gotten great results. Maybe next year.

More Trade Show Tips for Exhibitors

- Read the exhibitor manual carefully; make sure your signs and displays fit the show's format, and be aware ahead of time of upfront charges for carrying in the display, storing it ahead of time, hooking up electricity and telephone, etc.
- Many shows offer tables for small exhibitors; they're much cheaper and easier to set up than a full booth space.
- If you are exhibiting in a union hall, you will be hit with a hefty "drayage" charge for the teamsters to move your materials from the loading dock to the exhibit space. Find out ahead of time if you're allowed to carry in your own display—and if you are, *bring it in by the front door* (not knowing this cost me nearly three hundred dollars at the ALA show—*ouch!*)
- When you're setting up, if you encounter a problem with the union or the hall's decoration and setup company, find your liaison at the sponsoring organization—let him or her suggest a solution that works for all parties. Don't try to work things out directly with the decorator or the union.
- Don't overprint literature. Many people are traveling by plane to attend a national trade show, and they want to keep their burden as light as possible. Have a couple of thousand brochures on the show floor, but figure most people will not take them. Collect names and mail or e-mail your information within a few days after the close of the show. Assemble your ready-to-mail packets ahead of time, and just print out labels and slap them on the envelopes when you return. If you bring a laptop computer, you can enter the contacts into a database while booth traffic is light—or let a nearby secretarial service do it for you. (Obviously, how much literature you bring to the show floor will depend on how popular you expect to be. If you've nationally announced a really hot product that invents a whole new market niche,

you'll need lots of brochures. Otherwise, especially if your location is less than central, you'll just carry a lot of boxes in and out for no reason.)

- If you're lucky enough to get a booth location near a public entrance, print up at least one thousand plastic or paper bags (with handles) big enough for people to throw all the literature and freebies into. The larger and more rugged your bag, and the more comfortable its handles, the more people will continue to use it throughout the day. But don't make the mistake so many people do; this should not just be a time for branding. Instead of just your name and logo, treat it like a display ad and use your copywriting skills. Give people a benefit, a reason to learn about your product. Include contact information: address, phone, e-mail, Web site—but not necessarily your booth number. That way, if you have any left over, you can give them out to your customers (or save them for the next show). If you do retail, use the bags to pack customer purchases at your store.
- Food definitely brings booth traffic—though not always qualified booth traffic. If you can tie the food you serve in with your product, so much the better. Cookbook publishers can do demonstrations, food vendors should put out samples, travel agents could feature recipes from exotic locales. An outdoor equipment seller might serve trout or wilderness-ready dried foods . . . Unless it's your product, avoid candy; you'll compete with two-thirds of the booths offering munchies. You'll be appreciated more for something healthier: springwater or fruit juice, fresh fruit, toasted sunflower seeds, a casserole, cheese cubes, homemade bread, even bagels. For sanitation (and portion-control) reasons, avoid self-service—unless the item is individually wrapped. Or spear each item with a toothpick. Otherwise, you'll need one staffer just to serve your goodie. And *please* have a trash can and plenty of napkins! It's horrible to

have to search booth after booth for a place to throw your empty cup or wipe your hands.
- Mark your contacts' business cards as you acquire them. Don't expect to remember the exact kind of follow-up they need; write it right on the card.
- If you're selling on the floor, get the show office to set you up for local sales tax.
- Provide incentives for ordering soon—but let your show discount run at least two weeks after the close of the show.

Lisa Pelto <mailto:peltol@boystown.org>, marketing sales supervisor for Boystown Press (a large nonprofit publisher that relies heavily on trade shows), adds more suggestions:

- As soon as you are assigned a booth number, put it in all your correspondence with anyone in your industry, even on your packing slips and postage meter greetings!
- If you expect at least a couple of hundred leads, rent the show's automated lead-retrieval system. It's cheaper and more accurate than a typist, and can be used to mail-merge your follow-up letters.
- Categorize your leads *as you receive them* (e.g., wants a review copy, media contact, add to general mailing list). "I can respond to three hundred to four hundred trade show leads within two or three days of my return," she reports.
- Before you go to the show, write appropriate follow-up letters. Send them out right away when you get back.
- Invite key customers and vendors to your booth—ahead of time! Many people map out their routes before they arrive and see nothing outside their planned itinerary.
- Offer a show special.
- Have *something* to hand out—and keep samples with you at all times, including parties, trips to the bathroom, hotel shuttles . . . Start conversations and see where they lead. Have a twenty-

five-word, benefit-oriented description of each of your products or services. If you give out business cards, write your booth number on the back.

- Keep a "portable office" at your booth: Include camera, staples, tape, scissors, box opener, pens, business cards, mailing labels already addressed to your office, a fat black marker, index cards, lead sheets, date book, calculator, stamps, paper clips, pushpins, Velcro dots, masking and packing tape, string, a sewing kit, small first aid kit, breath mints, dusting cloths, lint brush. Keep a disk or clean original of your trade discount schedules, stationery, and logo [and the sales literature you're handing out!]. Purchase a container to keep all this stuff together all the time so you don't have to repack it every time you go to a show; refill when you get back from each trip.
- Bring nutritious snacks, bottled water, and very comfortable shoes.
- Store your shipping boxes with address labels and paperwork—to make it easy to send your exhibit back home after the show.

Some more tips, from the members of the Small Shop PR Agency discussion list, October 17 and 18, 1999:

- Ned Barnett <mailto:interned@accessnv.com>: A sofa and coffee table provides a low-key place to meet—and a sharp contrast to everyone else's booth. . . . Provide a literature packing service; people will remember you gratefully as they drop off pounds and pounds of stuff. . . . Stand out in the crowd; if most people are wearing suits, wear T-shirts. If most are in T-shirts, wear suits.
- Joan Stewart <mailto:jstewart@execpc.com>: Provide a water cooler, paper cups, and a wastebasket.
- SuzanneJackson<mailto:sej7@mindspring. com>: Create a photo opportunity or do something else "low-tech, but high-touch."
- Gail Robinson <mailto:infotechcom.com>:

"Ensure hardware has been booked if computers are involved. . . . Order the right number of electrical outlets and power. . . . Test the computers prior to booth setup and again after booth setup. "Send invitations. I've had clients who went from ten hot leads a day to thirty or forty just by personally inviting prospects and customers to a booth." The invitation should build on the booth's theme and offer a giveaway. "If time and budget permits, have the sales force follow up on the invitations about a week before the show." And kick off the show with a breakfast pep rally and instructional meeting for all your booth staff.

- Michael Stewart <mailto:mstewart@ana.org>: For groups concerned with public policy issues, set up a computer and printer with several boilerplate letters to the editor, and a database that can merge them with the addresses of various newspapers and politicians. Generate hundreds of support letters for your cause from the show floor (track them so that each newspaper only receives one copy of the same letter, and only one letter from each sender). Stewart even set up a map of the United States with pins for participants, to foster friendly geographic rivalry. "Last time I did this, we sent 125 letters in five days, and 27 of them were published!" Stewart also offered to UPS home each visitor's large, heavy resource binder—but in return, the visitor had to fill out a form.
- Terri Firebaugh<mailto:firebaugh@firepub. com>: If you'll be using custom order forms, make pads of them, about fifty thick. If you need to collect sales tax at the show, keep a tax chart with the local sales tax (which will be different from your home location). Bring a business card scanner, if you have one. "Trade shows are big, bustling places with tons of people everywhere. They're loud, crowded, and sensorily overwhelming. So, anything that you can do to make your place an oasis away from the crowd, relaxing, comfortable will stand out. People will come there for that alone."

— Get People to Your Booth —

Since your booth is small, it won't be easily noticed in the throng. So take out a quarter-page ad in the program guide and/or do some targeted direct mail, advertising a show special: a premium, drawing for a free item, discount . . . Whatever it is, it must pull serious prospects to your booth. Of course, your booth number should be prominently mentioned in the ad, along with a landmark such as "near the snack bar" or "just three booths down from [major vendor with enormous glitzy booth]."

David Sams Industries, an infomercial producer, took out a full-page trade journal ad, highlighting its tiny, plain trade show booth—and its qualifications, results-driven focus, previous successes, and so forth (but oddly, not the show name or booth number). The ad concludes, "Don't call us if you're looking for a fancy brochure. But do call us if you want the best-looking, best-performing show on the air!"

Interestingly, this ad, heavy on text, with primitive, hand-drawn graphics, is effective in promoting a glitzy, highly visual product: infomercials (*Electronic Retailing*, September-October 1995, p. 5).

Highly visible, inexpensive giveaways, such as buttons, balloons, automobile sunshades, and imprinted literature bags, can all help draw crowds to your booth. T-shirts and tote bags cost more, but will generate visibility long after the show. You can use these as purchase premiums, rather than just handing them out to everyone walking by—or sell them as part of your booth merchandise. Doing product demonstrations? Use them as incentives; throw a hat or a T-shirt to anyone who answers a demonstrator's question, or give one away with a drawing at the end of each demo. Keep in mind, though, that a lot of people will sit through your demonstration just to get the prize, then toss your literature into the next wastebasket.

Jeffrey Lant suggests that if you write articles, you'll vastly improve your pull at trade shows if you get a problem-solving article into the sponsoring organization's magazine or newsletter, to appear shortly before the trade show. But why not take this further? Do a series of articles and put them in for three or four months in quick succession, culminating in the issue just before the show (remember to leave several months' lead time).

Track Names

Above all, collect prospect names; this is the most important reason to exhibit. More and more trade shows are making follow-up easier for participating vendors. Registrants are issued a credit-card-style badge with their name and address or an ID number, and vendors run the names of interested people through a card reader or imprinter. If your show is still old-fashioned, try a fishbowl for business cards and a pad to gather additional names.

The face-to-face sales and product demonstrations are an added bonus, and you should treat each person who visits you as if they're really important to you. But the real dividend is your list of sharply qualified prospects who now have some exposure to your products and services.

Keep it to serious inquiries. If you have several products, identify who's interested in which ones. Don't collect names through free drawings, contests, or premiums other than for your own products; use those tricks only to attract booth traffic. You want to qualify your follow-up names so that you don't waste your time and money following up nonprospects. In other words, separate out the cards you'll be following up from those who just want your prize—or use some sort of instant-winner system so that you don't even collect the nonprospect cards.

Of course, if you give away your own product, contact all your prospects to not only announce the winner but disseminate his or her testimonial.

Once you get back to your office, follow up immediately, while the show is still fresh in prospects' minds and they haven't made a decision among similar products. Get information and pricing out within three days of the show's end. Include a coupon offering a special show-attender's price, with a rapid expiration date. Follow up by telephone within two weeks; time is critical.

Your Own Private Show

Here's an interesting recent trend: the private trade show. A company with a dozen or so products can set up tables for each in the lobby of its own building, throw in a speaker or a conference panel, and publicize the daylights out of it to existing customers and prospects, the press, and the general public.

Also, it's easy enough to organize a small-scale trade show beyond your own firm. For instance, I joined a local barter network at a Main Street outdoor trade show featuring a dozen or so worker-owned businesses. Then the barter network put together its own trade show at a community center a few months later, and ensured a great turnout by announcing some of the popular food vendors and live folk musicians who were participating. Both of these were small scale and took relatively little work to set up, and both shows reached hundreds of people with minimal investment from participants. In fact, they were a refreshing change from the glitz and roar of traditional trade shows—just a few people sitting at simple tables and chairs, talking directly to potential customers.

34

A Storehouse of Tricks

If you have a store, you need this chapter. Your store serves three crucial marketing functions:

- Making customers out of passersby
- Organizing and hosting special events to bring in customers
- Up-selling those who are already in your store

A store doesn't have to be a ground-floor retail space with a big plate-glass window facing a main shopping street. It could be in a basement, a loft, or even a portion of your home (zoning permitting). These days, it could even be a Web site. But with high visibility, your job is easier.

— Make Customers out of Passersby —

Part of your job is to make your store enticing: to attract the attention of people walking or driving by so that they stop and enter. We've already talked about signage in chapter 16. Indeed, a comprehensive program of signs over the door, on a sandwich board, and in a store window, all designed to work smoothly together, is a logical first step. But you can do a lot more.

Store Window Merchandising

The store window provides a marketing vehicle at no extra cost, and a nice, big, three-dimensional one at that.

Consider some of these options:

- A display involving mannequins or stuffed animals using your product
- Seasonal/holiday displays—including some obscure ones, too—for example, an agricultural display in midwinter for Tu B'Shvat, the Jewish new year for trees (If you commemorate traditional holidays, please acknowledge cultural differences; not everyone is Christian or Jewish, and it can be very alienating to feel ignored in the excitement of a major holiday that you don't celebrate)
- For craftspeople, a window opening directly into the artisan's studio, so that people can watch products being made by hand
- A contest to guess the contents of a mystery box or number of items in a large jar; prizes inside
- An exhibit about life in another culture, whose products you sell

- Live product demonstrations, with free samples
- An art, historical, or special-interest exhibit that continues inside
- A mannequin with a mirrored face, so the browser sees his or her own face wearing the latest fashion
- If you offer great selection, stack several each of thirty different competing products in some kind of creative shape—perhaps even use the cans to spell out something like "We Have It All"
- A clearly visible, well-maintained bulletin board of community events
- Children's activities while the parent is shopping: a maze, coloring area, tire swing, basketball hoop, blocks
- An elaborate display of your product, in an elegant setting (example: a local toy store filled a huge window with an intricate 35 x 8-foot model train layout)
- A banner promoting an event
- A contest in the window (a bookstore or office products shop could have three writers racing to finish a short story, for instance)
- Color, light, and texture, providing visual interest
- A continuously rotating three-dimensional display to highlight several products at once
- New arrivals or unique items, prominently displayed
- A continuous-loop videotape of products in use
- A camcorder or mirror that lets passersby see themselves—perhaps superimposed on your product

In short, the window is your strongest tool for attracting passersby. There is no limit to what you can do even in a small window; a large one can be a billboard for your store from a long way off. In fact, your displays may even become a tourist attraction. An example: A music store near me has had a series of window displays featuring cartoons of "Downtown Joe," the owner, for over a decade; people come from far and wide to see the latest incarnations.

A few final tips on window merchandising:

- Change your display often enough so that passersby don't get bored, but not too often— perhaps once a month.
- Always make sure the window display will help you get people into the store; it's not enough just to be clever for the sake of cleverness.
- Consider using promotional materials supplied by your manufacturers.
- Remember that a window can either be a unified whole or be subdivided into several smaller displays.
- If you're in a shopping mall or other area where you share space, work out displays that highlight several stores, using a unified theme (identify each store's material by store name).
- Let your marketing message work even when your store is closed. If you use a full-protection security gate that blocks view of your window when your store is closed, paint a permanent display on the metal panels. If your window is visible at night, illuminate it. You can even use nighttime lighting to create a separate display.

Find out your customers' reactions to your displays. But remember, people's likes and dislikes vary. Don't deliberately offend large numbers of people (i.e., avoid sexism, racism, obscenity, trashing of any group, defamation of any religion, or just bad taste). But don't be afraid to be unique.

Other Methods

We've already talked about handing out fliers or coupons, but consider more active solicitation. In developing countries, store workers often stand out on the street, actively encouraging people to come in and shop. When business is slow, stand out in front and give people a reason to come inside. It could be a polite "Would you like to come in and try a cup of our new Turkish coffee?" or a high-energy shout of "Twenty-five-percent off sale—come in and find a bargain!" (Don't use taped enticement recordings—that's impersonal noise pollution, not effective marketing. Ditto with blaring loudspeakers.)

The tone that is right for you will depend both on your business image and on the tone of nearby stores. Nobody is offended by a high-pressure pitch in Times Square, but along the elegant shops of Rodeo Drive in Beverly Hills, it wouldn't earn you any brownie points.

Don't forget something very obvious: the sparkle. Floors and counters should shine, employees should look like people a stranger would want to do business with, and the store should convey a general sense of orderly functionality. At the same time, every store should have its own distinct personality, its own decor, in keeping with the image you've worked so hard to develop. Casual clothes may actually make a better impression than formal wear for many businesses—but torn or dirty clothes will not.

Particularly in food-handling establishments, sanitation is vital. Says Bread & Circus store manager Dave Lannon, "The first thing people look at is the floor. You can have the greatest products in the world, but if your store is not clean, you're going to go out of business. Cleanliness is a major, major issue."

— Hosting Special Events —

Create intentionality. Get prospects to leave the house headed purposefully for your place of business. Sometimes you can do it just with great products and terrific service. But sometimes you need more. Go back to the chapters on publicity for idea-starters on how to create and publicize a special event.

— Up-Selling from Within —

Up-selling is the art of selling a customer on a larger purchase. The hardest part is getting your prospect in the door. Once the customer is there, you rely on both shopping with intention (coming in to buy a particular item) and impulse purchasing of additional items. But impulse purchases will only occur if the prospect is caught by something he or she hadn't previously considered, or didn't know was on sale.

There's a whole science of point-of-purchase marketing (marketing at the place where the buyer is present). Visit a few stores with your observation antennae turned on. Notice how merchandise is displayed and stacked, where the manufacturer or distributor provided posters, stands, and other point-of-purchase displays, how the store uses sale pricing, in-store coupons, and product layout, and whether there is a way to "try before you buy" (for instance, fitting booths, stereo listening rooms, free samples, money-back guarantees, demonstration models on the sales floor). Which of these methods will work in your store?

Let's break down the major in-store purchase aids according to the primary senses they reach.

Visual

Product displays themselves—on the shelves or in the aisles—fall into this category, as do notices on a bulletin board, stacks of sale brochures, signs on the shelves, posters, stands, and fliers. Supermarkets, superstores, and budget-oriented variety stores (e.g., Kmart, Woolworth's), all of which have very little sales staff support for a large customer volume, often use these techniques as their primary in-store marketing.

Make sure products are displayed attractively, exude freshness, and are easy to grab without causing an avalanche!

There is a reason why so many stores display their specials in huge stacks. Dave Lannon, store manager of Bread & Circus, explains: "It's psychological: People buy from a full display; they will not buy from a small display. Big displays connote that it's bountiful and they want to buy it."

Aural

Sound can be an important marketing tool, but only if it's used properly. If you barrage your customers with marketing messages or play music that jars with your image, they will rebel. And if you assault them from outside your store, they'll simply go elsewhere. Think of sound as a form of telemarketing—provide messages your prospects want to hear, at the right time. If you play music, avoid the extremes of either too sappy (so-called easy-listening) or too discordant.

Break in gently over a public-address system to announce a special, a product demonstration, or a new shipment arriving on the shelves. But use a live announcer. Stay away from continuously broadcast canned announcements; no one listens to them! If your store emphasizes personal service, let the person speaking identify himself or herself. "Shoppers, this is Bob in housewares. We've just gotten in a new style of trash can today; it looks like an elephant and comes in eight colors. Come to Aisle 6 and check it out."

The tone that is right for you will depend both on your business image and on the tone of nearby stores.

While shopping at a small, family-run supermarket, I once heard this announcement: "Ladies and gentlemen, we just got in some star fruit. I don't know exactly what it is, but it sure looks interesting. I'm going to try some and maybe you'd like to try it, too." This was years ago, but I still remember it, because it was so refreshing compared to the bland, prepackaged announcements in chain supermarkets.

The best use of aural marketing I ever saw was under a big tent at a county fair. Like many other people, I heard frequent laughter and applause emanating from the tent, and stopped in to see what was going on. There were rows of chairs, nearly all of them filled, and in the front was a man demonstrating a food processor.

You'd think that would be pretty mundane stuff, but he made it extraordinary. His pitch was a forty-five-minute running patter of product benefits and natural-foods education—disguised as high-spirited jokes. The whole time, he was also throwing all sorts of strange things into the machine and handing out samples of instant homemade sherbert and vegetable juice shakes. I'm pretty hard to sell to. But he was so good that I almost wrote out a $250 check.

Any time you're doing any kind of in-store demonstration or event, be sure your customers know about it! You don't have to use a P.A. system, either. Send one of your employees up and down the aisles to individually invite customers.

Taste/Smell/Feel

Participation is a powerful tool. Get people involved, by tasting a product, seeing and smelling it as it cooks—or by putting their hands on your computer, sitting on your furniture, wheeling your stroller. Let the prospect experience the momentary feeling of ownership; if the product is good, many of them will make it permanent. Let the customer experience things firsthand, demonstrate the product in a way that feels like being there, or—best of all—combine these approaches with a product demonstration followed by a chance for the user to try it out, ask questions, and receive hints from the expert demonstrator.

Even if you don't have a store, up-selling and/or cross-selling is possible. The University of Massachusetts Division of Continuing Education's Honoré David actively markets other programs to her tour participants. "When you get all these people on a bus, it's a good way to talk about other things that we do."

Consider Amazon.com, the online bookseller. When you click on a book title, you get not only description, but also a list of similar titles. And if you buy from them often enough to establish some patterns, Amazon will e-mail you if a book that fits these patterns becomes available.

Warning: Sometimes what you really need to do is not up-sell, but down-sell: to help a prospect find a scaled-back alternative rather than leave in search of something cheaper, for instance.

— An In-Store Marketing Master —

The most consistent, well-done, and successful in-store marketing campaign I've ever seen was at the western Massachusetts branch of Bread & Circus, a huge natural-foods supermarket in rural, college-oriented Hadley, Massachusetts. (Note: The observations in this chapter were conducted before the chain was purchased by a much larger conglomerate. After the buyout, there were many changes in the store's approach. Since I believe the original patterns were more effective, I am leaving this material as it was before the merger.)

The largest branch in a chain of six stores, this store uses nearly the full range of in-store marketing devices—and uses them well. Some of its marketing is developed in the branch store, and some in the corporate headquarters near Boston.

The other stores are in Greater Boston and Providence. But the Hadley store, with its wide aisles and huge square footage, uses its physical space to market more effectively than the smaller, more crowded inner-city stores.

Can a natural-foods store compete as a supermarket? Judge for yourself. Bread & Circus opened its first store in 1975; Hadley opened in 1983. The chain is the largest organic produce purchaser in the United States. Although it doesn't attempt to compete on price, the Hadley Bread & Circus has comparable square footage and dollar volume to a general-purpose chain supermarket.

Bread & Circus in Hadley is blessed with a huge store window, facing a large parking lot and clearly visible from the major local traffic artery. The store's marquee is legible from about half a mile, and drivers with keen eyes can read the specials highlighted on seven-foot-high posters in the windows as they drive by. As a customer pulls into the parking lot, those posters are clear and easy to read. Also legible are smaller posters calling attention to regular features (wide cheese selection, salad bar).

A sign in the lobby states the company's pure-foods policy—and a 100-percent-satisfaction guarantee. Underneath is a magazine rack with the current *Whole Things Considered:* a magazine and monthly specials list rolled into one. Reinforcing the store's image as environmentally conscious, it's printed on coarse recycled paper with soy-based ink.

This month, the magazine includes notices of a festival to fight world hunger and an herb seminar; a call for volunteers for a different hunger program; an illustrated nutritional comparison between peanut-butter-and-jelly sandwiches made with Bread & Circus ingredients versus traditional ingredients (sharing the page with a blurb advertising peanut butter on sale); a profile of the founder of a nationally popular natural-baked-goods line; and feature articles on several staple foods, with recipes. Also, articles on a vegetarian replacement for the traditional four food groups, promoted by an international physicians' group, and revisions of federal food labeling laws, with a sidebar providing the new definitions; recipes for quick and easy lunchbox meals; and—on every page—descriptions, pictures, and prices of the month's specials. In short, something customers will want to read and take home.

Next to the magazine rack is a stack of fliers with six money-saving coupons. And rounding out the lobby is a chalkboard with the day's restaurant specials.

Entering the store proper, you'll see the produce department—with perhaps the best-looking vegetables in New England—gleaming on the left. Store employees police this section so thoroughly that there is no visible trace of anything even a little bit past its prime. Says store manager Dave Lannon, "If you came in blindfolded, you'd never get anything bad. Produce is very much a pride issue. If you wouldn't sell it to your mother, we wouldn't put it out. If somebody buys something that's bad, we run the risk of them not buying it again."

On the right is an information kiosk, with brochures on products and on sustainable farming practices. Stacks of recipes on 3 x 5 cards are also here. Above the kiosk are a sign announcing gift certificates and a Retailer of the Year Award plaque from *Whole Foods* magazine. The courtesy booth is immediately next to the kiosk, as is a recycling bin for aseptic juice boxes (with a poster of the company president describing his delight in finding that these boxes can be recycled into building materials instead of thrown into the landfill).

Past the courtesy booth, opposite a row of cash registers, are endcaps with large displays of monthly specials—one or two between each set of aisles. More specials displays are along the back wall. Specials are also stocked in their regular places on the shelves, with signs noting the discount price.

Throughout the store, signs answer questions, provide information, and cross-sell. Here, for instance, is the sign on the almonds bin in the bulk foods section:

RAW ALMONDS

To dry roast, place in a 350° oven for 8–10 minutes until lightly browned. To blanch, pour boiling water over almonds and allow to cool. Slip from skins.

Almonds are rich in protein, iron, calcium, and Vitamin B2. Add roasted and chopped almonds to cookies, breads, vegetable and chicken stir-fries and stuffings. Store in an air-tight container in a cool, dark place.

This is a small, permanent, typeset sign, roughly six inches high by four inches wide, and has a sticker with the current price attached to it.

A larger (8½ x 11) sign attached to a small wooden display stand in front of the seafood case shows how the store uses cross-selling. This sign is handwritten in green (uppercase) and black (lowercase) marker, on preprinted stock with a gradated white-to-yellow background, a bright orange border, the word "Special" in the same orange, and a background graphic of a human face inside a sunburst:

Arrowhead Mills
QUICK BROWN RICE!
Try adding our
PEELED SHRIMP,
also on special, the last 3 minutes of cooking for a quick and delicious meal.

One staffer is employed full time just on point-of-purchase sign making, using both hand and computerized methods. Another employee works exclusively on window posters. Finally, the central office provides many of the permanent signs.

Some of the signs have no sales function, but are purely customer service oriented. For example, this one in the dairy department certainly furthers the store's hard-won perception as customer-focused:

FOR YOUR INFORMATION
Although some Stonyfield Yogurts claim to be cholesterol-free, they do in fact contain less than 3% cholesterol. The law, however, allows manufacturers to state otherwise.

The seafood display is past the bulk foods section and the salad bar, which includes several deli items. Past the seafood case are deli and bakery areas, each with an item or two on the counter for customer samples. Both departments create everything from scratch each day.

Across the aisle is a product sample/cooking-demonstration area, that runs weekday evenings and all day Saturday. The schedule of upcoming demos is posted. Around the corner, in the cheese department, are more samples. As Dave Lannon points out, "It's very hard to turn down a product once you've tasted it."

Dairy, soy-based dairy substitutes, and frozen whole-foods entrées fill out most of the far aisle, which ends with a gourmet beer and wine section. A huge black coffee roaster is in an alcove behind the wines, permeating the area with the smell of roasting beans several times a week. Finally, there's the restaurant, where people can buy a variety of hot foods, or purchase and eat items from the deli, bakery, cold-drink cases, and salad bar.

That's just the perimeter of the store. Between the produce and dairy sections are several aisles, all wider than in most supermarkets—and well staffed with employees who can answer questions about the many exotic products on the shelves: not just food, but books, cooking utensils, bulk herbs and spices, natural soaps and cosmetics, recycled toilet paper . . . all in keeping with the goal of providing one-stop shopping.

Bread & Circus also works hard to attract new customers, through such events as food-tasting fairs, seminars with experts, and coupons in print ads. Plus, of course, its customer service policies and vast product selection are all geared toward generating repeat business. Finally, the store is active in community service: giving otherwise wasted food to food banks or organic pig farmers, donating items for raffles, providing scholarships at a college organic agriculture program, and involving customers in a holiday charity food drive through a coupon program.

In short, every aspect of the store worked in concert to reinforce the store image and the marketing message.

Selling Through Others' Outlets

You can have a retail presence without your own storefront. With the right product, others will be happy to sell your items to their own customers, both in stores and through other channels such as catalogs or Internet sites. Consider a few among many possibilities:

- Airport, bus, and train terminal stores
- Campus stores
- Catalogs
- Corporate or foundation sales (as a premium or for internal use)
- Door-to-door
- Flea markets
- Gift shops
- Government offices
- Human-services agencies
- Libraries
- Mail-order clubs
- Museums and galleries
- Network marketing organizations
- Nonprofit organizations
- Outdoor markets
- Professional associations
- Pushcarts
- Specialty stores
- Tourist attractions
- Wholesale clubs

✁

Even if you don't have a storefront, many of these options may be open to you. And whether or not you have your own retail outlet, your own customers can be your very best salespeople. Read on for the inside scoop on enlisting their help.

35

Repeat and Referral
Customers

Word-of-mouth referral is absolutely your best marketing tool. A positive recommendation from a friend or colleague, although it may only reach one person at a time, is worth more to the person hearing it than any advertisement. And that same friendly recommendation can reach thousands of prospects on the right Internet discussion groups.

But if you do a bad job, or allow an alienated customer to go away mad, a lot more people will hear about it—and that's the worst publicity you can get. Typically, an unhappy customer will tell about seven times as many people as a happy one, trashing your reputation all over town (or cyberspace). So strive always to be a problem solver, not a product pusher—even if you have to give an occasional refund.

— Increasing Referrals —

Ask for referrals! As each client leaves, we say, "Oh, and by the way, we're grateful if you tell your friends and colleagues about what we do." We also hand the client our business card and sometimes our brochure.

Often, we get responses like "Oh really? I'd be glad to—I hadn't thought of that," or even "There are three people in my office who could use you, and I'll make sure to tell them."

Does it work? Referral business typically draws in 20–25 percent of our new clients. Some months, if a client is an enthusiastic networker, it's been 50 percent or more. Referrals are our second-largest source of first-time clients.

Honoré David, at the University of Massachusetts at Amherst Continuing Education Division, estimates that 60 percent of her department's customers are repeaters. "That's why it's important to maintain a good relationship with our audience." Referrals are also important to her. "The best publicity we can get is word-of-mouth—that is what brings us our students. It's people to people that does the marketing."

The activist group 20/20 Vision routinely asks its subscribers for names of friends who might like to join. Mentioning the referrer's name, 20/20 mails information to these people. A jaw-dropping 14 percent join the organization.

If someone sends you a client, acknowledge the effort. A written or telephoned thank you is in order for any referral. Little touches such as sending candy or flowers—or even a card—go a long way toward showing your gratitude.

Your thank-you gift can be something directly related to your business, too. In my business, I've given free lifetime résumé storage to people who've sent several of their friends. It's an ideal gift because it costs me nothing. But if it's been a few years since the last update, it could save the client money.

Also, consider referral incentives: Offer a concrete reward. Ideally, your incentive should require the original client to come back in order to claim it. For instance, if someone sends you three clients or $150 worth of new business, give a coupon for 10 percent or $25 off their next order. In a sense, you're paying the marketing cost directly to the referring client, rather than to your printer, your sales force, or your ads.

But if you think that's too crass, look for some other kind of incentive—a bottle of wine, dinner at a local restaurant, free copies from a local copy shop. Hold down costs by working out some sort of mutual premium program with another business.

Incentives work only if your existing customers know about them and if you efficiently track how new clients find you. So spread the word!

Repeat Business

By some reports, it costs five to seven times as much to bring in a new customer as to sell to an existing one. Let's look at that statement in a less conventional way: If profit = revenues less expenses, holding down your expenses yields a much larger increase in profitability. If new client acquisition lowers your profit by 30 percent per sale, and an existing customer's expense is only 5 percent (one-sixth of 30 percent), every existing customer who reorders yields 25 percent more profit. When you get reorders, your profits increase. So do the best job you can, treat your customers right, and sell quality products at a decent price—you should have a steady flow of repeat customers

As your services or products expand, and as your clients grow in their own ventures, you should be able to up-sell past customers—if they had a good experience the first time. When Frank Fox began a separate professional association for résumé writers, some two hundred members of his secretarial services association joined immediately. "They knew we would do what we said we would do."

But to count on repeat business, you must remind your clients and customers of your existence and your continued desire to serve them. Ask clients their birthdays and anniversaries, and send a card—or better yet, offer a freebie on the special day. You'll stand out from the pack that sends December greetings. Send out a "preferred-customers sale" flier once or twice a year, only for existing clients.

⚞

Whatever you do to harvest the bounty of your satisfied customers, you won't be sorry.

36

Who Do You Know?

We've already talked about getting referrals from clients—but that's only the beginning. My business gets referrals from people who've never even used my services. The more people who know what you have to offer, the more referrals you'll get. Word-of-mouth incurs *no* marketing cost. You have nothing to lose and lots to gain.

Think about it this way. When you need an ear doctor or appliance repair person, wouldn't you first ask friends for recommendations?

Consider all of these, and more:

Friends, Family, and Neighbors

Harness parents' natural pride in their children! It's not a big step from "My son, the accountant, just started his own business" to "My son, the accountant, just started his own business. Would your daughter, with her new toy shop, be interested in having him set up her accounting?"

Make sure everyone in your immediate and extended family knows what you do—*and* knows that you welcome referrals! Tell friends, neighbors, the world.

Community Groups

Being active in the community not only builds your image, but also gives you person-to-person contact with potential clients. When you participate in social, cultural, political, or charity activities, make sure the members all know what you do—and that you know what they do.

Don't be shy about donating your professional talents or goods once in a while, too. Volunteer action rewards you with good feelings. It's enlightened self-interest, ultimately. If you want your community to be a better place through arts events, social service programs, or new legislation, then help bring it about. You get a world that more reflects your interests and concerns, and your business gets the benefit of exposure.

People You Admire

Experts and stars in any field started out as ordinary people. Knowledge, willingness to learn, regard for their clients, and smart marketing set them apart from others over a period of time.

Surprisingly enough, outside the rarefied air of the entertainment industry or state and national politics, it's often easy to make contacts with well-known people in most fields. You can learn a lot from an expert in your field. But he or she can also learn from you; you have a toe in the water of the everyday world, which your V.I.P. may have lost sight of.

You can often find celebrities listed in local phone books or professional association directories; others can be contacted through a publisher or employer, or by searching the Internet. An approach should be honest, direct, admiring but not sycophantic. Don't begin the relationship by trying to get favors; let them grow naturally out of a relationship.

Here are a few ways to get to know celebrities:

- Call or write and say you've admired their work. Be specific: What made an impact? Why? Where could the expert improve? Then ask for an appointment just to chat.
- Secure an assignment to interview the expert for an article. (I've talked to Joan Baez, Madeleine L'Engle, Tom Paxton, Pete Seeger, and many other of my heroes this way.)
- Invite the celebrity to participate on your radio or TV talk show.
- Approach your target after he or she has given a speech or presentation at a professional meeting or trade show. Invite your star to join you for a meal. (This also works if your expert is simply attending, not presenting.)
- Review a book or article by or about this person, and forward a copy.

Remember, famous people are people, too. They want friendship, in-depth conversation, a social life, a chance to participate in and play in the real world. Don't be a groupie; be a friend. If this relationship is going to work, it must be a peer relationship. If you exploit this person in any way, the friendship will dry up and your name will be spread around negatively. Be genuine, be helpful, and go behind the public mask to the real person underneath. Also,

remember that celebrities are often very careful to protect their privacy. You should protect their privacy, too; never give someone else a celeb's phone number or brag about how the person helped you.

What can a well-known person do for you?

- Throw business your way directly, because of other commitments or lack of adequate compensation
- Work collaboratively with you (for instance, on writing an article)
- Provide testimonials, jacket quotes, or a forward on your next book
- Spread your name around as a respected peer
- Assist you in avoiding or redressing grievances with others
- Help you meet other influential people in the field

You can go pretty far in approaching famous people. Writing in *Computer Currents* magazine, David Needle describes how software entrepreneurs Skip Franklin and Dan Elenbaas, of Amaze, Inc., secured "Far Side" cartoonist Gary Larson's involvement in a computerized version of the "Far Side" calendar. First they tried standard channels. But Larson's agent brushed them off, saying the cartoonist didn't license much and disliked computers. Undaunted, the two men tried a different approach:

They had heard [Larson] often played basketball in a certain schoolyard, so they hung out at the court for a week, dribbling a basketball. He didn't show. . . .

Ready to give up, they asked a teenager at a nearby gas station if Larson ever played basketball at the schoolyard. Yes, they were told, but Larson . . . was home recovering from arthroscopic surgery.

Having found out where Larson lived, the Amaze, Inc., executive team swung into action, figuring out the best get-well gift. "First it was a crazy collection of flowers, with cactus and all sorts of stuff," said Franklin. "Then we said, 'Nah, this isn't "Far Side" enough.'" So they went to a local entomology professor (luckily, a big "Far Side" fan), got a collection of strange bugs, pinned those to the flower package along with separate recipes of how best to prepare them to eat, and headed for Larson's house.

They got to the porch, dropped the package off along with their business proposal, "rang the doorbell and ran like hell, like we were back in the third grade," says Franklin.

The rest can now be recorded in PC history as one of the most unusual paths to a celebrity endorsement. While impressed with the Calendar program itself—sans "The Far Side"—Larson says he was especially captivated by the animation potential. "The thought of the things I draw actually starting to move was both frightening and exciting."
. . . Now, Larson is actively involved with the Calendar program, helping with refinements to his artwork after it's scanned into the computer.

The program, incidentally, quickly became popular once it was released, and its sales clearly hinged on Larson's contributions. Perhaps its success is due not only to the persistence of its creators, but to their clever marketing, spreading their story with articles such as Needle's.

Professionals in Other Fields

People from every walk of life can send you work—if they know you're out there. Not only should your accountant know what you do for a living; so should your hair stylist; your letter carrier; the waitstaff in your favorite restaurant; the doctor, nurse, and receptionist who treat you . . . Make this a nice, long list, and—as always—let them know you welcome referrals.

Other professionals may also help you, even if you don't use their services. If, say, you do home repair, put your card up at every hardware store and lumberyard.

Complementary Businesses

What don't you do that your customers often need? What suppliers have you built up relations with? Make sure they know what you do! I get many of my clients through local printers, reference librarians, photocopy shops, and typewriter or computer stores. I put notices on their bulletin boards and also supply business cards, so when someone asks if the clerk knows a writer or editor, he or she can just hand out my card. Consider providing a small commission to the person who referred you.

Competitors

Surprising as it may seem, they can be a great source of referrals. Businesses have to turn down work when they're already stretched too thin. Or competitors may find a job too much trouble and send it to someone else. Also, firms often define different niches and specializations. It makes sense to send a client to someone who can do exactly what he or she needs, if it doesn't quite fit your mix. Sending your overload to a competitor makes the customer remember your thoughtfulness, rather than grousing about your unwillingness to help. Furthermore, your competitors may send work to you.

Networking with the competition may feel strange at first. Trade association director Frank Fox notes that resistance is only natural. "People are leery of their competitors. There's a fear of . . . losing trade secrets." It can take awhile to get used to "the concept of openly talking and sharing experiences and ideas on every facet of running this business." However, for Fox, the benefits of networking are worth the effort. "The collective power of everybody working together for the common good makes a lot of sense and ultimately benefits every individual member well beyond their individual dues contribution."

Maintaining good relationships with your competitors allows you to share supply orders and get a better price for your bigger volume; turn to them if your equipment breaks down, or if you have a personal emergency on deadline; work together on a large rush job neither of you could have handled alone; subcontract to each other when one is overwhelmed and the other is slow; warn each other about "bad apple" suppliers and clients; find someone to take on work you can't do, and thus avoid alienating clients

Finally, if a competitor's business goes under, you may be in line for all their clients. Over the years,

I've inherited all the business from six firms that closed their doors. When I see a new local firm listed in my professional association directory or in an ad or on a bulletin board, I call up for a get-acquainted chat. Sometimes I've referred work to some of these businesses. Some of my competitors have worked for me as freelancers. Only one of them turned out to be a turkey, and he went out of business after about eight months. So call your competitors up or drop by to say howdy. Better yet, join a networking group of professionals in your field—or start one, if none exists. There really is strength in numbers.

Formal Networks

There are groups whose sole purpose is to have people meet to form networks and help each other out. In addition to trade-specific groups, these can range from the Chamber of Commerce to by-invitation-only networking parties. Evaluate costs and benefits carefully before joining.

Networking Online

Special-interest groups over the Internet are incredible resources for networking. Do a good job for one listmate, and the word is likely to spread (especially if you can get your client to write a public thank-you note). Within short order, you may even get referrals from people who've never used you.

To get this benefit, participate actively and ap-propriately, as we already discussed—and let people know what you do without beating them over the head with it.

Casual Acquaintances and Strangers

If you get into a casual conversation with anyone and you can turn it around to the subject of your business, hand that person a card—or reach into your bag and show off a copy of your latest book. You'll never know when you might get a big order. Or, perhaps, your conversationalist will tell someone else about you. Some people keep cards for years; when they finally call you, they may not even know how they got your card.

Whether you join a conversation on a bus, chat with the person behind you in line at the bank, or talk to a stranger at a party, any resulting business—or friendship—has a marketing cost of zero. Keep your ears open when people talk about your line of work; politely enter the conversation and hand out your business card.

⤴

Networking is only one way to find clients who are predisposed to work with you. The next chapter will show you how to grow your business by developing and promoting your expertise.

37

Climbing the Marketing Mountain:
Selling Your Expertise

To achieve the greatest return on your marketing investment, be seen as an expert. Then you can package and sell your expertise as one more set of commodities.

Eventually, your image will begin to create its own momentum. The recognition you will gain will build upon itself and spread outward in new directions; the more publicity you receive, the greater your credibility. As you become better known, people will increasingly turn to you—to quote in an article, provide advice . . . and solve their problems. These activities will add to your reputation as an expert and enable you to reap even more publicity.

At its best, this snowballing effect can lead to a juggernaut of useful publicity. While you will still need to cultivate your market, your enhanced reputation and stronger credentials will make your selling job easier. And more people will seek you out and present opportunities to you.

Think of it as a spiral or a pyramid. As you climb higher, you still conduct the same activities. But now you breathe rarefied air, above most of your competitors. But with each turn of the spiral, your audience increases. You can see ahead, to places that were not previously possible. For instance, you might have done occasional interviews in your local newspaper; now a major national magazine calls.

But never lose sight of where you've come from and how hard it was to make that climb. When an expert starts acting like a superstar—isolating himself or herself from the world below, burying customer service under a wall of arrogance—there's going to be trouble. You're not a rock-and-roll or movie celebrity, but a business owner or service provider. You and your fame exist to help others. If you forget that, your certification as an expert won't stop the world at large from bursting your balloon, and you'll be worse off than you were before.

— Define Yourself as an Expert —

The opportunities to build on past successes and create future ones are almost unlimited. Rather than name all of them here, I'll examine seven approaches—writing, lectures/performances, teaching, consulting, creating a holiday, running for office, franchising—that can:

- Enhance your credentials
- Increase your visibility and prestige

- Raise your income
- Lead to more opportunities

Not coincidentally, these activities are all news-worthy—and the organizations that engage you should help you promote them. Publicity is multiplied when different media releases, from different sources, promote an event. For instance, when you teach a college class, your firm and the college should both send out publicity.

— Writing —

We have already discussed writing articles or columns for local media and for online publications. But there are many other possibilities:

Trade and Technical Journals

We've looked at articles in mass-market publications; now, how about the trade journal market?

If you've done or researched something unique and innovative in your field, or compiled tips to pass on to your colleagues and customers, submit an article in a trade or academic journal or newsletter that serves your own or your clients' field.

Syndication

Once you have a successful column in one paper, try syndicating it.

Syndication is particularly useful for consultants, who rely on their reputations as a significant marketing tool, gain visibility as experts through publishing articles, work with a geographically diverse clientele, and often rely on a few lucrative, long-term accounts to carry much of their cash flow.

Syndicates make columns available very cheaply to many newspapers. Because syndicates rely on high volume, your column must have very wide appeal before a syndicate agrees to take it on.

You can also bypass the syndicate and market your column yourself. However, newspapers are much more likely to buy new material from existing syndicates—and building up to fifty markets or so in order to make the column provide a decent

return on your labor will take quite a bit of marketing work.

Consultant Jeffrey Lant uses his self-syndicated column to reach audiences in a whole new market niche: "I hear from at least one newsletter publisher per day. They say, 'Would you like to run your column in our publication?' I say, 'I'll give you copy—I'll fill up your newsletter, and all you have to do is run a resource box from me.'"

Editors send Lant a blank computer diskette, which he fills with articles for the editor to select. "Twenty-five articles fit on a disk—that's two years' worth of columns." For under a dollar, "I have two years' worth of publicity."

Books

When you publish a book (even if you published it yourself), you're automatically an expert. Use your book credential to solicit lecture and other writing contracts, speak at conferences, and so on—and sell your books at these events!

Direct-Mail Information

Any how-to article can also be sold directly through the mail—provided you didn't sell all rights or do the piece as a "work for hire." Jeffrey Lant and many other marketing gurus republish articles as "special reports"; Lant even uses his computer to personalize them with the name of the recipient. He uses the reports as premiums to reward large or prompt orders, but also sells them for seven dollars apiece. They cost him about a dollar to print and mail.

— Lectures and Performances —

This category includes public speaking, films, slide shows, gallery talks, cooking demonstrations, performances, and so forth, either live or on the air.

You are there to share some of your skills, insights, and anecdotes; educate your audience on new developments; and/or convince them that you can supply the solution to their problem.

Particularly in speaking, it's okay to be funny, or to run with your audience's mood—if you work well under the pressure of spontaneously revising your speech. One crowd may roar over the same jokes that leave another audience flat (and restless). Reach each audience where they are, at that precise moment.

I once gave a speech to a group of contractors. I noticed that the men's room was decrepit—and threw away my planned opening paragraph. Instead, I started, "How many of the men here have used the bathroom tonight? And how many of you saw the marketing opportunity for contractors in there?" After that, I could say anything I wanted; they paid attention!

Feed off the audience reaction. If they like your jokes, make more of them. If they're ultraserious, either lighten them up or use that solemnity to emphasize the importance of your points.

While I don't generally recommend prepackaged audiovisual presentations as sales tools, they can be valuable for education—if done well. A picture/sound combination is often a lot easier to grasp than words alone. Tip: If using overheads or slides, distribute them as a handout as well.

Planning Your Speech

When listening to the spoken word, few people can pay total attention 100 percent of the time; most people absorb only about 30 percent of what they hear. Also, your audience doesn't already know the material.

So, to get your point across:

- Speak slowly and distinctly—let the words sink into your listeners' consciousness.
- Tailor your remarks to each audience; a speech on the same topic will be very different to paying seminar attenders than to students required to attend.
- Know what *you* want from your audience (immediate product sales, visibility as an expert, long-term consulting clients, names for a newsletter mailing list, etc.).
- Start immediately with an attention grabber, for instance a question.
- Involve your audience as much as possible.

- Concentrate on no more than three major points, and restate these in different ways.
- Keep your presentation fairly brief (ten to thirty minutes is great).
- Vary your tone of voice and sentence length.
- Draw on emotions, not just intellect.
- Liven up the speech with examples, jokes, or visual examples.
- Provide a handout that repeats your most important points.
- Leave plenty of time for questions.

Practice your speech several times before the event. Even tape your rehearsal and then play the tape to see how you could have been better. Use a large-print outline instead of a full written text; only read your speech if you need to be 100 percent accurate for legal reasons.

If you're speaking longer than half an hour without a break, or if you are one lecturer at an all-day conference, break up the thick air; lead the audience in a "light and lively"—a quick thirty-second stretch, shaking out the arms and legs, maybe even a group shout. Everyone will be a lot more energized and have more concentration to sit through another big chunk of talking.

— Teaching —

A class is more sustained, covers more ground, and can permit a more intimate acquaintance with your students than a one-shot lecture. While a lecturer can prepare one or just a few presentations and repeat them endlessly, a teacher needs a topic for each session—all connected in a coherent plan.

Classes can be limited or ongoing. Modify your old lesson plans to reflect current students' needs, past participants' evaluations, and your own increasing knowledge of the subject.

Opportunities to Teach

Though you usually need a master's degree to teach regular college classes, there are many other avenues: adult or continuing education programs (at local colleges, vocational institutions, and high schools); distance learning programs on the Internet or through teleconferences; skills networks (groups of qualified people who offer many different classes in their homes or in a central location, but share administration, costs of catalog printing, etc.); cooperatives—similar to skills networks, but focusing on one profession (for example, graphic arts); private, specialized schools (in cooking, foreign language, dance/fitness, etc.); for-profit seminar companies; corporate training programs; independently offered courses (you set up the class, location, and all logistics—and keep the entire fee); affiliated classes offered through a local business; after-school programs for children; seminars on video- or audiotape (get them professionally produced, please!); professional conferences . . .

— Consulting —

As a consultant, you help solve specific problems for one individual, department, or organization, monitor their efforts, and follow up. You check in frequently, suggest new courses of action, make sure your advice is followed (or help the organization actualize its own decisions), *and* make sure your advice works. If there's resistance to your ideas, find out why people don't want to implement them, and come up with appropriate new or modified plans. If your plan isn't working, develop a new solution. Consulting is a highly individual process, can be quite in-depth, and may last a number of months.

Those who make their living consulting full-time to large companies and agencies find it incredibly lucrative. But even if you're getting $20 an hour working with a small agency, rather than $500 an hour for work with some wealthy corporation, you still develop a reputation for expertise.

Evaluate every consulting opportunity to make sure you *can* solve the stated problem. Consulting over your head alienates your client and gets you a reputation as a bumbler. Instead, turn down the job or call in additional consultants to address other areas outside your expertise.

— Your Own Holiday —

Everyone knows you can get a lot of marketing mileage by riding on the coattails of holidays and topical events—but do you know how easy it is to start your own holiday?

As I wrote this, I was preparing for the first International Frugal Fun Day, October 2, 1999. I sent in a form to *Chase's Annual Events* and e-mailed the editor of *Celebrate Today,* establishing the first annual National Frugal Fun Day. (See the resources section for contact information for those two publications.) Almost immediately, I got an e-mail about the new holiday from Japan; from then on, all future publicity changed "National" to "International." I also sought community involvement by posting reader suggestions on a Web page <http://www.frugalfun.com/frugalfundayideas.html>.

My goal for this year: two stories in national print media, ten major regional publications, and at least a dozen radio interviews. And next year, I expect even more.

As it turned out, I got coverage in the *Japan Times* and several newspapers in my area. I also targeted newspapers in the Upper Midwest United States, where I tend to do well with radio appearances. Some of these may have used the information; I don't have a clipping service, so I don't know for sure.

More importantly, the holiday was mentioned in several publications within the frugality niche, resulting in a significant increase in traffic to my Web site and in subscribers to my monthly tipsheet.

Best of all, Frugal Fun Day opened the door to a conversation with a reporter at a major women's magazine. Though her article is not about Frugal Fun Day, I'm expecting to be prominently featured in an article about frugal holiday gift ideas.

I didn't have a chance to do much radio marketing, even after being picked up by one of the "prep services" that supply radio producers with guest ideas. I netted only two radio appearances tied to the holiday.

Of course, now I have a full year to build for the second annual International Frugal Fun Day.

Even though I didn't make my radio goal, the press I did receive built visibility for my book on low-cost fun. It gives the news media a nice, easy hook.

Charles Hayes, whose book on lifelong learning was the subject of the sample press releases in chapter 8, sponsors Self-University Week every September. He also has a thorough Web page on his holiday, at <http://www.autodidactic.com./selfweek.htm>.

— Running for Office —

For people with an issue-focused agenda, running for office offers sustained publicity, and thus continuous attention to a cause. Particularly in smaller communities, running for office is almost unequaled as a way to market ideas—and actually make a difference locally. And you don't have to win in order to make an impact!

Political campaigns can further a business, social service, or community activist agenda; you gain media coverage, community support, and perhaps accomplish your goals. Organizing is possible for or against any number of causes; some possibilities include: industrial growth; equitable taxes; alternative housing and social support services; better schools; funding for arts or social services; traffic safety; changes in laws regarding advertising signs; minority rights; zoning, planning, and conservation issues; ethics and/or efficiency in government; a need for youth programs (business owners: campaign for a youth job-training corps!).

I've run for citywide office twice, on an affordable-housing and traffic safety platform. Both times, I had a major impact on shaping the discourse. Each campaign resulted in significant changes: the appointment of two mayoral committees, new legislation, and a tilt by swing voters toward addressing these concerns. Furthermore, my campaign helped defeat a longtime incumbent who had blocked progress on a whole raft of issues.

Each time, I garnered about forty articles in the two main local papers, numerous appearances on local radio news, and occasional TV coverage—

nearly all of which mentioned my business, as did my campaign brochures. Over a decade later, my business continues to grow as a result of my political exposure.

These campaigns not only put me before the public, but made me a known figure within local government. If I have something to discuss with our mayor or a city official, my calls are put through and my concerns are heard.

Did I win the elections? No. But one campaign I managed and several I advised did win—completely changing the political power structure in town. Did I accomplish my goals? To a large degree, yes.

You don't have to win in order to make an impact!

A friend ran for Congress on a shoestring campaign. He had no intention of winning. But he wanted to focus attention on campaign finance reform. He received substantial press coverage, participated in some debates, and received even more publicity when he was denied access to other debates. Since that campaign, his grassroots community group has been considered important in the local political scene. In fact, when that group ran a debate in the next election, it was cosponsored by three major media outlets. His run for office certainly helped to secure this kind of legitimacy.

Advice to Prospective Office-Seekers

- Think through your positions.
- Run to focus the community on your issues and beliefs, not to get personal glory.
- Take it seriously—get out there and knock on doors, submit press statements at least twice a week, and participate in every debate and candidate forum.
- Address your concerns to city officials even after the election—win or lose.

- Get to know the important people in your government—not just elected officials, but department administrators.
- Treat voters' concerns seriously; listen well.
- Never slander your opponent or any group of voters.
- Keep scrupulously clean and honest.
- Avoid blatant self-aggrandizement, but don't hesitate to build recognition for your business, community group, and/or accomplishments.
- Have fun!

— Franchising —

In this scenario, you train others how to do what you do; provide them with promotional materials, authorized decoration and architecture schemes, equipment, and ongoing technical support; and charge a one-time fee plus a percentage of sales. The franchisee not only buys training, but a recognized brand name. Don't franchise unless you can say yes to all four keys to successful franchising:

- Others can duplicate what you do.
- Franchise holders can't continue duplicating it without help from you.
- Once it is well established (say, after six months), the business should be able to run successfully with minimal intervention from the central office.
- Each franchise will generate sufficient revenues to be worth your investment of training and materials, and the owner's investment of time and money.

There isn't that much damage you can do if you teach a bad class or write a mediocre article. But a bad franchise agreement could bankrupt you. Have all sample agreements looked over by a franchise lawyer, and examine the consequences of your agreements. If you're not sure what something means, ask!

— Doing It Right —

Obviously, a full discussion of any of these methods is outside the scope of this book. If these avenues appeal to you, research them thoroughly. Nonetheless, here are some brief pointers in order to get you started as an expert:

- Ask an *honest* friend to critique your article or speech ahead of time (you want critical feedback, not a pat on the back).
- Be clear and direct.
- Judge your audience.
- Be a good listener.
- Finally, evaluate the end product.

Consider criticism as a kind of market research. And for more about that, just turn the page.

38

Tick Them Off

Even though your publicity program will cost far less than a traditional saturation approach, it adds up: You'll probably spend somewhere between $100 and $50,000 each year on marketing—realistically, in most cases, from $1,000 to $20,000. Thus, you need to keep track of what works and what doesn't. You must develop a system to monitor your responses—and incorporate the data into your publicity and marketing planning! Don't skip this vital step! Without this small effort, you're wasting your far greater marketing investment.

Jere Matlock <mailto:jere@gte.net> cites a one-eighth-page ad that he ran for years; it continued to outpull every other ad in a magazine (as measured by reader response cards), because the ad was based on an informal customer survey and thus addressed his audience's actual needs. The ad wasn't fancy, and he was under great pressure to monkey with it from ad sales people. But every change lowered the response, so he kept going back to the original format.

Ultimately, it's not enough to know what brought you your customers. You also need to know what they want. Why did they choose you instead of a competitor? Which benefits pulled them in? And most importantly, what else do they need that you can potentially supply?

Here's an example from my own business. When we started offering multiple copies of résumés on our laser printer, at a price substantially higher than photocopy shops, we didn't know if there would be a market for it. Rather than invest in a huge inventory and hope for the best, we asked clients if they'd like us to offer that service. When we got a strong positive response, we invested in one hundred dollars' worth of specialty paper. We also put up a flier in our office giving two reasons to get copies from us instead of a photocopy shop, and posted samples of a résumé in each of four types of paper. And at the end of each appointment, we asked the client about copies. By the end of the first month, we had sold over a fourth of our paper stock and had already made back our one hundred dollars, so we ordered a larger inventory. A decade later, copies continue to be a profit center.

— Points of Interaction —

You interact with your public at several stages. Each of those interaction points allows you to check on how the word is getting out. Monitor at least one cross section.

*Y*ou must develop a system to monitor your responses—and incorporate the data into your publicity and marketing planning.

I monitor my publicity when a client makes an appointment, sends in a work order, or orders a book, rather than at the initial inquiry—that way, my record reflects where my publicity draws real clients, not browsers. We log the source directly on our appointment book, then transfer it to our income spreadsheet. Thus we can also track which publicity generally brings in the most lucrative clients.

But organizations much larger than mine can track just as carefully. For example, 20/20 Vision has over eleven thousand members, and its staff knows how each one learned of the group. Director Lois Barber explains: "All of the brochures have a place on them that says 'Where did you hear about 20/20 Vision?' So whenever someone subscribes, we just enter the source into the computer. And we do weekly tallies on the number of inquiries and the number of subscriptions from each source."

— Techniques of Monitoring —

Direct Question of Each Client

Simply ask, "How did you hear about us?" Follow up if you don't get a complete answer; when a client saw a flier, ask where it was. If you have several different ones posted, ask what the headline said. When a friend recommended your company, ask the name of the friend. Instruct your cashiers or salespeople to ask about the source of the customer's knowledge about you, and either write the information or check a box off on the sales slip. When someone subscribes to a newsletter from your Web site, the sign-up form can ask what led the visitor to you. Warranty or response cards are a variant: You ask through a printed form.

For retail business where it can be hard to track, advertising consultant Michael Corbett suggests an

Date	Amt. Collected	Type of Work	Source
4/1	$90.00	Marketing	wom (word-of-mouth)
4/1	$23.00	Book Order	DUC (Internet discussion group)
4/1	$500.00	Marketing	prev (previous client)
4/2	$50.45	Résumé	wom
4/2	$46.25	Résumé	pvpb (Pioneer Valley phone book)
4/2	$56.60	Résumé	Hamp (Hampshire phone book)
4/2	$90.00	Marketing	I-Sales (Internet discussion group)
4/3	$44.03	Résumé	wom
4/3	$9.90	Copies	prev
4/4	$51.50	Résumé	wom
4/4	$18.00	Cover Letter	prev
4/5	$20.00	Book Order	PMA-L (Internet discussion group)

alternative: Create spreadsheets of daily floor traffic, average ticket, closing percentage, and gross sales against all your advertising and promotional efforts.

Show of Hands

At any gathering, ask people to raise their hands every time you mention a way that they heard about the event. Encourage people to raise hands as many times as appropriate. For example:

"How many people heard about us on the radio? Which stations—anyone hear us on WXYZ? How about WAAA? WPNQ? Great. How about newspapers—anyone find us in the Springfield paper? How about the *Daily Democrat*? Anyone see the write-up in "Tyrone Trevor's Best Bets?" What about posters? Where'd you see them? Who heard about this event from friends? Several people didn't raise your hands at all. What brought you here?"

Tracking Codes

When using direct response—mailed orders, discount coupons, Internet clicks—you can track automatically. Code your return envelope, order form, and/or coupon.

For classified or display advertising, code each insertion. If an ad runs in four consecutive issues of a certain publication, you might want the first month's mail to go to Department B-1, the next to Department B-2, and so on. Meanwhile, another magazine ad running at the same time might be coded C-1 through C-4.

Codes can be as elaborate as you need them to be. When you need to track several variables, your code might be several digits long. For instance, if you're tracking by publication, issue, placement, headline, and body copy, you'd need at least five digits. Change the first two digits and track the same offer as a direct-mail piece, by mailing list and date mailed.

When using coupons, always include the words "limit one per purchase," to keep customers from stocking up on coupons and getting your products virtually free. And use an expiration date.

Codes can cover many media, too—not just print ads. If you're using a direct-response phone number, track by listing a specific extension. On the Internet, either use question marks embedded in the URL or set up mirror pages, where only the URL changes. (For a more in-depth explanation of Internet tracking, visit <http://www.frugalfun.com/keyingemail.html>.)

Discount or Premium for Mentioning Ad

With electronic media, you rely on the client telling you why he or she came to you. So pretend your radio or TV ad is a coupon: Announce a discount or give out a premium for mentioning the ad. Each cashier should have a notepad to mark off how many were claimed.

Build Marketing Power from Your Database by Tracking RFM

To take tracking a step farther, consider setting up your database so you can extract information on "RFM"—recency, frequency, monetary: when and how often they buy, and how much they spend.

If you haven't heard from someone in a while, drop a note that says you'll take him or her off the mailing list unless you hear otherwise.

Now you can organize your list into three groups: prime customers, deadwood, and the middle. If 20 percent of your customers bring you 80 percent of your sales, obviously it makes sense to do a lot of "valued-customer" promotions to them. Mail less frequently to the 60 percent or so who might make up the next 15 percent of your sales, and only mail occasional offers—with genuine value—to the low-priority 20 percent folks who give you your last 5 percent of sales.

Your numbers will be different from this hypothetical example, of course—but many marketing analyses do use some sort of 80/20 formula. If you can do 20 percent of the effort to achieve 80 percent of the results, you're being cost-efficient and will have more money to grow your business.

Another slant: If you haven't heard from someone in a while, drop a note that says you'll take him or her off the mailing list unless you hear otherwise—or offer a "get-reacquainted" deal. (If they do respond, keep them on, even if they're not buying right away. It would be a shame to get rid of "deadwood" and miss a big order.)

— Use the Data—

If an ad doesn't draw, drop it or rewrite it. When press releases and PSAs to certain newspapers or broadcast stations never seem to bring any return, drop them from your active list after a few months.

If you had only a handful of inquiries from one of your listings, drop it. And if one category seems to work particularly well, spiff it up a little more.

When they change format, or if you have an event that's of more interest to their readers, try them again. When a particular Internet discussion group proves effective for you, post often! If your best bulletin board notices get covered up or torn down quickly, replace them enough to keep your message visible.

When you renew your Yellow Pages listings, examine which brought in responses. If you had only a handful of inquiries from one of your listings, drop it. And if one category seems to work particularly well, spiff it up a little more.

39

Branding: The Buzz

Every marketing effort should reinforce your other marketing and build brand recognition for you and your services. Remember Jeffrey Lant's formula: Successful marketing reaches each prospect at least seven times within eighteen months or less, with different, complementary approaches. If you use several marketing strategies as part of a fully conceived overall plan, the whole will far exceed the sum of its parts.

You may not use the full range of marketing methods. But always choose at least three to five complementary marketing methods working together. Among many possibilities:

- Yellow Pages, press releases, posted fliers, a simple Web site (to promote a small service business at minimal costs)
- Classifieds, radio ads, brochures, and letters to the editor (a good combination for an ethnic or specialty store)
- Display ads, in-store marketing, radio (the traditional, costly approach)
- Articles, talk show appearances, Internet discussion groups, a comprehensive Web site, seminars, trade shows (great for consultants)

Select the methods that best fit your goals and marketing plan, think about how they will work well together, back them up with the best products and service you can, and you've got a winning combination.

— "Creating the Buzz" —

Your total marketing will build on itself; if you use several of the techniques you've learned, the whole will be more than the sum of its parts. Concert promoter Jordi Herold calls this "creating the buzz. . . . The thing that's more important than anything else is the perception that this event matters. That's more important than all the other things, although it's harder to quantify, less tangible. But that's what we aspire to. You can create the buzz for any event—it's a question of marshaling resources toward creating that sense that something's happening. I'll ask how many people heard about a show on the radio, newspaper—three hands go up. But a hundred people will raise their hands for word of mouth. Once I've created that [word-of-mouth] buzz, I almost stop advertising." Herold notes that his customers don't even know where they heard about a show or why people are talking about it—it's the cumulative effect of all his other promotion.

If you can get people to talk about what you do or sell as part of the general discourse, you've created the buzz. It could be an event, a product, a reputation for service—whatever it is, if people are hearing good things about your offer from many sources, they will think of you first when they want what you have.

Movies are a great example of this phenomenon. For instance, when a friend of mine mentioned the movie *Thelma and Louise* to me early one summer, I'd never heard of it. But by the time I saw it less than a month later, it had entered the discourse. Not only had I heard quite a bit about it from various friends, but I'd seen letters to the editor, mentions in Op-Ed columns, even a political cartoon.

If you can get people to talk about what you do or sell as part of the general discourse, you've created the buzz.

In less than a month, *Thelma and Louise* had become an archetype. The mention of those names immediately brings to mind the image of two spunky women traveling together in an old convertible.

Movies have often played this role: Think of *Life Is Beautiful, The Wizard of Oz, Titanic, Rainman, E.T., The Godfather,* or image creators such as Charlie Chaplin, Humphrey Bogart, Katharine Hepburn. Each of those specific movie titles or actors will bring to mind a strong image, whether or not you've actually seen the movies.

Clearly, most of you will not position yourselves as a household name throughout the English-speaking world. But you can create the buzz within your own market niche. If you run one of three hardware stores in town, you want to "brand" your store for product selection and customer service. If you sell discount camera equipment, you want people to automatically think of you when they want the lowest prices. If you write marketing materials as I do, you want to be associated with breaking through the mental clutter. Big corporations spend millions on branding. Because you know your market—and have read this book—you can brand in your own niche—for a pittance!

To promote an event, create a buzz within a short time frame—begin perhaps a couple of months ahead with a low-key presentation just to get it in the background, and then intensify the campaign in the weeks just before the date. What works is not so much any one promotional activity, but the total of all of them. As Jordi Herold puts it, "It's a question of repeating your message in as many media as possible. Someone might read a newspaper blurb and think it's somewhat interesting, then they hear the DJ talk about it, then they read our calendar or see a poster and they go to an event."

Products, as opposed to events, require a more sustained focus. Naturally, you'll contact your prospects through multiple venues. Each will reinforce all the other messages, until ultimately the customer no longer knows what convinced him or her to buy—only that "everybody" was talking about it.

— In Sum —

A quick recap, now. Successful marketing:

- Reaches the exact people who are most likely to want what you've got
- Hits them several times with a variety of approaches
- Stands together thematically across the different media
- Gets the biggest return for the smallest investment
- Is clear and to the point, as well as visually striking
- Stresses benefits to the consumer—and consequences of failure to act
- Makes it easy for the prospect to take the next action step

- Fully exploits opportunities for free publicity
- Provides additional opportunity for later follow-up
- Assures the prospect his or her money will be well spent (and provides a guarantee)
- Is backed by quality in all facets of your operation

In short, successful marketing makes an impact on the person exposed to it.

After all, as Jeffrey Lant puts it, "What is the alternative? Spending my own money on expensive paid ads that may or may not work [or on] direct mail that may not even be delivered! . . . instead of drawing from my major capital resource: my brain."

The amazing thing about good marketing is how easy it is to do it. Therefore, it's a surprise that so many marketers continue to produce bland, ineffective, egotistical marketing.

You hold in your hand the key to getting away from those ineffective approaches. You have the power to make every marketing dollar count, and you have the skills to either create the materials yourself or scrutinize the work of others you may hire. You can do it!

Good luck, and let me know how you make out. You'll find full contact information, along with other resources, in the resources section. Peace be with you.

Resources

Without trying to be comprehensive, I'd like to leave you with a few places to go for specific kinds of help. Where the product is not widely available, I've listed complete addresses (all in the United States). Otherwise, your local bookstore or librarian ought to be able to help.

— Accurate Writing & More —

My firm can provide several kinds of assistance—and you can request to work directly with me. Also, because we focus on affordability, we keep our prices affordable, too.

Contact us at:

Accurate Writing & More
P.O. Box 1164
Northampton, MA 01061-1164
(413) 586-2388 Fax: 617-219-0153
Outside Area Code 413:
1-800-683-WORD (683-9673)
e-mail: info@frugalfun.com
URLs: http://www.frugalfun.com
        http://www.accuratewritingandmore.com

Strategic Marketing Planning

We'll work with you to conceptualize a company name, an image, a marketing program, or a public relations campaign, or help you develop a reputation as an available speaker or talk show guest.

Copywriting Assistance

If you get stuck trying to write your own materials, or if you want your own efforts critiqued and/or edited, we'll be happy to help you out. We will write press releases, brochures, newsletters, direct mail, advertising copy, fliers, Web site copy, or just about anything else you need in the way of marketing materials, informational resources, technical assistance pieces (we're great at translating jargon into everyday English), correspondence, career aids (résumés, curriculum vitae, cover letters, media/publications summaries, etc.), or grants and proposals.

Public Speaking

My partner, D. Dina Friedman, offers classes and tutorials in Public Speaking for the Terrified. Also, I can speak to your community group or appear on your talk show, on a wide range of topics related to marketing, writing, careers, and having more fun for less money.

— Internet Resources—

I know you are budget-conscious, or you wouldn't be reading this book. So under this heading, I'm only going to list resources that are absolutely free.

Of the vast number of great e-mail newsletters and discussion lists that deal with marketing, a few stand head and shoulders above the rest. I don't pretend to be comprehensive here; these are places that I personally have found very useful:

Ralph Wilson's *Web Marketing Today,* archived at
    <http://www.wilsonweb.com>
Internet Sales Discussion List, archived at <http://
    www.mmgco.com/isales/>
Internet Advertising Discussion List, archived at
    <http://guava.ease.lsoft.com/archives/
    i-advertising.html>
VirtualPROMOTE Gazette, archived in a zip file at
    <http://www.virtualpromote.com/gazarch.zip>

My own site, <http://www.frugalfun.com>, contains over three hundred articles to save you money, enhance your quality of life, and help you run your business better. If you printed out the entire site, it would be over two thousand single-spaced pages of information. The most important pages for entrepreneurs and marketers are *Down to Business* magazine, <http://www.frugalfun.com/dtb.html>, and Marketing Resources, <http://www.frugalfun.com/marketing.html> (this page includes the complete archives for my Monthly Frugal Marketing Tips, among other goodies). There's also tons of information about frugal fun, which is the topic of my other book, *The Penny-Pinching Hedonist: How to Live Like Royalty with a Peasant's Pocketbook,* as well as the name of my domain. (Contact me if you'd like to get your own copy of this 280-page road map to living better and spending less.)

If you publish information for a living or as a marketing tool, the Pub-Forum discussion list is invaluable. This is a large, unmoderated list of independent book publishers with a strong internal culture and a typical volume of fifty to one hundred messages per day. To sign up, send a blank e-mail to: <mailto:pub-forum-subscribe@onelist.com>

— Calendars —

If you tie any marketing gimmicks to current events or anniversaries, look into these:

The Timetables of History, Touchstone/Simon and
    Schuster. Great if you want to have promotions
    pegged to long-ago events. For instance, 2001
    marks the hundredth anniversary of ragtime
    jazz, transatlantic telegraphy, and the motor
    bike—not to mention the four hundredth
    anniversary of Shakespeare's *Troilus and Cressida.*
    Also available as a CD-ROM for computers.

The next three do for each day of the year what *Timetables* does for whole years (my own Frugal Fun Day is listed in *Chase's* and *Celebrate Today*):

Chase's Annual Events, Contemporary Books, Inc.,
    180 N. Michigan Avenue, Chicago, IL 60601.
    (312) 782-9182.
Gale Holidays and Anniversaries of the World, Gale
    Research, Inc., Detroit, MI, 48277-0748. (800)
    877-GALE or (313) 961-2242.
Celebrate Today, (Open Horizons, P.O. Box 205,
    Fairfield, IA 52556. (515) 472-6130, <http://
    www.bookmarket.com>

— Directories —

This isn't intended to be a complete list; check with your reference librarian for specific needs. If you're serious about selling articles, you'll want to own the first one; most of the rest of them are very pricey and go out of date quickly, so work with your library reference department instead of spending several hundred dollars.

Writer's Market, F&W Publications. A must for serious magazine freelancing; also has a limited directory of syndicates. Be sure to buy the current edition, replace it at least every other year, and verify any contact information before you query; this one goes stale even before it's off press.

Bacon's Publicity Checker, 332 S. Michigan Avenue, Chicago, IL 60604. (800) 621-0561.

Broadcast and Cable Yearbook, Broadcasting Publications, 1705 de Sales Street NW, Washington, DC 20036. (800) 638-7827 or (202) 659-2340.

Feature News Publicity Outlets, Resource Media, Inc., Box 307, Kent, CT 06757. (800) 441-3839 or (203) 927-4616.

Gale Directory of Publications and Broadcast Media; Gale Encyclopedia of Associations; Gale Periodical Directory; Gale Trade Show and Professional Exhibits Directory; (all from Gale Research, Inc., Detroit, MI, 48277-0748. (800)-877-GALE or (313) 961-2242.

National Directory of Addresses and Telephone Numbers, World Almanac Publications, 200 Park Avenue, New York, NY 10166. Includes major media listings by category and city (although not pegged to individual names). Also lists computer database services, an alphabetical listing of corporations, associations, government agencies, and quite a bit more. This one you might also want to own; since it doesn't have specific contact names, its information will stay current for several years.

Oxbridge Directory of Newsletters, Oxbridge Communications, Inc., 150 Fifth Avenue, New York, NY 10011. (212) 741-0231.

Standard Rate and Data Service—Direct Mail List Rates and Data, Standard Rate and Data Service, Inc./Macmillan, Inc., 3004 Glenview Road, Wilmette, IL 60091. (312) 256-6067. They also publish an advertising rate book.

Working Press of the Nation (lists freelance writers by subject of interest), National Research Bureau, 310 S. Michigan Avenue, Chicago, IL 60604. (800) 456-4555.

— Books and Other Info Products —

There are literally thousands of useful books, tapes, and other tools for marketers. This subjective and very small list will get you started. I've had to leave many out so as not to overwhelm; feel free to expand this list.

General Marketing/Copywriting/Direct Mail

Abraham, Jay. *Getting Everything You Can Out of All You've Got.* St. Martin's Press, New York. A good overview on marketing creatively. Abraham's seminars sometimes run $5000. This substantial book is a lot of good ideas for $25. The chapter on barter is the best thing I've seen on the subject.

Kennedy, Dan. *The Ultimate Marketing Plan.* Bob Adams Publishing, Holbrook, MA. An unusually cheap introduction to the thinking of one of the gurus of the business opportunity set—and an awful lot of great, commonsense marketing advice.

Lant, Jeffrey. *Cash Copy.* JLA Publications, 50 Follen Street #507, Cambridge, MA 02138. If you do any marketing other than free media coverage and word-of-mouth, read this book before you write your first word.

Levinson, Jay Conrad. *Guerrilla Marketing.* Houghton Mifflin, Boston, MA. Widely considered a classic, this book is full of excellent tips. Provides the theory for which this book is the practice, according to *Home Office Computing* magazine. Many excellent sequels in the series provide not only useful information but an important lesson about successful branding.

Powers, Melvin. *How to Get Rich in Mail Order.* Wilshire Books, 12015 Sherman Road, N. Hollywood, CA 91605. Good coverage of direct mail, classified, display classified, and display ads.

Vitale, Joe. *Cyberwriting*. Amacom, New York. A master copywriter looks at successful online promotion, but his wisdom is applicable to any marketing materials.

Group M's Direct Mail Bootcamp. A four-day seminar with Ted Nicholas, Gary Halbert, and many other direct-marketing gurus, captured on twenty-four cassette tapes and a workbook. Not cheap, but if large-scale direct mail is going to be a big player in your marketing mix, this the single best info product I've come across. Available from me, at (800) 683-9673 or <http://www.frugalfun.com/marketingtapes-html>. (I was hired to write a sales letter for these tapes, and liked them so much I became a dealer for them).

Press Coverage and Public Relations

Baker, Bob. *Newsthinking: The Secret of Great Newswriting*. Writer's Digest Books, Cincinnati, OH. Aimed at reporters and writers, but his principles are sound in learning how to think like an editor and make your story come alive.

Hausman, Carl, and Benoit, Philip. *Positive Public Relations*. Tab, New York. Multitargeted, clearly written. Extensive coverage of graphic arts and photography. Minimal coverage of advertising. A good supplement to this book.

Graphics and Printing/Traditional Advertising

Corbett, Michael. *The Thirty-three Ruthless Rules of Local Advertising*. Breakthru Publishing, P.O. Box 2866, Houston, TX 77252. (800) 227-1152, PinBooks@aol.com. A must-read if you're going to spend any money on space ads.

Floyd, Elaine, and Lee Wilson. *Advertising from the Desktop*. Ventana Press, Chapel Hill, NC. Your graphic artist should spend some time with this book; it shows how design can support and enhance a sales message.

International Paper Co. *Pocket Pal*. 77 W. 45th Street, New York, NY 10036. Inexpensive printing and graphics primer.

Parker, Roger C. *Looking Good in Print* and *The Makeover Book*. Both from Ventana Press, Chapel Hill, NC. A clearly written pair with lots of examples on how to make your copy not only look attractive but stand out in the clutter. More attention to marketing concerns than in most design books.

Pickens, Judy. *The Copy-to-Press Handbook: Preparing Words and Art for Print*. John Wiley and Sons, New York. Another good guide to working with printers and artists.

Marketing Online

Kent, Peter. *Poor Richard's Web Site* and *Poor Richard's Internet Marketing and Promotions* (with Tara Calishain). Both from Top Floor Publishing, P.O. Box 260072, Lakewood, CT 80226 <http://www. topfloor.com>. Commonsense guides to Web site design and promotion.

O'Keefe, Steve. *Publicity on the Internet*. John Wiley and Sons, New York. The classic reference work for effective online marketing.

Face-to-Face Sales/Customer Assessment and Self-Assessment

Phillips, Michael, and Salli, Rasberry. *Marketing Without Advertising*. Nolo Press, 950 Parker Street, Berkeley, CA 94710. (800) 992-6656. Perhaps the last word on customer service as a marketing tool.

Siskind, Barry. *The Successful Exhibitor's Handbook*. Self-Counsel Press, Bellingham, WA. Detailed analysis of visual, auditory, and kinesthetic learning styles. As a trade show guide, it's more useful for large exhibitors than small ones.

Werth, Jacques, and Nicholas E. Ruben. *High Probability Selling*. High Probability, Philadelpia (800) 394-7762 or (215) 968-8827. Expounds on the theory that you'll sell more by targeting the people who are most likely to buy.

Yeager, Neil. *CareerMap*. John Wiley and Sons, New York. The best tools I've seen for self-assessment of skills and interests. It wasn't intended for business marketing, but his techniques are easily adaptable toward developing your own promotion strategy.

Audio/Video/Film/Multimedia

Byers, Judy. *Words on Tape*. AudioCP Publishing, 1660 S. Albion, Suite 309, Denver, CO 80222. <http://www.audiocp.com>. The definitive guide to bringing out informational products in audio formats.

Landen, Hal. *Marketing with Video*. Oak Tree Press, RD1 Box 378, Slate Hill, NY 10973 (914) 355-1400. If you're going to make a marketing video, this book will save you a pile. He learned his trade on *60 Minutes,* among other places.

Michaels, Bernie. *Writing Informational Video Scripts* and *How to Get Your Message Across: A Film and Videotape Primer.* These two inexpensive self-published pamphlets provide a good introductory course into effective audiovisual work, including a useful glossary. Bernie is an experienced industrial/commercial scriptwriter. For pricing, send a self-addressed stamped envelope to Bernie Michaels & Associates, 26 Homestead Lane, Ludlow, MA 01056, or call (413) 583-6080.

Book Production and Promotion

Bell, Patricia. *The Pre-Publication Handbook.* Cat's Paw Press, 9561 Woodridge Circle, Eden Prairie, MN 55347. This is the book to read if you're considering becoming a publisher and wondering if you have what it takes.

Kremer, John. *1001 Ways to Market Your Books.* Open Horizons, P.O. Box 205, Fairfield, IA 52556. (515) 472-6130, <http://www.bookmarket.com>.

Poynter, Dan. *The Self-Publishing Manual.* Para Publishing, P.O. Box 8206-240, Santa Barbara, CA 93117-1047. (800) PARAPUB, <http:www.parapublishing. com>.

Ross, Tom, and Marilyn Ross. *The Complete Guide to Self-Publishing.* Writer's Digest Books, Cincinnati, OH. Though they cover the same material, read both Poynter and Ross. Their perspectives are different on many technical and marketing issues, and you'll be a much more informed consumer if you absorb both.

Public Speaking/Media Training

Jud, Brian. *You're on the Air.* Marketing Directions, Avon, CT, (800) 562-4357, <http://www.marketingdirections.com>. Includes a video and two small books: *It's ShowTime*—for media training—and *Perpetual Promotion*—a guide to contacting media and booking appearances. The books are also available separately.

Otte, Miriam. *Marketing with Speeches and Seminars.* Zest Press, 1998, 8315 Lake City Way NE, Suite 139, Seattle, WA 98115. (206) 523-0302). The only book I've seen that focuses specifically on speeches and seminars as a tool for recruiting new business.

Naming a Business or Product

Barrett, Fred. *Names That Sell: How to Create Great Names for Your Company, Product, or Service.* Alder Press, P.O. Box 1503, Portland, OR 97207 (503) 246-7983.

— Final Words —

Your comments are welcome; if any suggestions you make are incorporated into future revisions, you'll be mentioned in the acknowledgments. I'd love to know how this book made a difference in your marketing—and also if you think there are places where the book needs improvement. Please write to me at the address on page 292. If you'd like a personal answer, please either use e-mail or enclose a self-addressed stamped envelope.

Thank you for staying with me all the way through.

Success, always!
Shel Horowitz

Index

Elenbaas, Dan, 276–77
e-mail, 184–96. *See also* Internet
 address, reading, 184
 America Online (AOL), 180
 articles, circulating, 188–89
 attachments, 187, 190
 automated, 193–95
 cost of accounts, 172
 data security, 195
 digest, 176
 direct mail, used for, 119
 etiquette, 186–87, 197–98
 faxes sent/received via, 167
 free, 180–81
 HTML, 176, 195–96
 mailing lists, 125, 188–93, 214
 mass mailings, 188
 media releases, 49–51
 multiple readers, access to, 188–93
 "on vacation" messages, 186, 193
 opt-in, 177
 participation, value of, 189–90
 programs, 181
 responding to, 187
 rich format, 195–96
 sig, 177, 185, 197–201
 targeted internal-list, 190–91
 targeted personal messages,
  184–86, 195
 trade show prospects, follow up
  to, 261
emoticon, 176
employees
 customer service by, 239
 sales force (*See* sales force,
  management of)
entertainment publications, 37
envelopes, direct mail, 106
ethnic radio programs, 160
events
 current events or anniversaries,
  marketing tied to, 293
 highlighted, 59–60
 reviews/previews, 60
expertise, selling, 279–84
 consulting, 282
 defining self as expert, 279–80
 franchising, 284
 holiday, creating, 282–83

lectures and performances, 280–81
 political office, running for,
  283–84
 teaching, 281–82
 writing, 280
eyeballs, 176
e-zine, 176

F
family, referrals from, 276
FAQ, 176
faxes, 167
 broadcast, 167
 for direct mail, 119
 e-mail, sending/receiving via, 167
fax-backs, automatic, 167
 publicity distributed via, 28
feature articles, 57–59
 collaboration on, 69
 examples, 66–67
 promoting, 64–65
 writing your own, 65–68
features, television/radio, 64–65
field (database), 39
fills, 22, 24
filter, filtering, 176
finance publications, 37
flags, 135
flames (Internet), 176, 187, 188
fliers, 105, 127–33
 color, 129–33
 cost, 128–29, 133
 design, 128–33
 example, 130
 exchanging with other companies,
  124
 gang runs, 133
 graphics, 129
 nonposted, 128
 posted, 127–28
 size/shape, 133
 tear-offs/take-aways, 128
 texture, 133
 type, 129
FlightLink, 167
floppy disks, 169
follow-up
 autoresponders follow-ups,
  194–95

direct mail follow-up to
  telemarketing, 120–21
 e-mail follow-up, to trade show
  prospects, 261
 sales, generation of follow-up,
  124–25
font, 22
Forbes Online, 195
formats
 classified advertisements, 83
 media releases, 43–44
forum, 176
four-color, 22
Fox, Frank, 99, 120, 235, 274
frame, 176
franchising, 284
Franklin, Skip, 276–77
Friedman, D. Dina, 292
Friedman, Stanley D., 31, 42, 44, 64
friendliness, assertive, 243
friends, referrals from, 276
frugalfun.com, 171, 178, 192, 210,
  218, 282, 293
FTP (File Transfer Protocol), 176
full-size page, 22

G
Gaines, Barry, 174
Gale Directory of Publications, 37
Gale Encyclopedia of Associations, 37
*Gale Holidays and Anniversaries of the
  World,* 293
general interest publications, 37
geographical advertising coops, 94
geographical market, 5
geographical media outlets, 36
Gibson, William, 171
Gidwitz, Teri, 51
GIF, (Graphic Image Format) 176,
  204
Gill, Peter, 51
Goodman, Danny, 213
GoTo.com, 212–13
graduated (gradated) fill, 22
grammar, 21
graphic element, 22
graphics, 22, 24, 295
 fliers, 129
 glossary, 22–24

CHELSEA GREEN

Sustainable living has many facets. Chelsea Green's celebration of the sustainable arts has led us to publish trend-setting books about organic gardening, solar electricity and renewable energy, innovative building techniques, regenerative forestry, local and bioregional democracy, and whole foods. The company's published works, while intensely practical, are also entertaining and inspirational, demonstrating that an ecological approach to life is consistent with producing beautiful, eloquent, and useful books, videos, and audio cassettes.

For more information about Chelsea Green, or to request a free catalog, call toll-free (800) 639-4099, or write to us at P.O. Box 428, White River Junction, Vermont 05001. Visit our Web site at www.chelseagreen.com.

Chelsea Green's titles include:

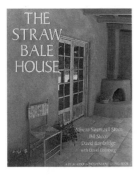

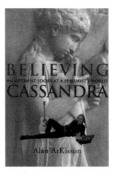

The Straw Bale House

The New Independent Home

Independent Builder:
  Designing & Building a
  House Your Own Way

The Rammed Earth House

The Passive Solar House

The Sauna

Wind Power for Home &
  Business

Wind Energy Basics

The Solar Living Sourcebook

A Shelter Sketchbook

Mortgage-Free!

Hammer. Nail. Wood.

Stone Circles

Toil: Building Yourself

Four-Season Harvest

The Apple Grower

The Flower Farmer

Passport to Gardening:
  A Sourcebook for the
  21st-Century

The New Organic Grower

Four-Season Harvest

Solar Gardening

Straight-Ahead Organic

The Contrary Farmer

The Contrary Farmer's
  Invitation to Gardening

Whole Foods Companion

Simple Food for the Good Life

Sharing the Harvest

The Bread Builders

Good Spirits

The Co-op Cookbook

Believing Cassandra

Gaviotas: A Village to Reinvent
  the World

Who Owns the Sun?

Global Spin: The Corporate
  Assault on Environmentalism

Hemp Horizons

Renewables Are Ready

Beyond the Limits

Loving and Leaving the
  Good Life

The Man Who Planted Trees

The Northern Forest

Scott Nearing: The Making of a
  Homesteader

Genetic Engineering, Food, and
  Our Environment

Seeing Nature